New Yiddish Library

*The New Yiddish Library is a joint project of the
Fund for the Translation of Jewish Literature and
the National Yiddish Book Center.*

*Additional support comes from the Kaplen
Foundation, the Felix Posen Fund for the
Translation of Modern Yiddish Literature, and
Ben and Sarah Torchinsky.*

SERIES EDITOR: DAVID G. ROSKIES

In

Those

Nightmarish

Days

THE GHETTO REPORTAGE OF
PERETZ OPOCZYNSKI AND
JOSEF ZELKOWICZ

EDITED AND WITH AN
INTRODUCTION BY
SAMUEL D. KASSOW

TRANSLATED AND CO-EDITED
BY DAVID SUCHOFF

Yale UNIVERSITY PRESS

NEW HAVEN AND LONDON

Yale University Press books may be purchased in quantity for
educational, business, or promotional use. For information, please
email sales.press@yale.edu (US office) or sales@yaleup.co.uk (UK
office).

Set in Scala type by Newgen North America.
Printed in the United States of America.

ISBN 978-0-300-11231-3 (alk. paper)
Library of Congress Control Number: 2015934206
A catalogue record for this book is available from the British Library.

This paper meets the requirements of ANSI/NISO Z39.48-1992
(Permanence of Paper).

10 9 8 7 6 5 4 3 2 1

♦♦♦ Contents

The ghetto writings presented in this volume might have vanished forever had their authors, Peretz Opoczynski and Josef Zelkowicz, worked alone and written in isolation. Instead, the men belonged to organized archives that encouraged journalists, amateur historians, poets, and ordinary Jews to compile a record of ghetto life, thereby providing future researchers with Jewish (and not just German) sources from which to construct a proper history of the times. Of the two men, one, Peretz Opoczynski, wrote for the secret Oyneg Shabes archive, founded in the Warsaw ghetto by the historian and public activist Emanuel Ringelblum. The other, Josef Zelkowicz, was a key member of the semi-official archive in the Łódź ghetto. Large parts of both archives were miraculously recovered after the war.

In the grim postwar judgment of Rachel Auerbach, a journalist and Oyneg Shabes member, the Ringelblum archive had better luck saving its documents than saving its people.[1] Of the more than sixty collaborators whom Ringelblum had brought into the project, only three survived. In Łódź, only one of the fifteen or so senior staff workers survived. Opoczynski's writings break off in January 1943, when he was probably deported to Treblinka with his wife and son. Josef Zelkowicz was murdered in Auschwitz in August 1944 during the final liquidation of the Łódź ghetto.

It is important to stress that the writings presented here are from ghettos, not from concentration camps. Despite a natural tendency after the Holocaust to regard the ghettos primarily as antechambers to the camps, in fact, as Gustavo Corni has pointed out, they formed a "unique social structure in which elements of the traditional pre-war Jewish society continued to exist."[2] For Samuel Gringauz, a social scientist who survived the Kovno ghetto and various German concentration camps, the ghetto, unlike the concentration camp, should be seen as "a form of Jewish national and autonomous concentration."[3]

Writers like Opoczynski and Zelkowicz knew that conveying the social experience of the ghetto—unprecedented, grotesque, and full of gruesome irony as it was—required resourceful reportage, a kind of inventive decoding that would make sense to future readers. While reportage had always been one of the most effective genres in Yiddish literature, in these writings it reaches a new level of insight and virtuosity. The cast of characters includes the entire spectrum of ghetto society, from rabbis to crooks. Taken into the nooks and crannies of everyday life, we see Jews not as anonymous victims or martyrs-to-be but as individuals, parents and children, neighbors and friends, relating to one another and the institutions of a Jewish community in crisis but not yet destroyed. In these writings, the Jews have names, not numbers.

Before the war, Opoczynski and Zelkowicz were journalists who knew the people they were writing for: the fractious, argumentative, opinionated Polish Jews who read the morning Yiddish newspapers. Good reportage was a virtual travelogue, deciphering the tumultuous diversity of Polish Jewry and explaining Jews to other Jews. Shtetl dwellers wanted to know what was happening in the city, and vice versa for city dwellers. Modern secular Jews loved to hear gossip about Hasidic rebbes; Hasidim avidly read exposés of crafty criminals. Yiddish-speaking Jews devoured biting satires of Polish-speaking Jews (*shmendrikes*) and their shallow pretensions. Wherever they lived, Jews were especially eager to know about the inner contours of the city: the milieu of specific streets, the exotic, secret world of the Jewish teamsters, porters, and butchers. They also wanted to know about the Poles, those neighbors whom they saw in the streets but hardly ever in their homes. Every self-respecting Yiddish newspaper also had its own court reporter, who somehow retrieved inside scoops from the police blotter.[4]

In the ghetto, Zelkowicz and Opoczynski no longer knew who their readers might be. They wrote in awareness that their words might vanish into oblivion. But they continued to write "as if"—as if, Rachel Auerbach recalled, their articles would appear in the morning paper.[5] As Opoczynski and Zelkowicz understood, an "as if" stance held out the best hope for leaving behind a convincing historical record. One could learn bare facts from dry, spare documents. But good reportage made the truth come alive, with emotional resonance. Writing fact, not fiction, Zelkowicz and Opoczynski touched all the registers of Yiddish speech in order to provoke, shock, preach, and even entertain.

Before they grasped the emerging contours of the Final Solution, writers like Opoczynski, Zelkowicz, and other ghetto archivists also thought of their reportage as prospective evidence for postwar stocktaking. Even as they revealed the corrosive impact of the ghetto on families and individuals, they did not hesitate to judge their fellow Jews, often harshly. Yet they also caught many moments of quiet heroism as Jews confronting the abyss of disease and starvation fought to keep their dignity.

Good reportage assumed a special bond between writer and reader. This was especially true when the language happened to be Yiddish, the language of the Jewish masses. Both Opoczynski and Zelkowicz came of age in the springtime of a Yiddish cultural renaissance that blossomed after the Russian revolution of 1905. As a folk language of hitherto uncertain status suddenly began to gain acceptance, Yiddish writers and playwrights became the new idols of the Jewish masses. Literary masters like Sholem Yankev Abramovitsh (Mendele Moykher Sforim) and Solomon Rabinovitsh (Sholem Aleichem) appeared on postcards and made triumphal tours in which they were feted and lionized.[6] Thanks to the new daily press as well as the Yiddish theater, urban Jews saw their problems and fears refracted in newspaper columns and onstage, were introduced to new models of heroism and villainy, and learned about the wider world as never before.

This renaissance did not come out of nowhere. Such writers as I. L. Peretz and S. Ansky had nurtured the vision of a cultural awakening in the years before World War I.[7] For both, East European Jewry stood at a fateful crossroads. Religious tradition and Talmudic law had come to seem rigid and hidebound. But assimilation and acculturation also led nowhere, especially in a time of pogroms and growing anti-Semitism. Their answer was to nourish a vibrant Jewish culture that could build on yet also transcend the religious tradition, and that would inspire Jews to embrace their people and reject assimilation. Aside from a dynamic theater and a vibrant literary culture, another element in such a rebirth was a solid sense of Jewish history. For the dramatist and ethnographer Ansky, culture was the "new Torah";[8] for the influential historian Simon Dubnow, a mastery of history would serve as the glue of Jewish national consciousness.[9]

In the years before World War I, Ansky had implored Jews to *zaml* (collect): to gather documents, record songs and stories, trace old tombstones, and recount popular customs dealing with birth, death, and the rites of passage in between. The act became as important as the final result, the determination to build an archive as vital as the archive itself; for it was through archives that a people without a territory and a state could find its voice and transmit it to others.

It was this belief in *zamling* that led in 1925 to the founding of YIVO, the Yiddish Scientific Institute in Vilna. Emanuel Ringelblum became a major leader of the YIVO historical section, and Josef Zelkowicz became one of YIVO's most enthusiastic and effective *zamlers* and ethnographers; indeed, one can regard the entire Oyneg Shabes archive as a continuation of the prewar YIVO. For his part, Opoczynski as a young man had decorated his room with pictures of the Yiddish and Hebrew writers who had inspired the new cultural renaissance.

At the same time, both Opoczynski and Zelkowicz were also steeped in Jewish traditional texts, receiving their inspiration from the religious tradition as well as the new secular culture. To quote Opoczynski, a real Jew had to "respect both the religious texts and the secular book" (*hobn derekh-erets farn seyfer un farn bukh*).[10] They and other archive writers brought this combined spirit to their work in the ghettos—work that reflected the vibrant civilization, complete with its internal and external struggles, of prewar Polish Jewry.

One cannot emphasize enough the degree to which not just culture but language itself was at issue for these writers—as indeed it was for

Polish Jews in general. Did one have to speak Yiddish to be a bona fide Polish Jew? In the interwar years, more and more Jews were answering that question with a defiant no. If Jews in France, Germany, or the United States could speak French, German, or English, why shouldn't Polish Jews have a right to speak Polish?

Indeed, by the 1930s Yiddish was in decline. On the eve of World War II, 80 percent of Jewish children in Congress Poland and Galicia were receiving their basic education in Polish. A new "Jewish Polishness" (to borrow Katrin Steffen's term) was emerging, whereby Polish Jews proudly embraced their Jewish identity but nonetheless insisted on speaking a non-Jewish language.[11] Daily Jewish newspapers in Polish, like Warsaw's *Nasz Przegląd* and Krakow's *Nasz Dziennik,* were gaining in popularity even as the circulation of the mass Yiddish dailies began to stagnate and decline. In its first issue, *Nasz Przegląd* defended itself in precisely the same terms invoked by Yiddishists—as a "gate through which Jews [will] return and come closer to their nation" and a vehicle for "strengthening the national feeling among our brethren and expanding the recognition of the creative power and spiritual legacy of Judaism."[12]

Yiddish writers and cultural leaders, feeling embattled, fought back hard. While the Polish-language Jewish press showed great sympathy for Zionism, supported the new Hebrew literature in Palestine, and extensively reviewed Yiddish literature and theater, the Yiddish-language sector stubbornly declined to return the favor. Writers for the Polish-language Jewish press were denied membership in the Jewish PEN club and were assailed, unfairly, as dangerous assimilationists. The Yiddish writer Yehoshue Perle called them *"mentshn on a morgn,"* people without a future, while Nahman Mayzel, the editor of the leading Yiddish literary weekly, assured them they would inevitably be forgotten. Had Sholem Aleichem chosen to write in Russian, declared Mayzel, he would have vanished into obscurity.

To defenders of Yiddish, linguistic acculturation threatened to split the middle classes and intelligentsia from the common folk and to destroy the very core of Polish Jewish identity. It was no surprise, therefore, that the battle over language would carry over into the ghettos, especially in Warsaw, where linguistic acculturation had been especially advanced. There, Ringelblum and others established IKOR, an organization dedicated to promoting Yiddish in the daily life of the ghetto.[13] Opoczynski, more outspoken, and convinced that now more than ever the beleaguered Polish Jews needed the bedrock strength of a folk culture anchored in a Jewish language, made no secret of his contempt and even hatred for Polish-speaking Jews. In Łódź, Zelkowicz likewise threw himself into Yiddish cultural activities. For both men, Yiddish was the language of the "social community" they set out to describe and memorialize—just as it was the language in which ghetto writers, singers, poets, and dramatists sought to reassure, guide, and entertain their people, and to make sense of the rupture and disaster that had overtaken them.

For this larger purpose, ghetto writers drew in part from previous models of Jewish writing in the face of disaster but also self-consciously sought their own voice and their own modes of expression. "In the City of Slaughter," a great cry of lament and denunciation by the Hebrew poet Haim Nahman Bialik, had stood out since the Kishinev pogrom of 1903 as the model of a modern "literature of destruction" (in David Roskies's phrase).

Bialik's bitter descriptions of the wanton slaughter of forty-three Jews are almost a parody of medieval Hebrew Crusade poems of Jewish martyrdom. The poet had not been in Kishinev during the pogrom, but he had no qualms about judging those who were: in particular, the Jewish men whose pitiful, abject passivity in the face of the pogromists formed the special object of his cutting scorn. His poem served as a clarion call to activism—and in literary terms as a challenge to later Jewish writers and poets. Forty years on, rereading Bialik in the ghettos, they had to wonder: would he dare to condemn us, too?[14]

One of Zelkowicz's closest friends in the Łódź ghetto was the poet Simcha Bunem Shayevitsh. In a poem aimed directly at Bialik, Shayevitsh convicts the great Hebrew poet, in Roskies's words, "for lack of empathy, for lack of historical imagination, and most of all for hubris, the hubris of a romantic poet who allows his own agonized voice to drown out the cries of the victims and the echoes from the hallowed past."[15]

Yiddish writers in the ghettos chose to write, not to keep silent. But they had to find a new voice, fashion new ways to articulate their rage and leave a testament for posterity. Josef Zelkowicz, for one, understood the gravity and difficulty of the task. Writing in the Łódź ghetto in September 1942, he exclaimed:

> Son of Man: even if, with all the years of Methuselah, you were able to invent the kind of language that is required, were able to discover the fitting words, to use pen and ink to express and describe everything your eyes had seen, everything your ears had heard, and all that your human heart had felt—what would you really have achieved? In the end, you'd finally get a grip on yourself and break out in a cry: "It can't be true!" Even after seeing it all, hearing it all, and feeling it all yourself, in the end even you won't believe it, for the limited capacity of your intellect will be unable to grasp what has occurred.

As Jews in the ghettos gazed into the abyss, they knew that their fate, and the fate of their beloved language, had become interlinked.

II

Peretz Opoczynski, one of the best writers and reporters in the Oyneg Shabes group, was born in 1892 to a very religious family in Lutomiersk, near Łódź.[16] (By coincidence, Zelkowicz also lived in that shtetl for many years.) He was only five when his father, a fervent Gerer Hasid, died. The local Gerer Hasidim failed to keep their promise to help young Peretz, his parents' only son, and he grew up in terrible poverty. Since his mother could not afford to raise him at home, he was sent away to study in yeshivas in distant towns where he ate in strangers' homes and slept on the hard benches of local synagogues.

In one of these yeshivas, in Lithuania, young Peretz encountered for the first time a world far different from the antimodern fanaticism of a Hasidic small town. The rabbi, an enlightened Jew, encouraged him to learn Russian and Polish and to study Hebrew grammar. When he returned home, word quickly spread that Peretz Opoczynski had become a "heretic." The Gerer Hasidim chased him out of their synagogue. He was now an outcast. For the rest of his life, even as he continued to respect the spiritual aspects of Hasidism, Opoczynski would resent most Hasidim as self-centered hypocrites—an attitude that surfaces in such pieces of ghetto reportage as "The Jewish Letter Carrier" and "Building No. 21."

A social outcast in his hometown, Opoczynski struggled to find direction. For a time he thought of studying in a modern rabbinical seminary in Germany, but he soon gave up that idea. Determined to pay his own way in life, he shocked his mother and four older sisters, who had always hoped he would become a rabbi, by informing them that he intended to be a shoemaker.

Leaving home, Opoczynski moved to Kalisz. These were turbulent and exciting times. In the aftermath of the 1905 revolution, new heroes and new attractions—Yiddish and Hebrew writings, improvised libraries, amateur theater productions—caught the attention of Jewish youth. Joining a "commune" of young men and women who pooled their earnings and heatedly discussed art, literature, and revolution, Opoczynski started to dream of becoming a writer.

When war broke out in 1914, Opoczynski was drafted into the Russian army. Wounded, he was captured and sent to a prisoner-of-war camp in Hungary, where he stayed until the end of the war. Moving afterward to Łódź, he tried to earn a living as a shoemaker while beginning to make his mark as a writer. Yehoshua Uger, editor of the *Łódźher tageblat*, hired him to co-edit a successful weekly, and for a time Opoczynski flourished. He was now happily married; he and his wife, Miriam, found a good home in the heart of Łódź and made many new friends in Yiddish literary circles. He became especially close to the well-known Yiddish poet Miriam Ulinover, and it is logical to assume that he also came to know Josef Zelkowicz, one of whose many projects was a history of Opoczynski's hometown.

But his luck did not last. His first two children died, casting him into a deep depression. In 1935 he moved with his wife to Warsaw to work for the newspaper *Dos naye vort,* the main organ of the Right Poyalei Tsiyon (Right Labor Zionists). As one of the paper's editors, Opoczynski gave his readers a rich menu of political news and literary works by Itzik Manger, Simon Horonczyk, Yekhiel Lerer, and other promising writers. Each edition also carried a page of fast-paced reportage about the Warsaw scene: accidents, fires, crime, and court cases. But as the paper's ambitions far exceeded its resources, it was forced to close in late 1937.[17]

In 1938, Opoczynski's sister Rena visited from the United States, leaving a valuable memoir that is one of the few sources on Opoczynski's life. Assured by his letters that everything was fine and that he had no need of her proffered financial help, she was shocked by what she found on arrival in Warsaw. Her brother lived in an attic apartment at number 21 Wołynska Street, one of the poorest streets in the city. The walls were covered with mold and damp. Still, his stubborn pride kept him from accepting any help from his sister: anyone wanting to make a living as an honest writer, he explained to her, had to accept poverty.

Indeed, Opoczynski cared deeply about his craft as a writer. He sought no fame and received none; one looks in vain for a mention of him in the various memoirs of the prewar literary scene in Warsaw and Łódź. Writing, for him, was a mission and a calling, not a career. But Opoczynski and his wife also had another chance at happiness with the birth in 1935 of their son Danchik. As his sister recalls, he doted on the child, showing him off at every opportunity.

Opoczynski was more than just a reporter. He held very strong views about politics and Jewish life, and these views would emerge in his ghetto reportages. Having joined the Right Poyalei Tsiyon while on the staff of its paper, he became a party activist and continued to work for it later in the Warsaw ghetto. The party combined Zionism with what one might call Diaspora populism, a commitment to fight for social justice and Jewish rights. As a self-identified workers' party, it tried, with mixed results, to gain a foothold in the Jewish trade-union movement.[18] It was also fervently pro-Hebrew, though, unlike some other Zionist groupings, it embraced Yiddish culture as well.

The Right Poyalei Tsiyon was also more moderate and tolerant than other, rigidly ideological political parties in the fractious world of Polish Jewry. Although closely allied with the labor-Zionist establishment in Palestine headed by David Ben-Gurion and Berl Katznelson, it did not entirely accept the Zionist school network (known as Tarbut) in Poland, with its emphasis on Hebrew only. Instead the party sponsored its own schools, the Shul-Kult, which put equal stress on Yiddish. By the same token, just as Opoczynski revered Yosef Khayim Brenner, one of the giants of modern Hebrew literature, he also venerated the Yiddish master Sholem Aleichem.

A prewar review by Opoczynski of a dramatic production of Sholem Aleichem's *Tevye the Dairyman* provides important insight into his politics and views on art. Too many critics, Opoczynski argued, had tried to use Tevye as a foil for their narrow political agendas. This was totally wrong. Tevye was an ordinary Jew, the symbol of the Jewish everyman. He lived his life by relying on his instincts and his innate Jewish pride. The last thing he needed or cared for was ideological guidance from intellectuals. In a repudiation of such intellectuals and ideologues, Opoczynski held out Sholem Aleichem's beloved character as a key to understanding the Jewish people. Would-be leaders who courted the support of the Jewish masses had to learn from Tevye's "integrity, his respect for both religious and secular sources, his faith in people and in justice, his love of work and honest human creativity."[19]

III

When war broke out in 1939, Opoczynski lost his meager livelihood as a Yiddish journalist. A few survivors of the Warsaw ghetto, which was established in November 1940, remembered him looking frail and tired, struggling against even worse poverty than he had known before the war. He took a job as a ghetto mailman, but it did not pay enough to feed his family. His feet, they recalled, were swollen from hunger.[20]

But Opoczynski refused to despair. Throwing himself into the work of the Poyalei Tsiyon in the ghetto, he continued to write in Hebrew and Yiddish for the Oyneg Shabes archive and also became an activist in his house committee at 21 Wołynska Street. Opoczynski was very much a part of what the historian Lucy Dawidowicz calls the "alternative community" of the ghetto, which saw itself as the true voice of the Jewish masses and despised the Jewish police and the Judenrat (the Jewish council).

It is not clear how Opoczynski was recruited for the Oyneg Shabes archive. Eliyahu Gutkowski, a key associate of Ringelblum and a member of the Right Poyalei Tsiyon, probably made the introduction. Hersh Wasser, one of the group's three survivors, would recall that the archive helped Opoczynski with small stipends; when he contracted typhus, another leader of the archive, Menakhem Kon, procured medicine for him.[21]

The Oyneg Shabes may also have gotten Opoczynski his job as a mailman—which gave him a bird's-eye view of a ghetto marked, like no other, by huge economic disparities, corruption, and cultural divisions. Other ghettos suffered from starvation, but nowhere else were the disparities so glaring that starving children and dying beggars lay in the doorways of fancy restaurants.

Conditions in the Warsaw ghetto changed very quickly, almost always for the worse. Ringelblum encouraged members of the Oyneg Shabes to describe what they saw immediately—not to wait. No day was like the preceding; images succeeded one another with cinematic speed, and what seemed important today might be totally forgotten tomorrow. It was therefore important to capture at once every event in Jewish life in its pristine freshness. Oyneg Shabes took it upon itself to grasp the moments as they happened, for it was such eyewitness, contemporaneous accounts that would give future historians some understanding of "ghetto time."[22]

No one was better than Opoczynski at capturing events as they happened. In 1941, when the pieces in this book were written, few Jews suspected the worst. Thanks to the Oyneg Shabes, he opened a window onto a community that was battered but still alive.

True, others were also reporting about ghetto life at the time, primarily in the Polish-language *Gazeta Żydowska,* the only Jewish newspaper allowed by the Germans. These stories were well written and often showed humor and insight. But this was "legal reportage" and, being written in Polish, could not capture the cadences and linguistic subtleties of ordinary ghetto Jews. More important, while "legal reporters" could chide ghetto bureaucrats, poke fun at ghetto agencies, and even hint at corruption in the Jewish police, they could not express anger or moral outrage. They were muzzled. By contrast, Opoczynski, like all other writers for the Oyneg Shabes, was encouraged to write from the heart.[23]

In "The Jewish Letter Carrier," he also wrote from firsthand experience. As Opoczynski the mailman walked his route, he encountered and described the diverse mosaic of Jewish Warsaw: Polish-speaking doctors, Hasidim, ordinary workers, housewives, destitute refugees. Jews envied him his job and offered bribes if he could help them get hired. Opoczynski deftly exploited humor to skewer their illusions. Before the war there had been no Jewish mailmen or Jewish police; now the ghetto had both—surely a sign of Jewish autonomy! What they did not know was that if he delivered 150 letters a day—a remarkable feat—he might earn nine zlotys, barely enough to buy half a loaf of bread.

What seems at first glance to be a straightforward relationship between a mailman and the people on his route becomes, in Opoczynski's hands, social and cultural material for skillful if often painful dissection. The mailman brought news from overseas and packages that might rescue a family from starvation. He delivered letters that might reestablish long-sundered family ties. His observing eye could take in the searing evidence of ghetto poverty, the "death houses" of Smocza and Mila where Jews lay in bed all day and slowly starved to death. In these wretched buildings, even the lowly mailman was forced to confront sometimes harrowing moral choices. If he handed over a letter without collecting the delivery fee of twenty groschen, the money would have to come out of his own pocket. If he refused to deliver the letter, a desperate Jewish family might curse him as a callous brute, a tool of the Judenrat.

In a normal society, the job of a mailman was routine. In the ghetto, it offered a microcosmic look at the rampant pathologies and moral dilemmas that dogged the Jews at every step. Even the mandatory twenty-groschen fee per letter served as an emblem, in this case of the obtuseness and corruption of the Judenrat, which taxed rich and poor at the same rate. Nor was this the only testimony to the wide social and cultural gaps in the ghetto. Polish-speaking Jewish professionals addressed their mailman in tones of arrogant contempt, exposing their own inferiority complexes. The Hasidim were no better, hypocritical misers who begrudged him a measly tip. The only Jews who treated him decently were *amkho:* ordinary, unpretentious people who spoke Yiddish and related to him with empathy. They were the ones who gave him decent tips—at least in the beginning.

As these instances described by the mailman suggest, Opoczynski was a dyed-in-the-wool populist, a strong believer in the essential decency of the common man. Incredibly, as can be seen in some of his Oyneg Shabes reportage, this faith in the common man even extended to ordinary German soldiers and Poles:

> Many German soldiers came to visit the ghetto because they were decent ordinary folk [*erlekhe folksmentshn*], workers and peasants, who had no interest in Hitler's ideology. . . . [T]hey would come to the Jewish street markets and talk to the Jewish traders in Yiddish-German. Like common people everywhere, they . . . began to feel comfortable with one another, and even began to say what they thought of Hitler and his gang.[24]

Although some ghettos—Vilna or Kovno, for instance—functioned almost entirely in Yiddish, in Warsaw the tension of language exacerbated existing social disparities. Opoczynski made no secret of his own disgust with the corrupt clique of Polish-speaking Jews who ran the post office as their own private fiefdom; but he also admitted that a mailman had to speak Polish on the job if he wanted to command respect. Of course, when Jews cursed him, as they did with growing frequency, they resorted to the choicest Yiddish. As hatred of the Judenrat deepened, the mailman became a scapegoat. Few noticed his tattered shoes and swollen legs. After all, he was an official, wasn't he?

IV

Before the war, Opoczynski had written that each courtyard in Jewish Warsaw was "like a shtetl." On hot summer days, when blazing temperatures drove people out of their homes, the Jews of "shtetl Stawki would loiter along the fence, shtetl Lubetzka would hang out by the gutters, shtetl Wołynska would arrange itself along the steps."[25] Such prewar writings paint a picture of languid poverty as women idly exchange gossip about recipes and children, interrupted by the cries of the hucksters who come by to hawk their wares; here Opoczynski writes in language that evokes Sholem Aleichem's ability to capture the voices and gestures of down-to-earth, everyday Jews: the kind of Jews who inhabited his grimy building and neighborhood.

His wartime reportage in "Building No. 21" is very different. This piece describes the first period after the occupation of Warsaw by Hitler's forces, before the enclosure of the ghetto. The building described is 21 Wołynska Street, which was the author's residence both before and during the war.[26] At first, after the Germans occupied Warsaw in 1939, a year before they chased the Jews into the ghetto, one could still hope that with enough grit and luck, it might be possible to hold out till better days. The great question at the time was whether to stay in Warsaw or head for the "other side," the territories occupied by the Soviets. Like their forebears trading legends about a "golden land" beyond the seas, the Jews of 21 Wołynska Street entertained dreams of Communist Russia. They avidly latched on to letters that described a better life, a place where Jews could work and live in dignity:

> The letter from Rivkeleh's son soon passes through the hands of everyone in the tenement. Everyone who reads it handles it like some magical amulet—as if it were a wishing ring. With each passing minute, another neighbor rushes in:
>
> "Good morning, Rivkeleh."
>
> "Good morning, good year."
>
> "Rivkeleh, do you think we could have another look at the letter you got from your son?"

But as with everything else in wartime Warsaw, things only got worse, not better. The Russians closed the border. The "other side" was revealed to be other than the paradise it was made out to be, and Jews returned to Wołynska Street broken and anguished. Still, like the "little Jews" of Sholem Aleichem's stories, they also retained their wry sense of humor—even when suffering the collective humiliation of the *paruvke*, the disinfection procedure in which their belongings were ransacked and ruined as they waited, naked and freezing cold, for a shower and the painful removal of body hair:

> It is, after all, the first winter of the war, when jokes can still be made. At two in the morning, when Jews finally leave the bath and walk out into the frosty, starry winter night, they pay no attention to their hungry stom-

achs and perform a mock toast to one another: "To health! We've been koshered and rendered pure. So where's the challah and fish?"

Opoczynski concludes his reportage on 21 Wołynska Street with the cynical statement by an army tailor that in wartime, everyone is on his own:

"If freedom doesn't mean saving me, just me—saving just my own hide, you understand?—from the claws of the beast, well then, so be it. There's no more freedom and justice. It's every man for himself—save yourself any way you can. Rob, steal, and fill your own belly first, because there's nothing better or more beautiful on the face of the earth than a good meal, and there never will be."

Opoczynski himself totally rejected that point of view. He deeply believed that Jews had to help each other. In essays on the house committees of the Warsaw ghetto (not included in this volume), Opoczynski fervently urged his neighbors to work together in mutual support. Precisely because wartime let loose unbridled egotism and selfishness, it was doubly important for Jews to show concern and civic responsibility.

Yet here, too, he had to report, the house committees found themselves fighting a losing battle against dwindling resources and rampant corruption. Forced to pay exorbitant bribes to protect their courtyards from the dreaded "disinfections" described in "Building No. 21," they soon ran out of money, bringing despair to many Jews who had seen them as a source of welfare.

Even as Opoczynski wrote about individual Jews with sympathy and humor, in hard-hitting reports like "Children in the Streets" he could excoriate the community as a whole for its moral failings. He also lambasted the Judenrat and the Jewish police for what he regarded as criminal corruption. It was bad enough, Opoczynski wrote, that the police sent the poor to brutal labor camps while exempting the rich. But what was truly inexcusable was the disregard shown by the Judenrat for the wives and children of the deportees. How could a Jewish community do so little to help the many Jewish children who were starving to death in the streets?

All sense of community began and ended with the four walls of one's own apartment. It is the tragedy of the Polish Jews that the war found them so unprepared, so unorganized, so incapable of rising to the needs of the times. Polish Jewry—divided into thousands of separate tribes (*eydes*)—and each person a tribe unto himself.

Here as nowhere else in his writing, Opoczynski demands a moral accounting and justice. Having lost two children of his own, he had no time for excuses.

As these lines are written [in November 1941], we find ourselves in a critical situation in the ghetto. New expulsions from apartments are taking place, new streets are being removed from the ghetto, and with our territory growing narrower, the noose pulls ever tighter around our necks. All we see are walls, new walls. Soon there will be nowhere left to turn: winter, dampness, cold, and death on every side. Will we still be able to save the Jewish child?

Even as he described the tough battle fought by ghetto Jews to stay alive, Opoczynski was struggling to feed himself and his family. No one could survive on the official rations allocated by the Germans, with their daily allotments of 184 calories for Jews (as opposed to 600 for Poles and 2,613 for Germans).[27] The ghetto was horribly overcrowded, with an average of seven people to a room. In addition, the Germans had dumped more than 130,000 refugees into the ghetto, cramming them into filthy and lethal housing that is described in macabre detail in "The Jewish Letter Carrier." Since the ghetto received little coal for heating, pipes froze, toilets ceased to work, and feces and frozen urine piled up on stairs and in courtyards.

Yet despite all odds, by July 22, 1942, when mass deportations began to Treblinka, most of the Jews in the Warsaw ghetto were still alive. More than a hundred thousand had succumbed to starvation and disease, but 360,000 were still holding on. In large part, they owed their lives to the massive smuggling of food that had begun as soon as the ghetto was sealed off, in November 1940. In his diary, Adam Czerniakow, the head of the Warsaw Judenrat, recorded that "we receive legally 1.8 million zlotys' worth of food monthly and illegally about 70 to 80 million zlotys' worth."[28]

Of course, the large-scale smuggling in and out of the ghetto raised many fascinating questions, which Opoczynski tries to answer in two remarkable reports: "Smuggling in the Warsaw Ghetto" and "Goyim in the Ghetto." How did the food get in? How did the Jews pay for it? What kind of characters were the smugglers? What did this arrangement imply for Polish-Jewish relations in the future?

> Smuggling certainly is a filthy business, a noose hung around the neck of the starving and swollen consumer, but in the horrific conditions of the huge prison the Jews have been driven into and enclosed by the ghetto walls, smuggling is the only salvation left for the surviving remnants. Who knows? Someday we may have to construct a memorial to the courage of the smuggler, who saved a good part of Jewish Warsaw from starving to death.

In Sholem Asch's story "Kola Street," written in 1906, the wealthy Jews of the shtetl sneer at the lowly tough guys, the brawny porters and teamsters who live on Kola Street. But when danger threatens, it is these "tough Jews" who defend the shtetl from harm. So, too, in the Warsaw ghetto: hundreds of thousands owed their lives to the smugglers.

Opoczynski also describes how smuggling and the underground economy drew Poles and Jews together. Of course, the Polish smugglers and traders were not saints. When they snuck into the ghetto, they knew they could drive a hard bargain. After all, the Jews were hungry. Yet not only did these Poles foil the German plans to isolate the Jews behind ghetto walls and separate the two peoples; they actually kept the ghetto alive.

> If you're looking for some higher value to this buying and selling, then you can find it only in THE BRIDGE that has appeared between the Jew and the Gentile. It's a bridge built out of bad material: speculation. But it has a good purpose: to keep a large part of the Jewish population from starving to death. . . .
>
> The smugglers maintain a link between Poland's loyal citizens; they extend a brotherly hand to the persecuted and thus erect a beacon of morality in a time of rampant demoralization. Yes, that's maybe how it is, maybe how it must be.

By their very actions, Opoczynski believed, the Polish smugglers re-futed the logic of the prewar Polish boycott that had aimed at expelling Jews from economic life. The war showed yet again that Poles and Jews needed one another, even if their relationship was marked more by mutual need than mutual love.

Written in late 1941, just as the first rumors of mass killings reached the ghetto but before any certain knowledge, "Goyim in the Ghetto" reflects a widespread belief that both Nazi and Polish anti-Semitism might be tempered by economic reality. Certain German decrees, Opoczynski notes, had been rolled back when the Germans saw their harmful economic consequences. Indeed, the very imposition of a ghetto, a political decision, made no economic sense. The Germans could not seal the ghetto off from the city; many of them, Opoczynski argues, did not really want to. When Germans needed Jews to provide a service—such as rag picking or scrap collection—they did not hesi-tate to use them. Perhaps when the war was over and Poland regained its independence, pragmatism would triumph again. Ringelblum wrote in his diary that "the tree of life" would prove stronger than an abstract anti-Semitism ungrounded in reality.

During and after the Great Deportation of 1942, in brief, laconic notes, Opoczynski continued to record in his diary the destruction of Warsaw Jewry.[29] On September 4, he reported the rumors that the Germans actually intended to wipe out all the Jews of Europe:

> Our end had come. This is the thought that is on everyone's mind. We're facing annihilation and no one has the courage to lead a resistance, so that we would at least die with honor.

On September 8, he described the bedlam at the "cauldron" where all the remaining Jews had to gather in a small area for a final registration and selection:

> The impression left by this registration was terrible and was symbolized by one- and two-year-old children sitting on a sofa in the middle of the road and crying "mama" while Jews, their hearts bleeding, were passing by, watching the horrible scene and crying. The Germans had probably done it deliberately. They could have taken the children away, but they did not. On the contrary: let the Jews see and grieve.

In the last months of his life, Opoczynski kept returning to the theme of resistance. Apparently unaware of the ŻOB (Jewish Fighting Organization) and its preparations for armed struggle, he gave vent to his anger in his diary. On December 4, 1942, he discounted a rumor sweeping the ghetto that Jewish workers in a labor camp near Lublin had killed their German guards. Some 180 Jews were said to have escaped.

> We are more than certain that this rumor is not true. It was produced by our deep sense of shame that in Warsaw, this mother city of Israel, in this city with its great masses of tough working Jews, and its traditions of political struggle, the Jews should have let themselves be led like sheep to the slaughter.

Even in his deepening despair, Opoczynski held on to his belief in the fundamental decency of ordinary Germans. For him, this lingering vestige of prewar humanism helped allay the growing sense of terror and isolation. On December 22, 1942, he noted the rumor that 50,000 Warsaw Jews were working in Bobruisk in White Russia. The Gestapo spread these rumors, Opoczynski believed, not to comfort the Jews but to deceive the ordinary German soldier, who would "tremble" in horror, or revolt, if the truth about the death camps became known to them.

The last diary entry is dated January 5, 1943. Nothing is known about his fate, or the fate of his wife Miriam and their son Danchik. They were probably seized during the roundups in the Warsaw ghetto that took place in mid-January and deported to Treblinka.

v

Like Opoczynski, with whom he shared many things in common, Josef Zelkowicz (1897–1944) was born and grew up in a small town near Łódź, in his case as the son of a well-to-do Hasid.[30] Like Opoczynski, he received a traditional religious education, earned rabbinical ordination, and then abandoned strict religious observance. He entered a Polish teacher's institute, briefly taught in a state school, and fought as a soldier in the Polish army during the Polish-Soviet war of 1919–1920. He also spent some time at the University of Berlin and developed a keen interest in modern German literature.[31] A fluent writer in Polish as well as Yiddish, he served some time on the staff of a Polish military newspaper.

After leaving the army, Zelkowicz moved to Łódź and in 1925 began to contribute feuilletons to local Yiddish newspapers while also taking an active role in the Yiddish theater. At some point he joined the militantly secular, Yiddishist, and pro-Soviet Left Poyalei Tsiyon party, which also included the noted historians Emanuel Ringelblum and Raphael Mahler. The party, which had a particularly strong presence in Łódź, was a staunch supporter of YIVO and the Central Yiddish School Organization (CYSHO), a network of secular Yiddish schools also supported by the Bund.

Developing a serious interest in Jewish ethnography and folklore, Zelkowicz helped found the Łódź branch of YIVO in 1930.[32] Although he lacked formal academic credentials, he turned himself into a serious scholar, publishing notable articles in the *Łódźher visnshaftlekhe shriftn* [Łódź Academic Writings] of 1938 on Jewish death and burial customs and on the politics of the Jewish community of Lutomiersk, Opoczynski's native town.[33] Combining ethnography and reportage, Zelkowicz not only made use of a wide array of documents and cited extensive passages from Yiddish literature, but also tracked down elderly informants for juicy details, anecdotes, and insights into Jewish folk practices. His vigorous prose brought to life the rich interplay of religious law, popular custom, social tensions, and local politics as seen through the microcosm of Jewish burial practices.

As YIVO expanded its activities in the 1930s, it worked closely with the Society for Landkentenish ("knowing the land"). The two organizations encouraged Jews to write the history of their towns and regions and become collectors (*zamlers*) of documents.[34] The monthly journal *Landkentenish* devoted articles to kayaking, skiing, photography, mountain climbing, and hiking as well as Jewish art and architecture. Whereas Polish tourist societies refused to admit Jews, and guidebooks for tourists virtually ignored Jewish artifacts and Polish Jewish history, *Landkentenish* and YIVO fought to instill in Polish Jewry a sense of *ayngefundevetkayt*, a deep connection to the Polish land. As one leader of the movement, Dr. Leon Wulman, wrote in 1933, "We want not only to learn about this land . . . but also to learn about our own part in the life of this land. . . . We want to know Jewish life in Poland through and through, we want to investigate it and understand it; this is a task that only we, relying only on ourselves, can do."[35]

Another major thrust of the *Landkentenish* movement was to encourage a strong regional consciousness. In a 1937 article for the movement's journal, the young historian Philip Friedman wrote that "the more diverse, the more colorful, the more creative the parts, the stronger will be the whole."[36] In particular, Friedman and Zelkowicz set out to encourage research on the Jews of the Łódź region, with Zelkowicz himself launching a major study of regional Yiddish speech and histories of the towns of Lutomiersk and Konstantin. All of these manuscripts were lost during the war.

VI

The Germans conquered Łódź on September 8, 1939, renaming the city Litzmannstadt and annexing it to the German Reich.[37] The ghetto, announced in February 1940, was supposed to be no more than a temporary holding pen until the Jews could be deported elsewhere. With the fall of France in June 1940, talk was heard of shipping the Jews to Madagascar. In the end, the short-term ghetto lasted four years, until August 1944. One of the first to be established by the Nazis, it was the last to be liquidated.

One reason the Łódź ghetto endured so long lay in the bizarre partnership that developed in 1940 between Hans Biebow, a crafty German businessman appointed to supervise the ghetto, and Chaim Rumkowski, whom the Germans anointed as "Elder of the Jews" in October 1939. When the ghetto with its 165,000 Jews was sealed off from the rest of the city at the end of April 1940, the Germans had no idea of exploiting the enormous potential of a skilled Jewish labor force that had helped make Łódź into Poland's leading industrial city. But as the plan to ship the Jews elsewhere collapsed, Rumkowski persuaded Biebow to turn the ghetto into a center of war production. That would benefit the Reich, help feed the ghetto, and, most important from Rumkowski's point of view, buy time.

Rumkowski was a brilliant organizer, and Biebow a canny business-man and opportunist. After procuring orders from the German army for the products of ghetto workshops, Biebow also convinced local Nazi party leaders that they could rake in huge profits from the enter-prise. A common interest of sorts developed between Rumkowski and the local German administration. Both had reason to maintain the ghetto in being; until 1944, this commonality helped foil SS attempts to deport all of the remaining Jews.

Few Jewish leaders under Nazi occupation have been more contro-versial than Mordecai Chaim Rumkowski (1877–1944). Before the war, Rumkowski, who had moved to Łódź from a small town in White Rus-sia, had tried his luck at different business ventures. With no formal education, and familiar only with Lithuanian Yiddish, he made up for his deficiencies with energy and ambition, and soon made a name for himself in Łódź. He became involved in local Zionist politics, served for a time on the Jewish community board, and became the director of Helenówek, one of the largest Jewish orphanages in Poland.

Opinions about the prewar Rumkowski were sharply divided. His enemies noted his coarseness, lack of culture, and naked ambition. There were rumors that he had molested some of the young girls in the orphanage. But he also had his defenders, who cited his vitality, organizational talent, and effective administration of the orphanage.

Rumkowski became even more controversial after the Germans ap-pointed him Elder of the Jews. For a long time, they humored him with promises of far-ranging "autonomy." They also granted him—for a while—a great deal of power over the Jews, more in fact than virtually any other Judenrat leader. For his part, Rumkowski lost no time in setting up the most regimented and rigidly organized ghetto in eastern Europe.

The Łódź ghetto was hermetically sealed off from the rest of the city. There was no smuggling, no "goyim" came in and out, and the only money allowed was a special scrip that was worthless on the other side of the fence. If, in Warsaw, more than 80 percent of the food in the ghetto was smuggled, in Łódź the Jews depended totally on German allotments whose distribution was supervised (until 1943) by Rum-kowski. His control over the food supply gave him enormous power to reward friends and punish enemies. Again unlike in Warsaw, no Jewish self-help agency, no network of house committees, emerged to rival the Judenrat. Postal service was greatly curtailed.

The Warsaw ghetto had a great deal of "social space" that included not only the house committees but a very large underground press, the Oyneg Shabes archive, and relatively extensive contact with the "Aryan" side. While the Poles did not particularly love Jews, they detested the Germans and eagerly welcomed the chance to do business with the ghetto. In Łódź, on the other hand, there was little "social space," little room for an organized life not under Rumkowski's control. And the people on the other side of the fence were largely Germans or ethnic Germans, not Poles. There was no such thing as an "Aryan" side. If, in Warsaw, several thousand Jews survived on Aryan papers, in Łódź one could count such cases on the fingers of one hand.

In Łódź, once the ghetto was sealed, smuggling virtually ended, and Gentiles, aside from German police and officials, did not enter. Rumkowski quickly shut down the house committees. Whereas a Peretz Opoczynski could present Warsaw Jewry as a community with some degree of moral agency and moral responsibility, Zelkowicz describes an atomized population with hardly any potential for independent social action.

Rumkowski boasted that his tightly regimented ghetto "worked like a clock." On a "state visit" to the Warsaw ghetto in 1941, he told members of the Judenrat that they could learn useful lessons from Łódź. The head of the Warsaw Judenrat, Adam Czerniakow, hated him, noting in his diary that Rumkowski was "replete with self-praise, a conceited and witless man, and a dangerous man, too, since he keeps telling the authorities that all is well in his preserve."

Upon returning from Warsaw, Rumkowski reminded the Łódź Jews how lucky they were not to be in Warsaw. The hellish scenes there—thousands starving in the streets, children begging at the doors to fancy restaurants—did not exist in Łódź. And there were indeed relatively fewer social disparities in Łódź, even if a small group favored by Rumkowski merited better rations and living conditions.

But while the Łódź ghetto may have been more "equal," it was just as deadly, and mainly because of the lack of smuggled food. The mortality rate was the highest of any major ghetto. Between 1940 and 1944, 43,743 Jews—21 percent of the original inhabitants—died of starvation and disease. Still, even in death there was a difference: in the Warsaw ghetto one could not take even a brief walk without seeing corpses in the streets. In Łódź, Rumkowski made sure the bodies were buried immediately.

Rumkowski ruled with an iron fist and showed no mercy to those who tried to defy him. The Jews hated and feared him but also accorded him a grudging respect. The war seemed to rejuvenate him: he rode through the ghetto in a horse-drawn carriage, married a woman thirty years his junior, and apparently continued to pressure other women for sexual favors. He had one message for the Łódź Jews: "his" factories were their only hope for survival. And they could only agree. By 1944, 117 different enterprises working for the Germans employed 95 percent of the ghetto Jews. Albert Speer himself, the Reich armaments minister, personally intervened with Hitler to keep the Łódź ghetto in being.

On the plus side, Rumkowski made heroic efforts, when the Germans allowed, to help the children above all. Childless himself, he organized the best school system in any ghetto and provided summer camps and extra food. For a time he encouraged Zionist youth movements, giving them parcels of land in semirural Marysin, near the Jewish cemetery. He also extended help to rabbis, promoted Yiddish in the schools, and tried to protect writers and intellectuals from deportation—as long as they did not cross him. Finally, he did his best, with very limited resources, to set up a system of social welfare for the poorest elements in the ghetto. That system is described by Zelkowicz in this book.

Over time, however, Rumkowski suffered a steady erosion of his "autonomy" and power. In October 1941 he had to close down his cherished schools in order to make room for 5,000 Gypsies and 20,000 Jewish deportees from the Reich and the Protectorate. The deportees endured even worse conditions than the Polish Jews, and serious tensions soon flared up between the two groups.

In early January 1942, the Germans told Rumkowski that they planned to deport 20,000 Jews. He could, if he wished, draw up the lists himself. Rather than rely on the tender mercies of the Germans, he assumed the task on his own authority, expelling the welfare cases, the unemployed, some underworld figures, and certain people whom he regarded as troublemakers. But on the whole he protected political leaders, rabbis, and leading writers and intellectuals. Did he know that the deportees were going to the extermination camp of Chelmno? In January 1942, perhaps not. But by May, when the Germans demanded another reduction in the size of the ghetto and Rumkowski ordered the deportation of most of the Jews who had arrived from Central Europe, there could be no doubt that he was aware of their ultimate fate. In the first six months of 1942, fifty-four transports with 54,979 Jews left for the killing vans of Chelmno.

Worse followed. In a bolt from the blue, the Germans demanded in September 1942 that Rumkowski help deport all children under the age of ten and all adults over sixty-five. Even for a ghetto accustomed to horror and trauma, the week of September 5–12, 1942, was a macabre episode of torture and agony. It is that unspeakable week that Josef Zelkowicz so brilliantly describes in his last piece here, "In Those Nightmarish Days."

VII

In the Łódź ghetto, Zelkowicz emerged as a major figure in Yiddish cultural life. He was a leader of the Yiddish Culture Society (Yidisher Kultur Gezelshaft) and organized literary readings in the soup kitchens.[38] He worked with the popular composer David Beigelman on musical and theatrical productions and participated in a circle of Yiddish writers and poets that met regularly at the apartment of Miriam Ulinover. He also remained an active member of the Left Poyalei Tsiyon.

But Zelkowicz's most important post was in the Łódź ghetto archive. While the Warsaw Oyneg Shabes was totally separate from the Judenrat, the Łódź archive was actually established on Rumkowski's direct orders in November 1940 in order to prepare material for a future history. Rumkowski ordered all ghetto officials and bosses of workshops to cooperate with the archive and furnish useful information. (His own private office, however, remained off-limits.)

Henryk Neftalin, one of Rumkowski's closest associates, supervised the archive and appointed its first three directors: Josef Klementynowski, Julian Cukier, and Zelkowicz.[39] When the deportees from the Reich and the Protectorate arrived in late 1941, Neftalin invited the German-speaking journalists Oskar Singer and Oskar Rosenfeld to join the staff. Neftalin defined the archive's main mission as the creation of "a base for future scholars studying the life of a Jewish society in one of its most difficult periods." He protected the archive staff from deportations, provided supplementary rations, and established an inconspicuous office that had a separate entrance and was safe from prying eyes. On the eve of the ghetto's final liquidation, it was Neftalin who packed up the documents and did his best to hide them.

Bernard Ostrowski, the only survivor of the senior archive staff, recalled in 1947 that the archive was "semi-secret."[40] Rumkowski and the Germans knew about it but seemed to take little interest. There is no question, however, that Zelkowicz and the other writers had to exercise a degree of self-censorship that was absent in the Oyneg Shabes archive. After all, one could never know when Rumkowski might decide to read the documents or, even worse, when the Germans might show a sudden interest. Therefore the staff refrained from directly attacking Rumkowski and mentioned the Germans only elliptically. Zelkowicz, Singer, and Rosenfeld skillfully conveyed important information without crossing certain dangerous limits.

Zelkowicz played a central role in all aspects of the archive's wide-ranging activities. Its major project was the *Chronicle of the Łódź Ghetto,* which began in January 1941, continued until July 1944, and ultimately ran to several thousand pages. Edited first by Cukier and then, beginning in January 1942, by Oskar Singer, the *Chronicle* provided an almost day-by-day account of life in the ghetto. Interspersed with dry statistics and dutiful reports of Rumkowski's speeches and activities were gripping accounts of family tragedies, orphaned children, demoralization, and a dogged determination to survive.

After Oskar Singer took over as editor, the style of the *Chronicle* became more journalistic. New columns appeared, such as "What's Said, What's Heard," an interesting and compelling digest of incidents, street scenes, and rumors of the day. Lucille Eichengreen, who worked as a young secretary in the archive and survived the war, would recall that the office resembled the editorial desk of a city newspaper. Trusted friends and staff members arrived to report the latest rumors, exchange information, and discuss future plans. Yiddish poets like Simcha Bunem Shayevitsh often stopped by to discuss Yiddish literature with Zelkowicz.[41] Thus, the staff was somewhat better informed than the average Jew in the ghetto—although, compared with the Oyneg Shabes in Warsaw, it knew very little about what was going on in the outside world.

In January 1944 the archive began another important project, the *Ghetto Encyclopedia,* intended to provide future readers and historians with a guide to the special language of the ghetto. As Singer put it:

> Nowhere on earth is there any other kind of society that resembles the ghetto. The transformation of social, economic, and cultural conditions has also brought about a basic transformation of concepts [and words]. . . . Language as it is usually used does not correspond to the reality of the ghetto.[42]

VIII

Zelkowicz not only contributed to the *Encyclopedia* and the *Chronicle* but also wrote dozens of reports for the archive on ghetto factories, strikes, street scenes, folklore, and the struggle of ordinary Jews to stay alive. Some of these articles read like official reports: factual, informative, and unlikely to offend anybody, even the Germans. In others, Zelkowicz boldly and angrily attacks the corruption and protectionism that poisoned the ghetto's atmosphere. One example is *"Dura Lex, Sed Lex"* (the law is harsh, but it is the law). In this bitter exposé of the unequal justice meted out by the ghetto court, Zelkowicz mentions the case of a Jewish tailor who had absentmindedly taken a piece of thread from his workplace, was thrown out of his job, and saw his family condemned to starvation—all while ghetto bigwigs guilty of worse offenses got away scot-free. Even in this attack on corruption, however, Zelkowicz was very careful to avoid any direct criticism of Rumkowski.

Zelkowicz also kept a diary. Here, like Rosenfeld and Singer in their own private writings, he allowed himself to be more critical. There is, for example, a striking difference between his terse, somewhat bloodless summary in the *Chronicle* of the traumatic deportations of September 1942 and "In Those Nightmarish Days," his diary entries on the same events. And even in his diary, one must assume, Zelkowicz could not entirely let down his guard.

Zelkowicz was keenly aware that the documents he handled every day could not tell the entire truth. Often, indeed, they concealed as much as they revealed. In the summer of 1940, a guard at the ghetto fence murdered twenty-four Jews in a failed business deal that involved the smuggling of hens. In "Twenty-Five Chickens and One Dead Document," an investigative report of this disaster, Zelkowicz gave future readers some pointed advice on how to read such accounts.

> History loves to repeat itself. Its nuances, however, can be found in documents, though it is the nature of such documents either to tell us too much, and so to hide those nuances from us, or to tell us too little, so that their story must be enlarged by oral tradition. Documents are often so laconic in their tone, so dry, and seem so devoid of anything important to relate that they might as well be discarded, with nothing to be carefully considered and nothing remembered. But beware of those little scraps of paper that seem to tell us nothing at all. Don't throw them away until you've examined and researched them thoroughly.

Zelkowicz begins his investigative report with three brief documents. The first listed the recipients of twelve chickens confiscated by the ghetto's Jewish police. The second, compiled by the Department of Vital Statistics, noted when and where thirty-five Jews were shot near the ghetto fence in July 1940. The third was a record of the approximately 1,400 Jews buried that month at the cemetery, a mortality rate far above the prewar level.

What the documents failed to spell out, Zelkowicz gleaned "from the mouth of the people" and reconstructed by nimble detective work. His cast of characters includes Janek, a low-class Polish porter, and Leyzer, a Jew who before the war had run a flour business. Janek had occasionally worked for Leyzer, but now their roles were reversed. Janek was now Johann, an ethnic German standing guard at the ghetto gate, while Leyzer was a pitiful ghetto inmate. In the months before the ghetto was sealed, Janek had pocketed big bribes from Jews who were smuggling merchandise and food. But now, forced to live on his meager guard's salary, Janek was furious:

> No dog likes having a muzzle placed on his snout. By then, all his twenty-mark notes were long gone. And with all Jews now having been forced into the ghetto, there was nowhere else to look. Somehow Janek had to get by on the paltry policeman's salary. And you can't go get drunk when you have to do guard duty—stand guard like a dog on a chain.

So Janek jumped at the chance to do some business when by chance he saw his old boss Leyzer near the ghetto fence. Leyzer told Janek to get him hens; he would sell the eggs, and they would split the profits. But the deal went bad. The moment corrupt Jewish policemen saw eggs and chickens in the ghetto, they knew they were being cut out of a lucrative racket. The police tracked down Leyzer and confiscated twelve of his twenty-five chickens. In turn, Leyzer deducted the twelve chickens from the payoff he owed Janek.

> Janek wasn't as upset about the money as he was about the nerve of those Jewish troublemakers who without his permission had made use of his method of "requisitioning" at will, and he thought to himself: Good enough—if the damn Jewish troublemakers take twelve of his chickens, he'll take out two Jews for each one he's lost. . . .
>
> Let the ghetto remember redheaded Janek: two months and two days after the ghetto was closed off, he began systematically, and for nothing—for absolutely nothing—to shoot down twenty-four Jews.

Just as Zelkowicz discovered the real story behind the terse documents in this case, so he set out to reveal the human tragedies that underlay the laconic monthly reports of the ghetto's welfare department. The neediest Jews in the ghetto could qualify for a monthly dole after welfare inspectors interviewed them and filed an evaluation. Serving as a welfare inspector himself, Zelkowicz left gripping reports of his interviews, during which he was accompanied by Riva

Bramson, an educated woman who knew little Yiddish and had scant rapport with ordinary ghetto Jews.

Fifty years earlier, in 1891, the great Yiddish writer I. L. Peretz had also gone, pencil and paper in hand, to interview poverty-stricken Jews in shtetls near Lublin. Peretz's fictionalized account of these encounters, "Impressions of a Journey Through the Tomaszow Region," clearly served as a literary model for Zelkowicz's reportage of his own journey through the nooks and crannies of the Łódź ghetto.[43]

Peretz's narrator was an enlightened, Europeanized urban Jew whose task in the shtetl was in theory quite straightforward. He would conduct interviews and gather statistics. Perhaps he might also indirectly encourage the benighted shtetl Jews to take some small steps to better themselves. Yet his very first encounters sparked feelings of emotional turmoil and confusion. Although these Jews lacked a university education, they were not stupid. In their provincial Yiddish, heavily larded with phrases from traditional texts, they mocked his interest in statistics, questioned his motives, asked questions that he could not answer, and raised objections that he could not refute. The narrator begins to question the whole purpose of his mission and his own assumptions of cultural superiority. In a time of growing anti-Semitism, rising Polish nationalism, and waning faith in liberalism, who was he to promise them a better future? At the same time, he could not take refuge in romantic delusions about the supposed vitality and vibrancy of shtetl culture and traditional Judaism. Thus did a routine trip to the provinces turn into a journey into the soul of a modern Jew who had lost not only his religion but also his faith in progress and concord.

On his own visits to the appalling apartments of the Łódź ghetto a half-century later, Zelkowicz also confronted unexpected misgivings and self-doubt. He was deeply shaken by his encounters with filthy apartments, shattered families, proud heads of households on the brink of collapse, religious Jews who had lost their faith, and married couples now set against each other. In this time of shipwreck and calamity, what was it that he, an educated Jewish intellectual, had to offer—aside from a wretched welfare payment? As the interviews progressed, Zelkowicz also realized how often his own instincts and first impressions misled him.

Zelkowicz's political and cultural choices before the war had underscored his dedication to Yiddish, the folk, and the "Jewish people." But now he had to reconcile abstraction with reality, his faith in the nation with his disquieting encounter of actual individuals who had lost their moorings—or, no less mystifyingly, who responded to terror with displays of love, devotion, true caring, and the determination to protect a family.

As compared with the ghetto reportage of Peretz Opoczynski, that of Zelkowicz conveys a much greater feeling of distance from the ghetto Jews. Opoczynski's style, in many ways so similar to Sholem Aleichem's, imparts a sense of shared community between the narrator and his subjects. In Zelkowicz's narratives, by contrast, one can sense a gulf—no doubt the result, in part, of his own emotional turmoil and disorientation.

That disorientation is reflected in Zelkowicz's multilayered and revealingly frank narrative approach. One dimension is provided by his encounter with the ghetto Jews. It came as a rude shock to Zelkowicz that many saw him not as a progressive and sympathetic activist but as a detached intellectual and, even worse, as a privileged and hated stooge of Rumkowski and the Judenrat. As one desperate Jew blurted out:

"Have no fear. And death won't miss you, either! People like us really don't have any wood to burn, but for you all, providers for the *kehillah*, community leaders, record keepers, bloodsuckers, and rule makers, firewood won't be in short supply. They'll hang you all in groups of twenty-five—hang you from the ghetto bridges like they were store windows. Twenty-five on each side of the bridge! From the posts of the ghetto fence! Two community leaders to a pole; one on one side and one on the other—ha, ha, ha!"

Entering this apartment, Zelkowicz and Bramson were overwhelmed by the terrible stench of heaps of rotting vegetables that this Jew and his one surviving child were eating. Health warnings by Zelkowicz did not impress the man.

"To you it's junk. To representatives of the community, who sit in their offices with their delicate noses, who establish commissions and go out and record what they see—for them it's crap, it stinks: to them it's ty-phus, cholera, dysentery! But for people like us, who live like dogs and root like pigs—for us it's food! . . . Our sort of people, sir, are not pigs—human beings like us eat everything."

Another dimension in these narratives is Zelkowicz's internal con-versation with himself, his own attempt to make sense of what he was seeing. Going through the ghetto with Riva Bramson, he often discov-ered that his first impressions were absolutely wrong. The ghetto had turned the Jews' world so topsy-turvy that his instincts and common sense no longer served as reliable guides. In one room, he assumed that a couple in bed were a man and wife who, for lack of anything better to do, spent the empty days making love. He describes what he understood as sexual passion with a frankness quite rare in Yiddish writing, acknowledging his own prurient interest in their goings-on and lecturing Bramson to overcome her prudish shame and "take a closer look at 'him' and at 'her,' lying in a single bed and looking as if they've spent last night in stormy passion, completely exhausted and satisfied with no further need for each other."

But Zelkowicz had completely misread the situation. He had stum-bled not upon two adults lost in sexual pleasure but upon a loving fa-ther sharing his bed with one sick daughter because his other daugh-ter was infected with tuberculosis and had to sleep alone. His wife had died four months earlier.

No, Riva Bramson, don't curse me now! Don't sling the truth at me, the truth you want to tell, don't throw it right in my face! You see how I'm burning with—aflame with—shame. I'm ashamed of myself. I haven't been able to uproot the culture of the city from myself. And I'm glad that I can't. As far as our conversation on the subject of shame, Riva—please forget all about it.

A third dimension, as this passage suggests, is Zelkowicz's ongoing dialogue with Bramson, the educated European of refined manners who knew little Yiddish and needed Zelkowicz as mediator. In turn, it was through Riva Bramson that Zelkowicz addressed his future read-ers, for how else could individuals who had never been in a ghetto understand it?

On her own, without Zelkowicz to explain and to translate, Riva Bramson was caught in the trap of her own European sensibility, unable to look beneath the surface, unwilling to show empathy, to understand what lay behind the squalor. She had to realize that the ghetto was a complicated place, a place where mere facts did not tell the whole story. After all, Zelkowicz himself had learned not to trust his first impressions. As he writes, in words perhaps half addressed to himself:

> Get rid of those rose-colored glasses, Riva, and start looking at the world with the eyes of a real human being: a mensch. . . . And don't stop there, Riva Bramson. Teach your eyes that in the ghetto it's never enough to examine things from a realistic, factual point of view. Looking, and even seeing, aren't enough! Here your eyes have to be taught to get to the bottom of things—or as the saying goes, to read between the lines.

IX

When he wrote these reports, Zelkowicz could not foresee that the Jews he interviewed would become the first to be deported from the Łódź ghetto in early 1942 when Rumkowski, on German orders, put together the deportation lists. At the head of those lists were the welfare cases and the unemployed. No sooner had the first twenty thousand been sent out than the Germans demanded more. In the first six months of 1942, transports carrying close to fifty-five thousand victims departed for Chelmno.

Then, in the summer of 1942, there was a lull. Even Rumkowski had no advance warning of the calamity that was about to strike the ghetto in September, which Zelkowicz described in "In Those Nightmarish Days." The basic facts are well known. On August 31, the Nazis issued an order to deport nonproductive elements. The first to go would be patients in hospitals, children under the age of ten, and elderly people over sixty-five. But all of these groups together fell far short of the required total of twenty thousand. (Moreover, children of the Jewish police, of the "white guard" in the Food Provisioning Department, and of the ghetto elite were exempt.) Other Jews would have to go. Anyone who looked weak or frail was in mortal danger.

On September 1, armed Germans, aided by Jewish police, surrounded the hospitals in the ghetto and threw their patients into waiting trucks and carts. Panic spread as patients tried to escape; many were shot on the spot. The hospital raid took Rumkowski by surprise, but worse lay ahead. On September 4, he himself publicly confirmed the worst fears: parents would have to give up their children under ten. In his speech, Rumkowski, sobbing, looked like a broken man; Zelkowicz noted that his tears were "not feigned: they are Jewish tears, the outpourings of a Jewish heart." The ghetto, Rumkowski declared,

"has received a painful blow. They demand its most precious members— the children and the elderly. I have not had the privilege of having a child of my own and have therefore devoted my best years to the care of the child. I have lived and breathed children. I never imagined that my own hand would be the one to bring them to the sacrificial altar. In my old age I am forced to reach out my hand and beg you: brothers and sisters, give them away to me! Fathers and mothers, give me your children!

"Early yesterday they gave me the order to deport some twenty thousand Jews from the ghetto, and if not, 'We'll do it ourselves,' I was told. This posed the question: Should I undertake the task myself, or leave it to others to carry out?"

Rumkowski told the crowd that he had to cut off limbs in order to save the body. If he didn't carry through the deportation, then the Germans would step in and do it themselves. Therefore the Jewish police would do the job.

On Saturday, September 5, the Germans ordered a *Gehsperre,* a total curfew until further notice. Everyone had to stay inside. No one could be in the streets without a special pass. All ghetto factories closed. The all-important record office was sealed so parents could not change their children's birth dates.

On the first day of the *shpere,* the Jewish police carried out the roundups. But the Germans soon lost patience and took over the job themselves. House by house, courtyard by courtyard, they announced their presence with shouts and pistol shots. Everyone had to line up for the selection. The Germans snatched children from their mother's arms and shot anyone who resisted. They also paid little attention to documents. In theory, people under sixty-five who could prove employment were safe. In fact, no one was safe because the Germans seized anyone at random. Hans Biebow, whom so many Jews had regarded as a protector, rampaged through the streets with a pistol. A distraught Rumkowski shut himself in his office. According to Oskar Singer, he was close to suicide.

"In Those Nightmarish Days" is quite different from Zelkowicz's reports of home interviews. There, what everyone feared was starvation and disease, not mass murder, and he was still a reporter, able to observe and convey information from a position of authority. Despite his self-doubt and uncertainty, he had a certain status as an interviewer, as a representative of the Ghetto Bureau of Statistics, as a *zamler* collecting important material for future historians and ethnographers.

Here, however, he was confronting something totally unprecedented. He was watching the slow unfolding of palpable horror from the inside, in real time. He knew no more about what would happen in the next hour or the next day than the average Jew trapped inside his apartment. Even as he made the tragedy tangible through brilliant descriptions of individual families and people, he could not forget for a minute that he himself was in danger. When, on the second day of the curfew, the Germans shoved the Jewish police aside and took over the selections themselves, people were sent to their deaths on pure whim.

> The whole time you stood there lined up in the courtyard, trembling in your petrified trance, you lost all sense that you have a child, a wife, a heart, and a brain. Your head is held in a sturdy vise, your neck surrounded by a coarse noose, and heavy stones weigh upon your heart. The dearest person to you in the world could be shot down in your arms, your own child could be ripped away from you, together with a chunk of your own breast, and you—standing there in your deaf and dumb, narcotic torpor—you wouldn't move a single nerve or show even the slightest twitch of a reaction.

Objectively speaking, Zelkowicz had reason to feel safe: Neftalin protected him and the rest of the archive staff. But nothing was certain. Far from being a sagacious narrator or an inquisitive reporter, he was now peering directly into a monstrous horror that he had to struggle to understand.

Making his accounts so effective is, among other things, his use of time, a minute-by-minute, hour-by-hour record of how the Jews in the ghetto came to realize what was about to happen to them. Zelkowicz makes palpable and real the terror of Jewish parents living through the mornings, afternoons, and nights when they knew they would soon lose their children. As death crept closer, they held their children tighter and counted the minutes before the Germans would arrive to take them away forever. They were frantic. They were totally helpless. There was absolutely nothing they could do but wait. In the moments that remained, they hugged their children and gave them the last of their food. But they were trapped. Escalating fear and horror were measured by the slow ascent of the sun, the onset of twilight, the race against the clock to procure food before the curfew took effect.

> Today, however—how many years of their lives would people gladly have given up if they could just keep the sun from setting once more, to draw out this day longer and longer and make it last without end, so that a terrifying and tragic tomorrow would never come? Today, where is the Joshua who will cry out, "Sun, stand still in the ghetto!"

Each passing hour saw wild swings in the mood of the ghetto as everyone sought some weak reed of assurance. In vain: Zelkowicz's account of the final deportation in those "terrible days" brilliantly combines striking images of the collective with heartbreaking vignettes of particular victims. On the level of the collective:

> People are screaming. Their cries are terrifying, dreadful, and pointless, just as terrifying and dreadful and pointless as the action that is the direct cause of those laments. The ghetto is no longer simply frozen in fear— now it twists in convulsions: the whole ghetto has become one huge, monstrous spasm, leaping out of its own skin and then falling back upon the barbed wire.

On the level of the individual:

> There are many children in the ghetto who belong not just to their parents but to the building as a whole. Such children as a general rule are

lovely and far more intelligent than their age would indicate. Rysiek Fein was just such a child, everybody's darling. No neighbor, whether male or female, no stranger could pass him by without giving him a pat on his clever little head. No neighbor, whether male or female, could pass little Rysiek by without offering some version of the following: "My little Rysiek, what will you do when the war ends and we all get out of the ghetto?"

. . . And since Rysiek Fein was one of those children who belonged not just to their parents but to the entire building, none of the neighbors were able to look on when his father smashed his head against the wall in wild despair, and no one was there to hear when his mother shrieked out her dreadful pain.

There was old Mr. Krell, an elderly religious Jew who had spent his entire life in prayer; there was Berkowicz, a tough tanner who together with his wife had built a sturdy home and raised a solid and loving family; there was a Jewish mother who refused to hand over her child and was gunned down in front of the entire courtyard. And there was also an arrogant deportee from Düsseldorf, full of contempt for the Polish Jews, who refused to hide her own children and threatened to inform on her neighbors if they hid theirs. And there was another German-speaking mother who went insane after they took away her child, Putzi.

Throughout the long night and eight hours of the burning hot and feverish day, she could not just cry out "Putzi." The name had probably lost its effect on her ears, which heard it as simply a wild, un-Jewish, animalistic kind of sound. At dusk she began to scream, or rather bark, a series of different Jewish names: "Perele, Peyle, where did I leave you, Pay-le? Who tore you from my heart?" . . .

The doctor's diagnosis was that she was suffering from a fit of insanity. Was the evidence behind this diagnosis that a Jewish mother was crying out in Yiddish, from her Jewish heart?

It must have been especially difficult for Zelkowicz to write about his close friend, the Yiddish poet Simcha Bunem Shayevitsh. Despite suffering hunger and privation in the ghetto, Shayevitsh had the twin consolations of his poetry and his family. He deeply loved his wife and six-year-old daughter Blimele. It was to Blimele that he had addressed his great ghetto poems "Lekh-lekho" and "Friling Tof Shin Beys." As fate would have it, just before the *shpere* began, a second child was born, another little girl. Shayevitsh lost all three: his wife, Blimele, and the baby too young to be named.

> These are the facts, and 100 percent true ones at that. But the writer of these lines would not hold it against anyone who harbors doubts about them, just as the additional fact will seem unbelievable: that the father, the Yiddish poet, ran about in circles, taking this enormity to heart, while retaining his clarity of mind, which made him believe that he would somehow see this weakened, feverish mother of his newborn child again. He believed that his most beautiful poem of all would be returned to him—his Blimele, and along with her a beautiful, fresh and kicking little girl, a newborn who would now have a name.

x

Throughout his report on these unspeakable events, Zelkowicz continues to show some degree of sympathy for Rumkowski. He is harsher in his judgment of the Jewish police.

> The Jewish police were bought. Then they were gotten drunk and given a kind of hashish: their children were exempted from the deportation decree, and they were provided with a kilo and a half of bread per day in exchange for this bloody piece of work, enough bread to eat their fill and an extra ration of sausage and sugar.

Even stronger is his anger at the porters who volunteered to help deport Jews in return for guarantees of their own children's safety:

> The so-called "white guard"—the porters who work at the Bałuty market and the food department—should have their names inscribed in black on the bloody page of history that records these events. Afraid of losing their soup during the period of the curfew, they offered to help in the manhunt in exchange for the same benefits enjoyed by the police: bread, sausage, sugar, and the exemption of their families from the decree.

Yet elsewhere, surprisingly, as if he were not quite certain of his own judgment, Zelkowicz tempers his criticism of the police. It was a fact, he admits, that in doing their dirty work, the policemen displayed more humanity than the Germans. One could talk with them, bribe them. They did not make superhuman efforts to discover hiding places. And as for the white guard:

> Who really knows? Who can plumb the depths of the Jewish soul? Perhaps they thought they were achieving something entirely different, were engaged in some act of rescue, if such were even possible. Perhaps.

Why did Zelkowicz moderate—if ever so slightly—his attacks on Jews who helped deport other people's children in order to save their own? Why did he treat Rumkowski with a certain degree of restraint, even with some sympathy? One scholar has argued that he was only practicing self-censorship, but this is unconvincing. The fact is that Zelkowicz, like most of his fellow Jews in the Łódź ghetto, saw no alternative to Rumkowski's course of action—a fact that only intensified their horror, their sense of being truly trapped.

Nowhere in "In Those Nightmarish Days" is there a call for resistance. Zelkowicz does not drop even the slightest hint that Rumkowski should have refused German orders or that Jewish parents should have attacked the Germans with hammers and sticks. With the knife at their throats, the Jews saw Rumkowski's strategy—buying time with Jewish labor—as their only option. It was for the same reason that Zelkowicz tempered his condemnation of the Jewish police. If one ruled out resistance and suicide, what was left? This was truly a time, in the phrase of the historian Lawrence Langer, of choiceless choices. Although Zelkowicz does employ some of the tone and literary approach of Bialik's caustic "City of Slaughter," he lacks Bialik's hubris and willingness to sit in judgment on his fellow Jews. Bialik knew what he wanted to say. Zelkowicz was painted into a corner.

The manuscript of "In Those Nightmarish Days" breaks off unfinished. But on September 14, 1942, two days after the *shpere* ended, Zelkowicz composed a long report for the *Chronicle*. With astonishment, he notes that people were already returning to their routine.

Is this some sort of numbing of the nerves, an indifference, or a symptom of an illness that manifests itself in atrophied emotional reactions? After losing those nearest to them people talk constantly about rations, potatoes, soup, etc.! It is beyond comprehension!

In fact, after September 1942, the ghetto experienced twenty-two months of relative stability. The archive undertook new projects. Rumkowski was stripped of much of his power by the Germans. He lost control over the distribution of food and to a large degree over the management of the ghetto workshops. Jews began to complain about him openly, and street singers performed biting lyrics about him, but all knew that nobody could take his place. The ghetto was deeply shaken when the Germans summoned him to Gestapo headquarters in December 1943, and breathed a sigh of relief when he returned.

Rumkowski told his ghetto critics that he would continue to do what was necessary to save at least a remnant. After the war, he would accept the verdict of a Jewish court. Did anyone have a better alternative to offer? When he gave members of underground political parties the chance to save their comrades from deportation, did they not do so without hesitation—even though they knew that to save a friend meant another Jew would take his place?

After the nightmare of the *Gehsperre*, and during the ghetto's almost two-year respite, the battlefront of the war was moving closer and closer. By July 1944, the Russians had reached the Vistula, only sixty miles away. At night the Łódź Jews could hear the distant thump of heavy artillery.

But then came the end. Hans Biebow had assured the Jews that they would leave the ghetto for work in the Reich. The trains took them instead to Auschwitz Birkenau.

XI

When members of the Oyneg Shabes in Warsaw buried the first boxes of documents, in August 1942, they were sure that after the war someone would find them and those pieces of paper would shake the conscience of the world. Unfortunately, the impact was much smaller than they had hoped.

Opoczynski's essays written in the Warsaw ghetto were first published in Poland in 1954 in a bowdlerized, heavily censored edition edited by Ber Mark. In 1970 Tzvi Shner edited a Hebrew edition of his essays that was more comprehensive and more reliable. A Polish version, edited and translated by Monika Polit, was published in Warsaw in 2009. Some of Zelkowicz's reportages were published in Isaiah Trunk's *Łódź Ghetto: A History*, which originally appeared in Yiddish in 1962. Yad Vashem published a Hebrew edition of Zelkowicz's essays in 1994, and this appeared in English in 2002 under the title *In Those Terrible Days: Writings from the Lodz Ghetto*. Excerpts from Zelkowicz's writings also appeared in Lucy Dawidowicz's *Holocaust Reader* (1976) and Milton Teichman's *Truth and Lamentation* (1993).

Since the end of the war, Opoczynski, Zelkowicz, and the other members of the ghetto archives have been largely forgotten. These extraordinary writers have failed to win the attention they deserve. One hopes this volume may help correct that wrong.

NOTES

1. Rachel Auerbach, *Varshever tsavoes* (Tel Aviv: Yisroel Bukh, 1974), p. 9.

2. Gustavo Corni, *Hitler's Ghettos: Voice from a Beleaguered Society, 1939–1944* (London: Bloomsbury, 2003), p. 2.

3. Samuel Gringauz, "The Ghetto as an Experiment of Jewish Social Organization," *Jewish Social Studies* 11 (January 1949), p. 5.

4. For an excellent memoir of Poland's most popular Yiddish mass daily, *Haynt*, see Chaim Finkelstein, *Haynt: a tsaytung bay Yidn* (Tel Aviv: Farlag Y. L. Peretz, 1978).

5. Auerbach, *Varshever tsavoes*, pp. 174–175.

6. See Jeffrey Veidlinger, *Jewish Public Culture in the Late Russian Empire* (Bloomington: Indiana University Press, 2009), pp. 114–196.

7. See, for example, Gabriella Safran, *Wandering Soul: The Dybbuk's Creator, S. Ansky* (Cambridge, 2010); Ruth Wisse, *I. L. Peretz and the*

Making of Modern Yiddish Culture (Seattle: University of Washington Press, 1991).

8. Nathaniel Deutsch, "When Culture Became the New Torah: Late Imperial Russia and the Discovery of Jewish Culture," *Jewish Quarterly Review* 102:3 (Summer 2012), pp. 455–473.

9. S. M. Dubnow, "Ob izuchenii istorii russkikh evreev i ob uchrezhdenii istoricheskogo obshchestva," *Voskhod,* vols. 4–9, April–September 1891, pp. 1–91; see also his autobiography, *Kniga Zhizni* (Saint Petersburg: PV, 1998), pp. 168–169.

10. Peretz Opoczynski, *Gezamlte shriftn,* edited by Rina-Opper Opochinsky (New York, 1951), p. 173.

11. On this subject of Jewish Polishness, see Katrin Steffen, *Jüdische Polonität: Ethnizität und Nation im Spiegel der polnischsprachigen jüdischen Presse* (Göttingen: Vandenhoeck and Rupprecht, 2004). See also Khone Shmeruk, "Hebrew-Yiddish-Polish: A Trilingual Jewish Culture," in *The Jews of Poland Between Two World Wars,* ed. Israel Gutman (Hanover, N.H.: University Press of New England, 1989), pp. 285–312.

12. Quoted in Shmeruk, "Hebrew-Polish-Yiddish," p. 307.

13. On IKOR and the fight for Yiddish in the Warsaw ghetto, see Samuel D. Kassow, *Who Will Write Our History? Emanuel Ringelblum, the Warsaw Ghetto, and the Oyneg Shabes Archive* (Bloomington: Indiana University Press, 2007), pp. 116–118.

14. David G. Roskies, "Bialik in the Ghettos," *Prooftexts* 25: 1–2 (Winter/ Spring 2005), pp. 82–99.

15. Ibid., p. 113.

16. On details of Opoczynski's prewar life, see Rina-Opper Opochinsky, "Mayn bruder Peretz Opoczynski," in Opoczynski, *Gezamlte shriftn,* pp. 5–60. This is virtually the only source on Opoczynski's pre-1939 biography.

17. For a good overview of *Dos vort,* written by an insider, see "Dos vort, Dos naye vort, Folksvort," in *Di yidishe prese vos iz geven,* ed. David Flinker, Mordechai Tsanin, and Sholem Rosenfeld (Tel Aviv: Orly, 1975), pp. 170–190.

18. One group of workers that it did organize was the *hoyzirer,* the rag pickers. Opoczynski wrote some vivid reportage on their trade before

the war, and his expertise stood him in good stead in the wartime reportage "Goyim in the Ghetto," included in this volume.

19. Opoczynski, *Gezamlte shriftn*, p. 173.

20. Kassow, *Who Will Write Our History?* p. 186.

21. Ibid.

22. Emanuel Ringelblum, "Oyneg Shabes," translated by Leah Robinson in *The Literature of Destruction*, ed. David G. Roskies (Philadelphia: Jewish Publication Society, 1989), p. 391.

23. For more on this "legal reportage," see Barbara Engelking and Jacek Leociak, *The Warsaw Ghetto: The Guide to the Perished City* (New Haven: Yale University Press, 2009), p. xix. This is the first ever study of the Warsaw ghetto that makes extensive use of this important and valuable source, the *Gazeta Żydowska*.

24. Peretz Opoczynski, "Megiles Parowke," in *Reportazhn fun Varshever geto*, edited by Ber Mark (Warsaw: Yidish-bukh, 1954), p. 26.

25. Opoczynski, *Gezamlte shriftn*, p. 138.

26. Peretz Opoczynski, *Reportazhn fun varshever geto*, edited by Ber Mark (Warsaw: Yidish-bukh, 1954), p. 9.

27. Israel Gutman, *The Jews of Warsaw* (Bloomington: Indiana University Press, 1983), p. 66.

28. Raul Hilberg, Stanislaw Staron, and Joseph Kermish, eds., *The Warsaw Diary of Adam Czerniakow: Prelude to Doom*, translated by Stanislaw Staron and the staff of Yad Vashem (New York: Stein and Day, 1982), p. 316.

29. Ringelblum Archive (Oyneg Shabes archive), Jewish Historical Institute, Warsaw, ARII, document no. 289.

30. Entry on Zelkowicz in *Leksikon fun der nayer yidisher literatur*, vol. 3 (New York, 1960), pp. 670–671.

31. Michal Unger, "About the Author," in *In Those Terrible Days: Notes from the Łódź Ghetto*, ed. Michal Unger, translated from the Hebrew by Naftali Greenwood (Jerusalem: Yad Vashem, 2002), p. 11.

32. Paweł Spodenkiewicz, *Zaginiona Dzielnica: Łódź żydowska, ludzie i miejsca* (Łódź: Łódźska księgarnia niezależna, 1998), p. 103.

33. Josef Zelkowicz, "Der toyt un zayne bagleyt-momentn in der yidisher etnografye un folklor" and "A bild fun'm yidishn gezelshaftlekhn lebn in a poylish shtetl in tsveytn helft fun 19tn yorhundert," *Łódźher*

visnhaftlekhe shriftn, vol. 1 (1938). The latter article was translated into English by Shlomo Noble and published as "A Picture of the Communal Life of a Jewish Town in the Second Half of the Nineteenth Century," in *Yivo Annual of Jewish Social Science* 6 (1951), pp. 253–266.

34. For more on *Landkentenish*, see Samuel Kassow, "Travel and Local History as a National Mission: Polish Jews and the Landkentenish Movement of the 1920s and 1930s," in *Jewish Topographies: Visions of Space, Traditions of Place*, ed. Alexandra Nocke, Anna Lipphardt, and Julia Brauch (Aldershot: Ashgate, 2008), pp. 241–265.

35. Leon Wulman, "Di ideologishe yesoydes fun undzer program," *Yedies fun der yidisher gezelshaft far landkentenish*, May–June 1933.

36. Philip Friedman, "Regionalizm," *Yoyvl Numer Landkentenish*, April 1937.

37. The best sources on the Łódź ghetto, from which the facts outlined below are taken, are Michal Ungar, *Łódź: aharon ha'getaot be'Polin* (Jerusalem: Yad Vashem, 2005), and Andrea Löw, *Juden im Getto Litzmannstadt: Lebensbedingungen, Selbstwahrnehmung, Verhalten* (Göttingen: Wallstein, 2006).

38. Löw, *Juden im Getto Litzmannstadt*, p. 212. Rumkowski himself declared his determination to promote Yiddish in the ghetto and stood ready to help ghetto intellectuals and writers. He even decreed that Yiddish would be the language of the ghetto schools and ordered teachers who did not know the language to learn it. Zelkowicz taught some of these courses.

39. Neftalin had been an attorney before the war. He was one of the relatively few members of Rumkowski's inner circle who commanded wide respect. Although he came from an acculturated background, he was also supportive of Yiddish culture in the ghetto. Klementynowski had been a prominent businessman before the war, with little connection to Jewish life. Cukier was an experienced and respected journalist who had written for the Polish liberal journal *Rzeczpospolita*. Both Klementynowski and Cukier died in the ghetto.

40. Archive of Jewish Historical Institute of Warsaw, 301/2841, testimony of Bernard Ostrowski, October 16, 1947.

41. Ostrowski testimony, 301/2841.

42. Löw, *Juden im Getto Litzmannstadt*, p. 402. Oskar Rosenfeld wrote that "the collection of new words and terms is an essential part of the cultural history of the ghetto. For those who want to study the ghetto in the future, such a collection will provide insights that would not be gained simply from factual descriptions." Ibid., p. 403.

43. These Peretz travel sketches have been republished in English translation by the New Yiddish Library, in "Impressions of a Journey Through the Tomaszow Region," in *The I. L. Peretz Reader*, ed. Ruth R. Wisse (New Haven: Yale University Press, 2002), translated from the Yiddish by Hillel Halkin, pp. 17–88.

SUGGESTIONS FOR FURTHER READING

Lucjan Dobroszycki, ed., *Chronicle of the Lodz Ghetto, 1941–1944*, trans. from Polish and German by Richard Lourie, Joachim Neugroschel, et al. (New Haven: Yale University Press, 1984).

Barbara Engelking and Jacek Leociak, *The Warsaw Ghetto: A Guide to the Perished City*, trans. from Polish by Emma Harris (New Haven: Yale University Press, 2009).

Israel Gutman, *The Jews of Warsaw, 1939–1943: Ghetto, Underground, Revolt*, trans. from Hebrew by Ina Friedman (Bloomington: Indiana University Press, 1982).

Samuel D. Kassow, *Who Will Write Our History? Rediscovering a Hidden Archive from the Warsaw Ghetto* (New York: Vintage Books, 2009).

Cecile Kuznitz, *Yivo and the Making of Modern Jewish Culture: Scholarship for the Yiddish Nation* (New York: Cambridge University Press, 2014).

David G. Roskies, *Against the Apocalypse: Responses to Catastrophe in Modern Jewish Culture* (Syracuse, N.Y.: Syracuse University Press, 1999).

David G. Roskies, ed., *The Literature of Destruction: Jewish Responses to Catastrophe* (Philadelphia: Jewish Publication Society, 1989).

David G. Roskies and Naomi Diamant, *Holocaust Literature: A History and Guide* (Waltham, Mass.: Brandeis University Press, 2012).

Isaiah Trunk, *Łódź Ghetto: A History*, trans. from Yiddish and ed. by Robert Moses Shapiro; introduction by Israel Gutman (Bloomington: Indiana University Press; published in association with the United States Holocaust Museum, 2006).

Michal Unger, *The Last Ghetto: Life in the Lodz Ghetto*, trans. from Hebrew by Naftali Greenwood (Jerusalem: Yad Vashem, 1997).

Josef Zelkowicz, *In Those Terrible Days: Writings from the Lodz Ghetto*, ed. by Michal Unger, trans. from Hebrew (in turn trans. from original Yiddish) by Naftali Greenwood (Jerusalem: Yad Vashem, 2002).

♦♦♦ *Reportage from the Warsaw Ghetto*

PERETZ OPOCZYNSKI

A peasant farmer drives into the courtyard with a little cartload of cabbage, bread, and potatoes; he sells the potatoes to one of the tenants, who'd been waiting for him by the road from Wola.[1] No one knows how much he paid for them, but the price he was asking barely five minutes later would make the eyes pop out of your head. Other tenants from the building buy the bread—cabbage and bread. There's pushing and shoving, and things get a little heated—but they pay the peasant whatever he asks: two guilders for a kilo of dirty black bread and the same for a kilo of cabbage. In all the confusion, one tenant snatches a small loaf of bread from the peasant when his back is turned; another pockets a half head of cabbage and doesn't pay a penny. When the peasant realizes that he's being robbed, he lifts a crossbar from his cart and threatens the crowd with it, full of rage and about to explode. Only then does the crowd start to back away. People keep what they've grabbed and keep quiet. The peasant stands by his cart, his eyes flashing like knives, while his wife heaps curses on the heads of the Jews, screaming that all their suffering is much less than they deserve.

1. Wola was one of the western sections of Warsaw, close to the Jewish quarter.

To the left, the Zelechower, who has himself filched two small heads of cabbage, rubs his hands together in glee: he lands on his feet even when everything around is burning down.[2] Now he's even begun to hope that things are looking up. His apartment is being rebuilt—the brick walls are already standing, though the roof hasn't been installed. With the fall winds beginning to howl, rainwater pours down from the upper apartments onto the heads of the tenants who live on the lower floors. The water has reached all the way to the bottom floor, flooding the floor where the egg dealer does business.

The landlady gets up at five in the morning to clean the courtyard all by herself. Her husband will sleep until late in the morning, but there's no rest for the weary. After the building janitor quit, she was seized by an overwhelming desire to work—to drudge away at her work and do nothing else. The effort lifts her spirits, reminding her of how she felt in her prime, when by toiling day and night she clawed and scratched her way to eventual ownership of the building itself. She can't enjoy it, however. Every second, the tenant from another ruined, flooded apartment bursts in to plague her with a another stream of complaints—telling her right to her face that, after all the hard work she's done, it's *her* fault that the place is a shambles and that the whole building will fall to pieces if she doesn't fix his place right away.

Hearing these claims against her, the landlady becomes extremely agitated. Not this; anything but this. Would she let her own building go to wrack and ruin, her own blood and sweat? She assures everyone that the construction will be completed as soon as possible; as soon as the bricklayers arrive, she'll speed things up, and while she's at it, she thinks to herself, she'll start demanding rent. Can she repair a building for free? She knows that the Zelechower, the shoemaker, and Pearl have stripped all the wood from the ceilings and walls of their damaged apartments and stashed it under their beds in their so-called shelters to use as firewood in the coming winter. But she doesn't say a word. She knows that sometimes, when you can't get in the front door, you've got to go around back, and besides, she's not about to start up with Pearl . . . no need to stir them up—they'll be paying rent soon

<hr />

2. This man is from Żelechów, a Jewish shtetl, or small town, near Warsaw.

enough. So she keeps it to herself and goes on with her work, cleaning and dragging the scattered bricks into the yard, sweeping out her apartment, then the whole building . . .

From every direction, the peasant farmers arrive with carts piled high with produce from the villages, carts filled with potatoes, cabbage, wood, and even with coal, for Jews are not allowed to get coal from the trains. Some people say that they aren't even real peasants but people from the outskirts of the city trying to make their living by trading with Jews. No one can say how they got permission to enter the city with their carts, but it makes sense—the local authorities are more likely to look the other way. After all, the German commandants in those places have to make a living too.

The whole length of Miła Street is crammed with these peasant carts; they wend their way onto Lubeckiego and Wołynska Streets. In fact, they pass through the whole neighborhood, especially the carts that are loaded with wood.

People stand in long lines in front of Wedel's shop on Marszałkowska Street and later on Bielanska—at the drop of a hat—each person keeping a watchful eye on the other.[3] If a passerby comes up and asks about the line, people answer that they don't know—they're simply waiting there, that's all. Eventually, word gets around that two guilders at Wedel's will get you a bar of prewar chocolate along with a little bag of candy. People buy these not to eat them but as merchandise that can be resold. There are still a few Jews left with enough money to treat themselves to a nice hunk of chocolate, though there are many more collapsing in the streets from hunger. So let there be chocolate—if it helps you stay alive.

In the city-run shops of the Christian area, like those far down on Marszałkowska, milk can be bought, and there's even candy for sale. The furrier's wife, along with the glove maker's daughters and the cobbler's wife, hear about it and spend whole days standing in line to bring home a few bars of chocolate and a little inexpensive milk. The milk that the peasants are bringing from the villages, along with butter, cheese, and sweet cream, is very expensive. Suddenly Jewish men

3. Wedel's chocolate factory had a chain of shops throughout Warsaw.

begin to appear throughout the city with yellow Stars of David on their sleeves and their wives with yellow patches sewn onto their shawls. Giant platform trucks arrive carrying Jewish men, women, and children, with noses red from the damp, cold fall weather. What's this? Who are these people?

As they pass, people on every street yell up to them: "What's happened? Where are you from?" The men, increasingly bitter from the constant questioning, answer back, "From Rózaniec, from Sierpc . . ."[4] Forty Jews from Sierpc arrive at Building No. 21 and settle themselves in front of a vacant storefront. The landlady doesn't put up an argument—on the contrary, she talks to the building commandant about ways to help them out.[5] Since it's Thursday afternoon, they come up with the idea of providing them with cholent to eat for the Sabbath (afterward, the commandant will boast that the cholent cost a whole hundred zlotys). After the Sabbath, the commandant makes the rounds of all the tenants who wanted to sublet places in their apartments and finds room for forty of them in the building. The landlady understands what this is all about. Her tenants are charging the Jews from Sierpc a pretty penny for places in kitchen corners or even for spots under the sink. What's this? she wants to know. And she's not supposed to collect rent?

The four thousand Jews from Sierpc and the same number from Rózaniec have already been housed in the city. Now there's news that expulsions are going on in other areas, however, and all at once Jews stop hoarding supplies. Katz, who'd already laid up a wagonload of coal in the cellar, refuses to take delivery of another; the butcher and the landlady quit buying up potatoes for the winter. The sausage maker buys no more salt and the shoemaker no more leather. What for? Does anyone know what tomorrow may bring? From eight in the morning on, a peasant with a cart stands in the courtyard of the building with a load of potatoes. Instead of getting the eighty zlotys a bushel he

---

4. These two towns were the first two victims of Hitler's expulsions from western Poland. In the western parts of Poland, Jews were forced to wear a Star of David on their clothing.

5. The commandant in charge of the building courtyard was one of the tenants.

was asking yesterday, today he's charging only seventy. By noon he's already down to fifty, and he stays there until dusk trying to drum up sales. Before long the price is down to forty-five zlotys a bushel—but still there are no takers. The peasant spends the night in the courtyard with his wares and in the morning sets off with a curse on his lips for the "kikes." Have they suddenly been possessed by a devil? What, they suddenly don't want to feed their faces? What gives?

The general state of confusion lasts another day or two, and before long the rumors start to fly, racing from one ear to the next: "The Russkies are on the move . . . they're not far from Praga . . . the border's been opened . . . Jews are crossing free as a bird to the Other Side."[6] All of a sudden the courtyard feels crowded. Not just the butcher, the Zelechower, and the volatile building commandant, but all the residents move into the street, talking about the same thing. Little knots of people cluster near the gates of the courtyard and discuss the news, and the same scene plays itself out at the front gate of every building. Every courtyard is jam-packed. In the street, you discover the latest developments even quicker by singling out a passerby and shouting out to him: "Tell me, do you know what's going on? Are they really coming?"

"What a question! You'll see. Tomorrow morning they'll be in Warsaw." The Zelechower is only waiting for his apartment. Then he'll figure out what to do. You don't have to draw him any maps. His sharp, squinty Kalmyk eyes shine with a shrewd sparkle, and his broad, foursquare shoulders stretch across his frame like a board as he cinches his belt and chuckles quietly to himself. The army tailor is also very secretive. He doesn't reveal even to his own wife, Pearl, that he's planning to leave for the Other Side with his son Zalman. Pearl, however,

---

6. In the first weeks of the German-Polish war in September 1939, rumor had it that the Russians would advance to the Vistula, thus including the Warsaw suburb of Praga, on the east side of the river. Soviet troops did in fact quickly occupy and annex eastern Poland, although the German-Soviet demarcation line was actually well east of the Vistula, along the Bug River. Anyone hoping to escape from Warsaw had to get to the other side of the Vistula and then make a dangerous crossing of the Bug in order to reach Soviet-controlled territory.

has already gotten wind of what he's up to and wastes no time in making it absolutely clear that she won't let him out of the house with their only son—he can forget about *that*. Besides, the whole idea doesn't seem worth much to her. No, you can make a living right here under the Germans—that's her guess—and even better than you can on the Other Side.

The building commandant toys with the idea of leaving to join his brother-in-law in Tel Aviv, but he knows full well it's nothing but a pipe dream. Yes, of course, the Germans are letting a few people out of the country for huge sums of money, and the Italian Jews provide the visas. The Italian consulate in Warsaw is not making any trouble, at least not yet. When Hitler and Il Duce meet at Brenner Pass things will certainly be different, but until then you still have to earn the good graces of the Germans—not so much earn it as buy it. He knows all sorts of stories of Jews who reached the Land of Israel and even points beyond, but always for a price: say, twenty thousand zlotys. With that much cash in hand, no visa is required. That much can even get you to America. How does it work? Quit asking so many questions! You just have to know the right people . . . But what difference does it make? He, the commandant, is one of the rich, and besides, he has a record of revolutionary activity . . . back in 1905. Still, he's thinking about sending his sons to the Other Side—he's got another brother-in-law in Małkinia.[7]

Then the Germans order Jewish shops to display signs in Yiddish—no, in Hebrew: *Ki beyver hanohor yoshvu avoyseykhem* (From beyond the river came your fathers).[8] This decree comes as no big surprise. Everyone understands it as a continuation of the prewar Polish government's policy, under the regime known as OZON, ordering shopkeepers to hang a small sign displaying the owner's Jewish, rather than his Polish, first name.[9] Not Hela Wierzbicka or Bernard Leczycki,

---

7. Małkinia was a town on the new German-Soviet border; as such it was the last stop for thousands of refugees before they crossed into Soviet territory.

8. Joshua 24:2.

9. OZON, or the Camp of National Unity (Obóz Zjednoczenia Narodowego), was the Polish political party that came to power in 1937.

but Chana or Baruch, in true biblical style. Suddenly, Hebrew sign painters are everywhere, flooding the streets with unintentionally comic signs: *Akhilo mezoynes umini* (various and sundry edibles), *Barzel yashan kone* (used iron goods), *Khayat bgodim ishi'im* (men's tailor), and other ridiculous phrases. Winebaum hangs out a sign: *Khanus lekhem mezoynes vekhol akhilo* (store for bread, food, and all things edible). His new wife, his late wife's sister and nothing like the wicked stepmother that Rukhtshe the baker's wife had predicted, argues with the dealer in knitwear—a Yiddishist—who twits her, asking her why they didn't put up their sign in Yiddish instead. She's wasted a perfectly good piece of signboard, he tells her, by mixing Yiddish and Hebrew together. What's he trying to do, she replies—stir up trouble for her with the Germans? If they want Khebrew, let it be Khebrew. Let them rack their brains trying to figure it out—as long as they leave her alone!

Train travel by Jews has already been forbidden. But the ban is not yet being strictly enforced. In any case, it's not much of a calamity for Warsaw's Jews! Only a few people travel by train to the Soviet side: most go by bus, by wagon, or on foot. Going anywhere else by train is simply out of the question, except for real daredevils and the bravest of the brave, like smugglers or those clever operators who know how to talk their way out of anything and who've spent a small fortune on false papers so they can travel throughout most of Poland.

There's a huge row taking place at the entrance to the building: the lottery agent's daughter, whose fiancé was killed defending the city—a volunteer in the battalion called "The Children of Warsaw"—has fallen in love with a thief and gotten married.[10] Her father, a Hasidic Jew, ran out on his daughter during the bombardment, when she took several other thieves into the apartment as subletters. She's actually gone and married one of them; her father fell sick from the heartache. And now he's dying. Pearl spares no frills as she dishes up the story to her listeners in all its sordid detail. "Didn't you just know how the whole thing would end up?" she cries. "The girl's a Hasid's daughter,

---

10. The Children of Warsaw was a volunteer brigade for civil defense set up in the first month of the war.

after all, isn't she? Not worth the dirt on the soles of your shoes. *Our children would never do such a thing!* Only the daughter of a Hasid could go and do something like that: get conned, then fall head over heels for a worthless crook." The shoemaker's wife listens to the tale, bubbling over with self-satisfaction, while the Zelechower tries to get his dull brain to figure out exactly what the moral of this story is: yes, they're all bunglers, those Hasidic Jews, they're not like us at all . . . of course it's not news to him. He already knew all he needed to know about their kind back in Żelechów.

Pearl continues to hash out every angle of the story in her "temporary quarters." She's squeezed herself in with the Zelechower and the shoemaker until her own apartment is finished. That way she'll keep the neighbors from seeing just how eager she is to move back into her renovated apartment with the few belongings she took with her, once it's fixed up again just like new. The kitchen is already finished, and she's been doing some secret cooking there in the afternoons. Why should her neighbors in her temporary quarters have to know about every morsel she eats? She also spends part of every day standing in the Wołówka, the flea market, selling jackets, patting her stomach with both hands in satisfaction as if to say, "When you know what you're doing, you've got it made: a newly refurbished apartment, the wood off the walls, and you're out of paying rent . . ."

Brodsky the baker's eldest son has gone to the Russian Zone, having set off by bus. There are buses still leaving from Nalewki Street. For two hundred zlotys they will take you as far as Białystok. Where on Nalewki? From which courtyard? The building commandant knows where. He wants to send his eldest son too, but he's come up with a better plan: he'll take him there himself on the train, at least as far as Małkinia. Rivkeleh's son, who makes lightweight shoes (*gandis*), is also headed out; a few subletters take off for the Other Side every day. Every discussion in every apartment centers on leaving—how to get away. The army tailor and the Zelechower, waiting impatiently for their apartments to be finished, fill the empty time like two school-boys—scheming and dreaming up different ways to realize their plan to escape to Russia. Their goal is to somehow find their way to a big city—Moscow, Leningrad, Kharkov—where you can get big, fluffy white bread rolls and bowls full of rice, fish, and meat. "Listen, neighbor, listen," the Zelechower stutters, racing to get out the words. "I talked to a young guy from the building at No. 10 who just got back from there yesterday to pick up his wife and kids. He says if you get a job where those Bolsheviks run things, you can earn up to five hundred rubles a week—and you can get anything you want to eat there. All you need is a little luck."

"And what if you don't get a job?" the army tailor asks him.

"You sleep in the House of Study," the Zelechower answers him, "and you'll get something to eat that way. Three portions a day of bread and soup they'll give you there—enough to survive." The army tailor was ready to try anything, even though his experience in the World War has made him skeptical of stories that sound too good to be true. He's also worried about how to deal with Pearl, his wife. Before anything else can happen he has to talk her into letting him leave. That won't be easy.

The Zelechower and the army tailor can't just sit on their hands in the apartment. They constantly go outside and stand at the gate of the building, trying to get news of the latest developments from the crowd that always gathers nearby. Sometimes a wagon with thatched sides rumbles down the street—the kind you might see in the little villages near Lublin. The wagon is packed to the brim with Jewish men and women, to all appearances looking like a group of in-laws traveling to a wedding. The wives are all beautifully dressed, each with a little valise in her lap; their faces are hot and flushed.

"Where are you heading in that wagon?"

"To the Other Side."

"Really! I don't believe it."

"Believe it or don't believe it—but that's where they're going. They're heading to the Other Side."

At present, the number of wagons coming down the street loaded with people headed for the Other Side is growing from day to day. None of the neighbors can sit inside their apartments all day long; business and work have, for all intents and purposes, come to a complete halt. People are selling what's left of their possessions to get by, all dreaming of traveling to the Other Side. The army tailor, having seen something of the world, knows all the different routes: through Małkinia on the train or through Otwock on the small-gauge before getting back on the regular train, through Kolbuszowa and Zamość, or through Siedlce by train and then on through Sokołów and Biała by bus. The line to Sokołów goes straight from Bonifraterska Street in Warsaw to Sokołów, except for one small catch: to buy the extra ticket, you have to stand in line for a week, and after all that you've got to pay double to get the ticket in your hand.

Rivkeleh's son, who didn't have the money for the bus, set off for Praga. He made it past the sentry at the bridge for a five-note, sticking the bill into the hand of the Polish policeman while the German guard looked the other way. So he took off for Małkinia on foot. From there, getting across the border was not supposed to be a problem. In fact, he ended up stuck in the same spot near the border for a whole week in No Man's Land until a more amenable sentry arrived and cried out *"Tovarishtishi, perekhaditye!"*—"Comrades, pass through!"—finally allowing him to cross the border. Now he's not living in Białystok but in a little village nearby, and he's got it good. He's found work and writes his mother that he'll bring her over soon.

The letter from Rivkeleh's son soon passes through the hands of everyone in the tenement. Everyone who reads it handles it like some magical amulet—as if it were a wishing ring. With each passing minute, another neighbor rushes in:

"Good morning, Rivkeleh."

"Good morning, good year."

"Rivkeleh, do you think we could have another look at the letter you got from your son?"

"The letter? It's not in the apartment right now; someone took it over to the cane maker."

The neighbor leaves without even saying good day. Slamming the door with extra emphasis behind him, he hurries down to the cane maker's place in the basement, where the apartment is already packed with neighbors. The Zelechower stands in the middle of the group explaining the letter to everyone, which in fact needs no commentary at all to be clear. "Dear Mama," writes Rivkeleh's son in Yiddish printed in German letters. "I'm working, and everything's going very well. I've got enough to eat, and I can go where I want. You can make a living here; people are singing in the streets. I've already applied for your papers, and God willing, I'll be able to bring you over . . ."

"Aha, so you see," declares the Zelechower, pointing his index finger as if he were about to spring open a lock. He sticks out the tip of his tongue, furrows his thick, narrow brows, and bursts out with the following explanation: "That's right—he's got enough to e-eat, and can go where he l-likes. Like I already told you—do you need it any cl-clearer? Here, the minute you go outside, they grab you up for forced l-l-labor. There—you can do what you want! N-n-neighbor—are you listening, n-n-neighbor?" he asks the army tailor. Completely carried away, he turns to the army tailor with moist eyes. "Are you with me? Let's take off this week."

The cellar is in an uproar. Everyone speaks at once, with each interrupting the other out of sheer excitement. The cane maker alone is silent.

"And what's the point of going, exactly?" the tailor finally asks. "The Russians are going to be in Warsaw soon anyway."

The day after the war broke out, the shoemaker had started fixing worn-out shoes and looking for a place to sell them until the Wołówka flea market was repaired. He has no desire to go charging out into the wide world. The little black bread he earns by getting up at five o'clock in the morning and hammering away at his shoe bench, just as before the war, suits him just fine. So he can wait until the Russians reach Warsaw. Though the cane maker, the Zelechower, and the army tailor all work and earn enough to keep body and soul together, each is drawn to the world Over There and isn't patient enough to wait for the Russians. They want to be free.

The cane maker stays silent for a day, then for two and three. He keeps going outside to hang around at the building's front gate, however, lending an ear to the rumors being discussed by every crowd that gathers. Then early one morning, and not a nice one but gray and foggy, he gathers up his wife and child and puts them on a small wagon that pulls up to the building. Along with other Jews and their wives and children, he sets off on his journey to the Other Side. Only his elderly mother stays behind in the basement apartment; she will make her living by renting to subletters.

Now there's only one subject of conversation in the building by day, in bed at night, in front of the gate, wherever people get together to talk: "Well, when are you going? What about Zelig? Already gone? Through Hrubieszów, or Małkinia? How, on the small-gauge?"

The whole city talks of getting out. Workers and artisans, merchants and clerks, teachers and writers, doctors and lawyers—there isn't a Jew who isn't thinking of escape. Groups of travelers form on the spot— this person grabs that one, he grabs another, and the deal is sealed. This group returned yesterday from Praga because the guard wouldn't let him pass, so he'll set off tomorrow to try again. That person paid a Gentile to guide him from Warsaw over the border, while another is afraid to go with a Gentile—they can rob you and abandon you in the middle of nowhere. Yet another has found himself a reliable Gentile, a peasant who lives near the border and speaks Yiddish: someone you can travel with safely, since he's got a secret place built into his wagon where you can hide gold and jewelry, safe as in . . . a bank. So that you won't, God forbid, lose the little nest egg you've socked away.

Already a number of brokers have been advertising their services, offering to arrange a trip with "reliable" Gentiles who live near the border. There's also a group of Jewish cart drivers who've decked out their rigs with platforms and who have improvised buses and vehicles of all kinds. From early in the morning till late at night, the little wagons rumble down Wołynska, Lubeckiego, Niska, and Zamenhofa Streets—where can you look without seeing one?

A little peasant wagon makes its way down the alley; a Jew with a short, blond beard sits next to a Gentile on the coach box. On the single passenger seat—improvised from a sack of hay—sit two young boys, six or seven years old, bundled up in scarves and shawls, looking around with sad, black little eyes. As soon as you begin to peer into them, a whole world of misery appears, gazing back at you as if to say, "Look at what we've seen and what we're destined to wander through again—the land at war, nothing to eat, you're not sure of your life . . . those murderers . . . those horrible decrees . . ."

In a lucky hour, Pearl moves back into her renovated apartment. The Zelechower is furious and paces the halls in distress. His own apartment isn't finished yet, and he needs it more than Pearl. The shoemaker has already moved back into his apartment; the Zelechower is all by himself. And now the tailor, the previous tenant of the "temporary quarters," begins to pester him: the tailor who left before the bombardment began. He needs the apartment back, or so he says. The Zelechower understands exactly what the tailor's after—he wants the apartment back to rent it out, not to stay there. He runs to the landlady three times a day, stamps his feet, and finally, to his great joy, he gets the apartment. The landlady isn't shy. Let him first pay all the back rent that he owes.

"How's that?" This makes no sense to the Zelechower. Rent? Who ever heard of paying rent in wartime?

He hurries inside to tell Pearl the news only to learn, oy, that she, Pearl—who raised the roof assuring everyone that even the plague couldn't force her to pay rent in wartime—that even Pearl has handed over a hundred-note in payment on her account. Of course, she never would have done such a thing if she hadn't heard that the reconstituted Polish courts had just ruled that rent must be paid; evictions however would not be executed for the time being. Now the Zelechower has no choice. He's forced to give the landlady a few zlotys, some of the last remaining in his pocket, and he moves back into the apartment. After living there for scarcely a week, however, he takes a look around, notices everything getting more expensive with no work in sight for him—with trade practically at a standstill—and concludes that it just doesn't pay. So he sends his wife and children home, back to Żelechów. He takes a subtenant into his apartment, a klezmer musician, and the "temporary quarters" he'd occupied is let to a rabbi from whom the tailor, with the landlady's agreement, collects rent.

The Zelechower, alone now, has all day to run around and find the best way to get to the Other Side. He tries to talk the army tailor into going with him. But the tailor doesn't seem to think much of the idea: he's vanished from the building so quickly that not even the roosters make a peep as he goes. Pearl curses him up and down: "What a grief of a husband, a load on my heart." But once she accepts the fact that he's gone, she eventually calms down and brings all the sewing jobs he'd left behind to sell at the flea market. Her eldest daughter can stitch up a few pant legs on the machine and mend a few garments, while Pearl continues to carry bread and potatoes up the stairs to feed the family.

As a neighbor, the rabbi who holds court in the building is very agreeable, especially to the landlady, who is always trying to get rid of the more disreputable tenants and replace them with more respectable company. The tenants feel the same way. The rabbi gets his first clients. The girl from Skierniewice, who sublets from the furrier's wife, has found herself a young man who will go with her across the border. She will pay the traveling expenses—that's her dowry—and in return the young man has agreed to take her under the wedding canopy before they leave. These kinds of marriages are taking place more and more, and not just in Warsaw: half of Poland longs for nothing more than to get to the Other Side. Everywhere, young women find young men, and her parents are happy to get a daughter out of the apartment and to see her head covered. And the living the rabbi makes from performing such weddings isn't bad at all.

The boys from Wołynska Street travel to the Other Side. They return several weeks later so that they can go back across a second time as old hands—as guides who would make a few zlotys. They stuff their traveling clothes with wristwatches, which are expensive there and dirt cheap here, as well as suits and shoes, which are also worth their weight in gold over there. Brodsky's son has already returned. He looks terrible, but he's eager to go back as soon as he can. He now knows all the different routes and gives people advice on how to make the trip, and he even tells them that he can get them across the border himself. He conveys greetings that the army tailor has sent, but Pearl just listens to it all and laughs. Ha! What did she tell them? Doesn't she know her own husband—Mr. Big Shot? And how did you think he'd do without her? Would he ever be able to get by on his own—even for a single day? So he was full of hot air about how he'd find a job on his own and make some money. Feh! He's got no idea what it takes to run a house, and if he does, let him tell this to his grandmother. She, Pearl, isn't having any—he'll never pull the wool over her eyes. She knows that at the first bite of hunger, he'll remember her cooking he loves so, her full pots, and won't be able to take it. So now he wants to come back. Didn't she try to tell him a thousand times he'd regret it—that you can scratch out a better living selling jackets here under the Germans than you can over there?

Outside, the rain pours down without stop. Though the streets fill up with mud and filth in the fog and gloom, the little wagons keep pushing their way toward the border. There are buildings with empty apartments. One can find a furnished apartment very cheaply. Places that used to cost two thousand zlotys before the war are now going for only three or four hundred. But there's also talk that the border has already been closed—that people are stuck in No Man's Land for a week, two, three—and that you can't get anything across. Many people have become sick from staying outside the entire time on these cold and rainy late autumn days and from still more nights spent out in the late autumn frost. Children are dying like flies. There's also word of hold-ups by the Germans. Pulling over the wagons as they arrive, they grab everyone's money down to the last penny, take their overcoats and boots, and give them a brutal German beating for good measure—and then drive them back. There's even been talk that the Russians are no longer welcoming the fleeing Jews but instead cursing them, beating them, and even forcing them back over to the German side. Sometimes they even arrest people. The woods are thick with bands of Polish thieves, waiting to ambush refugees as they are passing through, robbing them, beating them, and even ripping the gold fillings from their mouths.

The shipping clerk's young son has returned from Białystok without the diamonds hidden in the hollowed-out buttons sewn on his jacket. The Germans saw through the trick in a second and cut the buttons off. A neighbor, a barber from the next building who'd hidden a gem underneath a filling in a gold tooth, had the tooth ripped right out of his mouth. He returned a pale and broken man, with more curses spewing from his lips for the "comrades" than for the Germans themselves. But people have not stopped heading for the Other Side. The buses to Białystok have already stopped running, it's true, but people are getting there by every other possible route. And the weather keeps getting colder: in No Man's Land the frost has already arrived. The peasants near the border are demanding huge sums of money to spend the night in their stables and extra rooms. Everyone who arrives has already heard the news, but that doesn't stop them from coming.

The Lithuanians have already retaken Vilna, and a new path for refugees has opened up.[11] Lithuania is now a neutral country—under threat by the Germans but officially neutral—and the hope has sprung up that escape can be made from there to freedom. People head there with the clearly defined goal of sneaking over one of two borders: the boundary between the Germans and the Soviets or the Lithuanian/Soviet-controlled crossing. At first the Lithuanian guards could be bought, but it wasn't long before they turned strict and brutal and forgot all restraint. Any suspicious person found on the border now gets a quick bullet to the head.

Khayale Auerbach, that pretty young creature, married a little over half a year, succeeded in hiding her entire fortune in a large four-square, hollowed-out button on her husband's jacket. The false button contained her dowry, converted to the currency of diamonds. Her husband had managed to cross the border unmolested at Małkinia, with his treasure intact. After meeting up with him in Białystok, then trying to cross the border into Lithuania, she was shot dead with a single bullet to the heart. Her husband went mad from grief, and this is not the only tragedy that has occurred. Everyone knows the stories, but the stream of departures continues without stop.

When the army tailor finally returns, snow has already fallen in the building's courtyard. His hands and feet are frozen stiff, and he has to spend the next several weeks in bed, but he's happy to be home. It wasn't worth it, he says, to work for nothing: you can't make a living with the Bolsheviks. The landlady stands in the courtyard but no longer sweeps and cleans—she's ruling the roost, in charge of the building once more. She buttonholes every tenant who passes by, asking for the back rent they owe. At first she made her demands hesitantly, with a faint smile and quietly, in a soft tone of voice. "Well, Mr. Grauman,"

11. The Soviets signed a mutual aid agreement with independent Lithuania on October 10, 1939, and returned the capital city of Vilna as part of the package.

she'd say, "I've got to pay the water bill, you know, and the garbage collector. My husband's also a human being, and he's got to live too!" People would answer her calmly and with respect, and she's satisfied with a promise that they're willing to pay—with their word. The whole thing leaves her with a strange kind of pleasure. She never imagined it would be so easy. Just two months ago people would have stoned her to death for such nerve.

The next day she's a bit bolder and less tongue-tied, her tone of voice is already stronger, and with each passing day, it becomes a little more forceful. Now she can be heard far off in the courtyard grilling the "good for nothings" hanging around—those strong, sharp-tongued wives who won't have any of it and are spoiling for a fight! Where does she get off asking them to pay rent now—in wartime? Rent under the Germans? She should lie sick in bed for so long! But the landlady knows her rights. They won't pay? Then she'll just take them right to court, and they'll have to pay at the green table, they will! "You want to eat, to buy bread don't you? You rush to pay for that. Well, apartments don't come free either—at least not with me."

"Take a look at her—the worthless piece of trash," the wife of the guy who deals in stolen goods yells back from the basement. "She won't be satisfied until the money is in her grubby little hands . . . trust me though—you won't feast on the fruits of our hard labor—curses are what you'll get from me!"

"It means nothing that I watched over the building during the bombardment, stood guard all night at the gate," the butcher chips in. "Now, you rich bitch, a curse on your years—you think people don't know? You think we don't know exactly what you are? Everyone knows your fortune comes from Buenos Aires—not 'the sweat of your brow.'[12] You should choke on it all—shove it up your ass!" The landlady says nothing, but leaves the broker and the butcher behind and beats a hasty retreat back to her apartment.

Pearl stands there hidden in a corner next to the corridor near the window, holding her breath the whole time, licking her lips with

12. An allusion to the prostitution rings the city was famous for in Yiddish literature, as in Sholem Aleichem's story "The Man from Buenos Aires."

pleasure when she hears the swearing and abuse. She heads straight to the furrier's wife and belts out the news: "Did you hear all that hullabaloo? They really let her have it! I should live so long—to see everything they've wished her fall right on her head! The whole thing actually makes me feel better! She thinks she can screw us that easily, that disgusting glutton! Screaming she's taking me to court! Well, let's just see her bring it off; when the Germans say no evictions, let her croak trying." The army tailor, with his frozen hands and feet restored to health, now helps his wife take on the landlady. The hundred he handed over was never rent, he tells her: he paid the money just to keep from having to deal with the likes of her. Pay all the rent he owes? Fat chance—she can forget about *that*. When the war's over—then we'll see.

After receiving a detailed and exhaustive account of the army tailor's journey to the Other Side, the Zelechower immediately makes the rounds of all the building's tenants, letting everyone in on the secret. If the army tailor hadn't snuck off in the night without him, he informs each and every one of them—if only they'd set out together—he wouldn't have limped home with his tail between his legs. He, the Zelechower, would have shown him the right route to take. Not to mention the fact that he's got lots of family in Russia—aunts, uncles, and brothers-in-law—all of whom are doing fine, with plenty of money and good jobs to boot. He'll go alone if he has to, he tells everyone—he's still planning to set out—he's just waiting for a letter to come that a Christian is supposed to bring him any day now from the Other Side. Then we'll see who's the guy who can pull things off. He's not one for big talk, of course, but we'll all know soon just who is who, thank you very much.

And people did see—well, didn't exactly see, but *heard*—that the Zelechower had sold two of his three new machines and discreetly shipped the third on a wagon bound for Żelechów. And then—he disappears without a trace. "Where's the Zelechower?" each neighbor asks the other. "Is he gone? Did he really head to the Other Side?" Several weeks pass by, and then he's back; his machine was confiscated by the Germans en route. He no longer saunters about in his heavy winter coat with the sheepskin collar but wears a summer raincoat instead. His cheeks have been hollowed by the journey: he says he's come back to do some business and that he'll be taking off again soon. True enough, he's a man of his word: he leaves and returns and then departs a second time, after making a nice deal on his apartment with the klezmer musician, who's already performing at Polish weddings, just like before the war. And then—the back and forth comes to an end. The Zelechower leaves Warsaw once and for all to rejoin his wife and children in Żelechów. He'll gladly trade all the opportunities Warsaw has to offer for one bowl of garlicky Żelechów borscht with potatoes!

Pearl holds open the door of her newly restored, brand-new, brightly painted apartment, furnished with polished red flooring she didn't even have before the war. With her arms akimbo she glares at every passing neighbor, man or woman, looking daggers at each of them as they walk by. "What can you say about that worthless landlady now? She's taking us to court—she's already filed charges against ten of us. May every one of her years be a curse upon her head. Let's just see who gets evicted—may she be thrown from the highest roof! Father in heaven!"

The furrier's wife is also standing in the doorway of her apartment. Her red head of hair finely coiffed, she wears a sporty vest that takes inches off her already slender waist, as if she wanted to go exercise at the Shtern Sports Club.[13] Apparently her husband has given up on his wartime business: they're no longer traveling to Otwock for milk, she's not standing in line for the chocolate and sugar candies, and he isn't trading in German papers. He's sewing fur collars now, and his neighbor, the purse maker, who doesn't make purses anymore, is making a living selling the furrier's collars at the Wołówka flea market.

The furrier's wife, who is one of the ten summoned to court by the landlady, now restates Pearl's case in legal language: "Apartment rent is not paid during wartime. Such a 'procedure' violates every legal 'standard.' Sorry, neighbor, if she's already paid for the water and the sewage—that was her choice. Does that mean she was entitled to keep security deposits from before the war? Snatch the last bite of food

13. A Jewish sports club set up by the Left Labor Zionists.

right out of the worker's mouth? Let us all withhold our rent together. Solidarity forever—for in unity there is strength."

Suddenly Khavtshe, the shoemaker's wife, runs in from the street with the news: a *paruvke*—a disinfection—is about to begin! Pearl cuts her to pieces with her glance. In her mind, Khavtshe is the root of all her problems—she was the first one to bring her rent to the landlady, and she did it while the first bombs of the war were raining down on Warsaw. Hearing the terrible news from Khavtshe's own mouth, she steals into her apartment like a thief and quickly shuts the door behind her. Pearl forgets all about going to court, the landlady, about curses—a *paruvke* is about to start! Soon the noise of bureau drawers being opened and shut and the scraping of a couch being moved about can be heard from within the apartment. The sewing machines are quiet, but benches are knocking about and everything is astir, making all the chaotic sounds of people rushing about and things being packed up quickly, as if there were a fire.

Fifteen minutes later Pearl comes out carrying a bundle of clothing wrapped in a shawl, her daughters right behind with fabric and bedding. Before the entire building has even heard the news, Pearl has already returned with her daughters to make another trip, taking the bundles to her mother's on Smocza Street. Now that she's fully prepared, she can wait for the trouble to start. As the news races throughout the building, a full-scale panic is unleashed. Who could have known that the smooth-talking little doctor with the wispy black beard, after inspecting every apartment and seeing nothing but freshly scrubbed floors, nicely made beds, and recently shampooed heads—as even he would have to admit—who could imagine he would go and declare a *paruvke*? And where is the building commandant at this crucial hour? And the house committee? Didn't they collect enough money from everyone last night—or so they promised—to pay the officials off?

Everyone runs into the courtyard, the women with kerchiefs over their heads, the cold, cutting wind doesn't let them stand still. They're waiting to hear from the building committee that the situation really isn't so serious and that this is just another danger the building can escape. For the *paruvke* that recently took place one building over makes every heart tremble with fear. But the committee members—

what committee members? They've disappeared faster than yesterday's rain. The women race back to their apartments and try to follow Pearl's lead, taking whatever they can carry out of their homes and over to the apartments of neighbors and friends. Everyone scrambles to get it done quickly, for no one knows exactly when the brutes will arrive—maybe it will be today, and maybe tomorrow. Then, suddenly, the threatening, shrill cries of the Polish police are heard in the courtyard, ordering everyone to head down to the delousing bath.

Oy, they've had it now. People run to the window and peer down at the courtyard below. The gate to the street has already been closed: there's no way out and nowhere to hide—the police have got them by the throat.

Before long, screams and cries can be heard from the courtyard as the police start clubbing people and driving them back with their rubber nightsticks.[14] Every entrance to the building is blocked so that no one can get out, unless it's to go line up in front of the delousing bath. Some of the police guard the building entrance, while others work their way through the apartments, driving people out to the baths. Screams and cries can be heard from every direction. The stall keeper's wife, who is pregnant, tries to reason with the policeman, explaining that she can't go down to the bathhouse in that condition. The officer proceeds to crack her on the skull with his nightstick, and soon her agonizing screams can be heard echoing through every floor of the building. In fact, the brutal blows of the police work effectively as a tactic: the butcher yells to several policeman to come in, closes the door behind them, takes a bottle of vodka from the cabinet, lays out a plate of sliced sausage on the table, and then . . . opens up his wallet. Afterward, the policemen leave his apartment with red noses: everything is on the Q.T., *sha shtil.* The butcher stands there quietly at the window, looks down at the courtyard, and watches the crowd being forced to enter the disinfectant bath.

Pearl goes down with her daughters and her little boy and does some time standing in line for appearance's sake only. Her family will

14. Many of the Polish police, known as the Blue Police, helped persecute and murder Jews, others worked for the Polish resistance, and some did both.

not have to go. Both daughters have paid off the brutish policeman. He promptly opens the gate and lets them out. After that, the policeman guarding the gate becomes more and more brutal and strict. The building superintendent, who'd been watching for a moment like this, now becomes his helper—acting as the middleman, taking his cut from the bribes the building's tenants hand over to buy their way out. Large-denomination change only is being accepted—no singles—just five- and ten-zloty coins, enough for the policeman to buy large bottles of whiskey and kielbasa while the tenants with their wives and children are herded to the disinfectant baths on Spokojna Street—or the "slaughterhouse," as it is commonly called. On the way, a few people try to slip away quietly and escape from the line, but the policemen have eagle eyes. Before anyone gets more than even a step out of line, a policeman's club comes crashing down on his head.

One person is allowed to remain in each apartment, waiting until the bedding can be taken for disinfection and the rooms themselves can be disinfected. Meanwhile, a gang of Gentile hoodlums and riffraff—both male and female—wait in the courtyard with their spray hoses. They bring a list of all the residences to be disinfected—that is, a list of everyone who hasn't paid off the authorities with a bribe. Members of the building committee don't fool around; they point the doctor and fumigation crew to those apartments that require . . . fumigation. Whether the apartment is clean or dirty, or whether the bedding is tidy or not, has absolutely nothing to do with it. There's only one thing that counts, and that's money! The fumigators take special delight in smashing whatever they can, their faces almost insane with the desire to annihilate and destroy. They grab hold of bundles of clean bedding, wrapped in fresh pillowcases, and heave them down the filthy stairs. Later, the same bundles are taken and piled in the courtyard on the wet asphalt, lying there for an extended period until carts from the bathhouse arrive and carry them off. Sometimes the bundles sit there a day or two, and sometimes even longer, and no one cares if it rains or snows. Afterward they're loaded onto the carts, where people trample them with their muddy shoes in the packed vehicles. If a sheet gets caught on an exposed nail, the fumigators show as little concern as they do about the other little problems they run into on the job. After all, they're enjoying themselves by getting back at the "kikes."

Out of breath, the building commandant returns and tries to slither discreetly through the courtyard, but the few remaining women spot him and run after him, crying, "Mr. Bernholtz, Mr. Bernholtz, this is how you work for us? And for this you took our money?"

"Those who handed over big bribes didn't have to go. The members of the committee got out of it too," yells the seamstress from the fourth floor. "You just wait, just wait, your time will come, you won't be in charge forever!"

The commandant flies into a rage, narrows his eyes to a slit, and then lets them have it with both barrels: "I warned you all; I told you to keep your apartments clean."

"Oh yeah?"

"Anyone who handed over a filthy wad of cash as a bribe didn't get fumigated at all, and not one person on the building committee got fumigated, now, did they?"

The knitter's wife yells down from the fourth floor. "You'll get what's coming to you soon enough—you won't always be the boss!"

The building commandant is furious—he screams a curse back at her and disappears from the courtyard in a huff. That's the last time he'll try to do favors for the tenants. What is he, Moses, that he's supposed to shoulder everyone else's burdens? It doesn't escape anyone's notice, however, that his angry outburst is just a way of slipping out of the courtyard a bit more quickly so that he'll be able to return, together with the other building committee members, once the danger has actually passed.

On Spokojna Street, the building's tenants discover long lines of Jews who've been brought to the disinfectant baths from other buildings, where new signs have been posted. In yellow letters written in German and Polish, placards warn of "spotted typhus," even on buildings where no cases of typhus have been discovered. The Jews pushing and shoving in line to get through the disinfectant faster understand all of this quite well, bearing the humiliation patiently. What difference does it make whether we suffer from a few blows of the truncheon or from a—a bath? They make their impatience and bitterness obvious to one another, but only by pushing and shoving. It's not unusual for the conflicts that result from the jostling and jockeying for position to be settled with fists. "Look at Mr. Big Shot, the rag picker, cutting everyone in line—in such a hurry! What's the matter, you can't wait? What's the big worry—scared the Germans haven't purified you yet? May your brains rot in your head, you stinking piece of trash!"

In the middle of all the hubbub an attendant comes out from the bath and starts to hit people on the head with a broom, or simply rips the caps off those who've reached the door of the bath, and forces them to the back of the line. All told, only about twenty Jews are let into the bath, with the rest forced to keep waiting and form a new line. Those who can grease the palm of the bath attendant with some cash get in first; others sneak in through the back door or push themselves in through a window, with bribe in hand, to get in sooner. People without any money may have to wait outside or remain back in the first or second entry hall for half a day or longer before they're finally let inside. Those lucky enough to get in are then immediately forced to strip naked and hand their clothes over for disinfection, though their garments can sit around tied up in bundles for long hours on end. The crowd waits impatiently, and the machines are always busy. Naked, they remain standing on the cement floor: freezing, hungry, and shivering.

Then the shearing plague begins. A boorish Polish boy appears with a dull set of electric barber shears and shaves every head without mercy. He takes special delight in lopping off the hair of young men whose hair is done up in style. The Hasid manages to save a bit of his beard by paying him off with a couple of guilders, and the butcher's son rescues his fulsome locks by slipping the Pole a healthy chunk of change.

After the shearing comes the medical examination. The "doctor," however, is really just a barber surgeon, a young jerk who makes sure they shave down every hairy area of the body. Those who fail to meet with his approval are sent back for another shave. After being shaved and examined, people are then driven naked through cold corridors to rooms that lead to the bath. There, however, they're made to wait for the water to heat up. And since there's little coal, they're often left standing in the cold from eight in the morning until midnight, and sometimes even longer, until they get their bath, only to be forced to wait another few hours for their clothes to be brought out. After this all-day-and-night disinfection process, the authorities finally release them from the bath, giving them a little card with the following certification: "purification complete."

That's how the disinfection bath goes for the men. The women have it much worse. The Gentile women running the bath, performing the inspection of the hair of the Jewish wives and women, know how to hit a woman where it hurts—they're females too! For a large enough bribe, however, some manage to escape the bath with a dirty scalp intact. But those without enough money to hand over in bribes get shaved without mercy, whether young girls or mothers, as the choking gasps and spasms of their desperate screams and cries resound. Wives with shorn heads return home sick and shattered—shamed and humiliated. The next day, wearing their kerchiefs to cover their heads, they will look like dazed old women.

Pearl stands in the middle of the women, openly cursing the building committee; she takes the injustice personally. She herself, of course, knew what to do to protect herself: that is, to bribe her way out of the process and get her daughters off too. She's deeply sorry, however, from the bottom of her heart, for what everyone else has undergone. The wives of the furrier and the tailor were lucky. They took along some money. But except for them the entire courtyard returned broken and depressed. The girl who sold eggs collapsed from crying so much and for a few days did not show her face in the courtyard.

But the furrier and his wife are still young, just over thirty; both suffer from asthma and do their best to laugh away the pain. It is, after all, the first winter of the war, when jokes can still be made. At two in the morning, when Jews finally leave the bath and walk out into the frosty, starry winter night, they pay no attention to their hungry stomachs and perform a mock toast to one another: "To health! We've been koshered and rendered pure. So where's the challah and fish?"[15] The children, having endured a full day of torment with their parents, forget they are hungry and sleepy and are enjoying the stroll through the night: "Look, look, Papa, a shooting star . . . a star."

15. In preparation for Jewish holidays, men would immerse themselves in the ritual bath.

A few sinister figures can be seen from afar, leaning up against a lamppost. Although a nighttime curfew is in effect during wartime, members of the Polish underworld lie in wait for Jews coming out of the baths, hoping to steal a towel, a jacket, or even a purse. Many people come out of the baths half sick and chilled, but now no one has any bedding in their apartments; many long days, sometimes weeks, will pass until their bedding is returned from the *paruvke*. There's nothing to sleep on. When the bundles actually do come back, there will usually be several items missing, though people know they were lucky to get away with their lives.

The stall keeper's wife came back unharmed. Having suffered less abuse than others, her only hope is to give birth soon, before the next *paruvke*, because everyone knows that when these murderers get their hands on a building and go through it once, they're not likely to handle it with such kid gloves next time around.

The next day, those who remained home are hunted into the bath, a group consisting largely of the weak, the elderly, the mute, the disabled, and the mentally impaired. No one is immune. While they're being led away, the building heaves a collective sigh of pain in the direction of the *paruvke* and lowers its head.

For the rest of the next day as well, few members of the building committee are to be seen in the courtyard, as if they are ashamed to show their faces—though they feel nothing of the kind. They're shameless, in fact: What good would it have done, as one member puts it, if they had gone to the baths with everyone else—if they too had been forced to suffer a *paruvke*? But Pearl will have none of it. "If there's a *paruvke*," she screams, "everyone should have to go! No special privileges! To the baths—everyone has to go to the baths!"

"And your children went to the baths?"

"My children—*my* children?"—Pearl's eyes burst into flames. "Didn't my Samele go to the baths, didn't my husband—didn't *I* go to the baths? What nerve you have, you fat-faced bitch!"

"And what about your daughters?"

"My daughters too."

"You're lying."

"Well, look who's talking—a fine one you are, Mr. Backscratcher—you calling *me* a liar! And what if I did send my girls to another bath—what business is it of yours?"

"Oh! So you sent them to *another* bath," the committee member answers in a singsong tone. "That's a horse of a different color."

The crowd gathered round all understand exactly what kind of game is being played! In exchange for a payoff, Bernholtz gave Pearl a note from the bathhouse stating that her daughters had undergone disinfection elsewhere. That inside deal, however, doesn't stop Pearl from making everyone flinch with her foul-mouthed broadside, launched against the inhuman injustice she claims to have suffered. The fusillade will continue until the next *paruvke* so that the commandant will remember what a tough customer he's got on his hands and . . . strike her name from the list.

Now, after the merciless *paruvke* is over, even those who lagged behind want to escape to the Other Side. What kind of life is this? they ask. Over there, at least you're free. Of course, you might find something to eat, or you might go hungry, but at least you're a human being over there. And what are you here? Even the purse maker adds his voice to the crowd. Few, however, have actually left, and the number of those actually heading to the Other Side has been reduced to a trickle now; only gamblers by nature are taking off, or people without any family holding them back. The frost is already bitter at the border, and every day several people who've tried to make it through have turned up again in the alley with their arms and legs frozen solid. In the building directly across the street a young man came home broke with his leg frozen from his foot up to the knee. Who knows if he'll save his leg? The frost is bad enough, but the worse news is that the Russian soldiers guarding the border are now shooting anyone trying to cross. This report works like a cold shower on everyone's imagination: How can the Russians, who call everyone "comrade," fire at people trying to find their way out of hell? Shoot Jews, victims of Hitler's terror?

The shoemaker, who cannot bear to see his faith in human justice trampled in this way, does what he can to answer back. "Can't you see—what do you expect them to do? It's the Jews themselves that are to blame—bringing in goods to Białystok, speculating on the price, trading in bread, cigarettes, and all kinds of contraband, sneaking into one village after another, smuggling dollars and jewels into Russia—what would you do if you were them? You think the Russians should just stand there, take it all in, and just keep quiet? There's a war going on, and the Russians have to keep a close eye on the Germans too!"

As soon as the shoemaker mentions the Russians and Germans in the same breath, the faces of his audience turn dark and somber. The furrier's wife in particular wants no more fancy talk about justice and humanity: if Russia can sign a pact with Germany, well, the end of the world has certainly come . . . that's it—it's all over. What's left? The butcher, meanwhile, just laughs it all off. What difference does it really make whether you're under the Russian or the German heel? If you know what to do, a person can get by just as well here as he can over there—it works the same way everywhere. If you've got enough smarts, you can always figure out how to get by, and he points to Hershel the butcher as his example.

The army tailor stands at the fringe of the group, listening to this conversation in the furrier's apartment with his head cocked to one side and with a wry smile on his lips. *Oy*, he has seen these Russian soldiers stealing through the woods at night, ready to ambush anyone trying to cross the border. He has heard the cries of the captured ring across the frozen nights—although he was allowed to cross the River Bug in a tiny boat for the price of sixty zlotys. And no, they won't be able to pry any information out of *him*: "If freedom doesn't mean saving me, just me—saving just my own hide, you understand?—from the claws of the beast, well then, so be it. There's no more freedom and justice. It's every man for himself—save yourself any way you can. Rob, steal, and fill your own belly first, because there's nothing better or more beautiful on the face of the earth than a good meal, and there never will be."

The army tailor breaks out in a shrewd grin that appears beneath his whiskers. He already knows what he has to do . . . yes, now he knows for sure . . . he will begin to live a real wartime life—his *own* life . . .

"A Jewish mailman? God bless you! Tell me, my good man, who are you looking for? We know everyone around here, or we can find him soon enough so you won't have to waste your time hunting around. Jews, come feast your eyes! Can you believe our luck? We've got a Jewish mailman, just like in Palestine!"

With these or similar words, many Jews greeted the Jewish letter carrier on the first day he made his rounds in the ghetto. It was really moving to see their childlike smiles. They did a double take at the sight of him. "Really? A Jew working in a government job?" was the general reaction. "With *pull?*" For so long you've been a second-class citizen, treated like an inferior. So when you see a Jewish letter carrier in the flesh it can catch you off guard. All of a sudden, you forget the troubles of ghetto life and its condition of absolute deprivation, civil and otherwise, and you naively imagine that a new era of JEWISH AUTONOMY—if you can call it that—is being born.

"And will you also have a postman's cap? How about a ribbon? With numbers?" "And a leather sack with a strap too?" another neighbor wants to know. He would have greatly preferred if the Jewish letter carrier wore a sword or some other sign of majestic might. If not a postman's cap, then couldn't he at least wear some sort of hat with a shiny visor, marked with a number, stripes perhaps, you know, something more official?

The letter carrier was welcomed into every Jewish home with shouts of joy, looks of astonishment, and then with affectionate glances. Met with this reception again and again, the letter carrier's self-esteem began to grow. With this feeling of the importance of his office, though with somewhat less of a sense of the social responsibility that was part of the bargain, the Jewish letter carrier got off to a good start.

The job of letter carrier, in fact, stoked feelings of envy in many Jews, who treated him as one of the elect—one of the fortunate few on whom lady luck had smiled.

No one really knows why people felt this way. Does the letter carrier's job in itself have something romantic about it? Does he bring the scent of far-off lands, of oceans and deserts, and of ships and trains, along with him? Is it because he delivers the joyful news that sons send to their aged mothers or prospective grooms send to their brides to be? Is it because he delivers the news of happy events, of weddings and circumcisions? Or is it just because people remembered the healthy tips they pressed into the palms of the Christian mailmen before the war, even though that was not allowed? Because they believed the Jewish letter carrier would make a good living—at a time, of course, when the overwhelming majority of Jews in the ghetto couldn't dream of earning a penny and were supporting themselves by selling off their household goods? The idea was enough to get people to shoot envious glances in the Jewish letter carrier's direction, introducing the FIRST DROPS OF POISON into his goblet of joy.

Whenever he entered an apartment to deliver a letter, the letter carrier would be struck by the nonchalant way the recipient would toss it aside, as if the letter were of no concern, so as to focus on something far more important. With an air of indifference, he would then artfully steer their conversation to a point where he could slip in the crucial question: "Anyway, how did you get the job? Who had the juice? Who did you have to pay off?"

Hearing this, the letter carrier has to hurry on with his route: he's still got a lot of letters to deliver on a number of different floors. But no matter where he turns, someone runs up to him and asks the question with such a skillful mix of politeness and reserve that the question can't be dodged, and he is forced to respond. Usually, the indiscreet question gets asked just as he begins to make his way out of the apartment. "Could you put in a good word for me? I'm not asking for a freebie, God forbid, I mean, there could be a few hundred in it for you . . . how about giving me a break?"

Not to be outdone, another neighbor follows the letter carrier down the stairs and addresses him in an upfront, businesslike manner, speaking Yiddish and not beating around the bush: "Here's the deal, mister: you get two C-notes, and I get the job."

In some homes where the letter carrier doesn't get propositioned, people can't keep themselves from tossing off a casual remark that appears out of the blue, a total non sequitur: "Well, you're in good shape," they tell him. "You've got a *government job.*"

People really believed it. A Polish letter carrier they remembered from their recent past had gotten a monthly salary, free electricity and heat, work shoes, a uniform, and other perks—all paid for with government funds. Naively, they believed the Jewish letter carrier would get exactly the same, especially when the "Jewish community" charges an arm and a leg for letter delivery, on top of the stamps.

Others simply imagined that the additional charge for letter delivery went right into the letter carrier's pocket: Who would get it if not him? The government? It gets its money from the stamps! Who among them could have imagined that the Germans considered the "Jewish post office" to be a mere "mail storage depot"—that the real post office was on Napoleon Street, outside the ghetto, and that the Judenrat did not get a single penny from the Germans to run the "Jewish post office."

The delivery fee for a letter quickly became and then remained the greatest obstacle the Jewish letter carrier had to face. First of all, the public couldn't get its mind around the fact that the stamp didn't cover all expenses—that it would cost them another twenty groschen to get domestic mail brought into their apartment and thirty for mail from overseas. Second, people complained about the letter carrier having to come into their apartments in the first place. In prewar Warsaw, mailboxes could be found in each entryway, with a numbered slot for every apartment. Each tenant had his own box, and the Polish letter carrier would drop letters into the slot—for free, with no extra charges tacked on. In those days, the Polish letter carrier entered an apartment only when a letter looked especially important—say, when a Jew received a letter smelling of dollars that came from America. Why shouldn't the Jewish letter carrier do the same?

When the latter would tell the addressee that the fees he was charging were by the book, people flew into a rage. "Of course!" they'd storm at him, "the Judenrat is feathering its own bed, may they burn in hell! It's exactly the same with ration bread, with potatoes, and with coal: the community officials grab all the good stuff off the top—feast on it all by themselves! May they roast in the flames of hell!"

When the letter carrier had to listen to these and like complaints in every apartment he entered—when he had to confront the angry looks of faces twisted with rage, of people foaming at the mouth as they heaped their invective upon him as if it were he himself who represented the hated Judenrat—his life became a lot less happy. The letter carrier would work his way up and down stairs, only to be met in every apartment by enraged customers pouring a steady stream of demands on his head. To them he was one of the "powers that be," a Judenrat official. All this eventually ate away at the letter carrier until he was reduced to a constant state of desperation—a sack of nerves always on edge, making it hard for him to control his temper and stay polite.

ATTITUDES TOWARD THE JEWISH LETTER CARRIER were different in each social group. He was best received by the common folk, worst by the professional intelligentsia and the Hasidim. The ordinary Jew would not only pay the special fees but would also throw in a few groschen tip on the side. To them, the act was second nature and done without any ulterior motive: they knew that everyone has to make a living, after all. It was not unusual for a letter carrier to enter the basement apartment of a poor shoemaker with nothing but a domestic postcard to deliver and to receive fifty groschen in return. When he'd explain that the fee for a postcard was only twenty, the little shoemaker would respond with a hearty "Keep it, keep the change; the Judenrat isn't exactly paying you to overeat!"

Middle-class types, on the other hand—especially doctors—treated him with a contempt verging on hostility. The Jewish letter carrier always addressed them in Polish, as he spoke Polish in most homes, just a little reminder that he was somebody official. In this case, however, he had met his match, for the doctors were the ones closer to the wheels of power. A number of them worked in the organizations or offices run by the Judenrat, and from the start they treated the Jewish letter carrier as just another little underling and never coughed up a single groschen tip. After all, they were professional intellectuals who had read in the Polish-language *Jewish Gazette* (the paper that declared, after the expulsion of the Jews from Kraków, that the expulsion of forty thousand human beings had been carried out in a humane manner) the appeal of the Jewish Council to the Jewish population not to pay more than the official fee of twenty or thirty groschen for delivery of a letter. In their eyes, only a sucker would pay something extra; only an idiot would tip the letter carrier. Mr. High and Mighty knows better. He knows the "law" and has seen it all written down in black and white. The other reason for this attitude—and the more likely explanation for their behavior—is that doctors are used to getting paid huge sums of money and charging obscene amounts; but as for shelling out their own money?

The Hasidim, on the other hand, were mostly small tradesmen. Though not businessmen in the strict sense of the word, they were well versed in the horse trading that goes into making a sale, and none would lay out even a single groschen over the official price. What really set the Hasid set apart from intellectuals like the doctors was his insistence that the letter carrier speak Yiddish. But even this demand, it turned out, was political posturing, not a matter of natural instinct— more lip service to the Agudah than a real expression of their common Jewish humanity.[1]

The warm reception of the Jewish letter carrier soon began to cool, though not through any fault of his own. The decline was the result of the job itself and the kind of work it required. It was inevitable, given the demoralization brought about by the Judenrat thanks to the

1. The Agudah was the major Jewish religious party in Poland.

corrupt figures who wormed their way into its public institutions, a corruption that undercut the prestige and good name of the Judenrat's institutions across the board. The psychological effect on the masses was so profound that every employee of the official Jewish community came to be seen as the agent or emissary of a corrupt ruling clique. As a result, the mere appearance of a letter carrier in the apartment of people tormented by their experiences in the war was enough to push them over the edge and make them erupt in a torrent of vilification and abuse.

What was the recipient of a letter supposed to think when, in the period just after mail delivery began (the situation was different later on), he received his mail a whole week late, if not two? His first impulse was to blame the letter carrier: think that he was lazy, incapable of delivering his route on time, or simply stashing the undelivered mail in his bag at home until he got around to them. Later, when people had learned that the postal management was to blame and not the postman, things didn't get any easier for the letter carrier. The doctors and *shmendrikes* assailed him in management's place, and abused the postal service with disdain as the "Jewish post office."[2] These assimilated Jews would raise their fists at "Yid mailmen," as if they wished to exterminate the entire species of "Yids." Other Jews simply derided the letter carrier himself, mocked and ridiculed the fees he charged, or, comparing the current situation with the past, simply came to the conclusion that Jews were nothing but a bunch of hopeless good-for-nothings as a group, a worthless lot—just try to get something done with a measly Jew. This self-denunciation would usually end with the well-known adage "The only thing Jews are any good for is praying."

The public of course had a great deal riding on prompt mail delivery; not just merchants and small tradesmen depended on it but the broader public as well. The little scraps of paper they received in the mail, often written in a mishmash of half Yiddish, half German, often represented their last chance for salvation, providing them with bread or other support from relatives still living in the countryside at large.

2. *Shmendrikes* was Yiddish slang for assimilated, Polish-speaking Jews.

People kept a special eye out for LETTERS FROM RUSSIA. The vast majority of these letters came from Polish territory seized by Russia when the war began. Jews who had fled to these areas, once they gained an economic toehold in these new locales, began to send packages of food to their relatives in Warsaw. Men sent packages to their wives and children, sons and daughters sent food to their parents, and others shipped what they could to relatives and dear friends. Packages from Russia came tightly wrapped with seven seals in linen, so no one could poke their way in and steal the choicest morsels while the package was under way, as these were boxes filled with hard-to-get items that would fetch a pretty price on the open market. Packages from Russia sent by relatives contained rice, tea, coffee, chocolate, and in the early days even spirits and tobacco. People mailed smoked meats, salami, bacon, cheese, butter, and even caviar. When a Warsaw Jew received a package with items such as these, he would be able to take some of it—a portion of tea, coffee, whiskey, or tobacco, for instance—and sell it for good money on the open market. Selling part of the delicacies could bring in enough to pay for food for several weeks, and he could go ahead and consume the rest.

Jews who received these packages on a regular basis did not have to worry about going hungry. The influx of packages from Russia influenced the going rates on the black market, bringing goods into Warsaw that the Germans tried to ban and that otherwise would have been prohibitively expensive for anyone to buy.

Of course the senders of these packages from Russia would always alert the recipient with a letter stating that goods were on the way, usually arriving some time before the package itself. People therefore treated a letter from Russia as something much more than writing on a scrap of paper: it was greeted as if it were a living messenger of good news still to come. With trembling fingers elderly mothers would caress a letter sent by their sons that told them a package was on the way; they would press it against their hearts, their minds dancing with visions of rich and thick giblet gravy, and chopped liver mixed with tiny onions cooked with diced pieces of goose skin, which they shared with their children on happy occasions. By reading between the lines of these letters and by the kinds of foodstuffs they promised, wives could tell, with that special sixth sense that women have, whether their husbands had been faithful while away. "See, Rivke?" a woman would boast to her neighbor. "My Sholem knows I'm dying for a nice piece of goose, so he makes sure to send me goose salami in every package. We should all have such a good year!"

And then, all of a sudden, they establish a Jewish post office—may it burn down to the ground—and you don't see any letters, you don't get any packages. People sit and wait all day at the door, on the lookout for the letter carrier who never arrives anyway. If he actually brings a letter, then of course it's always for—who else?—that tenant who rents a room from you, that louse who doesn't even have any real relatives there, just some buddy who keeps sending him things. Who wouldn't get depressed? You need to have luck for everything . . .

Then it became the talk of the town: the Jewish population was in a terrible uproar, cursing and berating the Jewish post office, its mismanagement, and the whole miserable system, and after all that the ORGANIZATION OF THE JEWISH POST OFFICE didn't improve in the slightest. Weeks and months passed before service improved in any significant way, and letters kept arriving late. The situation could be explained in part by the gap of ten days between the discontinuation of the Polish postal service and the establishment of the Jewish post office. As a result, on its very first day in business, the Jewish post had to start a backlog in the form of sacks of mail stuffed to the gills. Making matters worse was the fact that the workers who had been hired were completely unqualified. They took forever to sort the mail. While the backlog was being sorted and delivered, fresh sacks of mail continued to come in, sit around, and get stale . . .

The answer? Hire temporary workers to help sort the backlog, gradually increasing work hours to make up the deficit. It was the great good fortune of the Jewish post office, however, to be blessed with a director who somehow convinced himself that he was the "energetic type," smarter than everyone else, a paragon of efficiency and—much to everyone's regret—someone who excelled in "organization" as well. The Jewish post office was blessed with him. Until he got the brilliant idea of hiring temporary personnel, several long weeks went by, doing so much damage to the reputation of the Jewish postal service that even after a period of months, when the incoming mail was dispatched and delivered every day in punctual fashion, the word on the street remained unchanged: any letters that went through the hands of the Jewish post office, according to the street, would disappear into the maw . . .

The Jewish population unloaded all of its anxious fury at the post office on the head of the letter carrier himself. Whenever he appeared in the courtyard of a building, people surrounded him right away, pulled at his sleeves, and screamed the same question into his ears over and over: "None? Really no mail for Greenberg? What about Rosenthal? Morgenstern?"

"Mr. Postman, sir," a Jew would yell down from the fourth floor, "you've got a letter for Tsemach, don't you? A letter from Russia— come on! . . . You don't? Take another look . . ."

Others were not to be outdone by this performance: running up to the letter carrier, they'd rip letters right from his hands, telling him they were trying to carry some of his load, show him the way to an apartment, or save him a trip upstairs. When they finally accepted the fact that they had no mail, the only possible reason had to be that the Jewish post office had botched things up: they used to get mail all the time!

The higher the cost of living climbed and the tighter the noose was drawn around the neck of the ghetto Jews, the stronger their clamor for mail became. Tens of thousands of Jews walked around with their hands in their pockets, all with a single idea in mind: Please—oh, please! If a letter does come, please make it from Russia, or America, and if not, Kónskowola, Przasnysz, or Kock will do—a letter from any part of the family would be fine. Couldn't they just remember and send us a little package? Some Jews get packages from little towns all over Poland. Why should they have all the luck? The constant wait for packages drove people out of their minds. Women would surround the letter carrier and deluge him with so many questions that he'd be physically exhausted from answering them:

"Mr. Postman, sir, isn't there a letter for me?"

"What's your name?"

"Goldstein."

"Apartment number?"

"70."

"No."

"Maybe you've got one for number 76? Maybe for number 30?"

"You live in all three apartments?"

"No."

The Jewish lady pesters him because she's curious about whether her neighbor, that piggish woman next door with all the filthy luck, hadn't perhaps gotten a letter. She just *has to* know.

Then there are times when a letter carrier comes into a street where he's never delivered mail before and where the locals don't know him. They do know that the Jewish post office doesn't always keep its carriers on the same route, changing them almost daily—but they let loose anyway, screaming at him from behind: "Hey, listen, Mr. Postman, excuse me, sir, do you have a letter for me? What? No? No letter from Russia?"

A letter from Russia, a letter from Russia: the sweetest dream of those who have been ruined, and their ultimate hope and consolation. Children infected with their parents' sense of anxious expectation would not let the letter carrier take a single unmolested step down the street, besieging and pestering him with the shrill shriek of their youthful voices until his ears could no longer hear. And if fortune smiled and he actually brought a letter for their parents, the same child raced head over heels up the stairs, screaming at the top of their lungs and crashing into the room out of breath: "Papa, Mama, a letter from Russia, from Srulik, from Tsirl, from Yocheved. I saw it myself: a letter with a Russian stamp!"

"Oh children, a letter from Russia, may I live to see it," the Jewish woman would say, clutching her heart. "Run faster, children, go bring the letter here quickly. Go, go—here's some money—dear God in heaven!"

The Jewish woman is dizzy as she waits: in her mind, the letter soon becomes a huge round of cheese, a fat salami, or a thick chunk of butter. Before long, her eyes can see nothing else, her ears hear nothing else, as she stretches out her two hands as if to grab the good, rich food and drop it into her stew.

The letter carrier is absolutely worn out by anxious people constantly tugging at his sleeve and by having to answer thousands of questions a day wherever he goes—not just about whether a letter will come or not but about every single postal rule and regulation. He is bombarded with questions about sending money, registered letters, airmail, the courts, police, taxes—was there anything they didn't ask? After all, wasn't he a crony of the insiders, with his government job, someone close to the wheels of power? One of the high and mighty?

In point of fact, the letter carrier lives an utterly miserable existence. Getting up every day at five in the morning, he works until nine or ten at night and still doesn't get a weekly paycheck. He's paid by the piece instead, at six groschen per letter. After all deductions for taxes and for "social insurance," whose services can't be used by Jews, as per the decree of the occupation authorities—though he's given the honor of paying for it—his take-home pay won't total five groschen a letter. Delivering a hundred, even a hundred and fifty, letters a day will land him a ridiculously paltry sum given that a loaf of black bread costs from twenty-two to twenty-four zlotys. And the few tips he gets don't make any real difference in what he earns.

THE WORKING CONDITIONS are so unbearable that they soon begin to destroy the letter carrier's health. The "energetic" director who takes a military approach to all problems carries on like a drill sergeant, then often orders the letter carriers to attend an *odprawa,* meaning a conference. There he sternly announces the new requirement that they arrive at work on time and no later than eight in the morning. If not, he'll have to crack down, and no excuses will be accepted—and you better believe he's serious. He hates empty talk, and his word will be law. Punishment for those who can't keep up will be severe, and he'll fire them if he has to: order is priority number one! Or so he pathetically concludes.

This new regimen requires letter carriers to come to work not at eight a.m. in the freezing cold and snow of winter but at six, because the earlier you come, the better it is. The reason is the sorting machines: though they run from early morning till night, they are never able to sort the available mail into enough bundles for every postman.

A few letter carriers always get the short end of the stick and are sent home without work after a whole day of waiting in the freezing corridors with the cement floors. The lucky winners who get a sack of mail to deliver are those who arrived at five or six in the morning, and most of those are members of the "battalion": a group made up of the director's inner circle—people he worked with in the German work sites.

THE GENTLEMEN OF THE BATTALION were a chapter all their own in the life of the Jewish post office. Members of the battalion spoke Polish only—they were the heirs of the *shmendrikes*. The battalion practiced the military discipline of the German work sites, where they had earlier been section leaders, and bragged about *przepustkas,* or special passes and privileges they'd been given.

There were whispers that some of the battalion returned the favor by providing the Germans with intelligence, working as informers. The battalion has its people in every institution run by the Judenrat, and many higher officials tremble, since everyone knows they're "Gestapo people."

With an excess display of enthusiasm, the men of the battalion also made a point of chattering in Polish—like the director himself. Some of them wouldn't allow a word of Yiddish to cross their lips under any circumstances whatsoever, and when spoken to in Yiddish they'd answer back in Polish. People were reluctant, but everyone had to speak Polish with them, and after the *shmendrikes* took over the majority of letter carrier positions, even the delivery of letters in people's apartments had to be conducted in the Polish tongue.

But let's be clear about one thing. No matter how dear Yiddish was to the letter carrier's heart, and no matter how close he might be to the language in moral and ideological terms, his practical sense told him that he had to speak Polish in order to carry out his duties by imitating the Polish letter carriers that preceded him. A Jew speaking Yiddish would not have been accorded the proper respect, and there was no doubt whatsoever that such respect was absolutely vital to do the job successfully.

As it happened, there were times when Jews, red hot with anger, would barrage the letter carrier with verbal abuse, lambasting him with the most disgraceful, shameful attacks without a shred of justification. It was pure jealousy—he had the plum of a job that hadn't fallen into their hands, and they hadn't gotten the job, they were sure, because they didn't have pull where it counted. They heaped their insults in Yiddish, of course, onto the letter carrier's head—did they ever! Could you really degrade someone's father to his face while cursing him up and down seven times to Saturday in any other language than Yiddish—our angry mother tongue who'd suffered a lifetime of humiliation, poverty, persecution, and oppression herself? Only a few Jews spoke Yiddish to the letter carrier, and he answered them right back.

The men of the battalion had their own moral system. Since they made up roughly sixty of the total of one hundred letter carriers, power was firmly in their hands. When mail bundles were handed out they'd place one of their men at the door, and the official distributing the mail was in their pocket. As a result, the men of the battalion received mail addressed to the wealthiest streets—with the nicest buildings, the safest stairwells, and the best tips. Those who did not enjoy the privilege of belonging to the battalion got bags of mail addressed to the poorest streets and alleys, meant for buildings with broken and twisted steps, dark cellars, and damp attic garrets where typhus liked to grow.

At first the men of the battalion took the trouble to keep this favoritism secret; later they practiced it brazenly and cynically in the full light of day. Their claim was that the gentlemen of the battalion had made great contributions to the Jewish community and hence deserved this honor in return, and those with the courage to disagree with them were threatened by a fist waved in front of their face.

It was the men of the battalion, as it turns out—a group with its own peculiar notions of right and wrong—who caused the residents of the ghetto to suspect the letter carriers of THEFT.

For instance, a Jewish woman went to the post office swearing that after the letter carrier left her apartment a watch was gone from the table; another complained that a letter carrier had swiped a pair of galoshes. In both cases, guilt was never determined. Not long afterward an official with the Jewish Council itself burst into the post office, yelling and demanding to know why a certain carrier had carried off his briefcase with his thermos in it.

Suddenly the official noticed his thermos standing on a table. There he saw the elderly father of a particularly clever letter carrier—one of the smoothest operators working for the battalion; the father was using the thermos to help himself to a glass of tea. As it turned out, the old gent had received the briefcase from his son. The official ended up leaving the post office with his thermos and the briefcase, which had been stashed to the side. The thief was immediately placed under investigation by the post office and was even handed over to the court, but nothing really came of it all.

But why bother with cases of petty larceny and domestic thievery when so many packages were being looted wholesale in the post office itself that it started to look like a clearinghouse for stolen goods?

In point of fact, the post office where the letter carrier got his bags of letters to deliver and the warehouse where packages arrived and were unloaded were located on two different streets. Since letter carriers bringing letters and packages both wore armbands with the same insignia, the average person could not make such fine distinctions. As a result, a letter carrier who entered a home with a letter in hand was liable to be met with a broadside of the most shameless insults, because the last package the tenants had received was half empty by the time it arrived. It was not unusual for the recipients to get salt instead of sugar in their packages (so the scale would read correctly). Instead of cocoa from Portugal, a package would be filled with wormy peas or be lighter than its face weight, with the carrier doubling the delivery fee and pocketing the larger sum. Though it was impossible to tell just how the scam was actually pulled off—since the packages first arrived at the real post office on Napoleon Street and were transferred only after that to the ghetto branch—there's no doubt that the officials of the Polish postal service stole to their hearts' content, knowing full well that blame in the end would fall on the shoulders of the deliverymen: that is, on the Jewish post office and its carriers. But you can be just as sure that plenty was stolen at the Jewish post office itself.

That much was obvious in the united front maintained by officials of the Jewish postal service whenever someone came to lodge an official complaint of theft.

The public in general, of course, did not make any distinction between the post office on Krochmalna Street, which expedited letters, and the office on Ciepła, which expedited packages, because many postal employees—especially the guys from the battalion—were stealing on a grand scale.

Jews who had relatives in the small Jewish towns that had been annexed to the German Reich often received a letter in which five marks had been enclosed (such currency mailing was strictly illegal in the *Gouvernement*).[3] The bills often disappeared from the letter. Whodunit? It remains a mystery to this day.

The terrible sorrows Jews suffered in the war, the anguish and excruciating torture they had to withstand: the house searches, arrests, and on top of all that having to live for months and years without bread, without any steady source of income, with their food shelves so bare that mice no longer scampered about looking for a crumb, going to bed on an empty stomach, then laying there the next morning until noon without any reason to get out of bed . . .

A terrible life lived at the edge of an abyss called for every position in the community to be filled by people of integrity, of SOCIAL RESPONSIBILITY, and the job of letter carrier was just as important as any other in this respect, though it might not have looked that way at first glance. The letter carrier had been given a crucial task. There were times when a card announcing a package to come would determine the fate of an entire family, deciding whether they would live or die. In general, Jews did not commit suicide during the war (though there were a few exceptions). Their drive to survive was an innate reflex of the Jewish instinct for self-preservation. Jews opposed Hitler's death

3. After invading and conquering Poland in September 1939, the Germans annexed most of western Poland to the Reich, including Łódź and Poznan. In the central portion of Poland, the Germans set up the Nazi-run *Generalgouvernement* to administer the region in October 1939. This area included Warsaw. (The Soviets occupied the eastern parts of Poland.)

campaign with a resolute and powerful will to live and to remain alive; their biblical watchword was "they made their lives bitter."[4] Years without bread and without a spoonful of hot food, however, took a shocking psychological toll; many Jews were reduced to a state of panic, lost all motivation, fell into an apathetic state, and went to bed and stayed there, laying there for so long that they were no longer able to, no longer *needed* to, rise . . .

A letter carrier received his bundle of letters not at nine in the morning, as was done before the war, but around four or five in the afternoon, and then had to deliver them in the poor Jewish streets, where the street numbers of the buildings were terribly confusing. For example, the front entrance to the building on the left wing read "No. 1" and "No. 64," while the sign at the last entrance to the building read "No. 3" and "No. 107." Doing his job conscientiously became a next-to-impossible task for the Jewish letter carrier, especially in winter, when walking up slippery, often broken stairs, still in ruins from the bombing of Warsaw, could become a deadly affair.

Adding to the problem were the Jewish building superintendents, who were new to the job.[5] When asked where a particular tenant lived, they often had no idea and would insist that such and such a person didn't live in the building at all, though it would turn out that the person in question was living right under his nose.

And not to mention the knock on the door in the middle of the night—what a torture that was! Jews trembled at the prospect of house searches and assaults, of course, even when the knock came in broad daylight. The fear was so great that in some of the larger buildings, where apartments had a separate kitchen entrance, people would lock the front doors tight with huge locks, as if to say, "No one home."

4. Exodus 1:14.

5. According to Ber Mark, "After the enclosure of the ghetto and the removal of all Polish inhabitants from the Jewish streets, the position of building watchman [*Struzhn*] in Jewish neighborhoods was filled, naturally, by Jews." See Peretz Opoczynski, *Reportazhn fun varshever geto*, edited by Ber Mark (Warsaw: Yidish-bukh, 1954), p. 87. Opoczynski's ironic point is that the Jewish "supers," as they would be called in New York City today, were far less familiar with the Jewish apartment buildings than their Polish predecessors.

Given their already shattered nerves, imagine what they must have felt in the middle of a snowy, murky, or rainy winter night, with the house cheerless, dark, and still, when the faintest noise sounded like clattering wheels on a cobblestone street. And then—a knock at the door. When no one answered immediately, the knocking became stronger: the mail, after all, must not be delayed. The blood ran cold in their veins, and the louder the knock, the greater their terror became. By the time they finally took their lives in their hands and asked, "Who's there?" in Polish and received the reply *"Poczta,"* or "Mail," they'd already been scared out of their wits. When they finally opened the door to let in their unexpected guest, there'd be no outburst of joy, even if he had a letter from Russia in hand. Their anger at the Jewish post office, and hatred for the Jewish Council, could not be contained, and they unloaded on the letter carrier with as many curses as they could.

IN HOMES ON KROCHMALNA AND OSTROWSKA STREETS, the charges made against the letter carrier made up a long, almost endless list: here, he knocked on the door too quickly, and there, he delivered a letter late. People complained about packages being stolen, and the most important and widespread complaint of all was about fees charged for the delivery of mail. This constant abuse became the bane of the letter carrier's existence, leaving him physically and emotionally exhausted, especially since the complaint about delivery charges struck home with the bitter force of truth. In some areas, 80 percent of his customers did not have the twenty- or thirty-groschen fee and immediately ran to borrow it from a neighbor. It was not uncommon to see a letter carrier knocking at the door of every neighbor on the floor—the floor above and the floor below and more if necessary, until he'd gone from the fourth floor all the way down to the parterre—until he could finally find someone to lend the addressee a few groschen. For almost no one in the house had a cent. If someone had managed to earn a few zlotys by selling a household item, they'd already have raced off to a shop for a quarter kilo, or in the best case a half kilo, of bread.

More typically, a letter recipient would ask the letter carrier to lend him a few groschen: "It's only twenty groschen," they'd plead in moving tones. "Anyone with half a heart would loan twenty groschen!" Or

"You're so heartless that you won't lend me a few measly groschen? You'll come through here again; I'll pay you back." When the letter carrier answered that he couldn't do it—that most of the homes on his route had no money and that he'd end up costing his own pocket several zlotys every day instead of making a living himself—no one believed a word he said. "You're worse than the goyim," someone would cry out in wild anger. "The Christian mailman always trusted me for it. Only the Jewish letter carriers from the Jewish Council and its bureaucrats are like that; may you all burn in hell like Cain."

But all this heartache and sorrow was nothing compared to the FRIGHTFUL PICTURES OF MISERY AND SUFFERING the letter carrier had to watch while following his route from house to house in the vale of tears known as Krochmalna, Ostrowska, Smocza, and Niska Streets.

In these streets the doors to every apartment stayed locked until late in the day and people lay in bed until two or three in the afternoon. Others never got out of bed, having no reason to get up. In winter, the letter carrier might see ten to twelve people in the home of one of the larger families—he'd often see young men or women lying in bed with pale faces and feverish eyes, swallowing their spittle. Mothers would lie in bed with two or three children, wrapped in red bed covers, without the few groschen needed for soap to wash the sheets. Things were scattered around the house in a terrifying disorder, a reminder of the truth of the old saying "like outside, like inside." What was obvious was that all were crazed by a single, obsessive idea: "Where can I get a little piece of bread?" The mothers were not the mistresses, and the fathers were not the masters, of these homes. Doors closed badly, stoves were broken, the tables and chairs had not been cleaned, and the floors had not been scrubbed. What for? Who cares?

The continual lying in bed made people decline that much faster, and many were soon unable to walk a single step; others were swollen with hunger to the waist and higher. With some it was almost impossible to make out their eyes behind the puffy swelling that surrounded their sockets, giving them something of the look of dark Mongols or ravenously hungry Eskimos.

When encountering people tortured by hunger the letter carrier was faced with two choices: either to return the letter to the post office, noting that the letter had not been claimed due to lack of funds, or to consider the possibility that the letter he brought might mean salvation for the ruined human beings in front of him, as in many such cases it was. It then became the letter carrier's responsibility to get the neighbors to pitch in for the letter fee: to become an activist, a community leader, and organize the donations. Of course it was no big deal to just take the letter back to the post office, say that so and so had no money and that he hadn't been able to collect a cent. The letter and its corresponding notation would be eagerly received by the clerk as if nothing had happened at all. The director, who could talk a blue streak and who never stopped rattling on about the letter carriers' social responsibility, was himself incapable of doing anything to fulfill it himself. It never occurred to him to suggest, for instance, that letters addressed to refugees at the collection points, beggars who were the poorest of the poor, and the sick and insane should have their delivery fees paid for by the Jewish Council. The director was smart enough to keep the budget balanced and to see that the post office did not run a deficit. Where social responsibility was concerned, let the letter carrier break his head over it—and that he certainly did.

When evening fell, the letter carrier returned to his cold home and wife and children with his measly daily earnings and agitated by the day's endless quarrels. The day's dizzying pictures of misery clung to his spirits like pitch and gave him no peace; he felt like a broken shard of his former self. It didn't take long before the letter carriers themselves were swollen with hunger and battered by hard labor, their hearts ruined from the continual climbing up and down the stairs. The Jewish Council and its institutions, however—they remained true to form, caring as little about the abandoned children littering the streets, and about the refugees and the indigent, as they did about the letter carriers, refusing even to pay for their shoes to be resoled. Little wonder, then, that the mortality of the letter carriers themselves soon reached a murderous rate.

If all that were not enough, the officials of the Jewish community heaped DENUNCIATIONS on the Jewish letter carrier's head. A Jew loves to demand his due: many boasted of their connections with top officials, loudly declaring that they wouldn't be satisfied to speak with a clerk and wanted to go right to the top. People ran every other day to the post office to complain about any and every kind of foolishness and every which kind of trifle—a cow had flown over the roof, as it were, and they demanded to see the man in charge, or the "director," as he was called. "The boss" would soon announce himself with much fanfare, tilt his head to one side, send one eye into a squint, and the mood would turn deadly serious. Like a furious Hebrew schoolteacher, he'd then proceed to rip the letter carrier who was the subject of the complaint to shreds. The director would start by announcing, at the top of his lungs, that the carrier in question would receive no mail to deliver until a full investigation of the matter had been completed. Next he'd start the investigation himself, trying to trap the letter carrier with his own words using insinuation and biting phrases. Soon the complainant would be bubbling over with pleasure. "He's a clever one, that Mr. Director (not to tempt the evil eye)," the accuser would think, and our Mr. Director would think all the more of himself, bubbling over with satisfaction at his own performance, quietly admiring, no doubt, his own heroic wisdom. The investigation would drone on in this fashion, often delaying mail delivery for two to three hours. Never mind: the Jewish director of a post office can indulge himself in such things.

After such a solemn inquiry, the director was in the habit of coming out to meet the public in the cold corridor with its cement floor: on those cold winter days he would be wearing his wife's stuffed white coat, reaching just below his knees, simply to let everyone know that a war was on and to show everyone that he was the frugal type, trying to save the community the expense of heating the post office. Then he'd make a serious pronouncement: that soon—may it come to pass in our day—he would see to it that benches were provided so that the public would not have to stand from five in the morning to four or five in the afternoon waiting on their feet.

The director would make his announcement with great decisiveness, in a voice trembling with emotion and indignant at social injustice. Then his anger would subside until, two weeks later, another such occasion would arise, and he would give a repeat performance of his solemn declaration. Until behold: after four or five months the Jewish post office finally had brought the benches to pass.

For the letter carrier with a truly committed attitude toward his work there were also moments of joy and inner satisfaction, partially outweighing the heartbreaking sorrows that filled his days. Such was the case when he succeeded in delivering a letter to an ADDRESSEE UNKNOWN.

Letters would arrive, for instance—most from overseas—with addresses fifteen or twenty years out of date. Jews had relatives in America or Argentina or Uruguay from whom they had never received a letter the entire time. But now, when relatives in such far-flung lands read about the hellish suffering Polish Jews were undergoing, their hearts grew tender. They quickly dispatched letters to their relatives in Warsaw, and most were probably ready, if they got an answer, to send help.

It was impossible, however, to find the addressee at the given address. Going to the building superintendent was of no use, since as we've seen, he wouldn't have the faintest idea of who lived in the building. What other choice was there except going from building to building and knocking on doors? This required patience, a sense of responsibility, and the desire to do what was right.

If the reader had only witnessed scenes such as these: a letter carrier, after a long search, finally gets hold of an old mother, with a letter from her daughter in Paris after a four-year silence. The letter asks if she needs anything, telling her that a package can soon be on its way. If you could see how the recipient of that letter wrings her hands, then bursts out in a torrent of tears and cries while clutching at her heart: "Oy, my Brokhe, my dear child has not forgotten her old mother!" If you had witnessed that scene, you too would agree with the statement that the letter carrier had been paid for his troubles: not with money but with the heartfelt look from a mother's eyes that is worth far more . . .

In another house he delivers a letter from a son to his parents. The son writes from across the sea that he's heard his family is still alive, saved by some miracle from the brutal bombardment of Warsaw. His sister, a bride to be, goes almost mad with joy, holding her brother's letter in her hand while her mother is numb from surprise. An elderly, gray-haired grandfather stands in the middle of the apartment, his face pale with astonishment and both hands raised toward heaven, as if he were a Cohen giving his blessing, gazing with deep gratitude at the letter carrier.

Someone from the household finally collects himself and hands the letter carrier a few groschen, but the carrier himself stands there stupefied, his eyes greedily devouring the unusual scene. What are a few measly few groschen worth when compared to such an expression of human solidarity and loving care?

The Jewish letter carrier is no longer simply a Jew, one of many at whom the roar of extermination has screamed its cry. He has a heart, and in every house where he delivers an unexpected letter to mothers waiting for one for years, he lives what the people live and experiences his own quiet joy.

And then suddenly: *boom!* WAR WITH RUSSIA![6] Thousands and thousands of homes that had regularly received precious packages from Russia are immediately on pins and needles. First they wonder what they'll do now: How will they live? Second, they think about the children in Russia, in the recently occupied areas, in Białystok or Baranowicze, right at the front lines.

He goes from house to house, from parents with a son right at the front to homes with two parents with two and three sons, all in Russia. Everywhere they ask him, since he's a person with "pull" on the inside and who would probably know, what threats are their children experiencing? What can they expect? Will they ever see their children again?

The first to return have already turned up on Smocza Boulevard, youngsters as sturdy as trees who didn't waste any time and hightailed it back to Warsaw. Other parents sit and wait for their children to do the same, while at the post office, all hell breaks loose. The letters that trickle in become fewer by the day. Thousands of letters sent to Russia over the last few days are being returned with the German notation, "Postal Service Suspended." It gradually comes to be understood that in a few days, postal service to Russia as a whole will cease and with it a large part of the income of the Jewish post office. The di-

6. This refers to the German invasion of the Soviet Union on June 22, 1941.

rector squints with his right eye and cleverly, oh so cleverly, observes: "And perhaps—who knows?—perhaps the post office itself will have to close up shop." That's his only answer, at any rate, to the letter carriers' many questions about inadequate food, backbreaking labor, tattered shoes, and failing health.

As the nightmare of Jewish Warsaw darkens, hope is gradually extinguished: no more letters from Russia, no more packages, just walls— drab, red, and cold ghetto walls, like the walls of so many cheerless prisons. Who cares about the Jewish post office or the swollen feet of the Jewish letter carrier now?

Translated by Samuel D. Kassow

The plan had been daring and wide ranging: cut off the ghetto from the Polish side, lock the Jews up, and wall them in so tight that not even a tiny bit of light could shine through. But fanatical plans by their very nature start to fall apart as soon as they bump up against real life. And so it was with the German plan to create the ghetto. The zoological hatred of Jews clearly called for a jail, a pit, a deep abyss where they would all die. But if the Jews went under, then so too would many, many Gentiles. So the Gentiles themselves wanted to sabotage this sinister plan. And they did.

GOYIM CANNOT LIVE WITHOUT THE GHETTO

In the years just before the war broke out, the Sanacja regime—which coddled and encouraged the Nara gangs and all kinds of Jew haters—trumpeted the call to make the goyim, so to say, economically independent of the Jews.[1] But despite everything, the regime failed to produce

---

1. The Sanacja (Polish for "cleansing") was the group led by Józef Piłsudski, who came to power after a coup d'état in 1926. Although Piłsudski was no special friend of the Jews, he resolutely opposed anti-Jewish violence. After his death in 1935 his successors, afraid of being outflanked by the nationalist right, began to veer in an anti-Semitic direction. The Nara was a violently anti-Semitic fascist group formed in 1937.

Polish entrepreneurs with initiative who would be able to compete with the Jews. For well over forty years Polish society had been subject—in bigger or lesser doses—to boycott propaganda from the likes of Rola, Niemojewski, and others.[2] Perhaps this boycott movement helped produce a class of Polish storekeepers. But it failed miserably at developing experienced and talented merchants who knew how to sell good products at a cheap price—not to mention skilled manufacturers, large or small, or Polish cottage industries.

Just as soon as the fighting was over in Poland, hordes of goyim descended on the Jewish flea markets, bazaars, and business streets—such as Kercelak, Wołówka, the Wola market, Nalewki, Franciszkaner, and Grzybow. Now, unlike the prewar days, they could buy from Jews and not have to face the hate-filled stares of the Nara gangs or the young Endek students who hung around with cameras and who threatened to put them on public blacklists and turn them into social outcasts.[3] Now trade was booming, and the Poles were happy to make deals with Jews. And the Jews themselves were desperate to make a groschen. The goods that the Poles bought from the Jews were in turn sold to the peasants. And so, just like in the good old days, Poles and Jews lived off each other.

And all of a sudden—stop!

THEY SEAL OFF THE GHETTO

The news that the ghetto was closed set off feelings of consternation not only among Jews, who had been producing and trading quite a lot,

---

It specialized in attacking Jews on the streets of major cities and assaulting Jewish students at universities. Opoczynski erroneously believes that the Polish government supported the Nara thugs. It did not. On the other hand it failed to stop their violence.

2. *Rola* was one of the first outspokenly anti-Semitic periodicals in Poland. It was founded in 1883 by Jan Jeleński. Andrzej Niemojewski (1864–1921) was the editor of *Myśl Niepodległa*. Niemojewski was a Polish progressive who had once believed in the possibility of Jewish integration into Polish society but changed his views after the 1905 revolution and began to stress the inevitable struggle between Poles and Jews.

3. "Endek" is a shortened form of Narodowa Demokracja (National Democracy), a nationalist anti-Semitic movement in prewar Poland that strongly supported an economic boycott of Jews. The Endeks were the major rivals of the Sanacja.

but also among goyim and even the Germans—or to be more precise, the Volksdeutsche, who had been eagerly smuggling raw materials and merchandise from the Polish territories that had been annexed to the Reich.[4]

In order to process textiles in Warsaw, the Volksdeutsche smuggled in raw materials from Łódź, where there were still large supplies from before the war, into the *Generalgouvernement*. On the return trip they smuggled money; the Jews paid the Germans in marks or Polish gold coins, which fetched a good price in the Reich. So the closing of the ghetto was a blow not just to the Jews but to the Volksdeutsche as well.

And did it make sense for the occupation authorities to create a ghetto? Did it suit the Germans' economic interests? No way! The Germans established the ghetto for purely political reasons. If you looked at it from an economic point of view, it would have been far better had the Jews not been locked up and thus been able to stimulate trade and industry. The Germans needed to shore up the new occupation currency, the *Emissionsbank* paper zlotys designed to prop up the buying power of the German reichsmark. They also needed the tax revenues that would demonstrate that in occupied Poland the economy was strong, prices were stable, and the Germans, here in Poland as everywhere else, had replaced chaos with civilization and order.

WHY DID THE OCCUPATION AUTHORITIES DECIDE TO ESTABLISH A GHETTO IN WARSAW—IN THE HEART OF POLISH JEWRY, SO TO SPEAK?

First of all the occupation authorities had to show that they embraced Hitler-Haman's crazy plan to "destroy, kill, and wipe out all the Jews."[5] Second—and this is most important—they wanted to deepen the rift

---

4. Volksdeutsche were Polish citizens who were ethnic Germans and signed a paper attesting to their German nationality.
5. In the original Hebrew, a well-known quote from the Book of Esther read on the festival of Purim.

between Poles and Jews and use any means necessary to maintain the anti-Semitism of the prewar period, symbolized by the ritual slaughter debate in the Polish parliament, which fanned Jew hatred all over the country. German agents worked behind the scenes to stir this up and thus divert the Poles' attention from the Nazi danger.

There was no better way to avert Polish resistance and sabotage than to drum up hatred of Jews, and the Germans played this card in order to gain the favor of Polish anti-Semites. "Look, we couldn't crush the Jews. And here comes Hitler, and he takes care of things in the blink of an eye!" The plan to establish a ghetto diverted the attention of the Polish masses from what was happening with Polish politics in exile.[6] People just wanted to talk about the ghetto. Some were for it, some were against it, but that didn't matter. The main thing for the Germans was to divert the Poles and dull their minds.

No, the ghetto really didn't make sense for the Germans if you looked at things strictly from the economic point of view. But where is it written that every jot and letter of a law has to be carried out? It was enough to talk loudly about the anti-Jewish law, but in fact all ordinances of the occupation authorities were systematically sabotaged, and the Germans themselves did not go all out to ensure that everybody would obey them.

Let's take for example the edict about prices, the first draconian decree that was issued in the beginning of 1940 and that threatened the death penalty for anyone caught selling food at inflated prices. At first glance you might think this was a sensible and rational way to fight speculation, but that's only how it seemed. This was really about the Germans' desire to confuse people, to disturb the stable relations between Poles and Jews. They did not want the population to be able to catch its breath lest it have the chance to reflect on what was really happening.

Now about that edict itself. Well, not only did it fail to achieve its purpose, but in fact as soon as it was issued food disappeared from

6. There was a Polish exile government that was based in Paris until June 1940, then in London, but it is not clear what was going on at the time that Opoczynski refers to here.

the market, prices skyrocketed, and you could only get bread or food through connections or in secret. From that point on, prices never returned to their previous level, inflation soared, and the value of money fell. The occupation authorities had to realize that once again they had sacrificed their economic self-interest in favor of political goals, so they looked the other way at the illegal trade in food. Technically, the edict remained in force, but the Germans did not impose one death sentence for food speculation. And the same thing happened to the edict about the ghetto.

This ghetto decree hit everyone, the Germans not less than the Jews and the Poles, so it could only be implemented gradually, against the will of the local authorities, who understood that

FRANK'S FANATICAL PLAN HAD DANGEROUS IMPLICATIONS
FOR THE ECONOMY

The decree establishing the ghetto was issued in the second half of 1940. There was a period of several months between the time the decree was issued and the actual beginning of the ghetto. During that time there was a tremendous amount of trade in Warsaw. Masses of peasants brought into the city all the products they could: potatoes, vegetables, dairy products, fats and other kinds of food, wood, peat, and even coal, which they had an easier time obtaining from the Germans than Jews did and which they sold for jacked-up prices. After the peasants sold their products they used their money to buy clothes, imported goods, and everything else that a peasant might think would come in handy in the long run.

Business was just as lively in the markets, where Polish buyers and storekeepers traded with the Jews. During this time many Jews became downright rich and others made more than enough to support themselves and their families. It was hard to believe that the Germans would see any sense in closing the ghetto.

In the city there were already special Jewish trams with yellow signboards that served purely Jewish streets, half yellow and half white for areas that were mixed Polish-Jewish, and just white for purely Christian areas. There was also talk about forbidding Jews to travel on the trains, but in the meantime the population—Poles and Jews—still believed that the decree would be annulled.

But things happened otherwise.

On November 15 the ghetto was closed. Jews could no longer leave. Gentiles were given a month to enter the ghetto with special passes, ostensibly to give them a chance to wind up their businesses.

During that month one could observe an interesting scene in the markets: small crowds of Jewish peddlers, men and women, would surround any Gentile they found and press merchandise for sale into their hands. The goyim would get angry and yell at them: Get out of here, go to hell, we don't need to buy anything!

But in fact that was not so. They actually did need to buy, but they wanted to exploit the opportunity and buy at rock-bottom prices. And they were able to pull it off.

From that time on the goy begins to play a particular role in the ghetto. He becomes the favorite, the big shot, everybody tries to flatter him. Jews argue over him, they try to get on his good side, they give him little candies for his children. In a word, the goy becomes

THE ONLY SOURCE OF A LIVELIHOOD

Jews, who until now had lived off savings from before the war and who still allowed themselves to buy something from time to time in the market, now stopped buying. They had run out of money and had started to sell possessions, coats, clothing. Other Jews, whose possessions would have enabled them to get along for many years, fell victim to informers, Jewish and non-Jewish, who sucked the marrow from their bones. The Germans would arrive, load all the clothing, furniture, and overcoats on trucks and carry everything off. If they found jewelry, silver, diamonds, or gold—not to mention money— they scooped it up greedily, and in fifteen minutes the owners were reduced to total poverty and were doomed to death by starvation. So Jews stopped buying. They were no longer able to support the market. The only buyer now became the goy.

Where previously the goy had been the major customer in the markets, now he became the only customer. In the early days of the occupation the goy bought everything that the Jews offered for sale. But now that the ghetto was closed, it became more and more the case that goyim forced Jews to sell their possessions for practically nothing, a dry piece of bread. Now the goy became picky, he turned up his nose at old rags, he wanted the finest and the best and at the cheapest price. If he didn't get it he would walk away.

THE TRADE IN USED GOODS

For as long as anybody can remember, thousands of Jews, peddlers, hucksters, and ragpickers would trade in the Wołówka flea market, and with a few zlotys in start-up money they could somehow put bread on the table for their wives and children. But the war dealt them all a terrible blow. Now nobody wanted this second-rate stuff, and the peddlers who would go from house to house died of hunger. Now the only traders who could make money were those who could offer goyim a good suit, a coat, nice linen and silk underwear, silk and velvet dresses, furs, good boots, and the like.

The Germans did not care about what happened to the traders, but they did want the raw materials that they collected. So they established big collection points and gave the rag dealers permits and issued them green armbands, just like state officials (pardon the comparison!). This allowed them to go pretty much anywhere, even outside the ghetto, and in return they provided the Germans with needed materials such as wool, old cotton goods, and other things that might help the war economy.

Jews cast envious glances at these traders with the green armbands. Many did pretty well, and Jews murmured that at least some of them made their money not so much from the rags they collected but from informing the Germans about Jews who had good things that they could rob . . .

Anyway, until the rag dealer became a privileged character the trade in old stuff was deep in the dumps. There was a long lean period until Jews suddenly got the bright idea to remake the old clothes. Sewers took old shirts, blanket covers, and sheets and cut them up to make new articles out of them. Tailors and shoemakers did the same with old clothes and footwear, and pretty soon the Wołówka flea market featured two kinds of business: old stuff that Jews acquired to redo, and new clothes, which the goyim bought.

But now a new source of trouble appeared.

THE BANISHMENT OF THE FLEA MARKET

The old Wołówka, which had been located on the corner of Stawki Street near the new, unfinished bus station, remained outside the ghetto. For as long as anyone can remember, this trade in old clothes and used goods had been a mainstay for the poor masses. But in the ghetto, no new market replaced the Wołówka.

At first the Wołówka sellers set up their little stores not far from the old flea market, on the corner of Zamenhofa and Niska. But they were driven away. Then they moved over to the corner of Niska and Lubecka. Once again, they were forced to leave. They then started to slowly shift along Lubecka to the corner of Wołynska and Gęsia—and had to suffer constant raids. Germans came with rubber sticks, Polish police with wooden batons, and they beat the daylights out of them. They didn't spare the women, and they made arrests. They also shot into the air—or at least that's what they pretended to do—but more than once they actually killed somebody. And so it went until the Germans took another look at things and realized they could profit from this Jewish trade. They made the new flea market on the corner of Gęsia and Lubecka "kosher" in order to squeeze money out of it.

The constant raids and arrests and harassments at the Wołówka had practically driven all the goyim away from this Jewish market. The Germans then closed off the ghetto, and the goy could enter only with a special permit, which needless to say meant handing out a lot of money to wheelers and dealers. And to get it he had to state a reason for wanting to go into the ghetto. Of course he couldn't just say he wanted to go there to buy something. And when you added the shootings, the arrests, and the beatings, the goy decided that going into the ghetto was too much bother.

when the goy did not come to buy? The answer is simple. One has to remember that legally it was not possible to totally seal off the ghetto from the rest of the city, and it wouldn't be possible in the future either. For the municipal authorities, whose headquarters was outside the ghetto, the ghetto remained an integral part of the city of Warsaw. The city government sent in its officials to collect taxes, it dispatched its conductors on the trams [that ran through the ghetto]; for a while it also sent postal officials, street cleaners, and workers from the electric and gas companies—in short, the municipality sent in all kinds of people to deal with public services. The city court was also in the ghetto. The hospitals also had to send in ambulance wagons to carry the sick; the municipal provisioning authority had to send in trucks with food. So all these trucks and wagons; the tram workers; the witnesses and defendants in the court; and last but not least the Polish police themselves—the same ones who hounded the Jewish vendors, beat them until their blood flowed and dragged them with terrible brutality into the police stations—all of them happily smuggled stuff in and out of the ghetto. And what's even more amazing—in return for a lot of cash, the Germans themselves smuggled things in and out on their army trucks.

The situation really changed only after the establishment of the new flea market, when the Polish traders and customers decided that once again it was worth it to take the risk, pay good money for a permit, and enter the ghetto to visit the Wołówka. So from day to day more and more goyim, male and female, came to the Wołówka as well as more and more Jewish traders to sell used goods and household items. There weren't many other ways to make a living in the ghetto, and even craftsmen brought the goods they produced to the Wołówka.

WAR WITH RUSSIA

Business in the Wołówka flourished. Now that they were planning to attack Russia, the Germans needed peace and quiet in Poland, and they started giving the population some small concessions in order to demonstrate the benevolence of the German occupation regime. Even the hated Jews, whom the Germans saw as the most disgusting and vile creatures, were able to feel a marked improvement, which lasted some months.

First of all Hans Frank sent a German commissar into the ghetto, and he started to look into the food situation there.[7] As if it were a big surprise, the Germans suddenly discovered that there was a high mortality rate, terrible epidemics, and thousands of people whose bodies were swollen from hunger. So they sent this commissar to sort things out. And you have to admit, as long as the situation at the Russian front was unsettled, the commissar imposed some kind of order. The public soup kitchens got more foodstuffs, as did the homes for orphans, the hospitals, and the centers for convalescents. And now, two days a week, the soup kitchens gave out a piece of bread along with the soup. Once or twice a month a little more bread appeared on the ration cards. Jews who had not stopped cursing and damning the Judenrat now saw living proof that indeed, up to now, the Judenrat had been devouring everything. Yes, now there was clear proof: a goy doesn't fool around, he gets things done . . .

There's a folk saying: "The way it goes with the Christians, so it goes with the Jews." Many concessions were made to the goyim, especially in matters concerning the ghetto. The guards at the ghetto gates started to look the other way and didn't check entry passes so carefully. Just as it became easier for goyim to enter the ghetto, so too did it become easier for Jews to leave. It wasn't just that now the Germans were preoccupied with the war with Russia to the exclusion of everything else. The war also served as a subtle warning to the Germans that they should be careful and try to win over the population. After all, who knows when you might need friends?

The goyim responded to the German overtures. Every day you could see thousands of goyim on the Wołówka, and they went home with

7. Hans Frank, a Nazi lawyer, was the governor-general of occupied Poland, appointed by Hitler in 1939. The German commissar given responsibility for overseeing the Warsaw ghetto was Heinz Auerswald, another Nazi lawyer and member of the SS, who was appointed to the post in 1941.

everything you could imagine. The production of remade clothes, shoes, and undergarments flourished as never before. Tailors would take out the cotton from old worn quilts and sew warm jackets and winter trousers, or they would use it as lining for windbreakers or winter coats. And the same process went on with other items.

Goyim, mainly young guys, would come into the ghetto on the transit trams that were not supposed to stop. They would jump off after giving a good bribe to the Gentile policeman who sat on every tram that transited the ghetto. The policeman looked the other way. So did the conductor and often the Germans themselves. The Gentile guys would wear POLISHED BOOTS, nice fur jackets, and golden rings on their fingers. Their faces were ruddy, clean shaven, and well fed: the very picture of good health. The same for the older goyim. Judging by their looks many seemed to be peasant women from the villages, with round cheeks that looked like thick Polish doughnuts, broad shoulders that you would see on a man, and feet nestled in sturdy boots. They would move about, just like experienced merchants, from one Jewish seller to the next and would buy up the best stuff dirt cheap.

Toward evening you could see an amazing sight on the corner of Zamenhofa and Muranowska. Hundreds of male and female goyim stood in a row carrying sacks stuffed with silk and velvet, padded clothing and coats, expensive underwear, shoes and boots, carpets, and quilts. They were waiting for the last trams, all the while glancing suspiciously in all directions, worried that a German might suddenly appear or that they might attract the attention of an undercover policeman.

If suddenly someone said *"O idzie!"* ("Somebody's coming!") everybody would quickly scatter into the nearest gateways, onto the steps of buildings, and into corridors. When Jews would tell them that the coast was clear, they would go back to the tram stop. Each Jew, who embodies the righteousness of the persecuted, believes that he is obligated to help the goyim when he sees them fleeing from the glances of the undercover agents. It is truly moving to witness the help Jews give them when that happens.

The goyim catch the exact moment when the tram stops, leap on quickly with their loaded sacks, and then go home happy, sated, and full of self-confidence because of the purchases they made—which hold out the promise of really fat profits. Because, you see, the stuff that the goy is carrying in his sack is just a decoy, meant to divert attention from the real loot, which he is concealing by wearing it himself.

The expensive silk underwear, the good furs, and the jewelry are hidden on their bodies. When the little stalls and shops went up in the new Wołówka, the Jews also put in little kitchens to prepare cold and hot snacks for the traders. The goyim could well afford to pay the Jews good prices to stuff their faces, because inside those kitchens there was a tiny space where the Polish traders could, for a few zlotys, undress from head to toe and put on all the good stuff they had bought.

THE POLICEMAN AND THE CONDUCTOR

Those who accompany them home at night from the ghetto don't really have to know about all this to the last detail; it's enough for them to see a sack of goods, and when there is a big enough crowd of traders—say, enough to fill two packed tram cars—then every bit of cash pressed into the hand of a policeman or conductor makes the whole deal worthwhile for them. They don't go away with nothing.

If the trip into the ghetto is successful—and ninety-nine times out of a hundred it is—then the traders return the next day. If they pay good money they can travel like princes in a nice auto, and nobody will notice a thing. These are the ambulances from the first aid or from a city hospital that come every morning into the ghetto to take out the sick and return those who have recovered. Or the traders can come in the autos of other city departments, such as the disinfection service. Yes, there are Jewish hospitals in the ghetto, but the number of sick is so great that a lot have to be taken out of the ghetto.

And then there are those who enter through the ghetto gates, where there's always some Fritz who does not say no to some hard cash; he knows even Hitler can't get along without money. And many goyim sneak in through cracks and holes in the walls or through attics and cellars. Because it's worth it—yes, it's worth it a thousand times over. Ultimately their customers, the peasants, will repay them quite well.

made great profits, and even though he had to hand over some of his crop to the occupation authorities, there was still more than enough left over to sell on the free market at inflated prices. True, there was one problem: they closed off the ghetto. So he could not come in with his crops and get the prices offered in the urban market. But not to worry—the peasant could sell to the Gentile smugglers who sneak in grain, flour, and vegetables on the trains going into Warsaw. Or on the other hand the peasant could hand over a fat bribe, take his wagon in himself, and make so much money that he did not know what to do with it—he didn't have much confidence in the new paper money issued by the Germans. His stubborn peasant cunning tells him that the wheel might turn again and the day might come when he'd be left with a worthless bundle of paper zlotys. He also remembers all the chaos and tumult of the First World War. So he wants to exchange his money for real articles, and indeed only for the best stuff that would be just like real money—not just gold and silver, which he buries in the ground, but also expensive clothes and other necessary items.

When the Polish traders, both men and women, succeed in making a great deal in the Wołówka, when they buy from the Jew "just the thing" that the peasant will love, then—as is common with ordinary people—they become superstitious and don't want to jinx their good luck. God might punish them, who knows? So they look to do a good deed to make up for their sins and faults.

And on the Wołówka such a good deed would be giving something to eat to a hungry Jewish child begging for food, a child who is smart enough, like any child, to sidle up to the Gentile woman just when her bosom is heaving in prayer to get safely back. The child holds out his hand like a little shovel and says in Polish, *"Kochana pani, zlituj się nademną, jestem głodny"* ("Dear Miss, have pity on me. I am hungry"). Then the "dear miss" takes her purse out of her bosom and gives the poor Jewish child a whole zloty, sometimes even two. Or even a loaf of bread, while she whispers in his ear that he should pray to the Jewish God that she should return safely to the Aryan side with all her stuff.

But sometimes things don't turn out well. First of all, there can be problems in the Wołówka itself. Sometimes, just when the deals could not be better, a truck full of Fritzes might suddenly appear, with all the Germans shooting in the air, climbing down to stick you with bayonets, beat you with whips, or seize somebody with a Polish face that looks suspicious and arrest him. As for the Jews—well, you can easily guess. Those who fail to run away in time get a blow on the head that sends them reeling; the Germans confiscate their stuff and often haul them off to the COMMISSARIAT, where they sit—sometimes for a long time, sometimes less—and always they come out stripped of everything, with empty pockets and broken bones.

And if the Germans don't descend on you, then the plainclothes Polish police might. Sure, with them you can negotiate; after all, they speak Polish, and they certainly understand the language of the market—money. With money you can get yourself out of any trouble.

But if this is how things were for a while after the start of the Russian-German war, then things got a lot worse toward the end of 1941, when the Germans reached the shores of the Sea of Azov and were telling the people back home that soon they would take Moscow. Now they didn't care so much about buying off the Poles with little concessions. Or who knows—maybe just when it seemed that they would capture Moscow they would not only get stuck but the Russians would actually counterattack. Or maybe it was out of sheer frustration. Whatever the case, the German regime in Poland became more brutal, more nervous, and more impatient. So German policy became much tougher, and along with the terrible punishments suffered by the Jews who left the ghetto, Poles coming into the ghetto now felt a wave of persecution.

The witnesses who came to the court building to testify at a trial were now ordered by a German guard to empty their pockets. If they found a few hundred paper zlotys, they would confiscate the money and haul them off to jail. A goy who bought a prayer shawl on the Wołówka—outside the ghetto the goyim would dye them and rework them into nice wool clothing—really had some bad luck, which served as a reminder of what the Jews had to go through.

The German found the tallith the goy was wearing under his coat with the fringes tied together just like religious Jews would do going to pray on the Sabbath. He ordered the goy to take the tallith off and wear it on top, then he had to gather the fringes in his hands, just like Jews do, and dressed like that he had to march down the whole street kissing the fringes.

Another time Polish police were sent to cruise the streets with a small pickup truck to catch goyim who had come to buy a permit to enter the ghetto. The police cast knowing glances on all sides of the sidewalk and picked out every Polish face, even if the male or female goy was wearing the white armband with the blue Star of David—the police could tell who was a Jew and who was a goy. The Germans themselves did not have a clue when it came to telling Jews apart from Poles. The male or female goy wearing an armband could march past a German without any fear; they knew they could fool the *schwab* and did not care. But they could not fool the Polish policeman. The only good thing was that the Polish police also wanted to live and actually to live very well, just like the old *strazhnik,* the Russian policeman, so he quickly lost interest in the hunt.

SABBATH IN THE WOŁÓWKA

On the Sabbath, which since the winter of 1940 has served as the official Jewish day of rest—it's not for nothing that the Germans want the Jews to observe the Sabbath—business is slow on the Wołówka. Few Jewish traders come even though the religious observance of the Sabbath has sharply declined during the war. And on Sunday—the official Gentile day of rest—the goyim don't come. After all, they want to rest one day a week. So what, do you think they'll miss out on something, that somebody else on the Wołówka will snap up the bargains? On Sunday it's just Jews trading with other Jews, but come Monday morning, the Wołówka springs to life. The Jewish dealers come early, and the goyim also hustle in. By eight in the morning it's already like a bustling fair, with deals going on like crazy. Jews stand around and happily look over every newly arriving goy; their beaming faces flash smiles and the kind of looks you might give to beloved members of your own family, as if to say, may we never have to part again, father in heaven! And the goyim sense this—they feel conceited, walk around like peacocks, as if they know that they are bringing abundance.

Sometimes it happens that a Gentile woman, who used to work as a servant in a Jewish home and now is doing very well for herself as a trader, confronts a Jewish woman who she thinks wants too much money. The Gentile can't help herself, and she'll say, "Sell, lady, and sell at the price I'm offering you, because if it weren't for me, then all of you here would croak from hunger . . ."

The Jewish woman gets scared; she hasn't heard that kind of talk from goyim since the days of the anti-Semitic boycotts from before the war.

But then again this kind of talk is not really unexpected. In their folk tales about bad kings, dishonest princes, and hostile rulers, Jews had already heard plenty about persecutions of Jews, about how princes would sic vicious dogs on them or toss an entire family into a pit; about troubles suffered by Jewish tavernkeepers, leaseholders, innkeepers; about calamities suffered by entire communities when they were uprooted and forced into exile, to wander the four corners of the earth . . . and still here we are, we're alive! So what the hell, let the goy spout. We know in the end that

THE BAD TIMES WILL NOT LAST FOREVER

Okay, maybe the Jewish woman did not think about all these things exactly in the same way, but it didn't matter, it was all there, and inside her heart, like lightning, her faith and all she had learned in a lifetime flashed by. In a second she forgets the vile talk she just heard, calls out to another Gentile woman and offers her bargains: wedding dresses of Jewish mothers thrown out in the middle of the night, from the homes they had lived in their whole lives, and forced to wander though dark forests; wedding presents received by young women—Turkish shawls, silk and wool prayer shawls, head kerchiefs, carpets and drapes—silent witnesses to terrible bitter poverty, to hearts weakened by hunger, to the first awful signs of SCURVY.

How many Jewish women find that they can't bear to part with the nice things and shed bitter tears before they take them away to be sold on the Wołówka? How many wonderful memories are bound up with every item?

But life has crushed us under its wheel and the world has turned upside down; the strongest countries, the freest countries, where everybody was an equal citizen and where nobody thought of discrimination, are now under Hitler's heel; he establishes ghettos everywhere. Will we someday be able to return to our old homes and rebuild them as bright and as neat as they were before the storm?

WILL SALVATION YET COME?

Yes, a woman thinks about such things, but then she makes a quick gesture with her hand: it's all the same, she realizes—the house is already destroyed, so what's the point of thinking about our possessions? So, Mister Jew, tell me—how much are you willing to offer?

And it's as if the Jew were listening in on what the Jewish woman was saying to herself. He offers her a low price, a merciless price. The war knows nothing about kindness, the war doesn't bother itself with morality. The war teaches you to look after your own skin. So the old Jewish woman takes the few gulden for her treasures, which are really more like abstract memories than actual possessions, and she goes home in silence. But she feels better when she sees how her husband and children eat the modest meal she cooks up with the money. As she watches them come back to life she tells herself her only regret was that she wasn't able to salvage more of their possessions to sell and keep on going . . .

The Gentile who comes later and buys the woman's things from the Jew doesn't feel a thing; what he's holding in his hands is just stuff that's worth money, fat pieces of LARD—nothing more than that. If you're looking for some higher value to this buying and selling, then you can find it only in THE BRIDGE that has appeared between the Jew and the Gentile. It's a bridge built out of bad material: speculation. But it has a good purpose: to keep a large part of the Jewish population from starving to death.

Look, it's possible that the Endeks, the Nara crowd, and all the other Jew haters with whose presence Poland was so abundantly blessed are lurking somewhere in their lairs and grinding their teeth as they watch this catastrophe. They are Hitler's faithful disciples and want to see our physical destruction. But the goyim of the Wołówka foil their plans and thwart their hopes.

And it's also possible that in another segment of Polish society, among the true Polish patriots whose hearts bleed as they feel the national disaster, there's a feeling of gratitude to these Polish smuggler-traders who are only thinking of their own profits but who nevertheless serve Poland's national interest. The smugglers maintain a link between Poland's loyal citizens; they extend a brotherly hand to the persecuted and thus erect a beacon of morality in a time of rampant demoralization. Yes, that's maybe how it is, maybe how it must be.

So for the time being the comprehensive plan to isolate us in a ghetto has not succeeded, unless the enemy becomes so barbaric that he lines us up in front of guns and shoots us all en masse like rabid dogs, just as he is doing to Jews in the occupied Russian territories. But in that case the Germans can be confident in our total victory.

THE LAST JEWISH CHILD will be the first of our future generations: the new Jew, proud, clear minded, pure, forged in the blast furnace of our era. The new Jew will blaze and burn with a determination to win the total redemption of mankind, to remove the mark of shame from the face of his own people, and to erase the plague that has beset the world: hatred between peoples.

Goyim in the ghetto: they too are a harbinger of our coming victory.

The ghetto wall cuts across Franciszkańska Street right at Koźla Alley. You don't see it from far away; only when you stand at the opening of the alley does the wall become visible, as it really is, in its entirety. In part that's because the alley is so short and narrow, lined on both sides with odd-looking, antiquated buildings that open onto little courtyards, twisting entryways, and decrepit, crumbling steps.[1] Here and there a narrow five-story structure with lots of windows shoots up between two older buildings, which suggests that once upon a time it housed small apartments for workers, artisans, and street vendors.

These larger structures—squeezed in between the ancient-looking buildings and shooting straight up—disrupt the pattern of the little alley; they give it a wild and wanton feel. In fact, this whole neighborhood had been neglected before the war, when the powers that be left the street to its own devices and let it go to wrack and ruin.

In front of every house there's already a crush of pushcarts selling fruits and vegetables. The food stands are minuscule. On a stool or

1. A few portions of the surviving manuscript of "Smuggling in the Warsaw Ghetto" are illegible. A listing of these sections, along with conjectures for their original reading, may be found in *A Holocaust Reader*, edited, translated, and with an introduction and notes by Lucy S. Dawidowicz (New York: Behrman House, 1976), pp. 197–207. This translation is indebted to Dawidowicz's work.

table an old Jewish woman sets out a few small sacks of flour, each weighing two or three kilos: cornmeal, rye, *bona* (the ration flour bakers receive from the occupation authorities to bake the ration bread), or sacks of groats, millet, or barley. Such items as beans, white flour, or dried mushrooms that you might buy in a store are not typically found at these little stands. The prices here, of course, are a little cheaper than in other streets—this is Koźla Alley, after all! Still, they're steep enough for most Warsaw Jews. The ghetto has robbed them of their livelihood, leaving them with empty hands dangling at their sides. That leaves them with only one way to eke out a meager living: by selling off their clothes and household items in the Wołówka, the flea market.

The crush of booths, food stands, and pushcarts blocks the street. Every booth is besieged not so much by shoppers as by onlookers, who would like to buy something, but they're broke. Sales are relatively brisk—but negligible in weight. The Jewish woman who can buy a whole kilo of potatoes, beets, or carrots is a sight seldom seen. People buy ten decagrams at a time, if not less. A quarter kilo? Fat chance! Anyone who buys a single apple, not to mention a quarter kilo, is looked up to as a model housewife, towering head and shoulders above the crowd. Others stop by the alley just to check out how expensive things are today and whether skyrocketing prices might not have come down. They lick the drool from their lips and keep on walking, aching with the burning shame that all they have left is—well—is nothing at all. But what can you do? There's a war going on. And when someone tells them that others are living it up and wolfing it all down while they're dying of hunger—they turn and walk the other way.

Rickshaws are the vehicle of choice here, that unique way of getting around in the Warsaw ghetto that the Jews—those "cosmopolitans," never slow to adapt what they need from anyone or anyplace—got from the Japanese and Chinese. The rickshaw was a huge boon to Koźla Alley, and not just because droshkyes and wagons disappeared right after the Germans confiscated the horses of Jewish drivers. That alone wouldn't have been so bad. A Jewish porter from Warsaw can, believe me, haul a healthy sack of flour on his back. But what's the use if he can't do it in broad daylight? For the police agent's eye is on the lookout. With the rickshaw, it's a whole other story. Jews have modified and perfected the design beyond the wildest dreams of the Chinese. Right under the seat they've installed an empty compartment where you can hide a few packets of flour while making yourself comfortable in the plush seat like nobody's business. Then off you go on a little jaunt through the streets.

But not everyone who transports food from Koźla Alley uses a rickshaw. Most go on foot, and they are in fact the mainstay carriers of goods. Known as "strollers," they can't afford rickshaws, so their own backs become their rickshaws—backs on which it's not unusual for them to carry three or four sacks of flour, groats, or other foodstuffs at one time. A sack typically weighs fifteen kilos—and off they go.

The strollers and other customers entering the street find their way blocked by the market at the corner of Koźla Alley, by the crush of vegetable buyers, and by the rickshaws that stand in the way. Every step they take brings curses from the crowd, and the stroller who hears them hurries about his business. He's in a sweat, gasping for breath as he goes, struggling to get rid of his load as fast as he can—often in a panic, since a police agent is never far away.

The degree of movement and danger in the alley are not constant throughout the day. The smuggler bringing in the goods can't keep them in storage. He's got to move the merchandise as quickly as possible—and just as feverishly as he moves the goods into his house he's got to unload and dispose of it to customers. Only then can he relax because he's removed all incriminating evidence.

SMUGGLING AT NIGHT

Nighttime smuggling provides the smugglers' shops with plenty of everything: vegetables and fruit, groceries, meat, chicken, honey, and whatever the heart desires—even good drink. The city needs something to eat in the morning, and the strollers need a whole day for their work. In the summer at five in the morning you can already see the strollers hauling bags of food or a sack of potatoes and cans of milk. Their faces freshly washed in the morning light and shining from their labor, these are working Jews who can eat their fill. They move with confidence and power—through a crowd of swollen feet.

Nighttime smuggling, however, is only a part of the network—it can't supply the ghetto with everything it needs in the few night hours. This is especially true in the summertime, when the smuggler never receives the goods he's ordered at the scheduled time. Ask the smuggler when he might be getting such and such an item and his answer is always the same: *I don't know—if they get it over to me, I'll have it. It all depends on when they can pass it over from the other side of the wall.* At night, smuggling takes place on the rooftops, through small holes, in cellars, and even over the ghetto wall itself—wherever possible. In daytime, by contrast, things work much more simply, though not without their own dodges and clever tricks of the Jewish brain: as the Mishnah says, "He who sees a place where a miracle was done for Israel."[2]

Koźla Alley has several even-numbered houses where non-Jews live, but the entrances to the houses and doors have been walled up. Their entrances are now on the other side of the wall, on Freta Street, meaning outside the ghetto. Only the windows of some apartments look down on the ghetto. This layout is a blessing, not just for the few non-Jews living in these homes but for the Jews as well, and let's be clear about it: not just for the Jews of Koźla Alley and its smugglers but for all the Jews in Warsaw. Smuggling certainly is a filthy business, a noose hung around the neck of the starving and swollen consumer, but in the horrific conditions of the huge prison the Jews have been driven into and enclosed by the ghetto walls, smuggling is the only salvation left for the surviving remnants. Who knows? Someday we may have to construct a memorial to the courage of the smuggler, who saved a good part of Jewish Warsaw from starving to death.

GRATED WINDOWS

The windows of the non-Jewish apartments were secured from top to bottom with wire grates, supposedly to fence the building off from the Jewish street. In fact, the wire bars were a great advantage to the

2. Partial quotation from the Mishnah that begins Tractate Berakhot 9 of the Babylonian Talmud: "He that sees a place where a miracle was done for Israel should say, 'Blessed are you that did miracles for our fathers in this place.'"

smugglers. Inside the Gentile places a wooden trough—the kind you see on a factory floor—right up against the grate. When the Gentile pours a sack of rye down the chute, the rye shoots through the grate right into the sack held up to the other end of the trough by the Jewish smuggler in Koźla Alley below. Before you can count to three the sack is full, and Meyer Bomke, the tall porter with the shoulders of a real Russian peasant, whips the sack onto his back as if it were stuffed with feathers and takes off in a flash.

Cereal, millet, sugar, and other foods are smuggled in the same way. Only flour gets smuggled in paper bags, though not of course stuffed through the window grates but passed through the windows of the upper floors. From there the Polish smuggler lowers a rope down to the street, where the Jewish smuggler catches it and ties paper bags on to the rope. The Pole hauls up the bags and fills them with flour, then lowers them one by one to the street, where they are quickly grabbed and spirited away. In order not to cut his hands, the Pole wears a pair of thick cotton gloves to let the rope slide through.

When it's time to lower the merchandise, the windows of the ground floor apartments are packed with people. Around the smugglers are their wives, sons, daughters, porters, and just plain Jews all milling about, talking with the Poles. Only those customers authorized by the smuggler himself are allowed to buy.

Often you can hear two smugglers bickering with each other at the "non-Jewish" window: "Yankele, you piece of crap—go fuck yourself. You'll never get near that window again. I swear, if it's the last thing I do, I'll fix your ass good!"

"Come on, Meyer, move it! Let's go, let's go, speed it up. Look at that guy working up a sweat!"

"Mendel, you should burn in hell! Why are you just standing there? Come on and take this into the store!"

Insults and curses fly back and forth and cut like knives. Goods shoot quickly from hand to hand as the smuggled items are whisked away. A heave here, a pull there, then a yank and the merchandise gets stowed in the dark, half-closed storerooms of Koźla Alley's medieval buildings. Broad-shouldered, red-cheeked wives with calloused hands look nervously from side to side, shooting quick looks toward

Franciszkańska Street at the end of the alley to see if the coast is clear or if someone is riding or walking by. At just that moment, a hoarse warning cry suddenly pierces the air: "Passover!"[3]

"Passover!" Everyone hears the call on both sides of the wall, and every door is slammed shut and bolted tight. Padlocks are placed on the outside. Other smugglers stay inside, while some keep to the street and remain on the lookout, leaning up against the store as if they had nothing better to do. The Poles above speedily yank up their rope, and Koźla Alley goes quiet; the air grows thick with anticipation . . . the smuggling machine is put on hold.

Because it's Passover. Some non-Jew with a briefcase has walked by. No one knows him, but he's probably an undercover agent, so they wait. When the Pole upstairs gets tired of waiting and has the audacity to lower the rope again, he cries out to the Jews standing below, *"Nie ma już pejsacha!"*—"Passover is finished!" With the contemptuous look of the expert, they shoot back a warning: *"Czekaj, pejsach jeszcze się kręci!"*—"Hold your horses, Passover is still going on!"

The Poles deliver milk to Koźla Alley around seven in the morning—elsewhere still earlier. Large tin cans, marked with the number of liters they hold, are pushed up against the windows of the ground-floor apartments. A thick tube with a measuring gauge is passed through the wire grate, and with a turn of the faucet a gushing white stream of whole milk spills out, still carrying the smell of the cow stall, and quickly fills the can. The milk can flies even more quickly from the windows to the stores, where Jewish milkmen and milkwomen wait with containers to bring it where people live.

BERL THE SOUSE

The Jewish smugglers taking delivery of the milk come with their own testers, who determine whether the milk is pure, unadulterated. But that's only to butter their own bread: they don't hesitate pulling the

3. The use of Hebrew and Aramaic by Jewish and Gentile smugglers goes back several centuries. The reference here is to the burning of the *hametz* on the eve of Passover, which serves as a cryptic warning to hide the contraband.

same trick on their customers. Listen, it's not about justice, it's about profit, at least according to them. A juicy drumstick, some gizzard, and the little belt on the side is something that a Jew like Mr. Berl just cannot do without. Berl, in fact, has prepared the cans at his place so that each contains unequal measures of water mixed with white foam. Here's the way it works: say a Jewish woman comes to the window to buy some milk and insists on getting it as it flows directly from the goy's hose. Berl warns her that if she wants to be doubly sure of its purity, it will cost her six zlotys. But just let her hesitate a moment and the tube is already filling Berl's can. Then he says, "Now you can have it for five."

The math is quite simple.

Actually, we've run ahead of ourselves: the work schedule—that is, the daily smuggling schedule—doesn't actually begin with milk but with vegetables. Not everyone can buy bread, but a beet, a potato, and a carrot during wartime are precious treats, and all are eager to get it.

Shloyme Yopke, a short Jew with rosy red cheeks like Simkhas Torah apples, his well-worn hands resting in his pants pockets, starts the day by selling smuggled potatoes, greens, eggs, creamy butter, honey, and sometimes nonkosher fats.[4] Rosie, a Jewish woman with a hefty backside, pouty lips, and rolls of fat on her ring-laden fingers, stands by the scale. Time and again she lifts a bag of flour, asks this person or that what they're buying, how much they're offering, and giddyap— we're off to the races. If she doesn't like the price being asked, she'll yell at them in her manly voice: "Beat it, you clown, save your story for someone else. We'll send you home with a cholent for Shabes, that's what you'll get! But you, of course, won't settle for less than the finest white flour . . ."

Shloyme stands nearby on stumpy legs; his squinty eyes with his whitish brows dusted with flour give him the sleepy face of a baker. His hands never leave his pockets, and the fob from his pocket watch

4. On Simkhas Torah, a fall holiday that marks the completion of the annual cycle of reading the Torah, children parade around the synagogue bearing paper flags with apples on top.

gleams splendidly as it dangles from his bulging vest, as if to say, "The hell with you all, you miserable scum! The hell I'll give you flour for that price!" Shloyme knows what flour is. After all, he was a baker before the war.

One of his six or eight partners, Izzy the Face, is two heads taller but has the same shoulders, wide as an oak tree. Izzy's got nothing to do and stands next to Shloyme with his hands in his pockets. In fact, he's there to keep an eye on things and to make sure his "capital" is growing. That's his people sitting over there at the counter doing figures, counting and taking money. The young man at the cash drawer keeps track, and after each transaction opens the drawer stuffed with paper bills and then pushes it closed. The Polish paper money, issued by the Germans with a picture of Chopin's monument and King Piast's portrait on it, is piled up in heaps, like a bunch of greasy rags: hundreds, five hundreds, and fifties, fifties, and more fifties—stacks and stacks of them.[5] The young man at the cash drawer is wearing a shiny pair of boots and enjoying a fancy smoke after his hefty breakfast. He looks with contempt at the money and the people who are forking it over. So much money lies piled up before him, so much inflated paper, that he imagines he's not hurting for cash at all. He too has forgotten what people without money look like, and he's impatient for the paupers to pay up in a hurry so he can grab it fast.

Izzy the Face has nothing to do either. He hovers around the shop with his flour-dusted bicyclist cap pulled down over his eyes and peers out like a ferocious dog. The third, fourth, and fifth partners are there in the shop. Once having worked as well-off teamsters, soft drink manufacturers, and tanners, they've now turned to the smuggling trade. One of them sits by himself, one leg propped up on the counter, calmly munching on a drumstick with a pickle on the side, casting lordly glances over his drumstick at the customers—if they're worth a look.

---

5. The only legal currency in the *Generalgouvernement* was issued by the German occupiers. Piast was the legendary peasant ancestor of the first dynasty of Polish dukes and kings. Some bills carried an image of a Polish mountaineer, and other Polish motifs.

The only nimble ones in the whole crew are the women, the partners' wives. The women know their way around eggs, butter, and other kinds of food much better than the men and are just itching to make it big. One complains to the other that for thirty zlotys she can't find something for her children to eat, which is of course a lie. The point is to look like a helpless wretch. Both women know full well that such talk is for public consumption only—to keep their customers from getting jealous. Look, you can take my word for it: even the top smugglers in Koźla Alley can't afford to lay out more than thirty zlotys for breakfast—that's the image they're trying to get across. But of course it's not even close to the truth. The current price for a kilo of bread tips the scale at twenty zlotys, not to mention the butter, cheese, milk, and fresh egg that a smuggler's child must gobble down for breakfast every day, all things that hundreds of thousands of Jewish children in the city can barely imagine in their wildest dreams. Charging everyone else twenty zlotys for a loaf of bread guarantees that no child of a smuggler will have to give up any of these items themselves. The price explains the attitude of calm that Shloyme displays toward his partners as well as all the nervous running around of their wives.

Meanwhile we're still at the start of the day, at the sale of potatoes. Soon other foods will go on sale, and then things will really cut loose. But you never know—miracles do happen. In an hour or two someone might spread the word that the Germans are invading Russia. After all, someone saw a column of troops marching over the bridge toward Praga just before dawn.[6] That's all it takes; the value of sensational news is well understood by the Gentile smugglers as well as the Jewish ones: suddenly, prices shoot sky high, just like that. And with the jump in prices, Koźla Alley becomes a hotbed in an instant. People start ripping the merchandise from one another's hands. Every sack of food lowered from the Gentile windows gets snatched by hands that might as well be pairs of pliers. The tough Jewish porters with their hands of steel grab up the merchandise immediately for the rich traders to bring to the market. And no one can compete with them.

6. Praga is a suburb of Warsaw, on the east bank of the Vistula.

Hundreds of Jews mill around in the middle of the tiny alley at times like these, the same way they gather on holidays in front of the synagogues: stout, well-fed Jews, making deals and trading political rumors. The street is littered with butts and half-smoked cigarettes, and this at a time when they cost sixty groschen, roughly ten to twelve times the prewar price.

Peddlers wearing sandwich boards pass through the crowd, carrying tins of little cakes, crying, "Step right up, who'll give it a whirl?" Numbers are drawn from a small sack; some lose, and some even win a small cake. A couple of young smuggler kids surround the cake seller, then gobble up his cakes with such nasty delight that it's sickening to take a look at their greasy faces.

Street singers and performers drop by, drawn by the prospect of earning a little something in this well-fed land of plenty. But who cares? The fiddler screeches out a tune, and the singer sings his ghetto song—"I don't wanna give away my ration card yet, I wanna live just a little bit longer"—but makes no impression on anyone. The alley begins to come alive only when a whisper moves from mouth to mouth: "Another quarter, half a zloty . . . and with two you can get . . . rye meal at twenty-four and a half." That talk is music to the alley's ears. Does anyone even notice the dead man—that is, the man in his death throes, who has carefully chosen a spot to expire right in front of Shloyme's shop so that when he's dead, he'll be underneath the smugglers' feet? Corpses lie strewn about on Ostrowska and Wołynska Streets, and even on Franciszkańska and Nalewki, as if they were right at home. Jews get up in the morning, go into the street, and know there will be corpses there—one, two, five, or ten of them. Some of them have fallen from hunger. Those are the bloated dead who hungered through the war, reaching a death they longed for and hated at the same time. But on Koźla Alley? A squashed fly or a bedbug—does anyone notice them?

The smugglers stand there in their gleaming boots, wearing their splendid burka jackets. The soft September sun shines on their smooth, pampered faces, as they snack on caramel and pastries that the candy merchant brings them, so that they don't even hear the whir of the fatal bullet as it flies.

"Hey there—hey, take a look: Auntie's coming!"

He means Basha, the redhead—one of the strollers—is coming. It's nine or ten in the morning. Food smuggling is going full tilt, and the strollers load up their backpacks with the abundance of Koźla Alley and carry it off to the bakers. Strollers earn twenty or at most thirty groschen per kilo of food and so need to pack a heavy load, even strollers who make ten trips a day into the alley after fresh supplies. They have wives and children, work hard, walk a lot, carry a lot, and want to eat: need to eat. Bread and potatoes alone cost fifty zlotys a day, even one hundred. And without them the smugglers could never do their work. The smuggler knows it, but he has to make a living too. He's no worse than anyone else who takes on hired hands, wouldn't you say?

Basha, a tall girl with big feet, strides across the street like a guy and zips like a demon through the alley with sacks of flour on her back. One, two, and she's already back with an empty backpack and a wad of bills in her hand. Before you look around, she's out and back again, and she keeps it up continuously. No slower than Basha is old Zelig, a Jew of seventy who's been carrying heavy loads since he was a child.[7] Sometimes he will make over twenty trips a day to Koźla Alley.

Not all strollers are so lucky. Some wives who work as strollers can barely manage to move their swollen legs. They have to beg for their eight or ten kilos, one at a time, and the smugglers treat them like a nuisance they can't get rid of. They act as if they're doing them a favor by tossing them a few kilos of flour to deliver, as if they're making a donation to these hardship cases. But even this is just for show. At bottom they size up the potential value of every stroller with a cold eye, whether he or she is helping him to empty the shop of contraband as quickly as possible or to avoid tangling with a stray gendarme, a Polish cop, or a *Junak,* the Polish auxiliary police.

Just yesterday that's what happened, or something like it. Right after a nice piece of business for everyone concerned, the German police appeared unexpectedly at night—different police, not the ones who'd been paid off—and put on quite a show, seizing tens of thousands of zlotys worth of food. It cost another small fortune in cash to stop the

7. A section of the manuscript is missing here.

losses there. In the midst of all the commotion, three boundary guards fell from the upper floors where they were perched and were killed on the spot. There's not much you can say about their fate except that they lived by the "border money" and died thanks to it as well.

The system of boundary money is extremely complex—reminiscent of the different instruments in which surplus capital is invested, with staggered maturity dates to maximize returns. Both Polish and Jewish boundary men take part. The Poles smuggle the merchandise brought by Christian suppliers to the Jews, after which the Jews transfer the goods to the Jewish smugglers on the other side. The watchers keep track as they go, making note of how many tons of foodstuffs get transferred, and for every kilo they get a percentage. The boundary men have their own people look on at every transaction, keeping a sharp eye as money changes hands, making sure that no one shorts them what they're due. These watchers have it tough: nonstop standing on the roof means they're continually risking their lives. But what won't a Jew do to earn his bread?

Koźla Alley provides thousands of Jews with what they need to survive—the barrowmen who cart away its fruit and vegetables and the porters who make a living from the same goods. A few porters can always be found hanging around every large smuggler's shop, ready to grab up every bag of flour before it hits the ground, along with sacks of grain and other staples, and take them where they belong. Besides their regular earnings, the porters have now come up with a new charge and require an additional package fee for every bag of food that passes through the alley.

Next to Franciszkańska Street stands Zelig the Paw, a short, stocky type wearing a shiny peasant's visor at a rakish angle, on the lookout for anyone with a package. "Stop!" he hisses through his teeth. "Don't be shy, Pops—fork over a fifty for your package fee."

"I owe a fifty?" the Jew passing by replies, trying to play dumb.

"That's right, a fifty, and hand it over quick."

He gives in quickly, and it's a good thing too. Otherwise Zelig would lay him out straight with a paw right to the face—hard enough to knock him silly. All pleas are useless against a strong argument like that, so he whimpers a few complaints and pays up.

Around noon the action in Koźla Alley grinds to a halt. Supplies of smuggled foodstuffs have sold out, the porters sit on the steps, the smugglers take a break on the tables in the empty stores, and the alley rests, getting itself ready for the afternoon's smuggling, which begins at four or five.

You never know whether prices will be the same in the afternoon as they were in the morning; they will only be set once new supplies have been lowered through the windows. From the spirits of the first smuggler as he carries his sacks of flour, and from the mood of the porters and the border watchers, the whole alley can sense a change in the going rate. Just as a sudden wind rises across a grain field in the heat of summer, a murmur passes through the crowd: "Prices are up!"

It's not just the barrowmen, porters, strollers, milk Jews, and boundary watchers who depend on Koźla Alley for a living. Thousands of small food shops are also partially dependent on it, raising their prices when it does. Thanks to its trade, some tens of thousands of Jews are able to survive who would have perished from hunger with money in their pockets if Koźla Alley had not served as their storehouse.

ONLY TIME WILL TELL[8]

Whoever endures, whoever survives the epidemics that race through the ghetto due to the horrific overcrowding, the filth and unsanitary conditions, the selling of your last shirt for half a loaf of bread—whoever survives will be a hero, able to tell the harrowing tale of a generation and an entire era, when human life was reduced to the existence of abandoned dogs in a city laid to waste.

Warsaw Ghetto
October 1941

8. In Hebrew in the original text: *Yamim yagidu.*

♦♦♦ Children in the Streets

Perhaps you can find some reason for the poverty you see on the streets and even find a way to explain away the corpses: a riot, an epidemic, a fire, or some other disaster must have taken place. Children on the streets, however, are the war's darkest stain, and it can't be washed away. If someone crossed the ocean and saw the way we live now, of course he'd be shocked. But after seeing the horrific spectacle of children abandoned on the pavement he'd be dumbstruck with terror and fright.

Children on the streets confront us with a bizarre kind of tragedy, and seeing them does more than rip your heart to shreds. The sight is something so shocking that the horror can burn through closed eyes, making you unable to just walk on by: the sight cuts to the marrow and attacks the essence of who we are—the vision assaults our very nature.

Children have always meant something sacred to human beings. More than objects of our love, we regard them with a certain piety. The new generation has a touch of something beautiful and holds its secret, like the light of dawns yet to come or the charm and mystery of pristine dew on the freshest flower in bloom. As a result, seeing children starving to death on street corners thus fills us with shame. This degrading violation of every norm of human decency is a disaster caused by the war itself and stands alone as its greatest human tragedy and deepest disgrace. Let this most repugnant of human shames be etched in black blood on the white paper of the historical record as follows: "The Nazi Moloch devoured children and drank their blood." In 1941 the Nazis began their mass murder of Jewish children—an act that cannibals, in all their brutality, have never matched; let this crime go down in the annals of human history as the Nazi legacy itself.

In fact, the process had already begun in September 1939. German planes bombed poor, densely populated Jewish streets of no military value with a goal in mind: killing thousands of Jewish parents. The children were left behind. Confused, crushed, frightened, and exhausted, they took refuge in moldy cellar hideaways. With their tiny eyes stretched wide open, seeing everything but not understanding a thing, children searched desperately for their mamas, poking their little necks out from behind the stoops of the buildings like thirsty lambs looking for water or a piece of bread. When the fighting was over, the bomb shelters opened their doors; the situation had changed, and the children were allowed to go "free." They were entrusted to God's care: that is, left to spend their nights in the courtyards of apartment buildings, the stairwells of houses, and the streets. It had begun: THE HUNGER MARCH OF JEWISH WAR CHILDREN.

Everywhere you turn you see them: hungry, abandoned children, begging with outstretched hands: "Dear Jews, don't be heartless, I'm hungry . . ." As you walk you hear the deliberate words these children use, the steady and adult sound of their voice. You take note of their gestures and their grimaces, and you don't know what to do—whether you should admire the maturity and strength of these children confronting misery and poverty, and their transformation into mini adults, admire their childish cunning and resourcefulness after being abandoned, or appreciate their courage in the insidious war for a piece of bread: "A crrr-u-mmmb of bread! A crrr-u-mmmb of bread! A little crrr-uuuu-ssst of bread! A little crust. Just a little crumb."

The children stand there in heat and dust, rain and cold, snow and wind; just where does a tiny tot of seven or eight get such RARE COURAGE? What could the hearts of these little Jewish children possibly be feeling after being driven into this strange world that has nothing childish about it at all—a world so serious and lacking any hint of a smile, or childhood high jinks, or games? Take a closer look at their little faces, so covered with clouds of gloom that it's impossible to see any spark of childishness in them at all.

In the damp and wintry days of November, the children stand in the streets during rain, snow, and hail. They huddle together and shiver in the cold, their little arms and legs trembling and their eyes full of fear, pale as the color of parchment, touched by the horror of death. Jews on the street walk right by, however, without giving them a second look. What can they do? They've got children of their own at home—hungry children! Let the community worry about it, the Jewish community— our public institutions! The community, the community—if you can call it that: the sick, morally atrophied, and stone-deaf public has a feeling for the common good that ends at its own front door. It wasn't long before any effort to help the rest of society didn't reach beyond their own four walls, nor past a SELFISH CONCERN FOR SURVIVAL: the idea is to get hold of something, anything you can grab, and take it straight home from wherever you found it—from wherever you can lay your hands on any food at all, even if it comes from the kitchen that feeds starving children, whatever it takes to remain alive.

And who sits on the Jewish Council, the representatives of the official Jewish community?[1] Individuals—cunning, crafty individuals who know that starvation is a terrible thing, a lesson they apply first and foremost to their own well-being and that of their families. For them, self-interest is the same thing as concern for the community as a whole. It is the TRAGEDY OF POLISH JEWRY that the beginning of the war found it wholly unprepared. The community was completely disorganized and not up to its historic task. The huge Jewish community was splintered into thousands of subgroups and factions, with every Jew acting like a community of one, as if to say, *"Ad po tavo velo tosif!"*—"You may come so far, and no farther!"[2]

---

1. The Jewish Council (*Judenrat* in German) was the official governing body imposed by the Nazis and was responsible for carrying out Nazi dictates in the ghetto.
2. Job 38:11, the voice of the Lord speaking to Job out of the whirlwind, cited ironically in Hebrew in the Yiddish text.

If the Jews of Poland had been organized and ready to act, who knows what they might have accomplished? Can you imagine what could have been done during those first months when the occupation began?

Enough food for long months, if not for years, could have been stored for tens of thousands of Jews. Shoes and clothing could have been stockpiled and distributed to thousands of naked, barefoot Jews who'd been burned out of their homes. Instead, nothing was done. Everyone hoped—that is, anyone with means—secretly hoped that maybe, just maybe, they'd be able to get through by the skin of their teeth, by holding on to their wealth, their food stocks, their clothes and linens. But that was before the Germans arrived and bit by bit—helped by Jewish and non-Jewish informants—succeeded in confiscating every last scrap of what people held, down to the last morsels of foodstuffs. They loaded it all on trucks and shipped it off to feed the hungry Reich.

Jews went on with their normal lives. Yet by the time we Jews, in the form of the weakened "Joint," realized that we could actually keep something for Jacob and not give everything to Esau, there was nothing left to give, and certainly no tithe left to share with the poor.[3] How many of those tens of thousands of orphaned and abandoned children could have been helped for part of the war with these plundered Jewish fortunes!

Whatever happened to JEWISH RESOURCEFULNESS, that famous native Jewish foresight and smarts? After all, wasn't the example of the German Jews right there in front us, not to mention the Jewish predicament in Austria and Czechoslovakia? These were nothing but previews of what Hitler's occupation of Poland held in store. But no one grasped the obvious. Instead we all sat on our hands until everything had gone to waste, plundered and picked clean to the last crumb like Passover *hametz* before the holiday.[4]

---

3. The Joint was the American Jewish Joint Distribution Committee, a worldwide Jewish charitable organization whose existence preceded the war and which continued to operate through the war years. Jacob (Israel) and Esau (Edom) refer to Israel and non-Jews, respectively, in traditional Jewish thought.

4. *Hametz* is leavened bread or bread crumbs, forbidden to be in the house during Passover, and therefore cleaned up before the holiday begins.

Thousands of Jewish children wander the streets—no roof over their heads or spoonful of hot food available to them, shirtless and barefoot. Thousands of Jewish children—an army of them—and all this occurs in front of our eyes, after the complex bureaucracy of CENTOS had been set up.[5] With its hundreds of officials, clerks, "big-shot" supervisors, and caretakers, CENTOS tries—both well and badly—to care for almost forty thousand Jewish children, most of whom are orphans. CENTOS is responsible, in part or in whole, for serving these forty thousand children, with thousands more wandering the streets—and the Jewish Council finances one institution, the single dormitory at Śliska 64—for sixty children![6]

The effort was a blot on the name of Warsaw's Jewish Council. The fat cats on the council made only halfhearted efforts on behalf of the children—efforts that were either empty or lacking authentic imagination or initiative. They were blind to every sign of the times, and they responded to the shrieking, urgent cries coming from the streets by turning a deaf ear.

Why didn't Warsaw's Jewish Council—why didn't the Jews of Warsaw *themselves*—rise to the challenge and use every ounce of strength at its disposal to deal with the GALLING SHAME of thousands of children starving in the streets? How can Jews, fathers of children themselves, walk into the streets every morning and see dead children on the sidewalks covered with sheets of packing paper—the tiny, frozen feet of the children sticking out from underneath? How can those same Jews go back home, walk in the front door, and sit down for a bite to eat, even if it is just a tiny piece of bread, knowing all the while that the shame of children starving in the streets has not been lifted from his—or from any of our—heads?

Adults die—yes, that's a fact. What can you do about it? What choice do we have? The fact is that seven thousand Jews die every month in the ghetto, and that is a truly bitter fate. But children are another case entirely: ten to fifteen thousand children in a population of half

5. CENTOS was the Society for the Care of Jewish Orphans, founded in 1924. It played a major role in helping Jewish children in the Warsaw Ghetto.
6. Judenrat chairman Adam Czerniakow showed much concern for children, but like CENTOS he lacked the resources to effectively deal with the problem.

a million Jews is really not an impossible number to manage: their housing and support could have easily been arranged!

Imagine what could have been accomplished if a Jewish baker, earning five or six thousand zlotys a week baking the official ration bread, had decided to give a few pieces each day to a starving Jewish child. And just think about the vendors at the little grocery stands, such as they are during the war, the wood and coal merchants who've gotten rich—and the smugglers who don't know what to do with the cash they've piled high. Couldn't they have contributed a more-than-healthy cut of what they've made to support the hungry Jewish child?

Roughly three thousand children are begging in the streets. Another ten thousand children, half of them orphans, have been abandoned, and another twenty thousand are beating down the doors of the soup kitchens and children's homes to find any miserable scrap they can eat. But all such numbers are approximate, thanks to A MORTALITY RATE that is shockingly high, thanks to hunger and epidemic disease. The mortality rate has climbed steadily, and today no one can say with any degree of certainty what the rate will be in the coming month. When an abandoned child dies, that's one thing, but when parents die, a new group of children has been abandoned and must take to the streets. The problem these children represent is fast becoming our most pressing issue—perhaps the central existential issue facing Jewish life in the ghetto. And how is this burning issue being addressed?

CENTOS did make one effort: establishing a Center for the Care of Street Children. Ten different children's institutions of different types were established: dormitories and half dormitories, children's homes, and more. But of all these institutions, the only one that's really effective is the dormitories, fourteen in all that provided a place for a little over two thousand children, providing them with food, a place to sleep, and clothing. In the other institutions, the children get only war rations and receive shelter for two hours a day at most. After that they're forced to return home to their cold rooms, if they're lucky enough to have one. If not, it's back to the street.

Many children who frequent these institutions have already developed clear symptoms of consumption, with another group of them showing signs of other diseases, in certain cases SCURVY—that terrifying form of malnutrition, known to people before this mostly as the disease suffered by those sentenced to life imprisonment in Schlüsselberg Prison in Czarist Russia.

Scurvy marks the frightening scene on Smocza Street, where a boy of about twelve sits on a stool on the sidewalk, half slumped over, and pulls his little shirt up to expose swelling that extends well past his navel, his swollen scrotum exposed as well. Is that painful image any better than scurvy?

Or is the image of a young girl on Nowolipie Street, who sits picking at her lice, who with a hardened, almost idiotic calm puts them in her mouth, any less frightening to look at than a case of scurvy?

And finally, is seeing those barefoot, ragged, and tattered children in the Wołówka market on a rainy, snowy, wintry November day, sleeping on top of each other trying to stay warm somehow, begging with chattering teeth from the biting, piercing cold—is this any better than scurvy?

What difference did four hundred servings of coffee and bread, or even coffee without the bread—the "Street Project" conducted by CENTOS—really make to the more than three thousand begging children on the streets?

What if any difference can the bit of roof over their heads and the few scraps of clothes provided by CENTOS's wash and tailor shops—the ones that are still open, that is—possibly make to thousands and tens of thousands of half or wholly naked children?

Every day you discover ABANDONED CHILDREN. You can be sure that the mothers of these children have not taken this drastic step casually or without serious thought. You can also be sure that their hearts were torn to shreds as they had to slink away after abandoning their dear little ones in a stairway or corridor at the CENTOS building or leaving them somewhere in the street. The Jewish Council runs an institution together with CENTOS for these abandoned children, but since their numbers are constantly increasing, the center is always swamped and its facilities are overrun. Winter, which came particularly early this year, points to a darker future. More and more mothers will be forced to take the same final, desperate step. Closing their eyes and covering their ears, mothers will push their own children away and abandon them—and with what result? We will still get up in the morning, walk down the street, and find dead children lying on the sidewalks, with their little faces frozen into a question: Why?

Can a community actually stare at the spectacle of its own destruction in such a terrifying and at the same time indifferent way—at the destruction of its own offspring?

Anyone who still hasn't seen the joy with which these children devour a tiny speck of groats in the community kitchen—not to mention a little slice of bread with "marmalade"—will never understand what it truly means to provide a starving child with even a miserable scrap of food.

When an adult eats a piece of bread and stills the pangs of hunger, you won't see anything unusual in his face. When a child does the same thing, however, it's more than just a meal—it's a celebration bubbling over with childish joy; sometimes it resembles a kind of mischievous children's prank. Children turn everything into a game. And when a child gets together with other children the same age in the community kitchen, the whole thing becomes a kind of holiday.

Let me briefly switch to the dry measure of statistics. According to the official CENTOS report, as of September 1941 twenty-six community kitchens and nine children's homes were operating in the ghetto, along with thirty-five other institutions. All told, 29,518 children were fed. This figure, of course, does not include children from the dormitories, half dormitories, shelters, or day centers (in the summer). During this period, roughly 44,941 children, and another 4,391 children from what were called CHILDREN'S CIRCLES, received assistance from CENTOS, located in institutions of different names and types. As of September 1 of this year, 164 children's circles were operating in the ghetto, run by youths from the apartment buildings. Young people from the buildings provided the staff, and they were supplied with a minimum amount of food from the local community kitchen. Sometimes, where the organization was more extensive, the circles provided lunch and dinner, with the necessary funds raised by the energetic efforts of the building's youth committee.

The children's circles were a welcome and healthy innovation. Eventually they could have been transformed into real homes for children, where not just a spoonful of soup would be provided but everything a child needs. The young people in the apartment buildings threw their hearts and souls into caring for the children from the streets. And in the early period, the innovation provoked a wave of enthusiasm, especially in the poorer streets. Young girls and boys would arrange the children in ranks and march with them down to a square on Gęsia Street, right by the Wołówka flea market. There they'd lead the children in exercise, songs, games, and dance, telling stories to the older ones and even holding small classes (the schools are still not open).

For the children who lived in the building, the circles became an endless source of enjoyment, strengthening their will to live and giving them an outlet for their enthusiasm. The circles worked like a kind of school, developing and channeling their energy into healthy social impulses, with the young people often undertaking the collections needed to run the project themselves.

In the poor Jewish streets, for instance, the children would collect potato skins and old bottles and sell them, contributing the money to the project. The circles would also put on little revues to provide an evening of distraction in the building, allowing the little ones to forget the war's anguish and sorrows for at least a few hours. Unfortunately, the great excitement didn't last, and the project petered out. The main reason for the failure was that the children's circles ran their activities in Polish, a foreign language to the majority of Jewish children they served.

Just who arranged for the *shmendrikes* to run these children's groups in Polish is hard to say, and it's just as difficult to explain exactly why the Jewish Council, CENTOS, the TOZ, the Joint, to a great extent ŻTOS, and the rest of the Jewish social welfare organizations conduct their business in Polish.[7] This is our illness—our self-suppression—and often it just makes no practical sense.

7. TOZ was an abbreviation for the Towarzystwo Ochrony Zdrowia (Society to Protect the Health of the Jews); ŻTOS was the Żydowskie Towarzystwo Opieki

What in other times could be chalked up to simple indifference or an oversight amounts to a crime in our current predicament. The children's circles' repertoire of Polish children's music, patriotic marches, and popular Polish folk songs have nothing to say to the heart of the Jewish child, and before long they lose interest or become sick of the game. The music selection also put a damper on the enthusiasm of the young people who cared for the children: the core, the emotional link, was missing. As a result, many of the children's circles simply fell apart. Only those led by young people with Jewish national feeling, working in groups sponsored by UNDERGROUND POLITICAL ORGANIZATIONS, still remained active by offering a rich and meaty program. Without any exaggeration, it can truly be said that for the period they existed, these circles served a great and important purpose. They organized youth choirs that would be considered excellent by any standard, featuring several children who were truly gifted.

If all the circles had been conducted this way, there would be more than a thousand caring for children instead of only 164 of them, tending not just to the children's cultural needs but providing them with food. If our leaders had given any thought to the organization of the circles they'd never have allowed them to spring up randomly and be run so artificially, like so much Polish wild grass. The circles would have reduced to an absolute minimum the number of abandoned children wandering the streets.

But that didn't happen. Today we have over three thousand children hovering in doorways, moving from floor to floor in every building knocking on doors, screaming wildly, and crying hysterically in their desolate voices: "A TINY LITTLE PIECE OF BREAD!"

Among the child victims of this terrible war there's a unique kind of child who shouldn't be passed over in silence when we talk of children on the streets. These are THE CHILDREN OF THE "LABOR CAMP JEWS," that is, children of fathers who have been nabbed and marched off to work in forced-labor gangs. The misery of Jews unable to evade the

---

Spotecznej (Jewish Organization for Public Care). The leadership of the ŻTOS, including Emanuel Ringelblum and Isaac Giterman, tried to have the institution use Yiddish for its official business.

forced-labor camps makes up a tragic chapter all its own in the history of Jewish suffering during the war. Their story is worth telling in some detail, using information assembled from different sources and verified. At the outset, let it be briefly noted that this German method of conscripting Jews into forced labor has a historical precedent. The practice resembles the infamous period of the Khapers, or Cantonists, in the Russia of Czar Nicholas I, well documented in Judah Steinberg's *In Those Days*.[8]

Someday the role played by the officials of the Jewish Council—spooning everything of value their own way—will be exposed in the harshest light. These were the corrupt civil servants who would obtain an exemption from forced labor for anyone who had enough hard cash, leaving those without any money to be deported in their place. When everything comes to light, it will also be impossible to hide the shameful role played by the Jewish police, which up till now has been completely silenced. The police come into people's homes in the middle of the night, nabbing them from their beds for forced-labor duty—unless, of course, their palms have been greased ahead of time with the proper amount, along with a cut for the Polish police. In that case, the police immediately determine that the person sleeping was not at home when they called, and they'd leave without anyone in tow. Those they did haul off were often half naked and penniless. At breakfast their wives had no idea what possessions to sell to get the children a bit of rye bread. Deportation to forced labor meant starvation for many such Jewish families, and before long everything that could fetch a groschen was sold. Wives were soon distraught, especially those with two or three small children, and many had children on the way.

Pregnant wives would go mad with despair, running straight to the Jewish Council's offices, to the Joint, and to the building committees, but it rarely did any good. At best they might get brushed off with a

---

8. Cantonists were Jewish boys in Czarist Russia kidnapped and forced into military service at age twelve and educated in canton schools of distant provinces. Opoczynski uses the Hebrew title for *In Those Days: Memoirs of a Cantonist*, by Judah Steinberg (1863–1908). The work appeared in Yiddish as *In yene tsaytn: zikhroynes fun a kantonist*, translated by Ber Karlinksy (Warsaw, 1910).

handful of zlotys, which was barely enough to buy enough black bread of the cheapest quality for two or three days.

What other choices did they have? Abandon the children, or just toss them away? Tell them to go begging? People tried every alternative, and every story was a little different. In the end, many of the children simply starved to death. When someone suggested that CENTOS could support them and collect them in specific locations, the children of those taken to forced labor were thrown together with refugee children: hardened, street-tough little Jewish kids who'd survived seven levels of hell, driven all the way to Warsaw from their little Jewish towns with their parents in the middle of winter and its sharpest cold.

Our relations with children who'd undergone these trials were naturally different from our dealings with the local children from Warsaw, and not just because they were assembled at these "collection points." The well-known collection centers, located in massive buildings on Dzika Street (from numbers 1 through 19), Niska and Stawki Streets, and others, became the worst kind of breeding grounds for infectious diseases.

THE REFUGEE CHILDREN

At these collection centers, the refugee children have been housed in separate rooms that have already become their "home." There, just like adults, they receive a bit of soup and a scrap of black bread with black coffee sweetened with saccharine. Children whose fathers have been deported to forced labor have been added to these groups.

Not all wives of the labor camp Jews have been treated so kindly; when you enter the street and see young women standing with teary eyes, children in their arms, begging in heartbreaking, moving voices, you can be sure that these are wives of husbands who've already languished for long months in the forced-labor camps. If they are lucky enough to experience the overwhelming joy of seeing their husbands return home, they'll first have to prepare ointments and bandages for their husband's feet, which will be swollen and full of pus from working knee deep in the rivers and swamps. With that day not yet arrived, their wives stand in the streets, begging in the name of their children.

In this situation the child can be used as a kind of advertisement but also as a practical shield. There are many cases in which the child, helpless and without anywhere else to turn, will allow an unscrupulous adult to use him as a ruse or a come-on for every kind of repulsive scheme, from fraudulent panhandling all the way to criminal cons. Though Mendele the Book Peddler's *Fishke the Lame* has already exposed and documented the way these traders in the souls and freedom of children operate in peacetime, lifting the masks from their faces, in the ghetto we've learned that the TERRORISTIC ASSAULT ON THE RIGHTS OF CHILDREN has reached a point where thousands of children are now little more than putty in the hands of adults—often their parents—and their unscrupulous schemes.[9] The children are worked to death as part of the bargain, forced to stand on the street from before dawn till late at night and beg on command, on the hottest days of summer and the coldest days of winter. This pitiful chapter in the history of the neglected Jewish child is perhaps the most tragic of all, because no one has yet been interested enough to take up the cause of these tiny wisps of children who, according to the judgment of the current legal system, in fact have no "rights" at all.

We are reaching a stage in the wartime degeneration of human standards that will provide a treasure trove of data for the study of mass behavior in the future. The ghetto's upsurge in criminality and other indices of social collapse make up a small part of the material at hand. Here we must simply record the fact that the child—the poor, neglected child—is now victim and prey for every sort of con man.

CHILD VICTIMS OF CON MEN

As soon as a poor child can hold a bit of bread in his hands, a "snatcher" accosts him and snatches or rips it out of his hands. If a child still has a pair of decent shoes on his feet, a friendly "nice auntie," with the piercing eyes of a witch, will spot them. In no time, she's used

9. *Fishke the Lame: A Book of Jewish Poorfolk* was a novel by S. Y. Abramovitsh, originally published in *Tales of Mendele the Book Peddler* in 1869; translated by Ted Gorelik, edited by Dan Miron and Ken Frieden (New York: Schocken, 1996), pp. 3–298.

every con and filthy trick in the book to make off with the child's tiny clothes.

This sort of operator never lacks a new set of cons. They're especially good at using the guise of an elderly aunt or a grandmother who caresses the child in lullaby tones. The old crone spies the child on the street, and her sharp eyes can tell whether he's a refugee in a flash. The look on the child's face gives her all she needs, and by the time he answers her first question, he's done for. The answer lets her know right away that he's not from here since it lacks the city's famous *"yakh"* [Warsaw Yiddish for "I"], and so she goes right to work. "My child, my child," she tells him, "would you like someone to take you to the children's shelter? You would? They'll give you something good to eat and drink there. I've arranged it all—they'll take you right away. And there's not just food: there are toys to play with. Here, I've even bought you a bike, a pretty one. But it's starting to rain now: we've got to get the bike covered so it doesn't get wet. Hmm, let's see—what shall we cover it with? I don't have anything with me. Tell you what: Let's cover it up with your overcoat, okay?"

The child goes right along with it—what kid wouldn't? Especially a child from a little Jewish town who's been offered a bicycle for the first time in his life. The little old hag takes the coat and goes into the building to get the bike. She'll be back in a minute, she tells him, and so the little child waits . . .

The father, a refugee to whom the child later runs crying, is helpless in this situation. A Jew from the countryside, he understands nothing about what goes on in "evil Warsaw," the big city. How could he know, since it's the war that has created this outrageous form of evil, sweeping like the wind of death over the head of the poor, helpless Jewish child?

And while the child is always and in all ages a helpless creature, wartime heaps all the sorrows of the biblical plagues on his head. The whole Jewish tragedy—all the persecutions inspired by a merciless hatred—have been placed upon his weak little shoulders. What sort of affliction *hasn't* battered the Jewish community—from expulsion to arrest to murder? The Jewish child has suffered the most from them all.

When you enter the rooms of Jews on the verge of starvation, and you look into the mournful little eyes of the children, noticing their pale little faces and sluggish movements as they play and the halting steps as they drag their feet across the floor, you will be seized by a sudden shudder. At that point, your political perspective or affiliation will make no difference. And whether you stand back to take a long-term view of the situation or not, the biblical curse uttered by the author of the Psalms will still leap to mind—the oath he spoke that rose from his heart when viewing the disaster that had befallen his people and their land: "A blessing on him who seizes your babies and dashes them against the rock."[10]

It almost seems as if our brutal enemy had planned it from the beginning, to destroy us in a radical and comprehensive fashion. It was as if the Germans knew that by cutting off our finest flowers, they could at the same time attack our deepest roots. Seen this way, the bombs that fell on the Medem Sanitarium for Children in Otwock on September 1, 1939, could not have hit their target by mistake, since they killed—in the first hours of the war—seven Jewish children, leaving scores of others with serious to minor injuries.[11] The bombing represented a carefully plotted assassination. It symbolized the deliberate act of mass murder to come: the infanticide and death of the Jewish child—the offspring of the Jewish people—and hence the physical extermination of the next generation of Jews!

As sorrowful as that is, the people as a whole could not comprehend the vile, mute language of the murderers. Their signs of fire, however, have already sketched out a plan of plunder and murder, whether the bombs were delivered by aircraft or artillery. If we had all understood the fundamental truth that the murderers were setting about their work systematically, it would have been impossible for us to remain so indifferent to the misery borne by the Jewish child. We never would have waited for the miserable aid provided by CENTOS—a plate of

10. Psalms 137:9.
11. This orphanage was named after Vladimir Medem (1879–1923), a founder of the Jewish Labor Bund, and was connected with the Central Yiddish School Organization in Poland.

grits and a few drops of milk for one child in a hundred, if not less. Instead we would have already found a way to establish large children's shelters—clean and healthy ones—not the homes they provided for the refugee children and the children of the labor camp Jews, with their horrid stench. We never would have stood for their rations, made up of little more than black coffee with sweetener. If we had understood, the children would have gotten what they needed to meet their basic needs. Above all, it would have been impossible for us to stumble on those dying or dead young martyrs of ours every day in the streets: the little Moishes or Shloymeles, with the light in their tiny kosher eyes snuffed out once and for all.

The bombs that fell on the heads of innocent Jewish children would have shocked us all, roused us from our numb complacency, and inspired us to stand together as one in defense of the Jewish child.

In the meantime nothing has been done. As these lines are written, we find ourselves in a critical situation in the ghetto. New expulsions from apartments are taking place, new streets are being removed from the ghetto, and with our territory growing narrower, the noose pulls ever tighter around our necks. All we see are walls, new walls. Soon there will be nowhere left to turn: winter, dampness, cold, and death on every side. Will we still be able to save the Jewish child?

Warsaw Ghetto
November 1941

♦♦♦ *Reportage from the Łódź Ghetto*

JOSEF ZELKOWICZ

The scene is a small shop—no larger than a Torah academy for poor boys run by an obscure rabbi. The room is empty and hollow, as are the stomachs of the Jews in the ghetto. Darkness descends like some sinister evening in an abandoned field in late summer. The hoarse creak of the door opens angrily, admitting you to the tiny room with its single, low-set, dust-choked little window.

On the right, an iron bed with twisted, rickety feet. The bed is piled high with baggage that reaches up to the blackened ceiling. On the left: a single, peeling wall. The whole room is crammed to the rafters with an unidentified material that produces a terrible, fearful stench, a cross between the reek of a kennel, a cow stall, and a slaughterhouse.

Hell must have dispatched a pharmacist specializing in poisons directly to the ghetto to concoct this special toxin, its murderous, moldy vapors saturating so many of the ghetto's dwellings. A pharmacist straight from hell! For you will never be able to imagine that the terrible odor emanates from the vegetables and refuse stuffed into these tiny rooms!

He sits alone on a corner of the overloaded bed. He's the man of the house, the head of household—the person whose name must stand at the top of the questionnaire. You'd have to say he emerges from the bedding like a snail from his shell, for he assumes a twisted, grotesque pose and just stands there, offering you the following reception: "Ah, what important guests we have today! If I had a stove, I'd roll it right out!" And wringing his hands in despair: "But unfortunately, we don't have one . . ."

And so you stand there, stunned and amazed. You're unsure whether it's Mephisto in a brand new getup who's crawled out of bed and now looks back at you mocking your awkwardness, or whether it's Kievele, the clumsy little cobbler, who wishes to assist Your Excellency in any way possible, an official from the welfare department.

His face gives nothing away. Dark and embittered, despondent and pale like every face in the ghetto. His left eye twinkles with an uncanny little flame—the same look you see in the eyes of everyone who's hungry in the ghetto, glinting with that little flame; it's probably the same look you'd see in the eyes of hungry wolves on a bitter winter night. His right eye, with the watery, turbid color of an egg white, sits extinguished in its socket. Around the eye, as clear as day, you see a growth that resembles a blue-green, unripe plum, surrounded by several red currants along with two or three bluish wine grapes and a brown, juicy raisin, like the ones pious Jews use to make their wine at Passover to be sure it's strictly kosher, so they can say the blessing over it.

"Who gave you that bruise on your eye?"

A grimace spreads over the interrogated face, which slowly turns into a broad, waggish smile and then widens like a flood, first reaching his good eye, then the dead one, and finally overtakes his pointed, ash-gray little beard.

"For God's sake, don't talk so loud about whacks in the eyes! The walls have ears, and my former wife—may she guard me from above—could get it into her head to rise from the grave and pick up where she left off: pick up a cobbler's last and give me a whack right in the eye! . . . Oy, if you could have only seen the fun she had giving me a poke in the eyes! I just didn't have the heart to stop her . . . it put years on her life! I just don't understand why she died so young . . . maybe she was just mad that I burned all the lasts, and she couldn't find anything to hit me with?"

"When did she die?"

"Who? She would be dead now—seven weeks."

"Is she the one who left you this inheritance, so to speak?"

"God forbid! An inheritance and her? The next thing you know, you'll be trying to blacken her name! But you won't get anywhere with me! The dead must be treated with dignity and respect; they've certainly earned it. Just imagine, an inheritance and her! She left two sons and rattled on about how they took after her, and she took them with her too—and you talk of an inheritance? On the day she sensed it was time to 'throw in the spoon' she took her forty decagrams of bread into bed, turned her backside to me and her face to the wall, and devoured the bread down to the last crumb, and . . . and you talk of an inheritance! It's nothing more than slander, as I am a Jew!"

"Okay, then, but what happened to your eye?"

"To my eye? That's a pretty tale. So you're asking for the gist of it, the short version, of what happened to my eye? Not me, my friend— wait a second, be patient—you know, doctors come sniffing around here like dogs to a rich man's wedding; they make a fuss over my eye and carry on about it as if I were the ghetto's only child! You go right back and tell those bums in the ghetto administration what's going on with my eye."

"Fine, so don't tell me. But you have to tell us what the doctors said about your eye, because we need to record the information."

"Oy, oy, a foolish Jew! You stand there and ask me—you'll pardon the expression—like a silly old Jewish woman. I have a neighbor here, fat Rosa we call her—although sorry to say she's already in her grave, dead as a doornail—Rosa loved to stick her nose wherever it didn't belong. She was also asking me, 'So, what did the doctor say?' The foolish cow! What the doctor says? You think he talks? A doctor shrieks! A doctor scolds! One was not happy at all that the wound was a greenish color. According to him it should have been blue . . . am I supposed to tell him he's wrong? Let me be perfectly honest with you: I myself, when you approached me, would also have preferred to offer you a blue plum! The kind of plum you pick, toss the pit, and pop right into your mouth when you've already got a mouthful of sweet, juicy meat, not like the meat in the ghetto (may my talk not get me into trouble). And then there was the other doctor, who liked, it seems, sweet and sour—who thought the red currants should leaf out and redden a bit . . . so I asked him, 'Mr. Doctor, sir, what's it to you that my cur-rants aren't red? How much money have you put into my garden any-way?' And that really ticked him off: 'What would a numskull like you know?' is what he told me. 'If the currants were red, they'd be typical.' Well now, isn't that really the question here: Which of the two of us is typical, and which one is the typical fool? And I'm nobody's fool! My old lady saw to that; before the war she'd already opened up my head with an iron last. But have pity on me—I know I'm such a nuisance. Who are you really, and what do you want from me?"

"We're from the control commission."

The merry little Jew opened his good eye, which gleamed wide in amazement. "No kidding? You mean you're not a doctor? And here I was, sitting here getting ready for an injection!"

"Why an injection?"

"When a bigwig comes to Kievele Tabachnik from the commu-nity, he is either a doctor or some scoundrel of an official. The doctor comes to write out a death certificate or to give him an injection or just to draw a little blood . . . the official comes to slap him with a fine for tearing off a board or for failing to keep the premises clean . . ."

"No, Kievele, we're only a commission, a . . ."

"You have to make a record? Fine, go ahead, write: you write stuff down, and people pay you for it. If I could do that and get paid for it, I'd do it too!"

The smile on his face has in the meantime disappeared, and his left eye has started to sparkle.

"Why do you keep so much junk in your room, Kieve Tabachnik? It's impossible to breathe in here!"

Kievele took a deep breath, as if eager to demonstrate that it was possible to breathe not only normally, but deeply. "To you it's junk. To representatives of the community, who sit in their offices with their delicate noses, who establish commissions and go out and re-cord what they see—for them it's crap, it stinks: to them it's typhus, cholera, dysentery! But for people like us, who live like dogs and root like pigs—for us it's food! For us it's cabbage greens, radish leaves, turnip greens, beet greens, or just nettles—who the hell cares? It's okay with us. You won't die from it . . . and if someone does die—so what? It won't bore a hole in heaven, and barely a tiny little hill in the earth . . . our sort of people, sir, are not pigs—human beings like us eat everything."

"But it still stinks, Kievele Tabachnik, it still stinks! And what do you need so many greens for when you get loads of potatoes?"

Kievele screwed himself up into a knot. Specks of foam appeared in the corners of his tightening lips. In a single swing he threw himself onto a pile, grabbed a hefty handful of leaves, and started chewing them like cud. "Potatoes? Who are you kidding? Who goes around wolfing down potatoes till their stomach pops? You two? Go ahead and treat yourselves to the lap of luxury! You've got money, can go out and buy yourselves bread, and radishes, and carrots, and beets, and pickles—you can scarf it all down to your heart's delight. Only the leaves are left for people like us, the leaves you all throw out in the trash. We eat up all the cholera, the typhus, and the dysentery, and there's none left over for you . . . we're your collection agents!" Kievele suddenly straightened himself and turned around, with his finger in the air. "Have no fear. And death won't miss you, either! People like us really don't have any wood to burn, but for you all, providers for the *kehillah,* community leaders, record keepers, bloodsuckers, and rule makers, firewood won't be in short supply.[1] They'll hang you all in groups of twenty-five—hang you from the ghetto bridges like they were store windows. Twenty-five on each side of the bridge! From the posts of the ghetto fence! Two community leaders to a pole; one on one side and one on the other—ha ha ha!"

The foam at the corners of his mouth bubbled as he spoke. His good eye sparkled and laughed along, and his sick eye joined in the fun—seemed to pour itself through the rest of his face. The green plum turned a bluish shade. The currants became red, making it a shame, really, that none of the doctors could be there who spent so much time fussing and carrying on as if his eye were the ghetto's only son, though they never arrived at a diagnosis. Maybe it's an inflammation, a virus, a draft, a breeze, a cancer, or just a growth . . .

---

1. *Kehillah* is the traditional name for the organized Jewish community, used here to refer to the officials of the Judenrat the Nazis imposed on the ghettos.

And you, Riva Bramson, don't tremble before the anger of this miserable, half blind cobbler, forced to stay the pangs of hunger by eating filthy leaves. For his anger is short, lasting no longer than the foam at the corners of his mouth, which bubbles up only when he comes to a boil. Try, Riva Bramson, to satisfy him this one time, and you'll see that his rage disappears as quickly as the foam on his lips.

The Kieveles, the Feiges—and everyone else there, whatever their names—don't hold grudges, and their memories are short. And if someone does remember, he dies, and once again there's nothing to fear.

"Why get all upset, Kievele Tabachnik? We didn't come, God forbid, to do you harm. We just came to check and see if you'll be getting your welfare support."

Take a look, Riva Bramson—he's eaten some more of the leaves, and the foam has already disappeared from his mouth. He's heard a kind word today, and his anger has already faded. The plum on his eye is green again, the currants have gone back to yellow, and Kievele once more stands before you, well disposed and at ease, with a little smile on his face already. "Whether I'm getting support? Wait, I don't think I lent you any money. But as you please—give it, or don't. I'm not stronger than iron! What could I possibly have given those doctors anyway, the ones who refused to visit without payment when my two sons were bedridden, clinging to life, and perhaps could even have been saved?"

"Are you alone now, Kievele, or are you still supporting someone else?"

Kievele beamed all over: "Hey Dobe. Dobele, get up and show yourself!"

On the other side, Dobe rolled herself out from behind the bed, something tiny, round, and pale, almost transparent, like a water candle: Dobe. Fourteen years old, like a snowflake. Blow on her, and she'd disappear.

Kievele looks at her with a father's pleasure. "Dobe, Dobe, would you like to be a grandmother?"

"Yes, Papa, a grandmother."

Dobe chuckles, then Kievele chuckles, and his good eye dances joyfully around his laughing face. "You see how sharp my little fourteen-year-old girl is, not to tempt the evil eye? All right, maybe not? I mean, she takes after me, until I'm 120 years old, as my wife used to say—may the living be separated from the dead. She belongs to me, which is why my wife left her behind . . . Yes, she had a good heart, she did, so have a little mercy on me! A wandering eye she didn't have; if something besides us was made of gold, she wouldn't touch it. The boys belonged to her, and so she took them with her. My girl—well, she takes after me, and so she's mine. That's why my wife left her with me, as if she were saying, 'There you go, enjoy the bargain, and try to keep an eye on her.' Are you hungry, my little Dobele, my wise one? Take a few leaves and chew—and as you love your life, chew like a little pig!"

Don't stand there rolling your eyes, Riva Bramson. Melt that frozen smile of yours with a little warmth, if you have any left. For a little warmth will do far more good for all the Kieveles, the Dobeles, and the Feiges, is far more urgent than any question on the form you're clutching in your hand, with its questions about furnishings, condition of the apartment, and the like. Under the heading "Is Welfare Support Indicated?" do not write "Immediately—at once." Put it off for eight days. You see what I mean, of course: Kievele has more than enough for eight days, and even if he never stopped chewing he'd never be able to down all those leaves in that time. And afterward: well, you know, God is great. In the meantime, maybe the war will come to an end. In the meantime, maybe he'll die! What can you do?

What is shame, Riva Bramson? Not an inborn trait but a feeling that civilization has imprinted upon us. When human beings are alone they do not experience shame, for the feeling does not originate in their own inner natures. When an intelligent person is by himself, it is possible that he thinks more logically than he does among others, for then his thoughts are his own—those inherent in his nature at birth.

Nakedness is man's original state. A person, like an animal, is born naked. And the animals, just like man in his natural state, as they carry that beautiful nakedness into the world, lack any sense of shame whatsoever. We have been taught otherwise, however, and shame is now a habit. In truth, Riva Bramson, shame is nothing more than a mask under which man hides his more authentic human face, nothing more than a card for fashion designers to play. They're the ones who tell us as much in blaring, screeching headlines: "If you feel shame stirring within you—and of course you must feel shame if you want to be taken for a cultured individual—you must hide your nakedness according to the following rules: garb your body in clothes, both woven and knitted, according to the formula established by this or that designer."

Shame, Riva Bramson, is just another name for fashion. In the ghetto, however, fashion itself has been canceled. In the city at large no trace whatsoever remains of your clothing style, now three or four years out of date. People stopped wearing that style long ago. In the ghetto, however—among its hungry and miserable animals—you can get away with your three- or four-year-old fashion cut and provoke envy in people who don't have anything of the kind.

In the city fashion taught us to be ashamed to reach out a hand to grab a gift from strangers. For a time, that shame drove a certain number of men and women to their graves. In the ghetto fashion continues to tell people to remain ashamed when someone sticks out his hand for a handout and it remains stuck in the air, empty.

In the city, Riva Bramson, you would never have gone for even the shortest walk without a hat on your head, and with a different one for every season at that. Without one you would have been ashamed. In the ghetto, however, you walk with me through the streets and alleyways, up and down buildings, and through apartments without anything covering your head whatsoever, and you arouse nothing more than envy at the gleaming sight of your silky hair. In the ghetto fashion has been canceled because its precondition—shame—has ceased to exist. In this regard, Riva Bramson, the modesty of your eyes when you avert your gaze, when stumbling upon scenes in Jewish apartments that provoke your atavistic feelings of shame—such modesty isn't necessary at all.

Animals and beasts of the field perform their physical functions in the open, before the eyes of all, and everyone looks on with indifference: that's how they're built. Human beings living in animalistic conditions—who've been robbed of any cultural outlet and whose basic cultural needs have been denied, then mocked with cynicism and scorn—such people are likely to become such animals, as it were. Thrown back into this primeval condition, they're like human beings in their original, natural state, with any sense of shame foreign to them.

If those who in performing their natural needs are still not too lazy to use the outhouse to relieve themselves, it's not out of shame but for comfort's sake and from a sense of habit. And those whose sense of comfort is not quite so demanding do their duty in the apartments themselves. The father in front of his daughter, the mother in front of her son; in the ghetto, such behavior is as normal and logical as the illogic of our collective life.

Raise your delicate eyes, Riva Bramson, so that I don't have to give you a lecture—so that I don't have to upbraid your excessive modesty and your overdeveloped sense of shame.

Raise your eyes and take a closer look at "him" and at "her," lying in a single bed and looking as if they've spent last night in stormy passion, completely exhausted and satisfied with no further need for each other—his head at the top of the bed, hers at the bottom.

Take a look, Riva, and see how they look back at you with their extinguished but nonetheless open, unashamed eyes, which make no secret whatsoever of the physical urges that have been satisfied, and—

But perhaps we are both mistaken . . .

The room: well enough lit, large enough, and wide. In the front, next to the window, stand two beds, one on each side of the window. The rest of the room stands empty. No sign of any table, nor any sign of a cupboard, and no trace of any other furniture. The little iron stove stands like a black, abscessed wound on the white floor but bears witness that a short time ago, this large and roomy apartment had not been so empty. There stand a table, several chairs, a cupboard, even a third bed; and the oven, with its cold, frozen snout hanging open, seems to be screaming "Food!" It is cold, horribly cold, and aside—

You don't think the previous situation is relevant, Riva Bramson, do you?

Three people are lying in the two remaining beds: in the widest one, made of wood, the one to the left of the window, can be found the "he" and "she," and in the other bed, the narrower one on the right side, lies a second, full-chested "she" with a double chin, red, heated cheeks, and two wide-open eyes that seem to shriek at you.

Here lies a wife of twenty-one or twenty-two. She's ripe and her breath is hot; her bosom is boiling and her body is aflame as she waits—

Maybe we've made another mistake.

But when you look at "him," with his shriveled skin and bony face—which looks something like a marten's or like the sharp snout of a hungry dog—when you notice his languid, slobbering mouth surrounded by thick curls that look like wild underbrush stealing its way through cracks in the fence and making its way into the garden, you automatically shift your glance to the "she," who lies there like something that's been tossed away at his feet. You look at the "she" who is not ashamed, neither for herself nor even for the presence of her daughter who lies on the bed directly opposite and who has heard everything that's happened next to her during the night, as the red in her cheeks makes clear . . .

When your curiosity has been stilled your gaze is fixed on the "she," whose eyes look straight at you: an old woman. But her face is that of a child, and a tiny one: a wrinkled face with the forehead of a freak who is neither man nor woman and a sunken breast and neck strewn with so many bumps that you'd swear she was covered with clumpy gray moss, the kind you'd find in an old, forgotten cave. And take a look at her hands! Yellowed like parchment, a skin that looks as if it were encrusted with mold. Her hardened hands look like dried sticks—little more than bones.

It's intriguing, of course. And something intrigues you not simply because it stirs your interest, making you want to satisfy your curiosity, but because you wish to know whether the know-it-all in you has ever seen this before, whether the matter really turns out the way your clever head had predicted, before you ever looked to confirm what you already knew. What's intriguing is the chance to affirm just how smart you really are! After all, didn't you get the whole story from a tiny hint? So you ask, in the tone of the victor, allowing yourself a touch of caustic irony: "An adult, lying around this long in bed?"

"Where do you expect an adult to be lying if he's alive—alive and swollen with hunger—where should he be, if not in bed?"

You, the all-knowing one, feel as if you've had a bucket of cold water dumped on your head, but your keen intelligence won't let it alone: Can lust really be that powerful? Can it hold this Jew so fast in its clutches that, even in his swollen condition, he keeps sleeping with his wife, clinging to her well into the day?

"How old are you?"

Fifty-six, you note, as you weave your wiles a little further. Fifty-six years old! The years of peak sexual performance! He probably doesn't have any other pleasures left. Maybe he's not as swollen as he claims. Maybe—

"How did you get it into your head that you're swollen?"

"How do I know? Maybe I talked myself into it. If a belly as big as a barrel and green as the grass doesn't mean I'm swollen with hunger . . . maybe I'm just pregnant. Maybe a stomach like a barrel and green like grass doesn't mean it's swollen; maybe I'm just pregnant . . ."

And as the fifty-six-year-"old" man isn't ashamed in any way, he tosses the blankets from himself and pokes his belly with a yellow, pointy finger: "So what do you think: swollen, or pregnant?"

"Uh, yes, swollen. Completely swollen. But . . . hmm . . . how old is your wife?"

"What wife? Whose wife? My wife's been dead four months already!"

Don't stand there, Riva Bramson, on red-hot pins and needles—you don't have any trace of the petty bourgeois in you! Someone who is consistent and refuses to be ashamed can do whatever he or she likes. Isn't that what everyone means by "free will" and "freedom of conscience"?

"To be honest, the whole business interests me about as much as last year's snow. It's just that . . . the questionnaire . . . it has to be filled out, and the question has to be answered: Who lives here, with whom, etc. The woman—who's that lying next to you in bed?"

When an already dark face turns even darker, it takes on the color of burnt ashes that have been shoveled onto a trash pile.

"The one lying with me here is my girl, not my wife."

"Girl" he says, not even "daughter." The old woman with the aged face and wrinkled brow, with the fallen chest and the moss-colored dimples around her neck—to him she's a "girl"?

"How old is she, the girl?"

"At Shabuoth she became sixteen."[1]

"And why are you holding on to her in bed?"

---

1. Shabuoth is the Jewish holiday in springtime commemorating the giving of the Law to Moses at Mount Sinai.

"King of the Universe! Where else should I hold on to her when she's sick?"

"What does she need?"

"Blood."

"Blood?"

"It happened last winter. She stopped having her period. The doctors said this, the doctors said that—it all means nothing. A 'ghetto malady' was the diagnosis. Almost all wives, all young girls, are in the same boat. Never mind, I made my peace with it—so did my wife, God bless her; today it's a shame when any drop of blood is lost. And then, just a few days ago, she comes down with dysentery. Blood out this side, blood out the other—what's the difference? The problem, praised be his name, is that it runs, and nothing replaces it."

"And who's that one lying in the second bed?"

"My girl, nineteen years old, also sick."

"Why aren't both girls lying together in the same bed?"

"The other one has a different disease—tuberculosis. She has to sleep alone."

No, Riva Bramson, don't curse me now! Don't sling the truth at me, the truth you want to tell, don't throw it right in my face! You see how I'm burning with—aflame with—shame. I'm ashamed of myself. I haven't been able to uproot the culture of the city from myself. And I'm glad that I can't. As far as our conversation on the subject of shame, Riva—please forget all about it.

In the Bałuty Apartments, Łódź Ghetto

♦♦♦ A Special Him and a Special Her: In the Sixth Apartment

They were photographed on their wedding day. That session produced the photo hanging above the white, polished table. Husband and wife—how beautiful they were. Their wedding took place two years before the war broke out, and at that point their ages were twenty-four he, and twenty-two she.[1]

The room is a square one, on the first story of a Bałuty apartment building. The single bed, standing by the window, gleams a pristine white. The floor reflects the feet of the beds and makes them look prettier. The white hutch on the wall directly across makes you want to take it in your arms and press it to your heart. A room that is so quiet, tranquil, and serene, in all its woe—a room like a box of bonbons, with everything looking so much in its place that it might have sprouted right from the floor. If you moved something from its spot, it would be like taking a nice picture and punching it full of holes. The little couch standing near the cabinet winks to you gently, with warmth and devotion, as if it were the bosom of your beloved: "Come, this is the place to lay your weary head."

When you enter such a room, after visiting so many rooms bathed in tears, sadness, and melancholy, you catch your breath much more

---

1. Two years before: this reads two days in the original, but from the rest of the essay it is clear that Zelkowicz meant to say two years.

easily, and the sounds that emerge from your throat have a softer tone.

When you enter such a room, after so many rooms shrouded in darkness and poverty, you recover your human face and recall you were created in God's image.

And when you enter such a room, after entering so many rooms sunk in filthy abandonment, you recover your ability to reason and begin to think: how much loving care a woman must have invested in her belongings to clean them as if they were her own teeth! How much tender, loving female breath was invested in the bedspreads and the shiny nickel bed!

So tell me, Riva Bramson, for what kind of person would a woman devote such loving caresses to her home? For whom does she deck out her bed in such a dreamy red and white? And for whom does she hover about her nest, as the angels hover about the towers of paradise? For herself? Tell me it's not for her husband!

It's for her husband, the man in the photograph taken when they stood under the wedding canopy on their wedding day. For the young man of twenty-four who looks like the dreamy, ideal image of a poet in the picture, hailing from a land of legendary beauty. For the husband who gave her the blond little child with the blue, open eyes who lies on the couch and seems to look back at you with a curious stare! Only then, Riva Bramson, can women make life seem beautiful and tender—when they themselves feel such love. And when women love, it is with a love that is not so much intense, not so much faithful, as it is beautiful.

You enter this room where everything is buffed and polished with a young woman's breath, and next to the door you notice an unshaven male who squats like a mourner on a low box, looking neglected and filthy like one of the dung carters at work in the ghetto. In the tidy room his presence shocks and upsets you like a sudden, grating noise that bursts out in the middle of a well-played symphony. The filthy, neglected male clashes with the nice, clean room: he doesn't fit it at all, not with the young, buxom bride sitting at the opposite window as far as possible away from him, and so—

You ask him to leave.

The wild, unkempt male figure, his face already indifferent to the room that surrounds him, isn't even aware that complete strangers have entered his apartment and told him to go. It's only when you read his name from the apartment registry that he turns around heavily, like a bear, reverses his direction, and declares with utter indifference, "That's me."

You observe him carefully for the first time, the man with the wildly overgrown face who looks like a forest bandit who hasn't yet slept off a drunken binge, taking your first good look at the tattered rags that are his clothes, torn apart and exposing a much larger, wide body. You cast another glance toward the window, then take another look at the little bed, where the little one is lying with his blue eyes wide open. Secretly, you snatch another glance at the photograph hanging on the wall over the . . .

No—not any more. The little table is no longer white and polished! It's gray and dark, the color of ashes. The nickel bed glints like the ritual slaughterer's knife, and the gleam transfixes you, like the tang of a sword. The little closet hutch on the wall opposite the bed now stands there clayey and cold, as if it were a golem! Just then the fear begins to hit you: you will take a step into the room, and the two doors of the closet will fly open—smash you and knock your legs right out from under you, just like in the other apartments. The nicely made bed suddenly catches your eye again, and this time you see the overdressed bosom of an aging coquette, completely devoid of love and affection, replete with the repulsive ugliness of false appearance instead.

"Nooo!" you feel like screaming at the top of your lungs. "It can't be! The missus wouldn't go for someone like that! It's impossible—a violation of the laws of nature! A young woman like her, a beautiful bride— there's no way in the world that she could care for a man with ungainly, shuffling feet like that—like a bear on the skids. She'd never love a face with blue-red cheeks like that—they look like his giant spleen burst, then shot prickly blotches all the way up to his eyes, if that's even possible. She'd never love such a physical wreck of a human being, covered in those ragged clothes. He looks like a sack of cornmeal split open down the middle then quickly tossed to the side—the whole thing only stays in one piece as long as no one gives it a shove."

So tell me, Riva Bramson, wouldn't it be an outrage for such a face to be kissed by such red, warm, and luscious lips, by the young wife who's sitting there by the window? How unbelievable to think that, after caressing the little blond tyke lying there on the couch, those same hands could touch that unkempt goon?

The only way to explain this is that she must love him. Otherwise, why would she have married him? She was young and pretty . . . look at the photograph . . . look at the happiness, the laughter in her face.

He tells the story this way: "I never went to school. They taught me how to read simple things and to write, but I forgot it all later. But it doesn't matter—be sure that you'll never hear a lying word from me. I'm not an educated person—but I'm an honest one. In the ghetto, honest people have to look the way I do.

"I never dreamed of any golden paradise for myself. My only dream when I was single was to make a home for my Brayndl—just for her, sitting there at the window. The only thing I dreamed of after the wedding was to have a nice, clean home.

"I'm not a learned man, but I am practical. I know nothing comes from big dreams—roast doves don't fall into the pot all by themselves—so I worked like an ox. Like a horse I worked, and I swear to you, as I'm a Jew, that in the two years I knew Brayndl before we got married I never wasted a single groschen. I smoked—and then I gave up smoking. I didn't drink. Card playing, absolutely not—but I did sock away groschen after groschen, they turned into zlotys, and from ones I made tens and from tens, hundred-zloty bills. Eventually I was able to get a hold of this apartment, and bit by bit I was able to pay for it all. After a while I'd managed to furnish it, and then we got married.

"Why did I do it? Do I need to say it? I loved her—just ask her, the one sitting right there. I was handsome. I was young, and a good provider too. I could have made fancier matches, with bigger dowries, with everything provided. And then I wouldn't have had to live the life I lived—not the life of the young, handsome, lively guy I really was but that of an old penitent denying himself so much . . .

"I did get married, and I thought I was the happiest man in the world. Though that's what happens to us human beings, I was never sick a single day. I don't mean I wasn't sick, of course—just that I was never too sick to get out of bed before she did, early in the morning, to take a look at how she looked asleep, so content and so at peace she was; her cup was so full to the brim. I should stop feeling anything at all, it all hurts so much. I wouldn't walk—I'd run to work! I knew I was working for someone besides myself, that I was accomplishing something with my efforts. Since I earned good money from my work, the things I brought home were only the best . . . not for myself! For me it was enough that I could put food on the table for her.

"Then the war broke out. I stopped working. My hands were suddenly worth nothing. But I didn't collapse. I thought to myself, 'How can this be? I'm still better off than the wealthy Jews from the center of the city—they're the ones who've been ruined, they're the ones who've lost everything, and they've been driven from their homes. They're not used to hard work and can't bear the hunger, but I've got everything: my apartment, my furniture, and I've got my wife, who's about to give birth to our child.

"In those days, when I looked at my wife, carrying my child in her stomach, my heart used to get a strange feeling, especially when I thought to myself, 'She's probably hungry.' Every time I got that feeling I'd grab something else, stash it under my coat, go out into the street, and sell it. What the hell, I could just pretend that the Germans had simply robbed me of the same item. The day she went into labor I'd just sold my last two pairs of pants for twelve marks. I used the money to buy a few pounds of coal so she should be warm at home—so that there'd be warm water when we needed to bathe the child.

"I couldn't rustle up any kind of job. I put my name in for every which kind of work. I banged on a lot of doors. But in the ghetto, apparently, there's not much to do for a pair of honest, experienced hands. In the ghetto the main thing is to have big shoulders.[2] So I began to swell up from hunger. The feet go first, then your hands, then it all falls apart. I've got nothing against my wife. She sleeps in her nice bed—I sleep in the little one of my own. She's got her nightclothes; I—I already sold mine. In return she's rearing a child. She sits there in her corner, and I sit in mine. But she sits by the window—while I sit by the door? What's the difference? She eats her bread, and I eat mine.

2. A pun: *shoulders* was the common ghetto word for "connections" or "pull."

I've got my soup pot, and she's got hers. I didn't do this, and she didn't either—life did this to us."

Her version is slightly different: "I don't have a single word to add or subtract from anything he said. There's no point in denying something as true as the day is long. But the part about us not choosing this life, that life made us this way—I don't agree with that at all. We make the life we want for ourselves. We do it on our own! If he hadn't gotten a move on and taken charge before the wedding, he'd still be a bachelor today, and maybe that would have been better for us both. If he hadn't gotten busy right after we got married, maybe we would have looked as bad after the wedding as we do today.

"That's really his fault, given the other conditions shaping our existence: he doesn't grab himself by the scruff of his own neck and get going; he just coasts along like everyone else and lets life run right over him. No wonder the stampede tramples him and that he ends up sitting there swollen with hunger. He's going insane from being by himself; he looks more like an animal every day. Oy, I can see what you're wanting to ask. How—why do I let myself stay and get trampled with him? Because I can't pick myself up and make it on my own; my hands are tied—I have a child."

She's said her piece. He's said his.

You, Riva Bramson, always so clever and cocksure in your judgments, do you stand on what you've heard? Who is really in charge? Does destiny dictate our fates—or do we make ourselves who we are?

Are we driven by the forces of life, or do we take the direction we choose?

Do you remember, Riva Bramson, once sitting in a public assembly in the ghetto, where a "senior" ghetto official stepped forth and delivered an oration—a speech that laid out his view of how our ghetto "kingdom" is supposed to work? Do you remember the usual enthusiasm he summoned when speaking about "our own" police, "our own" postal service, "our own" factories, and above all about "our own" currency? And do you remember, Riva Bramson, the comical effect that "senior" official produced on you—even on you, a normally serious person—an effect so strong that you couldn't keep yourself from asking the sarcastic question, "What reserves stand behind this currency of ours?"

Your question, Riva Bramson, was the kind that could only be posed after you knew the ghetto's length and breadth but not its depths, as you know them now. Today you know the answer: if the ghetto really is a state with its "own" police, its "own" offices, with its "own" high, higher, and highest officials—really a "state" with its own borders, guarded and carefully watched to prevent illicit crossings—then the ghetto must indeed have its own, hidden treasury reserves—natural resources backing up "our" currency as well.

What the ghetto is capable of deep down—now that's something you know all about, having learned about the yellow sand that ghetto housewives spread across their apartment floors to cover up their rotten squalor. You know all about what they're capable of when they dig deep and learn to make do now that you've seen the lime and clay people use to plug up the holes in the walls and ceilings in their homes. They're also capable of digging down deep for something else—and that's coal, for the ghetto's coal mines are a frenzy of activity right from the crack of dawn, like a heap of dung that is constantly buzzing with flies. The old and the young, the tall and the small, all go down into the mines. And there you dig in the muddy earth, groping, sighing, and clawing as you search its bowels. The "coal" they mine is then carried into the rooms of their households, where they sell it for forty, fifty pfennigs and more a kilo, depending on its quality, size, and, most important, on what the market will bear.

The "coal" itself is scraped out of sites where buildings, fences, or other structures once stood. This coal may be composed of any of the following materials: charred scraps of wood, bones, stones, and rags. This type of "coal" doesn't burn unless you lay it on wood that's already lit in the stove, adding it slowly to the action, at which point the already lit wood promptly burns itself out and begins to smolder. After a few hours of standing and blowing constantly in the stove opening so that the "fire" won't be completely extinguished, the pot cooking food on top suddenly comes to life.

That's right, Riva Bramson: Who said that life in the ghetto was easy?

And who, Riva Bramson, asks children in the ghetto to display adult intelligence and steadiness of nerve? No one.

A boy or girl leaves home early in the morning. In one trembling hand they clutch their carefully weighed and measured allowance of bread—their meal. The other hand holds their schoolbooks. Instead of school the young man in this case goes to the "coal mines." He's not a miner yet, but he watches from the side, and before long, he's made himself completely familiar with the "technique." Before long he's mastered it, and his hands are worth something. So he partners with someone who's already got a going "concern"—and before you know it, he's a miner.

As long as "coal fever" doesn't strike him, he keeps his wits about it. He returns home at the usual time each night, and his mother, if she has the time and patience to keep an eye out for him when he arrives, is astonished at the sight of her "student" coming from "school" covered with grime from cap to foot and looking like a filthy animal, and she sums up her reprimand as follows: "I'm going to have to get over to that school of yours to figure out how you're managing to get yourself filthy as a pig!"

It's just empty talk. She will not go; she won't find out. An empty threat, and nothing more! Just let her go ahead and try! When would she even have the time? She has to be there and line up at six in the morning just to get bread. At eight, the milk cooperative opens. She's got to get in another line there to receive her fifth of a liter of milk for her little child—which she then has to take and sell to other households for the thirty pfennigs she needs to buy enough tickets to get soup from the public kitchen. To get the tickets she has to go stand in another line, and to get the soup still another. Later, when lunch at the kitchen has been consumed, she has to go running once more to the neighbors so she can warm up a pot of stew. There she borrows a bit of groats and some beets, loosely understood, promising to return it all, and a little oil, when the next allotment of rations is received. She asks another neighbor for a pinch of salt, then she goes to yet another for a saccharine tablet as well as a match. And after putting all that together, she then has to stand in the kitchen by herself to make sure the pot gets warm. And by that time it's already night.

Just let her go check on her son! If she did, who would make the beds for her—her husband and her little child?

So the boy or girl wakes up another morning and goes out to mine "coal." The day after, they're late again coming home to the meager meal the mother has managed to scrape together with such torment and toil. Finally the cat's out of the bag, and Moshe, Chaim, or Mendel becomes an official "coal miner," with their mother's and father's permission to go.

Such an official, approved "coal miner" soon looks for his own saucepan, or some other old pot or pan, and works on it with a nail until it resembles a sieve, and he or she becomes the head of their own "concern." A Chaim or Moshe or Mendel then sits up to his neck in mud on a summer's day so he can bring the fruits of his labors home before nightfall. Soon he brings his younger, then his older, brother into the business, then his father, who hasn't found any better work, or even his mother, who'd shovel dung or carry bricks on her crooked back before she'd run a household on nothing at all.

When this same Moshe or Chaim or Mendel becomes an official "coal miner," he also becomes a derelict and lives a life beyond the moral pale. The coal mine is not like a house, where it's possible to hide nudity with the thin, spider web's veil of modesty that is sustained in the ghetto, though by the narrowest of degrees. In the "coal mine," young women who own no clothes other than the dress they're wearing will not, as a rule, wear them while slogging through the mud. Such clothes as they have are laid aside in a pile, and the naked bodies are covered with dust and mud just as fast. But a naked body covered in dust beckons all the more and only draws attention to itself. In these "coal mines," young boys of eleven or twelve, and girls of thirteen or fourteen, discover the secrets of their mothers and fathers. In the coal mines, a condition of equality obtains for everyone, and everyone satisfies their physical needs, even in broad daylight. Why waste time?

As the "coal mines" develop these "natural resources" of the ghetto "kingdom," they also give rise to conditions that produce a degenerate, socially stunted and crippled Jewish generation, matching exactly that image that the enemies of the Jews love to use in their propaganda so that they can say "Aha! You see? We were right all along! You see? We saw it long ago, when the rest of you were still blind!"

This is the room of a Bałuty resident who has not suffered like those from the central districts of the city. He hasn't been driven from his apartment, and his belongings have not been seized—he's just plain hungry.

It's a Bałuty apartment, and tidy Bałuty room, in a well-kept household filled with beds of all sizes, closets and cabinets, and tables, as well as chairs and benches. The room is its owners' pride and joy:

they're so attached to it that they'd rather die than remove any piece whatsoever from its cozy corner and carry it down to the street to sell.

A father and his four grown sons are pacing back and forth in the apartment. They wander from wall to wall, swallow their saliva, and keep on eye on the lady of the house, a short, shrunken Jewish woman who stands over a bucket and washes clothes. It's not the wash of some stranger—she has wash of her own to do, praised be the holy name—in an apartment, knock on wood, of eight people!

Yes, mister, she's seen better days. In the past, having another child meant another set of hands to share the work, someone else to help support the family, and another prop and stay for her old age. We were happy with what we had. Of course, if we'd been able to foresee the war breaking out, and that we'd be placed on the slaughterhouse table, and that every new child would mean just another mouth to feed and another shirt to wash in cold water without soap . . .

The husband sits there clumsily chewing on his wispy little beard that looks like a worn-out hairbrush missing most of its bristles. He stands up as if he wants to apologize. "Don't bother," he begins, "with the story about washing in cold water and no soap—that's my wife's business. I don't have anything to do with that—who cares if she washes in cold water, without soap? That's her business—that's not my fault. She can do laundry if she wants, and if she doesn't, fine— who cares? I never poked my nose into her business, and I don't want to start now. But as far as what she says about having another child, and then another—that's her story. Who could have ever known we'd reach the point where we don't know up from down, whether to go this way or that—don't know which way is life and which way death?"

Next to him stand four young men, as tall and thin as the poles on a wedding canopy, nodding their heads in agreement with their father as if to say, "Our father is telling you God's truth! You can take down every word in your notebook. It's not Papa's fault at all. There's no way he could have known that war was coming, and there's nothing we can do. But it's not our fault either! No one gave us an application where we asked to be born. And what difference would it make anyway? We don't even know how to write!"

"Where's Lipa? The twelve-year-old. Is he in school?"

Lipa is an entirely different kind of boy and has not followed in his brothers' footsteps. They are tall and thin with chestnut hair like their father's; Lipa is short and squat. He has dark hair and two wide, bright eyes, which have already seen an entire "world" and so never sit still in their sockets but constantly glance about.

"No, he doesn't go to school."

"Why don't you go to school?"

"Because I don't have any shoes."

"And what about the summer, when you can go barefoot?"

"I didn't go then either!"

"Why not?"

"Why should I? What's in school that's possibly worth running there barefoot to get?"

"Reading and writing and other subjects aren't worth anything?"

"If I knew how to read and write, you're telling me I wouldn't be hungry?"

"And staying home made you feel full?"

"It was better than school: I went and mined for coal!"

"And how much did you make as a coal miner?"

"Well, sometimes a mark and sometimes a mark and a few pfennigs. Depends on my luck."

The father stands up, a smile spreads slowly across his face, and his wispy little beard points upward as if to say, "And what of it, Mr. Jewish Council big shot? Some nerve you've got standing there and arguing with my Lipa! My little Lipa is worth ten of your wise guys, and that's with one hand tied behind his back!" The two grown boys stand there nodding in agreement, like lulabs at the end of the Sukkoth holiday, when "his steadfast love endures forever" is pronounced.[1]

His small, emaciated wife doesn't know what to use to dry her eyes—her sopping apron or her dripping hands. So she lets the tears

---

1. The ritual performed during the Feast of Tabernacles, in which palm fronds (lulabs) are waved and the Hebrew *Ki l'olam khasdo* (Psalms 106:1 and elsewhere) is pronounced. The scripture is given in Hebrew in the Yiddish text.

drain down the corners of her face and apologizes. "You see what we've come to, mister? The older ones stand there like bed wetters, while this one whom I've struggled to raise as a human being, he becomes the breadwinner for this poor family. May my words not come back to haunt me—this one . . . ," and she points to the twelve-year-old "coal miner," Lipa.[2]

2. Four pages here are missing from the manuscript, which concludes with a mock version of the questionnaire the narrator has to fill out for each apartment.

A rebbe from a long line of Hasidic rebbes is clothed in velvet and silk: spoiled with gifts of oranges and cakes to his heart's delight.[1] He's never laid his head on mere chicken or duckling feathers—that is, on the dry pages of the Gemara and its biblical commentary—but always on the down of the living swan: on books of Hasidic lore and legend and its wisdom tales.

To what, Riva Bramson, can such a rebbe be compared? To a paper dragon, which children let fly through the sky, seeming to hover there though it can be pulled back to earth thanks to the long tail they attach to it and the string held by a childish hand?

Such a rebbe, that embodiment of spirituality in his velvet and silk attire, has had his heart anointed and caressed with holy oil, making his mind fluffy and light so that he soars over the mundane chaos—the *tohu vabohu*—of life, just like that children's kite. His only ties to the earth are that long tail made up of Hasidic Jews, who latch on to him from the one side, and his acolytes and servants, who tether him to the ground on the other, preventing him from disappearing into the air.

---

1. A rebbe is the spiritual leader of a group within Hasidism, a religious revival movement that began in eighteenth-century eastern Europe.

And just as a kite sometimes breaks its string and sheds its tail as it soars through the sky or somehow tangles its tail in a wire like a pigeon snagged in a net—and just as children never treat it as lost for good and instead go on to make a number of smaller kites from its remains, which they soon launch into the air—so, Riva Bramson, are rebbes treated by their flocks.

When a rebbe dies, his Hasidic followers never treat him as lost. From the long tail of his sons and nephews he has left behind, the Saving Remnant, a number of smaller rebbes are made.[2]

Just as children must have their kites because by themselves they're unable to hover through the air, Hasidic Jews must have their rebbes to explore the upper realms in their name, since they're unable to do it by themselves—they simply haven't got the time.

And just as children quiver with excitement over their kites, so the Hasidic Jews tremble over every aspect of their rebbes' worldly existence: the rebbes' tables are stocked with every kind of delicacy, their every word is written down, their every thought is contemplated, and their every step is measured and watched.

Rebbes, Riva Bramson, live a hovering existence, and they die in the same hovering fashion as they fall from on high. Happy are those rebbes who know how to cloak their materiality in the garments of the spirit. These rebbes hide their plump, overfilled bellies with a stately beard, and their fat, greasy lips are hidden under the shadows of the high, genial furrows of their overarching brows.

Woe, however, be unto those rebbes who have sullied their spiritual aura with conspicuous material greed. Such rebbes tumble like shares of stock from a bankrupt firm. No self-respecting Hasidic Jew would so much as extend his hand to such rebbes, who are referred to only with contempt and are at best visited only by women.

The Glodziner Rebbe was probably not clever enough to make his materiality look spiritual, but neither was he foolish enough to allow his spirituality to look material. For him, the spirit was one thing and the flesh another; he chose the path of the golden mean, surrounding himself with neither too many serious Hasidim nor too large a clutch

2. *She'erit-hapleita:* from Isaiah 10:20 and Ezra 9:15.

of women. His flock was composed of everyday, chattering Hasidim, all making a solid living, with a few minor rabbis from the little Jewish villages providing the cream of the crop. Once a Jewish woman came to his circle even though her husband, a respected Hasid, followed another rebbe. But they did not throw her out.

The Glodziner Rebbe did not soar in the air, and the string tethering him to the ground did not break; maybe that's why he stayed in the ghetto. And when stranded in the ghetto like everyone else, the rebbe was for a short time able to live off the remains of his former spiritual and material wealth. He managed to salvage a few little books, and these, insofar as their quality would permit, sustained his spiritual hunger through the empty days. At first he could still numb himself with the teachings of the *Kedushas Levi,* relax over a tale by and about Reb Nachman of Breslov, fortify himself with the penetrating wisdom of the Kotzker Rebbe and the Vurker Rebbe, or chuckle with enjoyment over the cutting wit of Rebbe Meirleh of Przemyslany or Rebbe Naftali of Ropczyce.[3]

The rebbe's earthly hunger was taken care of by the food his friends managed to have sent to him through their connections and from the little bits—taken from their own last reserves—that his Hasidic followers gave him as they as they left the city of Łódź with him to go into exile in the ghetto. The rebbe himself, however, felt cramped in his single-room walk-up apartment in a Bałuty slum. He was accustomed to more spacious quarters and to the world's wide expanses. Only after recalling that even the Almighty made himself smaller after the destruction of the Temple did the rebbe's attitude change. Only then did he start to fall in love with the one-room apartment, with two large, soft rabbi beds, piled high with thick, musty quilts and bedding, and

---

3. The *Kedushas Levi* was a collection of sermons by Levi Yitshak of Berdichev (c. 1740–1810), a disciple of Dov Baer, the Maggid of Mezhirech, famed for bringing Hasidism to Poland. Rabbi Nachman of Breslov (1772–1810) was a grandson of the Baal Shem Tov, founder of Hasidism, whose kabbalistic *Tales* was published in Yiddish and Hebrew in 1815. The Kotzker Rebbe was Rabbi Menachem Mendl of Kotzk (1787–1859). Meir of Przemyslany (1780–1850) was a famed Hasidic miracle worker, known for his large court; Rebbe Naftali of Ropczyce was Naftali Hurowic of Ropczyce (1760–1827), a Hasidic rebbe known for acerbic wit.

with his sacks of feathers and goose down from the geese and turkeys that his Hasidim had sent to the rebbe's table at different points.

The two beds filled the little apartment with a smell that reeked of both the ritual bath and the slaughterhouse. The weekdays were a little gray and lonely because the rebbe was usually left alone, albeit in the constant companionship of the rebbetzin.[4] The female descendant of a holy Hasidic dynasty herself, the rebbetzin was for all that still a woman and would obey the call of nature right there in the apartment, as she had been wont to do from her childhood forward. As the Gemara says, you can get used to anything.[5] But the keeping of the Sabbath remained the strict province of the rebbe himself.

As always, the rebbetzin would kindle the Sabbath lights in her candelabra of six candles. It was true that the candleholders no longer held thick, heavy candles whose flame gave off the scent of that "extra soul" and taste of paradise that comes to us, as tradition teaches, on this sacred day. Instead the sockets of the candelabrum were filled with shrunken, whitish Hannukah candles, whose tiny flames flickered and guttered as if they were evil souls loitering about awaiting their redemption. She blessed the Sabbath lights nonetheless and always with the required six candles. The Sabbath table was bedecked with a tablecloth, and that one overlain with another—and between them the Sabbath bread took its place of honor. By now, of course, it has already become obvious that the blessing was not pronounced upon the usual array of grand challah breads, arranged to resemble the twelve loaves in the Tabernacle. The "as if He can," however, looks just as kindly upon the pigeon and turtledove, the offering of the poor, as he does upon the bull and the ox, the sacrificial offerings of the rich.

And the Hasidim would flock to his table. True, it wasn't like the old days, when the rich, overfed faces were always crowding around the feet of the rebbe, their impulse owing something to an evil inclination.

---

4. *Rebbetzin* is an honorific name for a rebbe's wife.
5. This refers to the Talmudic story of a gnat that lodged in the brain of the Jew-hating Roman emperor Titus. Since only the din of a hammer brought relief by disturbing the gnat, Titus paid a blacksmith to bang away nonstop. But the gnat resumed its tortures. The moral was that one could get used to anything.

Now they arrive with black and bitter faces full of despair, albeit more honest ones. Serious faces with an urgent mien—the faces of those who cling to the shepherd when an evil, threatening wolf has found the flock. They even chant Hasidic melodies together. But the tunes were still and sad, sung in the heartfelt, honest tones that beggars give forth, not the loud, sated, and self-satisfied voices they had before.

That's how it was for the rebbe at the beginning, when life in the ghetto had not yet become so brutal and hard—when their souls still yearned for something more and searched for spiritual support. Later, when life became more difficult and bitter, as the souls within them shriveled to nothing, the Hasidim forgot all about their rebbe and left him to his own devices.

Instead of the Torah, everyone dreamt only of flour.[6] Spirituality became a spiritual ghost, and materiality took on the most crass expression possible—that is, it assumed its ghetto form. Now the rebbe conducts his Sabbath celebrations all by himself. His table hymns are sobbed, not sung forth. Of the six silver candleholders, only two glass ones remain, and they don't illuminate the Sabbath table long enough for the rebbe to laud his wife with a round of "Woman of Valor."[7] Never before has the rebbe sung this melody with the heart and devotion he now gives it in the ghetto—in fact, what would someone like the Glodziner Rebbe know about reciting "Woman of Valor"—what could it really mean to him, given his status, to have such a woman as his own? His wife bore him no children, and they raised none together. He lived with her mostly because he was afraid of offending her saintly ancestors, those holy ones, and because—well, because he was a man made of flesh and blood, after all, for his own life was bound up with hers.[8] When Hasidim had sent him geese and turkeys, and the ritual slaughterers killed them, the pluckers plucked and gutted them, and the cook broiled and fried them—it had been Lealeh, a distant relative who worked as the housekeeper, and not his wife who

---

6. Cf. *Wisdom of the Sages,* ch. 3: "If there is no flour, there is no Torah; if there is no Torah, there is no flour."

7. The *Eshet Khayil,* verses lauding Jewish women, from Proverbs 31:10–31.

8. Genesis 44:30, describing Jacob's love for Benjamin.

had brought it all to the table. When Hasidim sent wine and other beverages, the sexton opened the bottles and the beadle filled their cups. When Hasidim sent him their finest prepared delicacies, Lealeh took charge of it all. The most that could be said was that the rebbetzin had fulfilled the office of wife only in a supervisory capacity and was by no means a "woman of valor."

In those good old days, the rebbe's Friday night singing of "Woman of Valor" sounded nothing like the "Shalom Aleichem."[9] When Jews greet the ministering angels in that song—those honored guests who come to every Jewish table—and ask that they grant those assembled the gift of peace, it is customary to greet the woman of the house as well, the housewife who "keeps a sharp eye on the guests." In accord with the customs for treating the fairer sex, she should be complimented fulsomely, and often more than she deserves. In the ghetto, however, when the Glodziner Rebbe brings his prayer to a close and turns his eyes to his impoverished table, bedecked for the Sabbath with a tablecloth on top and another underneath, he may or may not find the customary two loaves of challah. And when the blessing over the food is pronounced, there will certainly not be any fish or meat to bless. That week, just like the week before and the week before that, other dishes will be served in their place. These substitutes will become their meat and fish, seasoned by the rebbetzin's own hand with her special "it must come from somewhere sauce," which summons up a memory of traditional Sabbath tastes.

It is then that the melody and words of "Woman of Valor" burst from his throat, and he pours them forth in a hymn of praise. After all, the two tiny Sabbath candles, the two olive-size loaves of bread, and the food that replaces the meat and fish, seasoned by the rebbetzin's own hand, are there thanks to her efforts alone. Everything that's there is the result of her cleverness and hard work, because—well, because the Hasidim have long since ceased sending the rebbe anything at all. No goose and no wine, not even a dry crust of bread. They have nothing to send, and to demand something from them at this point would for him be like someone removing an offering from the sacrificial altar or taking a holy object from the Temple itself. If there is anything

9. Traditional song sung on the Sabbath eve to greet the Sabbath.

at all on the Sabbath table now, it is there by virtue of the rebbetzin's own hand.

Like a true woman of valor, whose business it is to make sure that not a single speck of dust or the tiniest strand of hair would so much as think about falling on her husband, the rebbe's wife now goes from door to door. She visits everywhere a Hasid or his wife once made their home, looking for tiny crumbs and scraps of food worth less than a cent. And from these scraps, smaller than an olive or half an olive, she creates her Sabbath repasts. And now the refrains of the "Woman of Valor" sound forth more proudly, seriously, and with more enthusiasm than ever before. *The heart of a husband safely trusts in her—and the heart of her husband is safe with her.*[10] The heart of a rebbe who has such a wife will never weaken or falter at her side. And the heart of a rebbe's wife belongs not to him alone but to the community as a whole.

But when the voice of Solomon the Wise rang out in "Woman of Valor," never in his wildest dreams had he imagined anything like the ghetto. *She is not afraid of the snow for her household,* it is written, while in the ghetto, snow is precisely her greatest fear. *She makes garments and sells them,* according to Solomon; in the ghetto she most certainly will never rest from this task. The feathers from the rebbe's bedding have long since taken wing from the apartment, as if with a life of their own. The huge tablecloths and heavy bedspreads soon followed them out the door. More than one of the plush rebbe beds were likewise unable to wait for the end of winter: both were swallowed up by the wood stove. And then, somehow—it should never happen to you—the rebbetzin's legs gave out, and now she's less than a full human being, let alone any sort of woman of valor!

There's no month that goes by in such circumstances when one doesn't begin to squabble over trifles. It even happened to the holy Baal Shem Tov himself.[11] But while it was the Baal Shem Tov's destiny to be shown the way back to the path of peace, he, the Glodziner Rebbe, was left on the path of those "Forced to Fall"—and fall he did,

10. Proverbs 31:11, and following in the next paragraphs.
11. The Baal Shem Tov—"good master of the name"—was the founder of the Hasidic movement, c. 1698–1760.

step by step, until he hit rock bottom. In the end, all that remained of the rebbe was a simple Jew with simple appetites, with the plainest hunger of all. And like the most average Jew you've ever seen, he was made of flesh and blood.

Nothing of his great riches remains except his long, broad woolen prayer shawl and the two phylacteries he wraps in prayer. There he sits half the day, wrapped in this tallith and tefillin: perhaps he will manage a spiritual ascent.[12] At the present time, however, that spiritual ascent has not yet occurred. But the broad, woolen prayer shawl is certainly good for one thing: it has kept him warm. He's hungry—but he's not cold. And not far from him sits the rebbetzin, not in splendor but as a pale reflection of the splendor that was. The rebbe has fallen from his heights; the rebbetzin has lost weight, her powers, and her face as well. All that remains of the good old days, of those days of wine and roses—all that's left is a case of sclerosis. She sits there and doesn't understand why. The holiday is just around the corner, and there's not a single Hasid to be seen? Why isn't the cook slaving away? With so much to do, why is the kitchen so empty and dark? Why all of this, despite the fact that the morning sun has been up for a good long while and the blessing has already been said—and Lealeh, the housekeeper, that gluttonous old souse, still hasn't brought her even a sip of schnapps and a slice of cake? Who does that Lealeh think she is? Is she trying to force me to fast?

And there sits the rebbe, all wrapped and covered in his warm tallith and tefillin, serving the Creator like a simple Jew—like a tailor reciting his psalms. And like a tailor, he has doubts of his own whether such dry and simple prayers will be powerful enough to help his dry and basic needs, so he announces his prayer to us in a humble and simple fashion: "Might it be possible perhaps, young man, to send for a doctor for the rebbetzin and for the community to send the four guilders in welfare support quickly, for the holiday, because it's been over a month since I've seen anything faintly resembling a coin, and now, oy, I'm really—really in it up to my neck!"

12. Phylacteries, or prayer straps, are applied to the forearms and forehead by pious Jewish men as they say the morning prayers; "laying," or using two sets, is a sign of extreme piety. *Tallith* means "prayer shawl" and *tefillin* means "phylacteries."

♦♦♦ *A Mother and Her Child:*
In the Eighteenth Apartment

The only north-facing window—every pane is shattered—has its cracks stuffed with rags of every which sort of household trash. Entire pieces of the buckling walls have been eaten away by the damp, and a few lazy flies can be seen clinging to its pieces. The ceiling has been pockmarked with blotches of gray and brown and looks like the filthy, stained bed of a baby carriage.

The two iron beds in the middle of the room are covered with several pillows without their covers and by the tattered sacks of straw mattresses, each with whole bundles of straw sticking out the sides. A bucket is standing right next to the beds, and around it are strewn scattered pieces of both white and colored laundry waiting to be washed.

Filthy, poor, and neglected—the appalling, gruesome scene makes your skin creep as you remind yourself: human beings live in this hole. That there are human beings alive and breathing in this apartment—an apartment whose cellar, winter and summer, is full of water that tears chunks from the brooding walls. And that under the repulsive, disgusting blankets on the rusted, rickety iron beds there are people sleeping: real human beings with eyes of their own, which once gazed upon a different way of life. There are human beings here with mouths that can speak and cry and which nonetheless have chosen to remain silent, choosing resignation just like the flies lazily clinging to the wall until the moment arrives, one morning, when their wings give a final flutter and they fall lifelessly onto the dirty floor.

A loathsome-looking, husky, pockmarked Jewish woman is lounging about the filthy place, clutching another creature to her breast and stomach, a being almost as large as she is herself. The Jewish woman moves about the room holding the creature tightly in her arms as if the child had been born to her in happiness and peace—as if the table were not piled high with all kinds of pots, bags, and other items. She moves about as if the apartment were not so crammed full of filth that it's almost impossible to set a foot inside. Her face is thoroughly pitted, and every pit left by the smallpox has been blackened, like her hands, which look as if she had just been kneading mud: the same hands she places underneath the creature she holds, whom she carries around on her stomach and heart. Her mouth hides behind a round head of curly, light-colored hair belonging to the creature clinging to her as if she wanted to become part of her flesh. But no sooner have you entered the door than does this hidden mouth greet you with a verbal outpouring impossible to divert or stop. The Jewish woman's pitted face, with its shadow of a beard, has not forgotten how to affect the high-falutin' manners of those good old days now past—demanding that honored or important visitors be greeted with excuses for the sorry state of the household, especially when they arrive with an unexpected knock on the door.

Don't avert your ears, Riva Bramson; you won't hear those same excuses you've encountered scores of times in scores of other apartments and which you've already determined aren't worth a red cent! You've heard those excuses a multitude of times in the "households" of these ghetto apartments: that housewives are helpless given the situation and that the cheap walls are to blame, constantly dripping their moisture down from the ceiling with their tears of lime. You've heard the same story hundreds of times in homes where the beds remain unmade—that it's not the housewives' fault for having given up on dealing with the squalor but the fault of the inferior housing conditions themselves. When so many people are crowded into a room with two beds at most, the rest must sleep on the floor, and when everyone gets up at the crack of dawn, the bedding gets tossed on the beds. There's no time to tidy up because everyone has to hurry off to get in line—for bread, soup, potatoes, or other foodstuffs, to sign up for work, or simply to find out what happened to the relief money that has not yet arrived.

You've already heard it scores of times, Riva Bramson: that the fact that the bedding and the clothes covering the bodies of the ghetto's inhabitants are so filthy is not due to the laziness of the housewives but a result of the ghetto conditions in which they have been forced to live. There's no way to warm up any water to wash, and certainly no soap. The most important factor, however, is surely exhaustion: after hours and hours of standing in so many lines and not having anything to eat all day, no one has the strength to stand over a wash bucket and scrub the wash by hand in cold water, and with no soap at that. You've heard the Yiddish saying often enough by this time to know it by heart: "like outside, like inside." In a nutshell, that's the general excuse you've run into time and again for the disarray you've encountered within the ghetto's homes.

I've heard you say quite often, Riva Bramson, that you're not a person who likes excuses. And if you were the presiding judge in a ghetto court, passing judgment on the chaos and disorder that reigns in its apartments, you'd dismiss those excuses immediately, issuing the harshest sentence possible on housewives who failed to keep their apartments and their persons clean. I'm well aware of the various arguments you'd marshal to support those harsh judgments, and I wouldn't doubt their factual validity for a moment. But permit me as well, Riva Bramson, to consider the validity and justice of the claims made by this woman with the slight beard, since you'll have to hear her out anyway given the torrent of speech she has launched that is impossible to turn aside. "Let me," as she says, "finally tell you what's really going on here. If it means my child should suffer in the slightest, God forbid— then, well, let my nice clean house grow with its head in the ground like an onion for all I care. As long as no harm comes to my child!"

She's talking, of course, about the child who's clinging to her as if she wanted to merge with her flesh, a child already almost as big as her mother, who carries the girl wrapped around her chest. "For her," she declares, "I waited eighteen years." Since the mother's verbal tidal wave cannot be stopped, you are obliged to listen to the story of that eighteen-year wait: eighteen dark years in the life of this repulsive but completely average Jewish woman spent swinging between hope and fear. She was the only child of people from a tiny Jewish village, ordinary but honest folk, average people who toiled bitter hours day and night to set aside a dowry for their only daughter, with nothing that resembled a beautiful face but blessed with a loving heart. The sharpest cold could not prevent them from walking all night behind their cart so they could stand the whole next day at a market fair in a far-flung little Jewish town. And they never hesitated to stand all day long in the burning summer sun either if it meant an additional groschen or two.

Once the whole dowry had been earned, however, and once their daughter's hope chest had been fully provisioned and packed, her parents had to face that old Jewish problem—impossible to get around—of giving their daughter away in marriage. "To whom should we give our ugly daughter and the dowry we slaved to put aside? Should we find some modern young man who's after a nice makeup job and a set of 'perfect' lips—the kind of man who will stick by our daughter until the dowry runs out? Or give her to someone with a trade, who'll count the pits in her face ten times a day?"

The most sensible course was to marry her off to one of those pious Yeshiva boys looking for a source of support in his studies—to someone less concerned with her face than with the steady income she might provide. Since the matchmaker had just such a boy in mind, she soon became a lucky bride, and the family pulled out all the stops and put on quite a wedding: "Both Mama and Papa were completely satisfied, and I—I was also content . . . but every time I looked at him, my heart would explode into tears. The difference between his face and mine—well, it was like the difference between vinegar gone bad and the taste of a fine wine. He, truth be told, was quite elegant and refined. He never, God forbid, said a single nasty word to me. But how terrible it was when husband and wife needed to talk! For me, the way he looked at me spoke volumes, and every glance told the same story: that he hated me the way you hate bitter, incurable gallstones. It wasn't long before he couldn't look at me at all.

"As for me? I was still a Jewish daughter, and a Jewish daughter's job is to love her husband no matter what. And besides—what can I tell you?—I loved him anyway! Why not? His face was soft and smooth, his figure was a blessing from God, and the elegant way he carried himself—you just can't put it into words!

"I looked after every step he took—not as a wife but as a faithful mother. I never let a single speck of dust fall on his head. My mother, may she rest in peace, doted on him and fussed over him, clearing obstacles from his path so he wouldn't stumble. My father treated him as if he were the spitting image of a precious stone. My husband had a mother of his own, of course, a real, you'll excuse me for saying so, a real, you know—well, I'd rather not say what kind. Apart from all the good and well-meaning advice she gave me about how to run a household, she never, God forbid, gave me a single word of abuse. It's just that, I don't know, even a corpse wants to speak the truth—every time she came to visit, her presence felt like one blow to the heart after another, and I constantly felt ashamed. Every time she looked at me, it felt as if she was counting the pockmarks on my face. She made me feel like a thief, and I couldn't look her in the eye. And in every other word I heard her exchange with her son, all I could imagine I heard was the sound of 'divorce.'

"My husband spent every day in the Hasidic prayer house or in the house of study, and every moment was sheer torture for me. I always felt as if the other men, his friends, were making fun of him for having a face full of pockmarks for a wife and were trying to egg him into a divorce. Every night my face was bathed in tears. I wasn't lamenting the shame of my face but the disgrace about to take over the rest of my life. Let's not even mention the times when he was out of town, gone to see one rabbi or another. On those days my life was simply unbearable: every sound at the door, every stranger in the street, stopped my heart, took my breath away, and made me think, 'There he is, the messenger with the divorce summons in his hands!'

"I started to hate myself; I began to hate the world and everyone in it. Soon I was envying the dead and continually cursing the day I was born. My mother, may she always look after me, used to say to me, 'Why are you fretting yourself to death, foolish girl? You'll have a child and show them all!' But it's easy enough to say 'have a child' and another thing to actually get pregnant."

The torrent of words continues to pour out of this dirty, repulsive Jewish woman. You can't stop it. On she rambles about the death of her parents and the double blow of sorrow she was forced to bear. For with them gone she had lost the source of both financial and moral support. She continues her story by telling how she had to hitch herself up to the pushcart her parents used to make a living, how she pushed it all by herself through rain and mud, snow and wind, and through the heat and cold, because "how could I ask my husband to go make a living, with his elegant hands and delicate body—make a living for me, his pockmarked, ugly wife and an accursed, barren woman to boot?" So she traveled to market alone, working herself to the bone. Between one market day and the next she took care of her house, was a good wife to her husband, ran to doctors, and never gave up her dream of having a child. "Unlike my mother-in-law," she went on, "God have mercy, who never said a nasty word to me, just treated me like a bitter fate God had laid upon her blessed son, my sisters-in-law—may they be thrown from the roof of the tallest building in town—gave me plenty of bitter pills to swallow. Their little pieces of advice ripped my heart to shreds, one piece at a time. 'That's just the way it is, let's not fool ourselves,' they used to tell me. 'Everyone knows a man will act like a man. And a man—let's face it—likes a smooth and pretty face and a wife who can bring happiness to his home. It's a fact, my little darling—every man's got a wandering eye.'"

What else could she do, after little speeches like these, except cry herself to sleep? Her face was anything but pretty, she knew, and pockmarks are impossible to hide. And as the chief breadwinner, of course her housekeeping had to fall to the wayside. "After all," she'd say, "a person with one shadow can't dance at two weddings. And happiness? That's in God's hands." When the doctors and all their medicines made no difference at all, she turned to Hasidic rebbes, who allowed her to pour out her heart to them and would, for a hefty price, provide her with slender amulets and tiny little charms. When amulets and charms failed her, she paid a visit to the quack and laid out huge sums for dried medicinal herbs. "There's nothing they've recommended that I haven't tried. There's no treatment or medicine they've told me to take that I haven't used—including those medications that turn your stomach inside out and taste sweet as sugar at the same time!"

And so she stumbled her way through eighteen dark years. Eighteen years caught between hope and terror—eighteen years of shame. And in the nineteenth, her daughter was born. "Back then," she went on, "my life hung in the balance. The murderers, those midwives, tried to pull her out of me piece by piece. I was in labor five full days. And just when I was at the end of my rope, with barely enough strength left to breathe, I scraped up what little I had left and screamed at the doctors: 'Go ahead and tear me to shreds, but get my child out in one piece!' So they did a cesarean, and I gave birth to my little princess . . . she looks more like my husband than she does me."

She smothers the girl still hanging on her neck with kisses. And the girl, who looks as if she wants to crawl right back into her mother's body, starts to kick and struggle with her hands and feet, almost knocking her down as she goes on. "For five years, I never let a speck of dust fall on my daughter's head; I swaddled her in silk, bathed her in wine, and treated her with honey. I was sick for a year after giving birth, and my husband had to support the family. I laughed at his sisters and could have been the happiest person in the world! Well, then the war broke out, they made the ghetto, and . . . now they're coming to check to see if I need 'social support.'[1]

"Do I need support? Take a look at this place! Have you ever seen a more disgusting dump outside of a pig's stall? The kid's got no shoes on her feet, and of course she refuses to lie in that bed! Am I supposed to let her run around barefoot? You think I would let the girl I begged for those eighteen long, dark years, God forbid, catch a cold? That I'd let everything turn upside down and spin right down into the ground? The dirty laundry's been on the floor of the apartment three days now, and the bucket's standing there all ready. You know, I've been trying to wash that laundry for three days. But every time there's

---

1. Polish in quotation marks in original.

muddy puddles outside, all over the place, the child won't lie down in bed, I've got to carry her around with me. As far as I'm concerned, all that laundry can rot!

"You think shoes are the only thing she needs? You think she's got bread to eat? You think she's got soup? My child's hungry. My child's got nothing to eat—the child I begged and longed for all those years. And you're here to check whether I need social support! If I did have something tucked away next to my heart, you think I'd try to save it at the expense of my child? You think I'd let her go hungry? And another thing . . ."

The torrent of words that had been impossible to stop or turn aside has now been overrun by a river of tears, filling every one of her pockmarks and flowing down toward the bucket below. Before you there no longer stands a repulsive and filthy Jewish woman, just a mother weeping for her child. The Jewish mother of the ghetto weeps perpetually, both when she alone is hungry and when her children are hungry, and she has nothing to give them, because—

The Jewish children in the ghetto are hungry all the time.

◆◆◆ *Every Dwelling Has a Hidden Ulcer Spreading:*
In the Nineteenth Apartment

So that every room will be dark—it's a Bałuty slum room, after all!—
the single window can't be placed smack-dab in the middle of the wall.
Just in case the sun goes completely mad and suddenly decides to
shine inside with all its might, the window has to be positioned carefully, up in a corner always in shadow, so that its light will be blocked
by the building next door.

There are a few beds in this particular room, all still unmade at
noon, with several pale, emaciated faces peering out from them,
which is of course why they created the ghetto in the first place: so that
deprivation, hunger, and the various diseases that accompany them
could have unimpeded sway. When you enter such a half-lit room and
begin to walk through it, your eyes no longer struggle to see what's
in the darkened corners, and they don't even gape at the beds: they're
already quite accustomed to these sorts of spaces and skilled at seeing
in the dark. Your ears have gotten so used to the groaning and the
sorrow that there's nothing really surprising to observe. Your fingers
direct your pen so mechanically over the questionnaire you've come
to complete that they never hesitate for a moment before answering
the summary question: "Social support required?" Automatically, they
simply make the following entry, with an underscore to emphasize the
point: *"Yes—support required. Immediately: Now."*

Everyone, absolutely everyone, needs social support because everyone's survival depends on getting that handful of marks that are too few to live on and just enough not to starve! But then you enter a room that at first looks as if you've stumbled upon a wedding: the table is set, with men, women, and children sitting all around. A few loaves of bread sit in the middle and right next to them, several dishes of honey. And everyone is digging into the goods with tooth and claw.

A single thought takes hold of your entire being when entering a room like this: "Get something to eat." Captivated by the spell of the guests' appetites you see in front, in a flash you begin to feel hungry, terribly hungry, yourself—before long you'd give away half the kingdom of the entire ghetto to be able to join these people at their table and join in their meal, eating pieces of bread smeared with honey, dripping with honey, not carefully weighed out on a scale, and to be able to drink their hot, black coffee, sweetened with saccharine to the taste. Your tongue floats in your mouth at the very thought, salivating like a drunk after his booze.

Your wits, however, remain about you, and grasping the utter nonsense of this vision of utopia they push you to a different evaluation of the scene. "Ah!" you think. "These people sitting so pretty and eating so calmly—the same ones who despise officials from the Jewish community, the same ones whose hatred and envy cuts you like a knife every time they look at you! The truth's a little different than what *they* think: there's at least one hard-working community official who's been climbing up and down the stairs of these apartment buildings all day long. And these people, meanwhile, are just now having their breakfast and getting out of bed!"

You quickly abandon this theory, however, once the diners begin their explanation. "So you think we have it easy, do you? *We* were standing in line from seven this morning until not too long ago—we finally elbowed our way to the front and finally got our rations. Still, it's a miracle we got anything. We just got our support money yesterday—it's a miracle we got it at all!"

As it turns out, these people hadn't been sleeping in. So you weigh the next most likely possibility to explain the scene before your eyes. "Let's see," you think to yourself. "To determine the number of diners—not to tempt the evil eye—sitting around this particular table"—though your glance, more agile than your superstition, has already begun to count—"not one, not two, not ten, not twelve . . . seventeen times forty decagrams of flour, let's see, so just about seven kilograms of bread a day are eaten in this room, aside from the honey, coffee, and not including . . ."

No, Riva Bramson—your common sense finally dashes the fantasies behind these rough calculations. No, Riva—everything we've already learned in these ghetto apartments has taught us over and over that figures are only guidelines that must be adapted to the actual situation and that measures can be used for both good and ill. Everything we've seen in the ghetto has taught us such figures are prone to error and that the human eye, no matter how sharp it becomes through practice, is easily deceived. Not, God forbid, from malice or the numbing force of habit. The reason, Riva Bramson, is simply this: your eyes have been led astray by the generous habits of your heart, a good heart that was longing to discover just one intact family of seventeen members in the ghetto sitting down to a breakfast of bread and honey and dipping chunks of it in their hot coffee. That's what your decent, good-hearted nature yearned to see, and so that's exactly what your eyes found.

Your joy, however, has already been tempered by the two apologies that have reached your ears from the group sitting at the table. If you were just a little worse off than you are, those apologies alone would be enough to guess that the last time this family sat down to bread and honey together certainly wasn't yesterday or even the day before but a whole month ago—the last time community support payments were received. You'd also be able to guess that if this family hadn't experienced its "miracle" yesterday and received their payments, they wouldn't be eating bread today.

So even if you don't want to undertake your normally painstaking investigation in this case, Riva Bramson, grab hold of those kosher, Jewish eyes of yours and take a long hard look at the nitty-gritty of the situation that's right before your face. Get rid of those rose-colored glasses, Riva, and start looking at the world with the eyes of a real human being: a mensch. Take another look, Riva: there are seventeen people total but only three beds there. Think about it for just one second: How can all these seventeen people in front of you share three beds?

And don't stop there, Riva Bramson. Teach your eyes that in the ghetto it's never enough to examine things from a realistic, factual point of view. Looking, and even seeing, aren't enough! Here your eyes have to be taught to get to the bottom of things—or as the saying goes, to read between the lines. When your eyes have acquired this observational technique, you'll come to the conclusion that the seventeen people sitting around this table don't belong to a single family at all. The three loaves of bread, three plates of honey, and the three cups of steaming coffee standing in the middle will tell you the same thing as well. If these loaves, plates, and cups had mouths they'd tell you right away that these seventeen people at the table come from three different families . . . Their coming together in a single room is a simple result of the conditions that ghetto life has imposed. And since there are no idyllic scenes in the ghetto—a fact you've long since understood—you'll also be able to figure out the following all by yourself:

In ghetto conditions, it is simply impossible for three families, thrown together by fate and chance and totaling seventeen souls altogether—including the older and younger children—to be housed properly under a single roof. Especially when only three people have an actual place to lay their heads or, at best, six. In the worse case, with four people to a bed—two at the head and two at the foot—five living, breathing people will be sleeping on nothing but the floor. It all adds up: in a room like this—as the loaves of bread, the plates, and the cups all attest—three families have been making their home; one has four members, another six, and the third seven. It all adds up—almost. As it happens, the very eyes you've taught to look carefully and observe what's in front of them are working for a person who can't see what's right under her nose. In the corner just to the right, next to the door, your eyes never noticed an improvised bed that's been set up on the floor. On it sits an old, paralyzed Jewish woman who could well be a member of any of the three different families in the room. There she is: the common root from which all three families have sprung. But according to the regulations governing social support in the ghetto, she must be counted as a separate family and so must receive her ten marks per month of support by herself.

Even before Bałuty was decreed as the new Pale of Settlement for the Jews of Łódź, Dvorah Hannah lived in this same apartment.[1] In those days she didn't occupy the right-hand corner of the place, wasn't paralyzed, and wasn't waiting to be discovered on a pile of temporary bedding right next to the door. Before Bałuty became a ghetto she was already seventy-five years old, and together with her husband, Yosl the weaver, didn't look a day over fifty and kept her house clean to the strictest housewifely standards, with two daughters and a son.[2]

Just because she married off her children, however—for better and for worse, for richer and for poorer—didn't mean she stopped being their loving mother. On the Sabbath she would dust off her venerable old husband's caftan and hat and stroll into town to visit them, where she was welcomed as an honored guest in each of their homes: "Look who's here! Good to see you, Mama! Come in, dear mother-in-law!" A little time would be spent sitting together, then a bit of chatting and catching up, a bite to eat—and soon she'd be on her way. "Good Shabes, children—a good Shabes and a good year to you too!"

"What's the big hurry, Mama, what's the rush? You just got here!"

Back then, Mama was a real mother—may we never be without one though we live the proverbial 120 years! And children being children, she lived and died with every hair that fell from their heads. Later, six months before the war broke out, her venerable old husband passed away. One evening, right after coming home from the factory, he began to complain of a pain in his side, so she sent him right to bed and gave him something to make him sweat. "Tomorrow," she thought, "I'll get up early and make him some broth; that'll get him back on his feet." Instead she had to get up in the middle of the night, and by morning, broth was no longer required.

---

1. The Pale of Settlement was the region of Czarist Russia to which Jewish residents were confined, as declared by Nicholas I in 1835; the term is used here ironically.
2. Zelkowicz may have made a mistake here, as several paragraphs later it appears that the woman has three daughters and a son.

For the Master of the Universe, she had no complaints. Her husband had simply spent his allotted time in this sinful world, that's all; no one lives forever, so every life must come to an end. Dvorah Hannah, however, did have one request: "Do whatever you want with me, Master of the Universe—go right ahead. Just don't make me live so long that I become a burden to my children! And if it's my fate, God forbid, to have to depend on them, it would be better if you just let me join my venerable old husband, wherever he's gone: he was my best child of all."

The Master of the Universe heard her prayer—so there was no need for her to move in with her children. There was just one small problem: when the war broke out, the children had to move in with her. The city daughters were forced to move in with their overjoyed mother, who already had an apartment in Bałuty. They didn't come as a group but one by one: first came the middle daughter with her husband and their two little children, may they be strong and healthy. Mama gave them one of the two beds, where her son-in-law and the two children slept, while she took her daughter into her own. It was a few days later when her only daughter-in-law arrived. Her husband had been drafted into the Polish army, and he'd disappeared from the face of the earth. Since she was about to give birth at any moment, Dvorah Hannah gave up her place and slept by herself on the floor, not far from the two beds. Two or three days later the other two daughters moved in, along with the grandchildren: "Oh, thank God, we're all together," was Mama's only thought, forgetting, of course, that there was nothing whatsoever for her to do now but pace back and forth in the apartment and sit in the corner by the door. "But at least we've all still got our health."

When her daughter-in-law, alas, was about to give birth, she had to be brought to the hospital—like a real trip to hell—and it was a place from which she never returned. Her place in bed stayed empty. Dvorah Hannah wouldn't take it, though she was definitely the one who most needed it, since she'd caught a chill in her feet at her daughter-in-law's funeral, if you could call it that, took sick and soon could no longer walk. Thirteen other interested candidates, however, were right there waiting to take her spot.

A few weeks later they tragically brought home all that remained of her daughter-in-law—a strong and healthy child, in fact—and Dvorah Hannah, now paralyzed, took it into her corner, laid it on her bedding, and cared for the child as if it were her own. Leibish quickly grew into a happy little person with two lively, playful little eyes. He bounces around the room like a little ball and calls all the men there "papa," because that's what he hears the other children say. He also calls all the women "mama," because that's what he hears from the other children as well. And so Leibish has three fathers and three mothers. All are glad to play with him, everyone holds him dear, but it seldom—almost never—happens that any of his three fathers or mothers gives him a piece of bread, even a tiny little morsel, just big enough for little Leibish to hold in his tiny little hand. Even when one of the three fathers or three mothers can save a bit of bread and set it aside, they want to give it to their own children, who are closer to them, after all.

Little Leibish has three papas, three mamas, and many brothers and sisters. And so, in reality, Leibish has no one at all: no real father, no mama, no actual brothers or sisters. He doesn't even have a ghetto father, the so-called *Judenälteste,* or Eldest of the Jews, to provide him with social support.[3] Leibish doesn't receive any welfare, for the simple reason that he's too young. Then again, at eighteen months old, how is he supposed to stand in line at the welfare office and hand in a written request, since none of his three fathers has registered him as their child because no one can or wants to accept the responsibility of raising him in return for the seven marks a month they'd receive in social support?

So Leibish has no one but his old, paralyzed grandmother, sitting on her bedding in the corner right next to the door—with her two married daughters, two living sons-in-law, and eleven grandchildren. And just like Leibish, her grandson, she really has no one at all. None of her daughters and none of her sons-in-law can see clear to spare her a piece of bread from their rations, especially when all of her

---

3. "Eldest of the Jews" was a Nazi term, often used by the Germans to designate the member of the Jewish community placed in charge of the ghetto. In Łódź, it was Chaim Rumkowski.

sons-in-law and daughters have older and younger children of their own—screaming, crying, and faint from lack of food. Dvorah Hannah herself doesn't receive any social support: she's unable to rise from her bedding in the corner and go to the welfare office herself. Nor can any of her children manage to sign the old woman up as part of their own families—not for just ten marks a month.

So Dvorah Hannah has no one but Leibish, Leibish no one but Dvorah Hannah, and the two of them together—together, they have absolutely nothing on which to live. And yet, Riva Bramson, those same seventeen people you saw sitting at the table, eating their meager meal of carefully weighed and strictly measured out portions of bread—those seventeen people are still envious of Dvorah Hannah and Leibish, and critical of them: "At least *they've* got a place in the corner to lie on! A piece of bedding just for the two of them! They may be hungry, but at least they're not sleepy—hey, the seventeen of us have just three beds to share between us. So we're hungry all the time *and* cold all night. Can't we have a place to lay our tired heads? What about *us*?"

Listen carefully, Riva Bramson—listen to our Yiddish language that you understand so little and please understand that its wealth of expressions and nuance are richer than your wildest imagination could dream. There's absolutely nothing that our lively, juicy tongue can't find words to describe. Even so, I don't believe anyone has the power to find a fitting description for everything going on beneath the surface of the Nineteenth Apartment unless, perhaps, you transformed the old Yiddish saying "Every ulcer has its own color" into a new and different saying: "Every dwelling has a hidden ulcer spreading."

On the fifteenth of March in the year 1941, the following announcement, printed on yellow paper, appeared in three different languages—German, Polish, and bad Yiddish—and was posted on the
ghetto walls:

> Announcement Number 233: This notice constitutes official announce-
> ment that from 16 March 1941, at the location of 27 Franciszkańska Street,
> a court of summary judgment is hereby established, whose jurisdiction
> will include any and all types of criminal activity harmful to the essential
> interests of the ghetto community.
>
> This court of summary judgment will be fully autonomous of the ex-
> isting General Court, at 20 Gnieźnieńska Street. Verdicts rendered by
> the Court of Summary Judgment will be issued by two separate judicial
> panels, each composed of a judge and two auxiliaries, henceforth to be
> chosen by me from the ghetto's residents.
>
> This court's judicial procedure will not include any prior investiga-
> tions and will exclude the roles of prosecutor and defense counsel.
>
> The court panel will issue verdicts based on its own independent judg-
> ment of the case at hand.
>
> The Eldest of the Jews in Litzmannstadt.
> Litzmannstadt Ghetto, 15 March 1941

The above announcement bore the signature "Mordechai Chaim Rumkowski."

◆ ◆ ◆

Though it is certainly the case that *inter arma silent leges*—in wartime, the law falls silent—crimes do not. It is especially important, in fact, during wartime, when the smallest violation can unleash terrible consequences, to nip crime in the bud. When there's no time to fiddle with investigations and with legal niceties, a judicial authority must be established with enough power to keep time with the drumbeat of war. Courts of summary judgment must be established. If you've committed a crime—you pay! Pay with your head, with your freedom— whatever it takes! With so much innocent life being cut short at the battlefront, no kind of criminal activity whatsoever can be allowed to go unpunished behind the lines. When a crime has been committed, the price must be paid, and it must be a heavy one: *dura lex, sed lex*— the law is harsh, but it's the law.

Many serious crimes have been committed in the ghetto. The most grave of all occurred when people who had worked year after year, supported by their culture and its civilization—which themselves had taken thousands of years to produce—when those same people were transformed into beasts of prey after half a year of life under inhuman conditions. Overnight, every ethical impulse they possessed became foreign to them as they lost any sense of shame. Ghetto inhabitants chiseled and cheated at every opportunity, regardless of whether they needed the loot or not. While some starved to death, some rooted in the garbage like pigs, looking for any piece of trash they could find, hoping to pounce and gobble it up on the spot, while others took every chance they got to steal, pilfer, eat, and guzzle.[1]

Money was even stolen from the Jewish community's funds and from the provisions that people spent their blood, sweat, and tears laying aside, stolen from the food warehouses meant to be shared equally by the whole concentration camp—the ghetto itself. Two different

1. The language here evokes Deuteronomy 21 and its description of the defiant sons, whose punishment was death.

pictures of the social situation soon emerged. Like miserable horses, some people hitched themselves to little wagons, finding work by carting filthy objects, feces, and other trash. Working fourteen to sixteen hours a day and sometimes round the clock, these dung haulers clung to wagons whose stench could be smelled miles away—doing the worst kind of work to earn a few measly groschen, which wouldn't even buy them a decent meal. Meanwhile, other people sauntered leisurely about with their hands in their pockets. Having gotten the plum posts in the ghetto administration, their only real job was to figure out how much they could steal and where they could steal it from—that is, without anyone else noticing that they were stealing.

Serious crimes have been committed in the ghetto, where the normal rules that constrain human behavior no longer apply. The ghetto is now under the sway of the law of the jungle—the notion of "do it to the guy next to you before he does it to you." Whoever is stronger pushes ahead and shunts whoever is weaker into the abyss. Forcing the head of the other under is the price of keeping yourself on higher ground.

It was clear to everyone that crimes had to be dealt with severely, even if eliminating them meant a court of summary judgment that would levy punishments in an indiscriminate manner. For as everyone knows and as the Yiddish proverb puts it so succinctly, "as the Christians sing, so sing the Jews."[2] What remains incomprehensible, however, is why the ghetto cast its net so wide but never very deep. Why were such vigorous measures quickly enforced against the criminals but never against the obvious cause of their crimes? It's obvious that someone who gets a job in the ghetto—and hence the chance to support himself, at least to all appearances, then uses his job like a crook to butter his own bread or to load up his soup while others get gruel—it's obvious that such a person requires punishment. In fact, the punishment would have to be severe in order to set an example for

2. *Az es yidlt zikh azoy, vi es kristlt zikh,* a version of the Yiddish proverb that can be traced back to the *Sefer Hasidim* of R. Judah HeHasid of Regensburg (c. 1150–1217). In its German-Jewish form the proverb is commonly attributed to Heinrich Heine.

all those with similar ideas. But can anyone understand why no one ever tried paying the ghetto's workers and officials a wage that would allow them to survive in the first place so they wouldn't have to steal to live?

It's possible to understand how, with the overload of cases on the docket, a court of summary judgment might be required. A normal court runs at a plodding pace as it brings the guilty to justice, while a summary court could take swift and immediate action against criminals, keeping them from committing a second or third offense before their punishment finally took effect. What remains incomprehensible, however, is how life-and-death judgments can be handed out so quickly and casually and without careful reflection and consideration. In short, the people responsible make these determinations in the same way all such decisions in the ghetto are made.

It is perhaps understandable that people who no longer remember they were created in God's image would transform themselves into predators, wolfing down the food set aside for others, and that they would have to be disciplined, sent to prison, or even kept in a cell with chains around their necks. What is incomprehensible is the treatment of their dependents. Why should their wives and children, along with the actual criminals themselves, be sentenced to what was effectively death by starvation? Why would the harsh verdicts of the summary court against the accused include his dismissal from work in almost all cases and thus put an end to his family's sole source of support?

It is understandable—the name "court of summary judgment" already says as much—that such a court could not investigate every detail of the crimes on its docket, as a court in peacetime might. What is incomprehensible, however, is why those named as judges, even those of goodwill, were far from up to the task. It takes a certain kind of person to grasp the psychological makeup and motivation of a criminal and the circumstances of the case and thus be able to come up with a punishment that actually fits the crime. Those appointed to the court had none of these skills. In fact, the incompetence of these "judges" was exacerbated by the conditions in which the tribunal worked. Sessions were held only at night, after members of the court had already put in a full day's work themselves. In this tense and exhausted state, the judges ran the court of summary judgment as if it were a revolutionary tribunal. Just as incomprehensible is the fact that of the two youths chosen to sit on the court, one has no life experience whatsoever, no humanity, and lacks even the most rudimentary aspects of intelligence. It's also hard to understand why most of the toughest cases were actually judged by an insolent young man who defined "criminality" according to his own warped criteria. Nor can any answer be given as to how the net cast in the ghetto swamp to snare "any and all types of criminal activity harmful to the essential interests of the ghetto community" manages to snag only the tiny minnows, while the big fish, fat and revolting, were able to swim along to their heart's content, swallowing their prey as they went along.

◆ ◆ ◆

Here are some of the crimes sentenced by the summary court:

A tailor, for instance, worked in a ghetto *resort* at his own machine, using tools he had been forced to turn over to his place of employment.[3] As a result, he was no longer permitted to take his tools out of the shop. To run afoul of the court, all the tailor had to do was to stick a pair of scissors in his pocket to keep them handy, then absentmindedly forget to remove them before heading home. Workers are searched when they leave their place of employment, and in this case, a quick look was all they needed to discover the scissors and charge the tailor with a crime worth bringing before the summary court. Because this tailor was an average Joe of a tailor who couldn't invent some excuse on the spot that would satisfy that sharp-witted, arrogant youth then sitting in judgment over him, he was sentenced to death by starvation, together with his entire family.

Similar stories abound. A tailor who stuck a piece of thread in his pocket for a moment, to keep it from being used by another worker sitting nearby, forgot to take it out of his pocket when leaving work that day, committing a crime considered worthy of being brought before the summary court. Another tailor had learned at his father's knee

3. *Ressort*, or factory, was a shortened version of the German term *Arbeitsressort*, meaning "work section" or "workplace."

that downing a shot was not a sin but a way of "laying a good foundation," and so he made it his standard working procedure: he'd down a shot of schnapps before and after work. The same tailor took it for granted that in the ghetto he could use a bit of leftover thread to fix a torn pocket on his pants. Before long he was caught in the act, brought before the court of summary judgment, and sentenced. A carpenter who cut a piece of wood at the carpentry shop to fix a broken table or cabinet at home was also apprehended as a thief and was sentenced by the court.

Here, however, are some crimes for which no one was apprehended and for which, therefore, no charges were brought before the court. The managers of the food shops—with the help of the officials of the Jewish community, who were on the take—managed to take a cut of the freshest and best of the food meant for the population as a whole for themselves. To make up the deficit they'd deceive their "customers" with rigged weights and measures. These sorts of thieves, strolling the streets and alleys of the ghetto in perfect freedom, were never pursued by the officials of the court of summary judgment and never subject to justice in any way, shape, or form. The managers of the food department—from its leading officials down to the lowest clerk—let thousands of kilos of potatoes and other vegetables rot intentionally in order to hide the shortfalls in the warehouses that their thievery had caused and which the paperwork would have eventually brought to light. Hundreds of wagons laden with potatoes were diverted in the dark of night, their contents dumped in the ghetto trash because their rotted loads had gone to ruin: all this could be laid at the door of those who managed the ghetto's food. These officials had on their conscience hundreds of Jews who had starved to death. But they were never brought before the court.

People with connections took bribes to get good jobs for idlers and loafers. Meanwhile many residents of the ghetto with the best heads on their shoulders and the most skilled and healthy hands could find absolutely nothing to do and simply died of hunger. These same "well-respected" individuals were considered to be "admirable Jews" and were never brought before the court. The same was true of the shops. The owners who decorated their display windows with the best and

most attractive items were the same ones who gouged their customers. They bought themselves brilliant, precious gems and jewelry by
speculating in the basest way on items essential to survival, and all
this at the expense of the poor and the sick; these owners were considered upstanding citizens in the ghetto and were never charged with
a thing. Once—perhaps it was a mistake—the notorious and tragic
scam known in the ghetto as the "potato affair" came onto the docket
of the court. The arrogant young man who served as judge simply
used the occasion to demonstrate his unmitigated gall: he took a bribe
and declared the accused to be innocent of all charges.

Gedalia had worked as a tailor for as long as he could remember
and came to the ghetto after having been given ten minutes to vacate
his home. He brought a wife and four children with him, probably
carrying his thimble and tailor's tape in his pocket and little else, and
of course he also entered the ghetto with a pair of healthy, well-worn
hands. When the ghetto opened its clothes factory he had to wait several long months to get hired, had to wait until everyone who'd never
stitched a stitch with a needle and thread, and thus had to bribe the
manager of the *ressort* or had inside pull with them or their underlings,
had already been taken on. Only when all these unqualified workers
had their jobs guaranteed did Gedalia receive his seat at the tailor's
bench, and only then did he begin to earn from two to three marks for
ten or twelve hours work a day.

Gedalia worked all through the winter and was satisfied. At home it
was cold and dark, and when he worked in the shop it was warm and
well lit. After work he'd sit at his bench an extra half hour or hour just
to spend less time at home. Gedalia worked through the spring and
was satisfied. At home the walls, now exposed to the rays of the sun,
began to drip and weep with the wet, and as they trickled their tears
onto his heart and into his lungs, his life became cold and damp. But
in the shop where he worked it was dry and homey: the sun shined,
the machines hummed, and his life was dampened mostly by sweat,
not by tears. And Gedalia would sit there an extra half hour, then an
hour, after work just to spend a little less time at home.

Gedalia worked and was satisfied by the knowledge that his arms
were no longer useless appendages hanging limp on either side of his

body, like tens of thousands of others in the ghetto. He was equally satisfied with his backbreaking work and the paltry sum that he earned, until one day as he was leaving the shop, the man assigned to frisk him and all the other workers from head to toe by sticking his hands in their pockets discovered some thread. The sewing thread had not been hidden—the swath had been hanging on his shoulder while he worked, to be ready as needed. The only difference this time was how it looked: Gedalia had carelessly thrown his jacket on over his shirt when it was time to leave, with the thread still hanging there, invisible, between his jacket and his shirt.

For this crime, which was really nothing more than an oversight, Gedalia was immediately led away from work under arrest, with nothing to eat or drink, and sentenced by the court of summary judgment as follows:

1. Three months confinement and hard labor
2. Banishment from future employment
3. Cancellation of his family's social support.

A tiny piece of a swath of thread, impossible for Gedalia to have felt hanging on his shoulder, now pressed his head to the ground as if it were an enormous burden; the same tiny, insignificant piece of thread had meant his downfall—or so the court had held.

Dura lex, sed lex. And Gedalia, whether he wanted to or not, had to bow his head and submit.

But Menashe, his sixteen-year-old son, who'd been apprenticed to his father for three years, had not yet finished grade school and so hardly understood Latin at all. This same Menashe was also unable to understand what they wanted from his father. He couldn't understand why they'd printed his name in the "Pillar of Shame" column in the ghetto newspaper and treated him as if he were a common criminal—an out-and-out thief.[4] Menashe, however, refused to bow his sixteen-year-old head. But the sorrow that tore at his heart all day long

4. In 1941 a ghetto newspaper called *Geto-tsaytung* [Ghetto Newspaper] was published.

would finally get to him in his bed at night, where he'd tear his hair out. Hair, however, is light and easy to pull, unlike the stony sorrow he could never push from his heart. Menashe spent whole days running from office to office, pounding on every door and gate of justice in the ghetto. And finding no ear for his claims and his laments, Menashe found madness instead. Tattered, ragged, and barefoot, he haunted the ghetto streets, piercing everyone he met with the gaze of his fiery eyes, and whenever he ran into someone wearing a yellow armband on his wanderings he'd pose the question: "Excuse me, you look like a community official. Is the court somewhere nearby? Is it?"

He'd stop every official he met and ask each one the same question. But he'd stopped waiting for the answer. He already knew the answer by heart, having heard it a hundred times before: "A nutcase! Looking for a department of justice in the ghetto! You think we've got that kind of office here?" Menashe made his mad dashes up and down the ghetto until he reached the barbed wire. In his insanity, perhaps he was simply looking for madness on the other side of the fence. Or perhaps, in his despair, he had no idea what he was doing at all. In any event, the soldier standing guard at his post was indifferent. He simply took aim with his rifle, as if lining up a mad dog in his sights, and shot him down on the spot.

His mother voiced the following lament: "There were six of us when we came to the ghetto, and we starved. Now we are only four, praised be the Holy Name: my husband jailed like a common thief, my son shot dead, and once again we've got nothing to eat . . ."

I do not know the laws and regulations, Riva Bramson, on which the court of summary judgment based its decisions. Be that as it may, announcement number 233 stated in black on yellow, "The court panel will issue verdicts based on its own independent judgment of the case at hand." Since this was a matter of "independent judgment," we can assume that the judge was convinced of Gedalia's guilt and rendered a verdict consistent with the dictates of his conscience. Therefore, Riva Bramson, if you filled out your form with "social support absolutely necessary" for Gedalia's family—having been visibly moved by this women's tears—cross it out. Though you're unfamiliar with the following Talmudic principles—"Claims against the court of justice are null and void," "A ruling of the court is final," and "Let justice be done though the heavens fall"—you've been lucky enough, unlike Menashe, to finish high school and university and are quite a scholar of Latin, so you'll understand what the motto means: *Dura lex, sed lex.*[5]

5. Ironic application of the Talmudic phrase (B. Sanhedrin 6b) *Yikov hadin et hahar,* literally, "Let the judgment pierce the mountain."

In the Bałuty Apartments, Łódź Ghetto

♦♦♦ *The Messiah Will Be Very Late:*
In the Twenty-Fourth Apartment

It's not just the outer world, Riva Bramson, that looks different in the ghetto kingdom—not just the tattered faces that look like death masks. The pressure of ghetto existence has utterly transformed the whole Jewish attitude toward life.

Have you had a chance to observe the way burials are conducted in the ghetto? No people anywhere in the world speaking any language whatsoever have, under any circumstances, ever conducted their burials the way final rites are performed here. Decent people bury pet dogs with more dignity than human beings today receive in the ghetto. Do you think it doesn't hurt to see wagons moving down the street, just as industrial trucks rumbled down them in the good old days, carrying material to the city's factories? Doesn't it hurt to recall this today, when wagons stop at almost every other building, swallow up two corpses, then leave two more in a pile before moving on, returning half an hour later for the rest? The pain is immense, Riva Bramson! Do you think hearts don't shudder when someone comes to a cemetery and sees the endless rows of corpses stacked on the ground, wrapped in burial shrouds and waiting day after day to be laid to rest—all because the gravediggers can't keep up? Your heart expires in your chest, Riva Bramson! You think your head could bear the thought of the meager, shallow little grave they finally dig, which the tiniest cat or smallest dog could easily unearth? Your head explodes on the spot!

Eyes burst into tears when they watch the way a corpse is laid to rest here: tossed into the hole in the ground the way they used to dump a load of dirty laundry into the kettle to be washed. He's wrapped in rags with a rotten board under his back—a rotten piece of wood that will later be stolen to warm a spoonful of soup for someone still alive. Later they will frantically rush to fill the grave because there's a freshly dug grave right next to it; another corpse that must be hastily and frantically buried is already waiting and next to that a third, and a fourth, a tenth, and more. The gravedigger, who works on contract and gets paid "by the piece," or "by the head," as they say in his trade, has neither the time, the energy, nor the sensitivity to provide the kind of burial that even a pet dog would get.

That even a *dog* would get, Riva Bramson!

Who robbed the Jews of their sense of piety toward the dead, nurtured in their hearts for centuries? Who transformed their way of looking at the world so radically and completely—their very self-image?

Wasn't it the ghetto, Riva Bramson?

The ghetto—that denial of the culture and civilization the people had built over the centuries—has already, in its short existence, erased the boundary between holiness and crass indignity as well as the boundary between what is yours and what is mine, between the permissible and the prohibited, between right and wrong. But don't think for a moment, Riva Bramson, that this erasure of boundaries has not exacted its price in blood and spirit as well! Our ability to recall those limits has not been forgotten, just numbed and frozen—and how!

Take, for instance, the case of Jacob Eli. When the people of his town fled to the ghetto as if escaping from a raging fire, each person grabbed his most precious possession from among their belongings, since it was impossible to save it all. Jacob Eli took the most precious possession he could bring: his Gemara, the part of the Talmud that is commentary on Jewish law (the Mishnah). Others grabbed their beds, their bedding, jewelry, or their money. Wives took their laundry and clothes, their kitchen implements—but Jacob Eli took his Gemara.

Jacob Eli saw how quickly the memories people brought with them from home were erased. He saw people chopping their beds into chunks of firewood, selling their bedding and their jewelry for a tiny, rotten morsel of bread, and how quickly money disappeared. He saw how swiftly clothes became rags in the ghetto, how fast dresses grew mildewed and rotten from hanging on the wet ghetto walls, and how furnishings were abandoned, unable to fit in the small ghetto rooms. After seeing all this, Jacob Eli held fast to his Gemara, his remnant and survivor from another world, and pressed it all the closer to his heart. Though its pages had yellowed and faded, and the ghetto's dampness had swollen those pages into bulges at certain spots, looking like a handkerchief overused by someone with a cold, Jacob Eli still treated them as if they were fresh furrows in a fertile field. The yellowed pages reminded him of the yellow patch he wore on his chest and on his back: they reminded him of his Jewishness. So he chanted his Talmudic melody, his *nigun*, with a little more sadness but also more heart and inner devotion.

For the ghetto itself hadn't made Jacob Eli melancholy: he accepted it as a punishment he somehow merited, delighting like a child when punished by his parents: like a child who knows that after his punishment has been meted out they will love him the same as before. This was not the only reason, however, that Jacob Eli took delight in the ghetto. He saw in the ghetto the "beginning of Redemption" as he'd often dreamt of it. He'd imagined the ghetto as part of the "ingathering of exiles," a space peopled by Jews—just Jews, and he would be one of them.[1] And if it turned out not to feel anything like the true ingathering of exiles, that didn't bother him at all. He had time, Jacob Eli did, and he could wait. In the meantime, until the day of the Messiah's coming, he was more than happy to sit there, come what may, for he was far from alone. He was spending his time with his friends and teachers—with the sages Abbaya, Rava and Rav Huna, and Rav Ashi of old.[2] They'd gone into exile with him and would never desert him, just as Job's friends had never abandoned him in his sorrows.

1. In Jewish messianic thought, both the reestablishment of the sovereignty of Israel and the "ingathering of exiles" are seen as necessary preconditions for the coming of the messiah.
2. These are names of Talmudic sages frequently cited in the Gemara text.

Job, however, had meditated on his situation, challenged God, and cursed the day he was born. Jacob Eli, in opposite fashion, praised God and thanked him, taking delight in the punishment he had "earned," leaving out one small fact: that he was hungry. But when had Jacob Eli not been hungry? He had always fasted during the "in between" periods of his study regimen. Jacob Eli had always worked hard in the *shtibl*—and between tending the stove and the ritual washing of hands, he strove to tame his flesh, trying to teach it to contract to the smallest possible point![3]

Jacob Eli had his own method of controlling his material self with a logic of its own: since "'the more flesh, the more worms,' it stands to reason that the less flesh there was on which the worms can feed, the healthier the soul will be. Because we cannot be free of the flesh regardless of whether we care for its pleasures or not, while the soul is harried by terrors on every side, pushing it toward the nether world."[4] He therefore neglected his body entirely, letting it go until it dwindled to the size of a slat of wood, trying to transform it into nothing more than a framework to hold his soul, and took that soul into his hands. Jacob Eli walked around as if he were protecting a precious stone, treating his soul as if it were the apple of his eye. If his flesh now and then made its presence felt in a bitter feeling that rose from his empty stomach, he'd throw it a bone as if it were an angry dog. More often than not, however, with the help of his teachers and friends he'd chase the flesh away as he would an irritating fly.

Abbaya, Rava and Rav Huna, and Rav Ashi—he could count on them every time. And whenever he asked the sages for their help, they were sure to answer: "Oy," Abbaya said.

"Oy," Rava chimed in once more.

It never took much pleading for them to help him in his bitter struggle with the flesh, that angry bill collector who wanted to rip his soul from his hands and pawn it for a little slice of bread. That's how it was with Jacob Eli when he first entered the ghetto walls, when the stones

3. A *shtibl* (literally "little room") is a small, often informal Hasidic house of prayer.
4. Wisdom of the Sages (*Pirkei Avot*), a section of the Talmud often printed separately, 2:8.

of the ghetto streets did not yet echo with the story of his hunger. Even at the very beginning, however—when people still had possessions they'd brought from the city and could trade them for food—at the very beginning, when people were still getting food packages in the mail from relatives and gobbling them up—even then Jacob Eli went hungry.

But in those days he still had enough strength in his physical self to laugh. "The land (though disconnected fields) is one block" was his principle; that is, it's the same world everywhere—the city and the ghetto are one and the same.[5] "If I mastered the flesh in the city," he reasoned, "I can do the same, God willing, right here." All the more so, given that he hadn't yet been abandoned and was still being supported by his friends, just like before. Jacob Eli, however, had made an error in his calculations. With every passing day, he sensed his body getting the upper hand on his soul. His friends began to act more like strangers, a fact that caused him great pain. Soon Jacob Eli began to feel the agony of his death throes approaching, and he writhed in the clutches of hunger like a fly in a spider's web.

"Oy," said Abbaya.

"Oy," Rava chimed in once more.

Their sayings began to slip his mind the way the shoes on your feet slide out from under you while walking on ice. Lines from the Talmud were no longer fertile furrows, producing green fields through which he strolled free as a bird, but frosty chunks of plowed earth in his path, getting underfoot, tripping him up, and leaving him spent. Jacob Eli is exhausted, worn out from a hunger that bores through him like a dull drill, exhausted from his wife, who coughs and sighs the whole night through. He's exhausted from watching the sorrows of his three adult daughters, hanging around the apartment with downcast eyes that are full of shame. He's exhausted by his twenty-two-year-old boy, Aaron Meyer, who's got no idea what to do with himself. He's even exhausted by his youngest son, Mendel, who's barely grown up at all, already fourteen years old and still crying like a mama's boy: "Mama, I'm so hungry. Mama, if you only knew how hungry I am!"

5. B. Talmud, Tractate Baba Kama 12b.

Since he knew how to contend with his own hunger, however, Jacob Eli finally uttered the following declaration: "I will not accept any food from the public kitchen, since I can't be sure that they're strictly observing the laws of kashruth." So he took no food and ate none. But how could he force his views on others—the flesh of his flesh and blood of his blood, when he'd grown so weak that he barely had the power to utter a single word? Giving his shoulders a final shrug, he gave in when the women decided to line up for soup from the public kitchen using dishes from their own house.

Then it came out that his wife, his own Sarah, had secretly taken their youngest, Mendel, under her wing and given him some food from the kitchen that wasn't strictly kosher.

Men, Riva Bramson, are not generally prone to crying, and Jacob Eli was even less inclined in this direction. If he ever did break into tears, it was not to lament his sorrows and woes but only when pouring out his soul when swaying in prayer on Yom Kippur.[6] And though Jacob Eli hardly ever cried, he did so more frequently in the ghetto. The first time occurred when Mendel ate soup from the public kitchen. The second time, he cried along with Mendel when he heard him say, "Mama, I'm hungry."

At that point, there weren't even a few pfennigs in the house to give Mendel to go out and buy a little soup. The third time he cried was when he learned that Mendel had been accepted to school where, aside from the lunch he received each day, he would receive once-weekly allotments of horsemeat.[7] From that point forward his tears, along with his blood and mind, felt as if they were frozen, and he could no longer cry. As a result, he didn't cry when he learned that Aaron Meyer was eating food that was heinous and strictly forbidden—*treyf.* He didn't cry when his daughters brought food for the Sabbath from the public kitchen actually cooked on the Sabbath itself, and he didn't even shed a tear when his middle daughter, who'd worked for several weeks in one of the *ressorts,* brought home a ration of horsemeat she'd received at work.

6. The Day of Atonement, when Jews pray for forgiveness of their sins of the previous year.
7. Eating horsemeat is a violation of the laws of kashruth.

He didn't cry, but he did plunge his soft fingernails into his own heart, struggling with his last ounces of strength to sustain his soul and keep it from falling under the sway of the flesh. Until one day Jacob Eli fell from weakness, and after fainting became severely ill. He was taken to the hospital, where he lost consciousness and where, by giving him enough food, they were able to get him back on his feet and send him home. Since then he sits at home at his little table like someone who isn't really there. A Talmud volume lies open in front of him. He looks at the pages, and the lines of print dance before his eyes. Doesn't Jacob Eli understand the connection between his stomach and his vision? He doesn't wish to understand what the doctors tried to "convince" him to believe: that malnutrition has left his eyes dim and dark. Nor does he understand the injustice he has done to his friends, who no longer want to speak freely and openly with him, as they'd always done before. So he often asks Aaron Meyer for help.

Jacob Eli has already given up fourteen-year-old Mendel for lost. He treats him like a piece of his own heart that's been cut out. He's gone to a school where he receives a piece of horsemeat once a week, and there he gobbles it down. Mendel no longer cares about being Jewish, and who knows whether he ritually washes his hands in the morning and whether he says his morning prayers? To Jacob Eli, it feels as if Mendel were a living piece of him ripped from his flesh. The agonizing wound torments him, leaving his face continually distorted in pain. But Jacob Eli assumes these travails with love and devotion: he's not ready to give up on Aaron Meyer yet. So he holds Aaron Meyer in his hands as tightly as he once held his own soul. And each time that his eyes or his mind goes dark, he calls out to him, "Aaron Meyer? Hey! Where are you, Aaron Meyer?"

But what is so important about Aaron Meyer, alas, to him? The real question to Jacob Eli is a different one: Can he still get his failing mind to grasp intellectual giants like Abbaya and Rava and Rav Huna and Rav Ashi? Meanwhile, Aaron Meyer's sagging shoulders have taken on the full weight of the ghetto exile. His pale face has already turned a shade of yellow; not the yellow of wax—in fact, a healthy color—but the yellow tint of the thinnest straw, a feverish, sickly color. On his head, a few hairs shoot out from what looks like sparse, sandy ground, which before turning their normal color have already begun to turn gray. A twenty-two-year-old young man with a thin, wispy beard that has already started to go gray, sallow cheeks, and a childish-looking head who nonetheless can look you down with two fiery, uneasy eyes. What could Aaron Meyer possibly do to help in this situation? His father still looks at him and begs, "Oh, Aaron Meyer, Aaron Meyer! You must still have your wits about you! Your mind must still be sharp—so tell me, just tell me, Aaron Meyer, what is it that Abbaya and Rava and Rav Huna and Rav Ashi want me to do? Tell me, Aaron Meyer!"

What could Aaron Meyer possibly say to him with the expression his wide-open eyes give his face? His only thoughts are dark ones and his dreams more ominous still. With hunger plaguing him day and night without interruption, what wisdom could he possibly confide? Wouldn't his words lack all logical order, pouring out instead in a complete jumble like poppy seeds scattered in the wind? What could he possibly tell Jacob Eli when Abbaya, Rava, Rav Huna, and Rav Ashi are already screaming at the top of their lungs, "Eat, Papa! Just eat!"

The father and son both sit there like yeshiva students caught in the act: Aaron Meyer's words fail to communicate anything comprehensible, thudding against his father's inability to understand like blind birds striking their little heads against a strange net. Afterward the son sits there with downcast eyes, saying nothing at all. But Jacob Eli issues an apology. "Yes indeed, kind sir, a fine end we've come to here in the ghetto. As we sit here and go hungry, our wits go cloudy on us, and there's no way we can understand what, or if, we . . ."

Do you understand what he's saying, Riva Bramson? The same Jacob Eli for whom the ghetto was a kind of merited punishment, who entered its walls with joy—the same Jacob Eli who fought for months against hunger, his most bitter and intractable enemy, and who had battled the flesh for decades and always come out on top . . . Jacob Eli has finally broken down. Finally he's begun to murmur against the dark place to which the ghetto has brought him: he's cursed God's name, almost as if he were Job.

But all you've heard are his statements, Riva Bramson. You haven't seen the blood it's cost him to reach the point where such things could be uttered out loud. Perhaps your delicate soul will be able to sense the tragedy that's befallen him. Perhaps only the good-hearted can sense the pain that speaks when he no longer minces his words: "That's the way it looks now, kind sir. The children of my house are not in the best of health. They've lain there the entire winter. And as soon as that one gets up, she's sick to her stomach right away. And every time I hear her swallow, it's as if a hole gets drilled in my heart. And three grown women, hanging around the apartment—don't you think that drags my head down? All three ready for the wedding canopy, and just take a look."

Jacob Eli speaks as if something has broken; words pour out of his mouth as if his subconscious had suddenly been laid bare. "You know what I mean, mister—I'm someone who's been happy to be a Jew his entire life, to extend the golden chain begun by our fathers' fathers another link, to serve the Almighty and await the coming of the Messiah. Someone like me thinks to himself, "So I'll enter the ghetto and live as a Jew among Jews—just Jews—you know what I mean? And what do these Jews go and do? They've turned everything upside down! Even the Messiah!—the Messiah they've been awaiting for two thousand years! Now they've gone into the ghetto and made themselves their own messiah! Just like in the desert long ago. Moses, our teacher, was gone for just one day, and that's all it took for them to go make a golden calf and to start dancing around—'These are thy gods, Israel!'[8] Here they've made themselves a messiah, put a green band around his cap, and put a bag on his shoulders.[9] People spend a lifetime waiting for their messiah, wondering why he's late and whether he'll give them ten marks a head for those older than fourteen and seven marks a head for those younger. Then it's the next morning after his coming, and those few marks—which don't bring an ounce of blessing with them, by the way—have disappeared like salt into water. So you sit again and wait, and then you wait some more . . . and is there any end in sight?"

Such is the voice of Jacob Eli, letting loose with all the words that have collected in his unconscious: these words full of bitter despair

8. Exodus 32:8; Hebrew in original.
9. Jacob Eli is here describing the ghetto postman.

and saturated with doubt are ones that Jacob Eli, the faithful believer, could never have brought to his lips. So you address his conscious mind directly and ask him a question that it cannot evade: "And you— you're the only one who's not waiting for this modern-day messiah?"

His answer is sharp and unequivocal—both dismissive and serious as well: "What's the use of waiting for him? He almost never comes, and even then, isn't he always very, very late?"

What's the use of all the labor and energy Jacob Eli has invested over the years, Riva Bramson—what's the use if a year and a half of ghetto life has been enough to transform his innermost essence, bringing him to turn his back on everything he's lived for until now?

♦♦♦ Twenty-Five Chickens and One Dead Document

Through a cock and a hen Tur Malka was destroyed.
—*Babylonian Talmud*, Tractate Gittin 57a[1]

History loves to repeat itself. Its nuances, however, can be found in documents, though it is the nature of such documents either to tell us too much, and so to hide those nuances from us, or to tell us too little, so that their story must be enlarged by oral tradition. Documents are often so laconic in their tone, so dry, and seem so devoid of anything important to relate that they might as well be discarded, with nothing to be carefully considered and nothing remembered. But beware of those little scraps of paper that seem to tell us nothing at all. Don't throw them away until you've examined and researched them thoroughly.

Should you come across an unimportant, meaningless scrap of paper like the following, for example:

1. The line from the Talmud is quoted in the original Aramaic. Zelkowicz is referring to the Talmudic discussion of how seemingly minor incidents can have catastrophic repercussions. In this case an altercation between Jews and Roman soldiers over some fowls set off a train of events that led to the destruction of Jerusalem in the second century CE.

At approximately 7 o'clock on Shabbat, twenty-five live chickens were seized at 19 Podrzeczna Street and brought to the HIOD. In consultation with Rozenblat, they were disposed of as follows:

13 hens left on-site

6 hens to Drewnowska Street

1 hen—Rozenblat

5 hens, i.e., 20 meal portions—distributed to HIOD.[2]

Do not, under any circumstances—though it is unsigned, undated, and written in pencil—throw it away. Such a scrap of paper can sometimes be a very important document.

Though it says nothing at all, such a piece of paper can sometimes represent a crucial confirmation of the saying *Vox populi, vox dei*.[3]

Such a dry and almost mute scrap of paper, discovered among junky old books, will illuminate—if you know how to read it properly—one of the ghetto's most murderous and tragic stories and bring it right before your eyes.

It's the story of twenty-four who perished senselessly, for absolutely nothing at all—twenty-four Jews.

It's the story of twenty-four human beings whose lives came to an end in the street, as if they were rabid dogs.

It's a story of twenty-four human beings shot down by a beast over a period of several days.

The little scrap of paper, found by chance in the ghetto archive, makes no mention of twenty-four murdered Jews; it speaks only of twenty-five live chickens. The Department of Vital Statistics tells us a little something—numbers are its business. Shot and killed in July

2. The Jewish police organization in the Łódź ghetto was established by the Germans on March 1, 1940, and was called the Ordnungsdienst, or Order Service; its commander was Leon Rozenblat. HIOD was the Hilfsordnungsdienst, or Auxiliary Order Police, which was to supervise children in the streets, fight against prohibited street trade, and maintain order at ration distribution shops. It was dissolved on November 3, 1940. See Isaiah Trunk, *Łódź Ghetto: A History*, translated and edited by Robert Moses Shapiro, introduction by Israel Gutman (Bloomington: Indiana University Press, 2006 [1962]), p. 42.

3. Latin proverb: "The voice of the people is the voice of God."

1940: twenty men and fifteen women. Total: thirty-five people. The details: their given names, family names, ages, occupations, and causes of death can be found in the burial department of the Jewish community, if you rummage through the roughly fourteen hundred death entries recorded for the month of July.

The actual story, however—and the logical connection between twenty-five live chickens and those who were shot dead—must be learned from the mouths of the people and begins with a *sheygetz* from the city.[4] He was a *sheygetz*, a city boy, though born and raised in Zielony Rynek among Jews. It was there, in Zielony Rynek, that he came to be known by the name "redheaded Janek," and it was there, after considering his situation carefully one day, that he decided to become a turncoat and transform himself into an ethnic German, or Volksdeutscher.

As a Volksdeutscher, since all Jewish doors were open to him, he made it his business to barge in wherever he pleased, and without fear of any consequences, to plunder any Jewish possessions that caught his eye. And as a Volksdeutscher he was free to snatch Jews off the street for forced labor, with some paying him off willingly or having their pockets emptied by him when they refused. As a Pole bred and born, Janek was probably familiar with the Polish proverb *Nie masz gorszego chama, jak ze sługi pana*—that is, "There is no worse boor than a servant turned lord." And through his actions he labored mightily to confirm what the common folk have always known: from a lowly porter brought up in Zielony Rynek, and a life hauling sacks for the Jews, Janek had been reborn a prince.

In constant wailing and woe when the noose of hauling sacks had been pulled tight round his shoulders, Janek the Volksdeutscher could now saunter about midweek in his Sunday best and drink himself silly whenever he pleased. Where before Janek had hauled hundred-kilogram sacks for twenty groschen apiece, now his pants pockets—that once contained the beans he managed to steal from Jewish shops for his pigeons—are stuffed with twenty-mark notes. Before, Janek had to beg for the round beans or steal them. More often than not he

4. *Sheygetz* is a Yiddish term for a Gentile lad.

stole them. When caught, he'd get a rap right across his paws or a slap on the snout. Today those twenty-mark notes are handed over to him in a docile and willing fashion, and when the giver is not willing or quick enough Janek lays into him from head to toe.

When Janek received slaps for his petty thefts they were delivered with a sense of justice and mercy. The few beans he nabbed didn't amount to much, they were nothing—but the redheaded dog needed to learn what not to touch, so raps across the knuckles and little slaps were what he received. Janek was happy enough, since his punishment felt like little more than a fleabite to him and the Jews were satisfied as well, since they imagined they'd taught the thief a lesson. When Janek hits you, however, he understands neither justice nor mercy. He never goes halfway. Janek loves blood. Lots of blood.

That's our Janek: straightforward. A black-or-white kind of guy. As a porter, he carried sacks for a few groschen apiece, lived on dry crusts of bread, and kept the leftover coins from his earnings wrapped in a rag until Sunday came, and on Sunday, he'd use those savings to drink himself silly. As a porter he wouldn't hurt a fly, even when drunk. As a prince, however, a twenty-mark bill was suddenly small change to him, and every smack and blow he deals out as he walks about must be a wet one, soaked in blood. Lots of blood.

"Bravo, Janek! *Aut Caesar aut nihil!*"[5] Bravo, Janek! You've convincingly acquired the qualities of a real live German! Bravo, Janek! You've decked yourself out like the real thing, a young and wanton beast. You've transformed yourself into a dog who grabs what he wants even when you give it to him and snatches it away from you when you don't—into a dog that lusts for blood. Well done, Janek! You're a real German now! But woe be unto you, Janek! Now that you've played the young beast so convincingly, they've decided to place a muzzle on your snout. Woe be unto you, Janek! No sooner have you become a real live German than you have fallen prey to the Germans' own economic logic—to the Germans' special economic gift for not letting a single piece of trash or crap go to waste. And even for turning crap into merchandise!

5. Latin adage: "Either a Caesar or nothing!"

In the old days, Janek was such a sad sack that he couldn't even manage to carry one properly—he was little more than a stray and mangy dog. Still, he was good enough to protect German law and order. For as long as you could hang a rifle on his shoulder and place a policeman's cap on his head, Janek could be turned into a German police official—and stand guard over Jewish life in the ghetto. As a German policeman (it goes without saying that he now called himself Johann), he was posted in one of the guard huts at the ghetto boundary, with the job of preventing any Jews from escaping. Still, he never felt comfortable in his uniform, given how different it was from the tattered rags he was used to wearing. No dog likes having a muzzle placed on his snout. By then, all his twenty-mark notes were long gone. And with all Jews now having been forced into the ghetto, there was nowhere else to look. Somehow Janek had to get by on the paltry policeman's salary. And you can't go get drunk when you have to do guard duty—stand guard like a dog on a chain. Janek wasn't used to it—he was a street mutt who liked to grab what he could.

And street mutts hate having chains placed around their necks. They'll always struggle against it until one of two things happens: either the chain breaks or, if the chain is stronger, the dog goes mad.

So Janek kept pulling and yanking at his chain. The more rebellious and disobedient he became, however, the less he was able to show that rebellion openly, since he would have been shot down like a rabid dog. So he swallowed his gall and kept it muzzled until life became bitter in his much-reduced world. Though he stood on the other side of the wire with the entire world open to him—to him, that world felt as if it had been narrowed, as if he were one of those on the inside of the ghetto with only a pittance to eat, felt like those with only the tiniest crumb or the most minuscule scrap of garbage to call their own. Now the Janek used to scooping up cash with both hands and drinking it up even faster was thirsty ever since being stuffed into his uniform. It felt as if his tongue had dried out and been stuck to his palate: full of gall, his mouth felt like a dried-out piece of clay—gall mixed with clay.

Janek craved—he thirsted for—freedom. He longed for the days not so long ago when twenty-mark notes could be harvested with ease. Dim-witted as he was, he started to use his small, piggish blue eyes to look for them even there—even there next to his guard booth, to which he'd been chained like a guard dog. Even there, right at the border of the ghetto.

One day as he was standing there, his dry tongue hanging out of his mouth like a thirsty animal, he happened to notice the redheaded Leyzer. They barely recognized each other: redheaded Janek, crammed into his uniform, looked like an entirely new man. When redheaded Leyzer had his flour business in Zielony Rynek he knew Janek as a good-for-nothing *sheygetz* porter, dressed in tattered clothes and running around barefoot, his hollow cheeks studded with thick, reddish pig bristles. Only on Sundays would Janek put on his single decent black suit, bought four years ago off the rack in the Old Town; on Sundays, barefoot Janek would put on a pair of stiff red shoes. His chin would be freshly shaven, and the thick, reddish bristles he had for hair would be forced down into a kind of flattop, like nails forced back into the sole of a boot. On Sundays, however, Leyzer's shop had been closed, so he had never seen Janek decked out before. As a result, it never occurred to redheaded Leyzer that such a worthless wastrel— that sorry-looking scoundrel of a redheaded Polish *sheygetz*—could have become a German soldier with a rifle propped on his shoulder and could be standing guard duty over him.

When redheaded Leyzer had his flour business in Zielony Rynek, he also had quite a paunch. In summer he would wear a splendid alpaca cloak that shone like a polished mirror. His feet wore a pair of soft chamois boots with flexible toes. In winter he wore a fur coat made from beaver with a wide, skunk-lined collar. He wore felt-lined boots and sometimes galoshes but was always seen in his handsome, carefully tended red beard. As a result, it never occurred to redheaded Janek that the tattered, shabby, skin-and-bones Jew in front of him with the scraggly red, unkempt, and strange-looking beard was actually the wretched redheaded Leyzer from Zielony Rynek.

So they met, without either recognizing the other. But they had looked for each other too long not to recognize one another once they finally met up. To say that they had looked for each other doesn't mean, of course, that redheaded Leyzer had been looking for redheaded Janek in particular or that redheaded Janek had been looking for redheaded

Leyzer alone. Leyzer had been looking for a German soldier on the make who believed in the principle of live and let live—a soldier who, as they say in the jargon of the marketplace, would agree to get a little dirty and do some business on the side. Redheaded Janek, meanwhile, was looking for more Jews who might, before too long, supply him with twenty-mark notes.

They met face to face, albeit at a distance—with redheaded Leyzer on one side of the barbed wire and redheaded Janek on the other—staring at each other a long time, a good long while, the way a man and a woman look each other over on a deserted street at night. The man is not overly bold in his attentions in case she does not do that sort of business, while she strikes an offish pose so that, if he approaches her, she can demand a higher price. Only after they'd checked each other out silently—with Leyzer noting Janek's newfound stature and Janek recognizing Leyzer's steep decline—Janek looked around carefully, checked behind him and to either side, and when finally convinced that no one was watching, motioned to Leyzer to approach the fence: *"Jak się masz, Lejzer. Chodź, nie bój się"*—"How ya doin', Leyzer? It's all right, don't be afraid."

And so it went. Deep inside, Janek had not forgotten how enormous the gap had once been between them, and now he could address his former boss and employer *"per tu,"* in the same way he might talk to a child or to an inferior. Leyzer, for his part, wasn't shocked at all by this change in station and was even satisfied with this familiarity, this newfound proximity to the powers that be. Once our *sheygetz,* always our *sheygetz*—he's still just a farmhand. And so Leyzer approached him without fear. Janek, who had been raised on Jewish soil and had always lived among Jews and earned his living from them, had mastered several Yiddish expressions, such as *mamele* (mamma), *tatele* (daddy), a *shlak* (a bad turn), a *kholere* (a curse on you), a *kapore* (the hell with it), and the like. In an attempt to ingratiate himself, Janek thus used the following words: "You see how it is, Leyzer, the Jews have come under a *kholere;* it's a done deal. All your sacks of flour at Zielony Rynek, they're all ours now—it's all ours. The whole world is going to belong to us. I'm Johann—I'm a *pan,* a 'sir,' and you, Leyzer, are a mangy Jew, a lowly servant."

Leyzer got it right away: if Janek kept insulting him like this, it wouldn't be easy to make a deal. But tossing the insult back in Janek's face might cost him his life. Instead he needed to pass the time with him, carefully flatter Janek's ego ever so slightly, then give it a little nick—just a tiny one—and so start to lead him down the garden path. Letting a moment elapse before he answered, he emitted a deep sigh, as if to let him know, "You're right, Janek, we're in deep trouble." He then continued in Polish: *"Nie bój się, Janek. Tam, gdzie woda była, woda będzie, a gówniarz—gówniarzem się zostaje."* ("Don't be afraid, Janek. Where there once was water, there will be more water, and scum will always be scum.") That is, Janek, he who had money before will have it again, and a pig will always find the shit.

The conversation continued in this manner. With Leyzer trying to feel him out and Janek delivering a jab wherever he could, a kind of agreement eventually emerged. Janek would toss over the fence whatever he could buy in the city, Leyzer would resell the merchandise in the ghetto, and they would split the take. "You know how it goes, Janek: live and let live."

"Tak jest, panie Lejzer" ("That's right, Mr. Leyzer"), Janek replied in Polish. *"Tam, gdzie woda była, tam i będzie"* ("Where there once was water, there will be more"). "Money goes to money," he went on in Yiddish. "You'll get yours, I'll get mine," before going back to Polish once more. *"Jak kiedyś, pamięta Lejzer?"* ("Just like before, remember, Leyzer?")

The ghetto had just then been fenced in and cut off from the city, and the public had not yet grasped the real horror that awaited them. They were, so to speak, still in the honeymoon period of ghetto life and so resembled a young newlywed. Not yet having squandered his entire dowry, he chases one deal after another and eats his fill. Everything in the ghetto thus became a piece of merchandise. Everything the stomach could digest.

After all the turmoil in the city, the shooting of people in their homes during the *planmäßige Übersiedlung* (resettlement process), the kidnappings for forced labor, and the fear and dread of what the next day, or even the next hours, might bring, people in the ghetto—where Jews could be among their own—reveled in the *dolce fare niente,* or what the Italians call the pleasure of doing nothing. They gathered in the streets and alleys and exchanged good news, sat in the courtyards of their buildings playing cards, or stashed away the little bit of cash they'd been able to carry with them from the city and bought food. Prices rose by the day. But with so much Jewish property having been destroyed, and with the wedding having been so costly, as it were, a few more marks here and there hardly seemed like much of a sacrifice! There was food, and you could keep on getting it from the other side of the fence, though you'd pay a hefty price.

This was the period of "prosperity" in the ghetto—a prosperity in reverse. People were not earning, then spending, what they earned, for only a few were making anything at all: those who were shrewd enough to take risks and to engage in smuggling from the other side of the wire. Those without any income spent the last of their cash buying up everything they could, whether a piece of soap, a nail, sugar, flour, toilet paper, meat, and most precious of all, live hens.

Live hens, where your investment grew more valuable day by day and which paid daily interest—in the form of an egg. An egg in the ghetto—oh Master of the Universe—that means every day a fresh harvest: a daily income of two, two and a half marks! Leyzer's impulse was thus an obvious one: "Janek, by god, think about hens! Not geese, not turkeys, but hens!"

Janek really did in truth have a good head on his shoulders, and the best evidence of it was the police hat he was now wearing on it. But he used it like a banister on a flight of stairs or as little more than a prop for the heavy bags he had carried on his shoulders. Unable to follow Leyzer's plan in its depths, he interpreted what he heard for himself: "Ha-ha, so the little Jews have had to curb those appetites of theirs in the ghetto, have they? No more geese or turkeys for them, so they've got to make do with chickens." And so the peasant women, bringing their birds to the city, would have them "requisitioned" by him. Though Janek didn't scrutinize the merchandise all that carefully. While supplying Leyzer with the hens he requested, he sometimes mixed in a few roosters, especially since merchandise return had never been discussed as part of the deal.

So when eggs suddenly began turning up in the ghetto shops at two to two and a half marks apiece, when plates of quartered chicken pieces were suddenly for sale on the ghetto streets at fifty marks a plate, and when a live chicken walked down the street in broad daylight and the early morning quiet began to be broken by the sound of *cock-a-doodle-doo,* the Jewish police became restless. "How is it possible? Chickens are coming into the ghetto—eggs in the ghetto—without our knowing anything about it? People are smuggling in goods, getting rich—with no cut of the action for us? What chutzpah! These Jews have to be removed—cut out root, stock, and branch!" And who better for the job than the Jewish police? They searched until they discovered redheaded Leyzer along with twenty-five live chickens: those provided him by redheaded Janek.

What became of the twenty-five live chickens themselves has already been narrated by the aforementioned document: according to the "50–50" system, thirteen chickens were returned to redheaded Leyzer and the rest, have no fear, went to the Jewish *Hilfsordnungsdienst,* or Jewish police, which, modeling itself after the German police—the KRIPO, the SCHUPO, and the like—shortened its name to HIOD.[6]

Six of those chickens, as the document states, were sent to Drewnowska Street. Since the addressee was not specified any further, we may assume that this meant the hospital located there. It is difficult to make the further assumption, however, that the sick ever received the food. Rather, common sense tells us that the following possibility is far more likely: that the hospital brass devoured those chickens long before they reached the patients of the infectious disease wards. One hen was sent to the commander of the Jewish police, the chief guardian of justice in the ghetto, so that he would agree to the remaining five chickens being divided into twenty portions and distributed among the HIOD staff. So the principle of "one for all" came to be established. Said redheaded Leyzer and his paltry twenty-five chickens were thus able to supply the needs of an entire hospital and an entire department of the Jewish police, with its commander at the front of the line.

The second half of the aforementioned principle goes as follows: "and all for one." It was given systematic application by redheaded

6. KRIPO was the abbreviation for *Kriminalpolizei,* the German criminal investigation department or plainclothes police; SCHUPO was the *Schutzpolizei,* or German municipal police.

Janek, though the details do not appear in any official document, which only the oral lore can supply. Redheaded Leyzer did not want to pay redheaded Janek for the twelve chickens taken from him. Janek wasn't as upset about the money as he was about the nerve of those Jewish troublemakers who without his permission had made use of his method of "requisitioning" at will, and he thought to himself: Good enough—if the damn Jewish troublemakers take twelve of his chickens, he'll take out two Jews for each one he's lost.[7] And if those damn Jewish troublemakers think fifty-fifty is fair, he'll just have to double their return: twelve hens—that's twenty-four Jews. That way they'll remember who they're doing business with! So they'd remember redheaded Janek, the *sheygetz*, in the uniform he'd been crammed into: the sorry *sheygetz* porter who'd wandered off on his own like a mangy dog and was good enough to hang a rifle on and stand guard at the ghetto's edge.

Let the ghetto remember redheaded Janek: two months and two days after the ghetto was closed off, he began systematically, and for nothing—for absolutely nothing—to shoot down twenty-four Jews. Here is a list of all those shot dead by redheaded Janek—shot in their tracks in the middle of the street like wild and rabid dogs:

On the second of July in the year nineteen hundred and forty, he shot a fifteen-year-old girl in the heart.

Three days later, on the fifth of July, when sent to the same post again, he shot a twenty-nine-year-old young man and a young woman, age twenty-one. After a five-day break, on the tenth of July he shot a thirty-year-old woman in the head.

On the eleventh of July, a young man of thirty-three.

On the twelfth of July he blew out the brains of a sixty-seven-year-old man.

On the sixteenth of July he put away a fifty-year-old woman and a well-to-do, well-brought-up young man of sixteen.

On the eighteenth of July he shot a sixty-nine-year-old woman in the head.

7. Jewish troublemakers: here and below Janek uses the German epithet *Juden-bengel*.

On the nineteenth, he put a bullet in the heart of a sixty-two-year-old Jew.

On the twentieth he murdered a sixteen-year-old girl.

With murderous precision he waited until the next day, the twenty-first. That day he shot five victims total: a girl of seventeen, a boy of twenty, two twenty-one-year-old boys, and a young man of thirty.

On the twenty-second, he murdered a young boy of thirteen and a thirty-eight-year-old Jew.

On the twenty-fourth, two older women.

On the twenty-sixth he shot a sixteen-year-old boy in the head.

On the twenty-seventh, a forty-four-year-old Jew.

On the twenty-eighth, the last two of his victims: a seventeen-year-old girl and a fifty-year-old woman.

The details—surname, family name, age, and address of the murdered—can be found, as previously mentioned, in the official files of the burial department. But official documents often have the disadvantage of telling us too much, like a gypsy reading fortunes from the cards. By telling you everything they hit the crucial point by accident and then deny all the previous, irrelevant material, the way the fortune-tellers are wont to do. Or the documents simply remain silent. The official statistics, for example, record the fact that in July 1940, thirty-five people were shot dead, forgetting to add that of those thirty-five who were eliminated, eleven were shot down on the 23rd of July—not by redheaded Janek or anyone connected to him but by another protector of German justice.

Redheaded Janek killed twenty-four and not a single Jew more: took twenty-four with a German sense of precision. Not a single Jew more. Nor do those twenty-four Jews shot dead in his settling of accounts receive a single word of mention in any official document, just as not a single word is given that might tell us whether the Commander of Order and the Guardian of Justice in the ghetto enjoyed his chicken or, God forbid, not.

—In the ghetto, January 1942

Mendele produced a splendid symbol for his itinerant Jewish vagabond—the beggar's bag. And Sholem Aleichem hit the nail on the
head with his symbol for the little Jewish village of Kasrilevke, the
ever merry pauper.[1] But the great artist Hirszenberg was guilty of an
oversight in his famous painting *March into Exile*.[2] For whether we
notice the mothers with their tiny infants cradled in their arms (today
we've become used to an exile of a different sort) or the masses being
herded, we do not see the persecutors driving them, standing with ri-
fles raised, ready to fire directly at them, or with blackjacks held high.
A painter of ghetto life today would produce kitsch, or trash, were he
to leave out the soup bowl. Kitsch, because his work would not be true
to nature. Trash, because it would not be true to the demands of art.

Neither the bridge nor the barbed wire nor the gate stand as the
ghetto's fitting symbol. These are mere accessories; external, deco-
rative signs and nothing more. The ghetto's real symbol is the soup

---

1. These sentences refer to *Fishke the Lame* and *Mendele the Book Peddler* by S. Y.
   Abramovitsh, and the fictional shtetl of Kasrilevke, populated by the "little Jews"
   who figured so prominently in the works of Sholem Aleichem.
2. Samuel Hirszenberg (1865–1908) was a Polish-Jewish painter from Łódź who often depicted Jewish suffering. *March into Exile* is from 1904.

bowl, together with the wooden shoes the workers wear. But shoes are less fitting. Not everyone who walks or drags his feet along the ghetto streets wears these wooden sandals. There are people who still trod about in shoes. The managers of the ghetto's enterprises, for instance, wear boots as a sign of their noble distinction. No one, however, can avoid the soup bowl: it can be found in the hands of the great and insignificant alike, from the garbage crews and excrement haulers all the way to the ghetto's upper crust, the managers, the most distinguished figures among us. The official rises early and goes to work, returning home in the early evening hours. Alongside his weary body, next to his briefcase, he carries the symbol of his office: the soup bowl.

The laborer goes off to work before dawn, returning home late at night carrying, alongside his tools, the same soup bowl. When six, seven, or eight women push a garbage cart, six, seven, or eight soup bowls dangle alongside: a soup bowl for everyone. Four men cart away excrement in a wagon, and the same soup bowls can be seen dangling from their sides, banging up against the barbed wire, threatening to unleash havoc upon the ghetto. A woman goes out for a simple stroll down the street, dressed to the hilt in her last bits of finery. Finally, after long and difficult consideration, she slings her soup bowl next to her handbag and takes it along.

And how do you send a child out into the street to find out whether they're "distributing something" at the cooperative, the food allocation site? First you equip him with a bowl. And when thousands of Jews were deported from the ghetto, what was the only thing they were permitted to take along free and clear without being disturbed? The soup bowl! A Jew dies. In the ghetto, he may receive an old burial shroud, a coffin made of rotten boards, and a narrow, shallow little grave. But he will also take along the shards of his soup bowl, the same treatment a wealthy man receives. Not barbed wire. Not the bridge. Not the gate. And not the yellow patches we wear on our chests and back: none of these symbolizes the ghetto. All such paraphernalia are mere signs, the marks of external differences. The true symbol of the ghetto was the soup bowl.

An artist, of course, might paint the ghetto Jew covered in yellow, with a Jewish prayer shawl full of patches. But if he fails to depict him with a soup bowl at his side or in his hands he has produced junk, not art. The first and most crucial task of the artist is to see what is before him. And as soon as he misses the soup bowl he's blind, and a blind man cannot produce a painting that is art. The situation is yet more grievous for would-be artists who have not yet committed their visions to canvas or paper and are still tossing notions about in their heads. The work these artists produce will lack the essential, the symbol of the ghetto that was: the soup bowl! And just as suddenly, there are no soup bowls in the ghetto! Your eyes have searched for them in vain! But they are gone, stowed away! As of yesterday, the factory kitchens stand empty. As of yesterday, the kitchen crews' stomachs and mouths are empty as well and—alas, alas! And with them stand empty—as if orphaned, forgotten by god and man—the soup bowls.

Bowls which only yesterday enlivened the ghetto streets with their vast array of tints and colors, which only yesterday had the chutzpah to knock up against the ghetto's barbed wire fence. Bowls that were the sine qua non of human existence, symbol of the ghetto itself and its fallen human condition: today, those same bowls stand empty, hollow, and vacant. Alas, alas: *sic transit gloria mundi.*[3]

—In the ghetto,
2 June 1942

3. *Sine qua non,* or "necessary precondition," is in Latin in the Yiddish text, as is *sic transit gloria mundi,* meaning "worldly glory is fleeting."

TUESDAY, SEPTEMBER 1, 1942

CLEARING THE HOSPITALS

On the third anniversary of the war, the day broke over the ghetto like thunder out of the blue. At seven a.m., trucks rolled up in front of each of the ghetto hospitals, located on Łagiewnicka, Wesoła, and Drewnowska Streets, and all the patients were loaded on board. The reason was not immediately clear. Earlier there had been talk of emptying the hospitals, since the ghetto could hardly afford the luxury of housing the sick in buildings that could instead be used as industrial sites. Some claimed that the temporary buildings going up on Krawiecka Street were meant to replace this hospital space and that the patients were soon to be transferred there. So when the trucks arrived and patients were taken aboard, the move was understood to be a clearing of the site, and no one thought much of it. A few crowds of curious bystanders, however, had collected in front of the hospital buildings, and with no particular purpose in mind began watching the scene as it developed that clear day. The crowds soon became larger, and when the Jewish police tried to move them along their eyes took on a look of surprise, their looks turned to ice, and confused questions began to pour from their hungry mouths:

"Why would they be using military vehicles to move civilian Jews?"

"Why are they heaving the patients onto the trucks like slabs of unkosher meat?"

"Where are they being taken? To which buildings?"

"The construction on Krawiecka Street isn't finished by a long shot!"

No one could answer these questions, and everyone soon felt the blood running cold in his veins. The answer arrived in its own good time, landing on each of them like a blunt blow to the head. During the war, the Jewish hospitals had already been "evacuated" and emptied twice: first the psychiatric ward when Poznanski Hospital was still in the city, in March 1940, and the second time on July 17, 1941, when the psychiatric hospital on Wesoła Street was cleared. Since no word about the evacuees from either hospital has reached the inhabitants of the ghetto to this very day, it's no surprise that the ghetto as a whole was seized by the gravity and horror of the situation. "It's another liquidation! Another liquidation!" In the ghetto, there's no place for the sick and for "useless eaters." In the ghetto, only those fit to work are fit to live. Whoever cannot work is thrown out like a piece of trash. The morning of the anniversary of the war's third year was deluged with tears, which did nothing more than rinse the dust and mud of the ghetto streets.

It's impossible to know just how the news shot through the ghetto like lightning and precisely who was responsible for spreading it. "They're taking the sick from the hospitals!" And with that, a macabre devil's dance began. Who in the ghetto didn't have someone in the hospitals—a wife, a child, a husband, a mother, a relative, or benefactor? So no one walks through the streets to get there—they run! And who has the time or energy to run there? Nobody, of course. But they hurry nonetheless. Who knows where they've gotten the strength? Every limb aches, and it's hard for them to move. Still their withered legs make the journey . . . something brings them there in a flash. Buildings and streets suddenly empty; the whole ghetto, everyone—both young and old—is going to the same place. Not to the distribution points for rations, not to the place that hands out meat or the sausage store, not to the factories, not even to the potato distribution lot. Today the whole ghetto is mortally ill and knows only one path to take—to the hospital.

Why do they run? They're running so they can be there to see their sick relative one last time; maybe, they think, that will make the death easier for both of us. Or maybe—who knows?—maybe it might be possible to save somebody; but all the streets around the hospital and all access to them have been blocked. Hundreds of Jewish policemen are on guard; the hangmen can do their work in peace and quiet. No one will disturb them. So the sound of the wailing voices barely reaches them. But of course such cries can only move the hearts of human beings. Animals would hear them and act even more cruelly. The limbs of those assembled here are truly crippled, their legs like blocks of wood; all these Jews seem able to move are their arms. They trip and stumble and discover the strangest voices in their own throats, scarcely human, with such an excess of tears pouring from their eyes that it seems as if someone must have hired them to do so. It's impossible to grasp, to understand, just how such people reduced by hunger, fatigued and dissipated—people who can barely breathe—can produce such an abundance of tears.

All the sick patients lying in their beds, meanwhile—some with an arm or leg in a cast, some suffering from exhaustion, burning with fever, or unable to move at all—are overtaken by a fearsome and threatening panic. They're being tossed onto the wagons like lambs to the slaughter. A feverish, frantic panic also spreads among the patients who can walk. Trying anything to save themselves, they jump from the upper floors, clamber over fences, hide in the cellar, disguise themselves as members of the hospital staff—anything that might save their lives. And by using these stratagems, many of those able to control their fear and maintain an outward calm did, in fact, manage to survive.

WHAT IS SAID AND WHAT IS HEARD

The evacuation of the hospitals, like everything else that happens in the ghetto, gave rise to many different rumors and conflicting reports. According to one, the chairman, knowing in advance of the decree that demanded Jewish blood, alluded to it just a few days before during a visit to some of the factories.[1] "Dark clouds are gathering over Jewish heads," he declared. According to another version, not only did he know about the decree, he was also the moving force behind it. He was forced to make this sacrifice, according to this interpretation, because he had been ordered to deport the old people and children. In order to save the old and the young he decided to send the sick to their deaths. In a third version, the deportation of the hospital patients was as much of a surprise to the chairman as it was to the ghetto population as a whole. His advice was not sought, he wasn't consulted at all, and nothing was done on his instructions. Since for all this time—this being the third anniversary of the war—the Jews had been allowed to sit by themselves in the ghetto, the Germans had to do something, the rumor went, to remind them who was boss. "When the sheep are shorn, lambs will tremble," the old saying goes, and so the morning's events had wide repercussions. Terrifying rumors spread throughout the ghetto: what had happened in the morning, it was said, was nothing but a harbinger of a still greater tragedy about to unfold. According to these rumors, the deportation of the hospital patients was the opening move in the deportation of the elderly and the children that will begin any moment now, a deportation made up of those who were sixty-five and older and children under the age of ten. The story goes—it's all a secret—that the chairman has already convened the Jewish Deportation Committee to draw up lists of those who will be deported.

The threatened population took it as proof that these rumors of continuing deportations were true when the personnel department supposedly declared that no new workforce was to be dispatched to any of the factories. People think the real purpose here is to make it easier for the commission to deport those who have been unemployed up to now. Although news of this decree has not yet been confirmed officially by the personnel department, the ghetto population is still in

1. "The chairman" refers to Mordecai Chaim Rumkowski, the Elder of the Jews in the Łódź ghetto.

an uproar, and as in every period of unrest, every frightening rumor is dwarfed by the next. Another version has it that the authorities have issued a decree that every patient who managed to escape from the hospital by one means or another must report back within two hours. If they don't appear as ordered, not only will they be shot on the spot but so will those who hid them.

WEDNESDAY, SEPTEMBER 2, 1942

AND NOT JUST FROM THE HOSPITALS

The sick were rounded up and deported—only God knows where and to what end. So were the children from the child care centers and all inmates from the central prison. The latter included a large group of people who happened to land in prison entirely by chance—like, for instance, those serving a twenty-four-hour sentence handed down by an administrative judge because their houses did not meet blackout standards when someone saw a gleam of light on in the evening, or Jews deported from the outlying provinces who were temporarily being housed in the central prison because of overcrowding in the ghetto. The confusion this news unleashed is unimaginable. It seems obvious to everyone this decree is meant to include not just the sick and those incapable of work, and so hearts pound with so much fear, so much apprehension. In the meantime, the Jewish police are going to Jewish homes and snatching up the sick who yesterday, by some miracle, escaped from the hospitals, and are taking them away. Terrible, heartbreaking scenes are everywhere: crying, begging, kissing the policemen's hands—but how can this do any good? If they only knew that this Moloch would be satisfied with these victims alone, they'd wipe away their tears, turn their hearts to stone, and resign themselves to the loss of each as if he were already dead. Three short years in the ghetto, and the populace is now on such intimate terms with death that it seems much more natural and routine than life itself. But the question "Will that be the end of it?" is so distressing that it not only tears at their minds but makes the blood run cold in the veins of a ghetto population that thought it was inured to every outrage.

"Will that be the end of it?" The Jews from the provinces who are new to the ghetto laugh bitterly at the naiveté of the question. Ah, they've already had practical experience: knowing the answer, they'd rather not bring the words to their lips. Everywhere, in all the outlying districts, it always begins this way. First there were a series of "brandings," marking the victims. First they took the sick from the hospitals, then children and the elderly, turning the remainder to ashes: deporting them, shooting them, executing them en masse, scattering them to the four winds, tearing wives from husbands, husbands from wives, children from parents and parents from children—killing them in so many different ways, as if one way were not enough for the weakened, tortured Jewish population. Ah—by now they know the formula quite well, these Jews from the provinces! Everywhere the tragedy was staged and produced in the same way. Trembling, they didn't answer the question posed to them, too fearful to bring the words to their lips. Instead they just laughed their bitter laugh—the laughter of those who no longer have anything to lose. These Jews from the outlying towns have already lost everything. The miserable few possessions they carry around on their tortured shoulders are little more than dead weight and a burden they would gladly shed. It's easy for them to laugh, while the local ghetto Jew—who till now had been living together with his family, relatives, and friends—he doesn't laugh at all. The bitter laughter of the Jews from the provinces simply makes his blood run cold.

The patients who saved themselves from the hospitals and holed up in their homes or with relatives and were pursued by the Jewish police, then caught and delivered to the central prison, were today loaded onto trucks and deported.

THE CHAIRMAN KNEW NOTHING ABOUT IT

It turns out that the chairman knew nothing about the decree that patients were to be deported from the hospitals. In one hospital lay his own father-in-law and brother-in-law; he managed to save his father-in-law at the last minute, but his brother-in-law died from shock. The part of the ghetto population affected by the decree was envious of the chairman. So what if his brother-in-law has died? At least he passed away in bed, surrounded by human beings, and the whereabouts of his remains can be determined. But the poor, miserable sick who were simply thrown half dead onto the trucks and deported—who will ever hear where they ended up?

A TERRIFYING STAMPEDE

Yesterday did nothing to calm the ghetto's nerves. Just the opposite: the longer the day went on, the more the sense of unrest grew. The night passed sleeplessly, and early morning brought a flock of terrified swallows into the ghetto, fluttering with terror. The children who were well provided for in the colonies set up in Marysin, living in circumstances that were, relatively speaking, better than those of the ghetto as a whole, gave up their "good fortune" and came running back to the ghetto under the protection of their nearest of kin. The only children who remain in the colonies are those who have nowhere else to stay—lone, orphaned children with no relatives whatsoever in the ghetto.

A NEW AGREEMENT

The authorities insisted that all patients who escaped from the hospitals should be handed over. But since not all of them could be found, others could not be handed over, and since a number of them had strong shoulders, were people with influence, and belonged to a protected group with connections in the ghetto, an understanding was arrived at with the authorities. In place of these escapees, the community would agree to hand over two hundred other people instead. These scapegoats meant for hell were not sought from the group of escapees itself because, as previously mentioned, many of them, thanks to their valuable protectors, were not turned over, even when exact knowledge of their whereabouts had been obtained. The two hundred were instead selected from those who had once been sick and hospitalized and had long since been discharged, but had nobody with pull who could now exempt them. Included in this group to be handed over were even those who had never been in the hospital to begin with but who had been given admit papers by a doctor.

AND . . . THINGS FOLLOW THEIR NATURAL COURSE

The strength to go on with a dark and gloomy life is amazing! As long as people keep on taking breath after breath and have not yet closed their eyes a final time, and as long as their senses continue to function, they overcome every tragedy and sorrow—they go on living and sustain their wretched lives, thinking, "Maybe things will get better." Maybe they will be able to survive and become human beings once again.

So people begin talking: in a building once used as a hospital, a carpentry shop will be established; most people receive the information with what could almost be called indifference. Only yesterday they had a brother or a sister who was snatched away while fully alive, and today you might find yourself working in the same spot just to sustain your life and tortured body as long as possible. The rumor then makes the rounds that a general distribution of potatoes will take place shortly. And so the public becomes almost indifferent to it all. Here and there a sigh can be heard, or a groan, and people give a kind of thanks to the Creator of the Universe for the good news about the potatoes . . .

This odd kind of indifference can be found only in that kind of miserable pseudo-existence, as lived in the ghetto, where death is more of a given than life. No one can explain or even understand the force that keeps a person alive, though everyone sees quite plainly how it is that one dies. Death in the ghetto is such a common, everyday experience that it no longer surprises or terrifies anyone, and even if someone continues to live, he does so with the constant thought that he is leading a parody of life, a temporary affair until finally, if not today, then tomorrow, life will surely come to an end.

Every moment that the citizen of the ghetto remains alive, he longs for one final chance to eat his fill. To be able to gorge himself just once and then let the chips fall where they may. For this reason, whenever talk arises of a potato distribution, all that has happened suddenly gets shunted to the side and everyone awaits the official announcement that will be given in black and white, with no guesswork involved. Will potatoes actually be distributed? Or have uninvited consolers spread the rumor just to set people at ease, to quiet a public that has seen its nearest and dearest patients sacrificed and shipped off as scapegoats bound for hell?

The announcement finally arrives. Written in black on yellow, it states that potatoes will be distributed. It's a fact: beginning tomorrow, Friday the fourth of September, the ghetto population will be given an additional five to eight kilograms per capita. The public is deeply satisfied, and in a terrifying way: "We'll be getting a whole fifteen deca-grams of potatoes more per day than we did last month." Everyone's satisfaction runs deep—but not the calm. Something is still in the air, and the atmosphere remains explosive. Agitated, the public can do nothing else but express a common wish: "May the Lord help us, and let us devour our potatoes in peace."

GOD HELP US! WHAT WILL HAPPEN NEXT?

It turns out that the ghetto population has learned to give up the realms of both the spirit and the flesh. But its blood has still not atro-phied, at least that of the majority of the ghetto's citizens, who have al-ready learned to live at something close to the level of animals, though their minds have not yet wholly descended to that level. Everything still brings their beating hearts to a flutter, and they wait with bated breath for the future. God help us, what will happen next? There's an ominous sense within the ghetto: the sky is covered with dark, threat-ening clouds that weigh like lead on the heart. The eight kilos of po-tatoes are not powerful enough to drive away their terror of the day to come and their dread of the coming hour. Potatoes? All mention of them has disappeared; no one remembers them. They're no longer discussed and have ceased to be a matter of interest. The number one issue and chief topic of conversation—the central matter of concern—has become the children.

At the gated entry to 4 Kościelna Street, the records department has hung up the announcement that the vocational training committee has begun to register not just, as until recently, children ten years of age and older for work but children ages nine and up. Immediately the office is besieged by mothers and fathers, and by children, looking for certificates attesting that their children have reached this lucky age, looking for the chairman's "passport to peace"—a work permit. People tremble and shake at the prospect, terrified at the fate that awaits the children: "Will they be allowed to register? Are they too late?" This dread at being late is continuous and never subsides. Exactly what there was to fear becomes apparent soon enough. With complete certainty and clarity, the news passes from mouth to mouth: children and the elderly are to be deported from the ghetto, children under ten and the elderly sixty-five and older. People pass on the news not as a possibility but as fact, the result of a meeting the night before held at the Bałuty Market by the chairman that discussed the matter. Children and the elderly are to be deported, and said deportation would total roughly twenty thousand souls.

So began the "resettlement" of the month of September in the year 1942.

FRIDAY, SEPTEMBER 4, 1942

THE DEPORTATION OF CHILDREN AND THE ELDERLY IS A FACT

The ghetto fell into a dreadful, monstrous terror today when surprised this morning by the fact that what just yesterday seemed an improbable, unbelievable report has unfortunately revealed itself to be the case: children ten years old and under will be torn from their parents and siblings and deported. The elderly sixty-five and older are being ripped from the last refuge they've clung to so desperately with all their strength, with both hands—their four walls and hard beds. Like extra ballast, they're being deported from the ghetto.

If deportation were only the end of it—if only the slightest indication existed that these "deported" will actually be sent someplace! If they were actually to be sent to a definite location under some kind of specified conditions, given some kind of accommodation and subsistence, the tragedy would not be so immense. Every Jew has always been ready to wander, and Jewish life has always been able to adapt to the harshest and most threatening conditions; every Jew has always been ready to take his wandering staff in his hands and, when ordered, to leave his home and way of life. All the more so in the ghetto, with no fortune or household goods or property, no rest and repose tying them to the place! Jews' lives have always centered securely on their ancient God, who, they believe, will never abandon them and of course told them that he would never leave them. "Somehow, everything will turn out fine," they say, or "Somehow, we'll scrape together a meager existence." If only they could find the least certainty, the slightest ray of possibility, that they would be sent somewhere, the ghetto would not be so shaken by this new and unknown decree. But never mind. So many unknown decrees have been handed down that everyone has had to accept, whether they wanted to or not, that it might have seemed natural to accept this decree as well. Except that now there is no doubt—it is certain those now being deported from the ghetto are not being "sent" anywhere. They're simply being tossed away, discarded like garbage. And with this being the case, how can anyone make his peace with the new decree? How can anyone be convinced to go on living, whether he wants to or not? No words are available—no power can summon the force necessary to convey the current mood: the wailing and shrieks that began to make themselves heard today from early morning in the ghetto.

If you were to say that today the ghetto is swimming in tears, it would hardly be a flowery expression—it would just be an unsuccessful description, a shorthand for describing the scenes and images that could be seen and heard in the Litzmannstadt ghetto, wherever you take a step and wherever you turn an eye or ear. No building, no apartment, no family escapes from the crushing weight of this ominous decree. This one has a child, the other an aged father. Another, an aged mother. No one has any patience, and no one can sit still inside their apartment—sit with hands folded and await his fate. Inside they suffer utter misery. Inside their apartments they feel alone, all alone with their unbearable sorrow eating at their hearts. And so the streets fill quickly, for in the street, no one feels quite as blind or quite so abandoned. Animals, they say, when they feel sorrow join together in a pack in the same way. Animals with mute tongues, unable to speak the sorrow in their hearts, do it, so why shouldn't human beings?

All hearts have turned to ice—all hands are limp from being wrung. All eyes are filled with despair. All faces are distorted. All eyes are downcast, and all are bleeding tears. Tears burst out of their own accord, and no one can stop them. And at the same time they know these tears are spilled in vain. Those who might be able to help them do not want to see them—and those who will see them, they themselves are bursting with tears spilled in vain and are unable to help even themselves. Worst of all, the tears that are shed do nothing to lighten the burden on their hearts. Just the opposite: instead of pouring from the heart, they fall upon it and make the heart heavier. Their hearts struggle and squirm amid the tears like fish in poisoned water, drowning in their own tears, and there's no one who can help even in the slightest. There's no one there to save them at all.

Is there really no one—nobody in the whole ghetto—who has the will and the ability to save them? Is there no one at all? There must be someone! Maybe they just don't know yet who that someone might be! Maybe he's gone into hiding somewhere because he can't help, can't save, everyone! Maybe that's the reason people are running around like poisoned mice throughout the ghetto. Everyone is looking for that hidden "someone." Maybe that explains why the ghetto Jews are pounding on the putrid walls—maybe the wall contains that longed-for "someone" within. Maybe it's this one, or maybe that one there. Perhaps that's why everyone runs on about their noble family tree, because today everyone's looking for someone with "connections"; perhaps a distinguished family tie will bring them mercy.

And then there are the children, who still, alas, know absolutely nothing at all. The small children have no idea whatsoever of the sword of Damocles now hanging over their innocent little heads, though they may unconsciously sense the great danger. So they cling all the tighter with both little hands to the thin, drawn necks of their fathers and mothers.

You, son of man, go out into the street and look for yourself, breathe in the unconscious terror of the tiny babies being readied for slaughter—look hard, and do not cry![2] Look good and hard, and do not let

2. An allusion to the opening lines of "In the City of Slaughter" by Haim Nahman Bialik, written in response to the Kishinev pogrom of 1903. See *The Literature of*

your heart burst, so that you will later be able to give a deliberate and considered account of a small part of what happened in the ghetto in the first days of September of the year nineteen hundred and forty-two! Mothers run through the streets, a shoe on one foot and the other bare, half their hair combed and the other wild, their kerchiefs dangling from their chests down to the ground, still clutching their children tightly—mothers who can press them all the more stiffly and firmly to their emaciated breasts, who can still smother their gleaming eyes and faces with kisses. But what will tomorrow bring—or what will happen in the next hour? The rumors fly aplenty: it's today that children will be taken from their parents. Another rumor has it that the children will be deported on Monday. The children will be deported—but where?

Deported as soon as Monday. Or today they will be seized. But for the time being, the present moment, every mother is still holding on to her child, still able to give it everything. The best that she can—that is, her last little piece of bread. Everything that she has in her heart, her best and most precious treasures! Today her child shouldn't wait for an hour and cry before mother and father determine it's time to give them a piece of their twenty-five decagrams of bread. Today the child will be asked instead, maybe, my little soul, you'd like a little piece of bread right now? And the piece of bread that child receives today is not, as per usual, dry and moldy—today it will be smeared with margarine, if a little morsel of it is left. Today it is sprinkled with sugar, if there's any still there—the ghetto is living on credit today. No one is weighing or measuring anything today. No one is holding on to their sugar or margarine today so that they'll last the whole ten days until the next "ration." Today no one in the ghetto lives with the future in mind. Today they live for the moment—in the current moment before it passes. Every mother still has her child by her side, her very heart and soul; what wouldn't she give to keep them there? And the children? What do children know? Most are naive creatures, and if one of them is a bit more clever, he asks, "Mama, why are you giving me so much good stuff to eat today, am I sick?"

Destruction: Jewish Responses to Catastrophe, edited by David G. Roskies (Philadelphia: Jewish Publication Society, 1989), sec. 47.

Can a mother respond to this question with anything other than tears? The child chews on the little piece of bread and chokes on the first bite. Without any answer to the question "Am I sick nor not?" he or she eventually comes to the conclusion, I'm probably sick. Because if the child weren't sick, it wouldn't be receiving such good food and in such quantities . . . if the child weren't sick, neither the father nor mother would be clasping it so close and so tight. And if it weren't sick, neither father nor mother would have wept so long and so hard while they did. Only one thing remains a puzzle for the child: if it's sickness, then why are they running back and forth through the streets together? Why not the usual bed rest instead? Why all this running about but no trip to the doctor? Of course they are sick, these poor little Jewish children. They are wretchedly ill, these little Jewish fledglings, and a final fate has been determined for these sick birds: slaughter.

There are children who already understand what's afoot. Ten-year-old children in the ghetto, for example, are already fully mature individuals who recognize and understand the fate that awaits them. They don't yet know why they're being torn away from their parents—that, perhaps, no one has told them just yet. In the meantime, however, the fact that they will be taken away from their trusted protectors—from their fathers and devoted mothers—is enough for them. Such a child is difficult to hold in your arms or even to lead by the hand; such a child walks alone in the street. Such a child cries alone, shedding tears of its own: tears sharp and pointed enough to pierce your heart like so many poisoned arrows. But hearts in the ghetto have turned to stone. If only they could break, but the poor things have simply become too hard, and that is perhaps their hardest and most bitter curse. That is how the most terrifying pain a Jew can imagine is produced: pressed on the one side by the ghetto and on the other by a Jewish—by a caring—heart.

The hurt becomes even greater and the pain more senseless when the situation is considered logically: okay, the elderly are, well, elderly. If they've lived out their sixty-five years, maybe they can persuade themselves, or others can persuade them, to come to a conclusion that looks roughly like this: "You know, I've lived, praised be the Holy Name, a good number of years already, both in happiness and sorrow—what's done is done. It's probably just a matter of fate. Anyway, no one lives forever, so what real difference does it make if the end comes a few days, a few weeks, or even a few years sooner? You've got to go sometime, and that sometime might finally be this time. Let it be—what's done is done." Perhaps the elderly talk themselves into it, or perhaps they are persuaded by their closest relations to come to this conclusion. Children, however, who have barely pecked their noses out of the eggshell—children who have seen God's world only in the ghetto, children for whom a cow or a chicken are nothing but strange shapes from some fairyland, children who have spent their entire lives without smelling a flower, seeing an orange, tasting an apple or a pear—fate has decreed that their lives are to come to an end! On these heads, the full black and brutal fate of death is to fall?

Bitter fathers and mothers gnash their teeth. "Mine won't go! No living child of mine will be handed over! They'll take our children from us as corpses!" The ghetto skies, like yesterday and the day before, are as clear as ever. The sun shines with the light of the month of Elul, as it did yesterday and the day before, and looks with a smile at Jewish sorrow and misery.[3] The sun looks down as if worms were being trampled or as if a decree against bedbugs had been announced. As if the Day of Judgment on rats had been proclaimed—to be annihilated and exterminated from the earth. And for all that, some in the ghetto still have their doubts. There are still enough people to be found in the ghetto who want to carry on confidently with their lives and even offer a logical explanation: "Here in the ghetto, 80 percent of the population is performing useful labor. We're not a provincial city they can make 'Judenrein' in half an hour.[4] We're needed for their purposes, since the work has to be done. It makes no sense that they'd take people from here and deport them."

Others who have no logical argument to make retain their confidence—they simply believe in miracles: "There are so many stories where it's happened. A bitter decree has hung over us more than once

3. Elul, in late summer, is when Jewish families traditionally visit graveyards and commune with the spirits of their departed loved ones.
4. Nazi term, in German in the text, meaning "clean of Jews."

in Jewish history, and every time we were saved at the last moment. And for the first time in the war, Łódź has just been bombed from the air. The deportation announcement can still be rescinded—how can we know what will be?"

The atmosphere has grown strange in the ghetto. People have already heard so much, so much good as well as bad, that previous experience should have taught them a lesson: good rumors have never proven to be true, and life in the ghetto never improves. Life here is meant to get worse, and the hundreds of evil rumors that have proven to be true prove the case. Nevertheless, people are eager to hear about the most distant prospect that might mean good news rather than confront the evil that faces them right here and now. So the public has allowed itself to be persuaded by logical arguments and permitted itself to be sung to sleep by their optimistic lullabies; the public has returned to the *ressorts* and to the everyday working routine.

In the *ressorts* themselves, however, they have awoken from their hopeful dreams and been led back to a harsh and cold reality. There was no work in the *ressorts* today. In the *ressorts,* as a result, no distribution of soup took place. There people made the following claim with the utmost confidence: "The official list at the records department of the ghetto was sealed last night." The only uncertainty that remained was, who sealed the records? Was it done by the authorities? No. The list was determined by the Jewish "Resettlement Commission," then sealed in order to prevent birthdates from being forged—to prevent children from being made to seem older or the elderly from being listed as younger. In this way the full bitterness of the decree has been preserved. Today no miracles of any kind will be possible that happened in the past, and the past has receded so far into the distance that none of the ghetto Jews can remember it in any case. For no ghetto Jew has experienced a miracle yet, and no ghetto Jew can tell a tale of a good rumor that proved itself to be true. Just the opposite: what becomes real and contemporary is always worse than what came before. Still, the following story is making the rounds in the *ressorts:* "The Resettlement Commission has already been formed."

People in the ghetto have been found, whether compelled or of their own free will, to take upon themselves the role of a Great Sanhedrin and to become the adjudicators of the laws of capital crimes.[5] The commission comprises messieurs Jakóbson, Blemer, Rozenblat, Neftalin, and Grynberg and will administer the deportation of the twenty thousand elderly and children.[6] They will be the ones to cut these limbs from their living bodies, the ones to slice Jewish families in two. Of course, they've received the assignment from the chairman to dispose of this matter. And of course a new, official body must be constituted whose task it is to carry out the decimation of Jewish families. For the same reason, no person with a conscience would undertake to judge such capital crimes.

This same commission, having assembled an entire staff of officials, yesterday worked through the night and produced a listing of the entire population broken down by street and building. The committee has established its offices at 4 Kościelna Street, at the records department, the focal point on which the entire ghetto population has fixed its gaze. Here people come to cry and mourn for their own and those near to them. But so much chaos and tumult prevails, so much disorganization and disorientation, that none of the aforementioned gentlemen of the committee knows what anyone wants from them; no one understands what his responsibility is or whether he can actually do anything for anyone. None of the gentlemen on the committee have any real understanding what the decree means in its practical application. One of them has declared that the age for deportation means children ages one through ten, making children less than one year old exempt. Another has followed the doctrine of "up to and including," making the decree apply to children from one minute old to nine years, three hundred sixty-four

5. In the period of the Second Temple, the Great Sanhedrin was empowered to adjudicate capital crimes.

6. Szaja-Stanisław Jakóbson was a trained jurist and chairman of the ghetto court; Zygmunt Blemer was head of the ghetto's Bureau of Investigation; Leon Rozenblat was chief of the Jewish police; Henryk Neftalin was head of the Department of Population Records; and Grynberg was "a legal trainee." For a different account of these figures by Zelkowicz, see "Litzmannstadt-Getto, September 14, 1942," in *The Chronicle of the Łódź Ghetto,* edited by Lucjan Dobroszycki (New Haven: Yale University Press, 1984), p. 250.

days old.[7] Another difference of opinion in the committee concerns the elderly. They were uncertain whether the age limit began with the completion of the sixty-fifth year or whether those already sixty-five years old were to be included. At the same time, no one on the commission knew whether a work permit should be considered a "passport to peace," as the chairman called it and on which he had founded the ghetto's very existence—making them a magic charm that works against deportation just as it had a few weeks ago, when they had been stamped—or whether the miserable thing will be of no use at all.

In any event, the personnel department has been besieged by hundreds of people who have not yet been lucky enough to come into possession of the chairman's "passport to peace"—a work permit. The majority of them are the elderly, the sick, and children who as of the present, thanks to their infirmity or age, have not been eligible to work anywhere. Now they want to work. Now they are asking the personnel department for a work assignment and work permit. No one knows whether this will do any good, but everyone is drowning and will cling to any possibility to stay afloat, no matter how small, precisely because no one knows for certain whether it will help or not. The personnel department, however, is not open, and people stand there with anguished hearts, ready to grasp at any straw, but the straw is now out of reach. Of course, why should the personnel department be any exception to the norm of all other institutions in the ghetto? How was anyone supposed to work? Who had the strength or the cast-iron nerves required to sit all day at a job? Has anyone been found among all those many officials or other workers in the ghetto who is not subject directly or indirectly to the decree?

FAMILIES OF FIREMEN, POLICE, AND *RESSORT* MANAGERS—
EXEMPT FROM DEPORTATION

Meanwhile the day takes its course—nothing stands still, and everything becomes more frantic. With every passing hour, with every

7. Talmudic doctrine of interpreting similar cases similarly, given in Hebrew as *ad v'ad bikhlal.*

minute, the unrest continues to grow. And with every passing minute something else happens to fan the flame. Every minute it's something new, and it doesn't matter whether the rumors are founded or unfounded—any report that sharpens the decree, that explains its different nuances and shadows, complicates it more and more until no system in it whatsoever can be determined—until the general agitation, tumult, and sense of disorientation becomes all the greater.

At the start of the day the rumor was that the deportation would begin on Monday, the seventh of the current month, and continue for seven days; that is, until Monday the fourteenth. The daily number to be deported would total roughly three thousand people, thus making the total for the seven days roughly twenty thousand. Later in the day there were a few reports that the "Resettlement Commission" had determined, based on information it had discovered, that even if all children and elderly subject to the decree—all without exception—were to be deported, the number involved would produce a figure of thirteen thousand souls; the remainder would be supplied, on a contingency basis, from the ranks of the unemployed and those unfit for work. Thus, while before the decree was seen to affect a small number of people who had been touched in isolation—as, for example, a miserable old man with no close relations or other potential savior in the ghetto, or a child or a lonely orphan with no relatives—the decree had spread. It now applied to every person—for what could be done if the "Commission" decided someone was unfit for work? For, in fact, what hungry, exhausted Jew in the ghetto is actually fit for work?

It turns out, of course, that there are no rules without exceptions. This decree does not apply to everyone. There will still be a considerable number of people in the ghetto who will not be touched by it, at least not directly. During the day, a rumor emerges that the deportation will take place without the intervention of the authorities. The deportation is to be carried out by the "Resettlement Commission," with the help of the Jewish police, fire department, and others. In return for their loyal and effective enforcement of the directive, they have been assured that their families—that is, their children and parents—will be exempt from the decree. The police will in this way be able to "work" with a clear head and calm spirits and will certainly carry out their labors well—on that you can depend. They've already proven their mettle several times in this regard. The promise of an exemption had already been made to the managers of the *ressorts* and other officials, and the reason was the same—to allow their work to continue undisturbed. The only remaining question is, who will pay for these privileges? If no exceptions are made, all the adults and children covered by the decree produce a total of thirteen thousand souls. Now, with exceptions to be made, including the families of the police and fire departments as well as other high officials, where will the deportees come from who are to take their places?

This is the reason that now, before the deportation has even begun, every Jew is eligible for inclusion. Since age will soon no longer play a determining role—and age alone, after the exceptions made for the privileged, would produce only half the number required—the other half will have to come from the community as a whole. How can anyone know whether this fate will befall him? So the public wanders the streets—since no one can sit at home any longer—like sheep without a shepherd, with no one to turn to, no one to ask for help, not even anyone with enough knowledge to give an answer or a piece of human advice. Those who should have known something—the Resettlement Commission—are themselves completely disoriented and unable to give any advice. They have no idea how to manage the huge size and difficulty of the task they have been assigned. They are, nonetheless, those charged with the task of applying the law of capital offenses, with deciding between life and death: deciding between who will remain and continue to be tortured, and those who are to be tossed away like so much garbage. The matter rests in their hands—but does it remain in theirs alone? Will they be asked for their advice, or their opinion?

The longer the day goes on, the greater the uproar becomes and the more uncannily it weighs on the soul, as the reports become increasingly ominous. Around noon a new report makes the rounds: to prevent a panicked public from leaving their residences during the deportation and hiding in the various places that have already been swept, everyone will be ordered to remain at home. The Resettlement Commission, it is said, is about to issue a decree that a curfew will be in effect for the entire period that its deportation is under way. No one will be allowed into the street, and everyone will have to remain at home. The furor this news has unleashed is impossible to describe. For a large part of the population, it felt as if the last board separating them from the abyss had been pulled out from under their feet. Many people had settled on precisely this strategy to save themselves from deportation—had hoped simply to hide out or just move from their own homes to areas where the Commission had already "worked." The news also set off a fresh wave of anxiety of an entirely different sort: if people will not be able to leave their doorsteps while the deportation is under way, they will still have to find provisions for that period. And what, if anything, in the ghetto—where people live from day to day, and even then on a meager ration—how would they possibly be able to lay away food?

Go ahead and think of "laying away food"! The prices for foodstuffs on the private market are climbing by the minute, especially once news of the curfew had gotten around. In order to lay aside enough provisions for several days, you'd need the wealth of the Korah.[8] The only possible thing to do in this case is to get to the distribution points as soon as possible and buy the eight kilos of potatoes that according to yesterday's announcement are supposed to be distributed starting today to the population at large from the vegetable vendors there. But in a perverse twist, as if to spite the Jews, by the time most of the population got the announcement, most of the distribution points were—except for those who lived nearby—no longer in operation. And of course the distribution points are run by residents of the ghetto, who are just as affected by the decree as everyone else. So how can you expect them to sit there and remain at their posts with nerves of steel and work as if everything were normal? And wasn't work even canceled for those in the factory *ressorts*? At the distribution points that have not yet been closed, the routine doesn't hum at a business-as-usual pace, as they are able to serve only a few of the huge crush of humanity pressing forward to find the only possible provisions they will be able to put

8. A common Yiddish expression: Korah, who rebelled against Moses in Exodus 16:1–18:32, was according to Midrashic tradition both wealthy and evil.

aside—potatoes. The "lucky" ones who manage to pay for potatoes and receive the appropriate coupon for one of the vegetable vendors had dropped everything at a minute's notice and run to the spot. There too, however, the protectors of public order are unable to control the situation. The shoving of the hastily formed crowd becomes so powerful that even those who manage to push themselves to the front receive their potatoes helter-skelter, in a crazy and confounded way. Most of the multitude, however, after an entire day of waiting in line, end up leaving with the same thing they arrived with—an empty sack.

MORE DETAILS ARE IN THE WIND

In fact, people already know what is to come. Both the proponents of logic and the optimists have been proven wrong. People are already convinced that the deportation will include not just children, the elderly, the weak, and the sick but others as well. Children, the elderly, the weak, and the sick are simply not enough to make up the quota of deportees. This fact is already well understood. What is not yet understood is the following: Who will be fated to make up the rest of the group? How many will this contingent comprise: twenty thousand people or more? All kinds of rumors are in the air! There is talk of a *Judenreinigung* on the order of Pabianice, Zduńska Wola, and other cities in Warthegau.[9] The most interesting question is this: Who will actually conduct the deportation? Will it in fact be the Resettlement Commission itself, without intervention from the other side, or will they themselves—God forbid—take part?

Around two o'clock, mimeographed announcements turned up on the ghetto walls: at three-thirty the chairman and other high officials will appear at Fireman's Square, 13 Lutomierska Street, and explain the deportation to the public. This was the first official announcement of the deportation, as if to spite the proponents of logic. The rays of the sun shine, as they do in the month of Elul, with the light of the approaching Day of Judgment, penetrating the skin as if they were pins and needles. The tremendous heat has become unbearable, and the

9. Warthegau, which included Łódź, was one of the districts in western Poland annexed to the Reich following the German invasion.

heavens look as if they've been covered with lead; any hint of breeze has disappeared. The crowd gathered at Fireman's Square numbers roughly fifteen hundred people—a completely different group than usually assembles for the chairman's daily address.

The chairman has already addressed many crowds at this location. The group that usually comes to listen does so out of curiosity, wanting to hear something new about food provisions, work, or other plans the chairman may have in mind. Those who stand in the usual crowd are, for the most part, those who have time on their hands and can do what they will—high officials or employees of the ghetto administration who can, if they like, take time off from the office and listen to his orations. The faces of the usual crowd appear well rested: their eyes are calm, giving no hint of anguished spirits. Today, however, a crowd has gathered with blood on its mind. No idle curiosity has driven them here—curiosity would hardly be strong enough to tear them away from their places in the potato line or from the distribution points and bring them here to Fireman's Square in such numbers. None of them have come to hear the latest news, and everyone knows there will be no good news to relate. People have come here to hear their verdict: whether they will live or—God forbid—whether they will die. Fathers and mothers have come to hear if judgment has fallen on their children's little heads. The elderly have expended their last ounce of strength to come, propped up by their thin canes or by the withered arms of their children, to find out what their fate will be. The majority of the crowd is composed of the elderly, standing with sunken heads and slumping over their canes, of young people clutching their tiny offspring, or of children who are alone. All backs are bent, all heads hung between the shoulders, all faces twisted, all eyes swimming in tears. All throats are sobbing. Taken together, everyone in the crowd of fifteen hundred assembled in the square resembles a huge congregation sentenced to death and facing its final moments.

They stand and wait, frying in the blazing sun. The chairman has not yet arrived. In the meantime, Kaufmann, the "kommandant" of the firemen, gives a speech: he, the only one who does not wish to, or is simply unable to, give any kind of reckoning that rises to the seriousness of the occasion. With all his harshness and tendency toward coarseness, he gives vent to his crudity in front of the crowd. He jostles them this way and that as if this were not a group of people suffering from heartbreaking sorrow but a group of animals to be herded to the slaughterhouse. Under no circumstances will he agree to let the crowd stand closer to the stage and a bit to the left, where a little shade can be had—the proper distance must be maintained. Instead he gives several commands for the crowd to be pushed to the right and away from the stage. He appears indifferent to the whole affair, as if the matter hardly interests him in the slightest. Presumably, what everyone says must be the case: the families of the police, the firemen, and managers will be exempt from the decree. Otherwise it would be impossible for him to display such nerves of steel at such a crucial moment and to be so tactless in bossing the crowd about. It was a good thing he had the savvy—perhaps someone gave him the idea—so that this time he avoided his usual practice of ordering everyone—in Polish, no less—to "look right" to greet the chairman as he appeared to speak.

At quarter after four, the chairman makes his appearance, accompanied by David Warszawski and S. Jakóbson.[10] His eyes show the great transformation that this man has undergone in the last few days, or perhaps hours. His head is bowed as if he can't keep it on top of his shoulders; his gaze is extinguished and blank. We see an old man who can barely hold himself up. An old man like all the other old men assembled there in the square—except that his face is fuller and not as emaciated as theirs. Unlike them, he's also decked out respectably, in fine clothes, rather than in their tatters and rags. The wild confusion of his white hair makes it apparent that he has endured a terrible ordeal, and the twitching at the corners of his mouth makes it equally clear that his mouth contains not a single consoling word for his public audience that has assembled—it will not bring forth a shred of happiness today.

The chairman barely pulls himself up onto the stage and makes an announcement:

10. Warszawski was manager of the central office for tailoring in the ghetto; Jakóbson was chairman of the ghetto judicial court.

He is no speaker, David Warszawski. In fact, he's almost entirely incapable of conducting a normal conversation with another human being at all. But who says a cup of gall must be drunk from a beautiful goblet? Poison taken from an ugly vessel works just as effectively as it does from a beautiful one. No one has come here today to enjoy and admire a display of oratorical eloquence. They've come to hear the truth . . . and David Warszawski tells that truth in all its bitterness, in his own plain and bitter words:

"Yesterday, the chairman received the order to deport roughly twenty thousand of the children and the elderly. Striking, the turns of fate that human beings must face! All of us know the chairman well. We all know how many years of his life, how much of his energy, how much work and health he has invested in the education of the Jewish child. Now he's being asked to provide the sacrifices with his very own hand. Him—the same person who has educated more children than the number in today's decree! But what's done is done. This is an order that is irrevocable. Sacrifices have been demanded, and the sacrificial victims must be supplied. We understand the pain involved and feel it—it cannot be concealed, and it cannot be hidden from you. All children must be handed over. Up to the age of ten, and all the elderly. The decree cannot be revoked. Our only way of softening the blow is to carry it out calmly and in an orderly way. The same decree was issued in Warsaw. It's no secret to any of us how it was carried out there. It happened that way there because it was carried out not by the Jewish community—the authorities themselves enforced the decree. We, however, have undertaken to carry out the decree ourselves, because we don't want to—because we *can't* let the carrying out of the decree take on catastrophic proportions.

"Consolation or words of calm? Unfortunately, I don't have any for you. The only thing I can tell you is that—and maybe this will calm you down or give you a bit of consolation—it looks, in all probability, as if we will be left in peace after carrying out this decree. It's wartime. The air-raid siren has to be sounded quite often, people have to run for cover; at such times children and the elderly are nothing but a hindrance. They must therefore be removed . . ."

Such was the speech of David Warszawski. With blunt and simple words he described a blunt and bitter truth. He is also a businessman, however, and in talking to the crowd was trying to make a sale, trying to convince them that the decree was not senseless and that it was motivated and had a logical foundation. That's why he came up with the idea of air-attack sirens, but the public listened to him as they would any other salesman—they took half of what he said to be true. As far as the motivation and logical foundation of the decree, however, no one believed a thing he said.

The floor is given to another speaker, the lawyer Jakóbson:

"Residents of the ghetto: yesterday an order was issued to deport over twenty thousand people from the ghetto and to take them from the children, the elderly, and the sick who have no prospect of recovery. None of the previous deportation decrees have been as difficult to carry out as this one. What makes the current decree even more difficult is that we do not have the means or opportunity to heal the wound it represents, or even to make it less painful. We have had to take upon ourselves the heavy obligation and great responsibility of carrying the decree out ourselves. We have had to take it upon ourselves because other cities have given us the example of what happens when such decrees are carried through by strangers, and by our own hand . . . [The sound of powerful sobbing can be heard in the crowd.] No sobbing or cries will, unfortunately, be of any help to us now. The statement has already come down from on high: 'Either you will carry out this order yourselves, or we will carry it out for you.' Any further discussion would be superfluous. We already understand everything, and all too well. The deportation will have to total three thousand people per day. The responsibility for carrying out the decree falls on the community as a whole. The whole community stands surety for its implementation and is responsible for the actions of each of its individual members.[11] Therefore no one will be allowed to leave his home, in order to avoid unfortunate incidents and to protect the community as a whole, which is responsible for what everyone does."

11. Ironic application of the Talmudic doctrine articulated in Shavuot 39a, "Lo, it is written, and they shall stumble one upon another, one because of the iniquity of the other; this teaches us that all Israel are sureties one for another!"

So went the speech of Jakóbson the lawyer, who had spoken more concretely still. He spoke not just of the elderly and the children but also about the sick. In truth, just of the sick with no prospect of recovery, but how is that to be determined? Who will be the final judge if a patient is beyond recovery or if he has some chance of getting well? And those who are not patients, those who are still going to work every day in one of the *ressorts,* pushing a cart or hauling garbage, using every last ounce of his strength to do so, or a ghetto official who sits in some office still at work today—can anyone assure them that they won't be seriously ill tomorrow and thus people who, given the living conditions and nutritional limitations of the ghetto, would have no prospect of recovery themselves? None of this was addressed explicitly at all! Everyone already understands how it will go. The patients with connections—they will be considered to have a prospect of full recovery, and their places will be filled by patients who have no one who can pull strings on their behalf.

For the first time the curfew had been addressed explicitly. No one will be allowed on the streets for the period when the Commission goes about its work. But the speaker's claim that this order was intended to avert a series of calamities from unfolding was understood by the audience as nothing more than a lawyer's excuse; everyone understands quite well that this measure was introduced by the Resettlement Commission in order to make its assignment easier to carry out. It's quite clear: make everyone sit ready at home when they come to get you, and they won't have to look for you high and low. Nothing in either speech made things any easier. Both David Warszawski and Jakóbson have clearly emphasized that nothing can be done. The former stated quite explicitly that he had nothing consoling to offer, and the latter stated explicitly that he had no remedy for their wounds, not even a means to ease their pain. Their speeches possessed only a single advantage: people had now been made aware of the truth—the truth about the number of those that had to be deported, the truth about who would compose the group, and the truth about the new *shpere,* or curfew. However bitter such truths may be, no matter how much despair they may bring, they are still better than dealing with the unsaid, with rumors, and with various conjectures. Yet everyone felt that everything had not yet been said. Everyone knew that there still remained something for the President Chairman to say. The crowd held its breath at the peak of the suspense so they could better hear the President Chairman have the last word.

THE CHAIRMAN SOBS

Here you have him, the proud Jew. The Jew who ruled his kingdom with a high hand in complete despotism: here is the Jew who never heeded anyone's advice, who did everything with his own hand and followed only his own lights. Here that Jew stands in front of the crowd as a broken man. The Jew cannot regain his composure because of his tears. The chairman cries like a child; people see how deeply he has been affected by the public's sorrows, how deeply the decree has touched him, though he is not subject to it either directly or indirectly. These tears are not feigned: they are Jewish tears, the outpourings of a Jewish heart, and have gained him a great, great deal of credit with the assembled crowd. Barely able to regain his composure, he begins with the following words:

"The ghetto has received a painful blow. They demand its most precious members—the children and the elderly. I have not had the privilege of having a child of my own and have therefore devoted my best years to the care of the child. I have lived and breathed children. I never imagined that my own hand would be the one to bring them to the sacrificial altar. In my old age I am forced to reach out my hand and beg you: brothers and sisters, give them away to me! Fathers and mothers, give me your children! [A tremendous, dreadful lament breaks out from the gathered crowd.] I had a feeling that something was coming at us; I readied myself for this 'something' and have remained on constant alert, like a guard on his watch, to try to avoid this 'something.' I have not been able to, because I didn't know what was awaiting us. I did not know what we had in store. The taking of the sick from the hospitals was a matter completely out of my hands. You have seen the best indication of that: I had my own close relatives there and was unable to do anything for them at all. I believed that that would be the end of it, and that afterward they would leave us in peace for which I have struggled so hard and for which I have always worked and striven. As it turned out, another destiny awaited us. Such is the fate of the Jews: always more and harsher sorrows to bear, especially in time of war.

"Early yesterday they gave me the order to deport some twenty thousand Jews from the ghetto, and if not, 'We'll do it ourselves,' I was told. This posed the question: Should I undertake the task myself, or leave it to others to carry out? Viewing the situation chiefly from the standpoint not of 'How many will be lost?' but only through the guiding principle of 'How many will we be able to save?' we have come to the conclusion—that is, my closest colleagues and I—that however difficult it may be for us, we must carry out the deportation with our own hands alone. I must carry out this difficult and bloody operation—must cut off limbs in order to save the body! I must take the children, for if I do not, others, God forbid, will be taken as well. [Dreadful wailing from the crowd.] I have not come today to console you. I have not come to calm you down today either but to uncover the fullness of your sorrow and woe. I have come as a thief to take the greatest treasure you possess in the depths of your hearts. I have tried with every ounce of ability to hold this decree at bay. I have tried, after retracting it became impossible, to cushion its blow. Just yesterday I ordered all nine-year-old children to be registered; I had hoped to save at least this group between ages nine and ten. This I was not allowed. I succeeded in one thing only—saving children ten years of age and older. Let this be our one consolation in our great sorrow.

"We have many sick with tuberculosis in the ghetto whose remaining life can be numbered in days, or in weeks at most. I don't know—maybe it's all the devil's plan, maybe not—but I can't prevent myself from saying to you, 'Give me the sick, and in their place, the well will be able to be saved.' I know how tenderly the sick are tended to at home—especially by Jews. But anytime there is a new decree, the following question must be considered carefully: Who can be saved, who should be saved, and who is it in fact possible to save? Common sense demands that we save only those with a chance to survive and not those who in any case cannot be saved.

"We live, however, in a ghetto. We live lives of such deprivation that we don't have enough for the healthy, much less for the sick. Each one of us feeds the sick at the expense of his own health: we give them our own bread, our little bit of sugar, and our meager piece of meat, and the end result is not to make the sick person healthy but to make ourselves sick as well. To make such a sacrifice, to be sure, is the most beautiful and noble of acts. At the point where we must make a choice: to sacrifice the sick, who don't have the slightest chance of ever regaining their health and who are liable to make others sick in the process, or to save the healthy. This was not the kind of problem that I was going to spend a long time thinking about. I decided to save the healthy. I have therefore assigned this task to the doctors, and they will be obliged to hand over the incurably sick so as to be able to save, in their place, those who still have a chance to live . . . [Dreadful sounds of lament are heard.]

"I understand you, mothers. I can see your tears quite well. I can feel what your hearts will suddenly feel, you fathers, when tomorrow they've taken your children away while you're at work when you played with the little ones only yesterday. I know all that and I feel it. Since yesterday at four o'clock—since I first learned of the decree—I have been a completely broken man. I live with your sorrow, and I live with so much of your pain that I don't know where I will find the strength to go on living. I must tell you a secret: they demanded twenty-four thousand victims in eight days, with three thousand people deported each day, but I succeeded in reducing the figure to twenty thousand, and even less than twenty thousand, only by agreeing to the condition that it would be children to the age of ten. Children ten years and older are safe. Given that the number of such children and the elderly totals roughly thirteen thousand, there is no choice other than to include the sick. It is difficult for me to speak. I don't have the strength. I simply wish to tell you my request: help me to carry out this *Aktion!* I'm trembling. I'm frightened that others, God forbid, will carry out the decree instead.

"A broken Jew stands before you. Do not envy me. This is the most difficult task that I have ever had to impose. I stretch out my broken, trembling hand to you and I beg you: hand over these sacrifices in order to prevent an even greater sacrifice, to protect a community of over one hundred thousand Jews. This is what I was told: if we hand over the victims ourselves, calm will be restored. [Different cries make themselves heard: 'Then we'll all go!' 'Mr. Chairman, don't just take the only children; take children from families that have more than one!'] Hold your empty words! I don't have the strength to hold a discussion with you! If the authorities were to come, there would be no such cries . . . I understand what it means to rip a limb from a living body. I have begged—I've begged on my knees, but it did no good. From small towns of seven or eight thousand Jews, barely a thousand have been able to reach us. So what is the better choice? What do you want: to let eighty or ninety thousand Jews remain here or, God forbid, see everyone destroyed? Decide for yourself, but my responsibility is to protect the Jews who remain. I'm not speaking to the hotheads; I am speaking to your ability to reason and to your conscience. I have done everything I can and will continue to exhaust every alternative to avert the use of firearms in the streets and the bloody scenes that would result. The decree could not be rescinded, only altered here and there.

"The heart of a bandit is required for someone to demand what I've demanded from you. Put yourself in my place, use logic, and you yourselves will come to the conclusion that there's no other way for me to proceed, because the numbers that can be saved are far greater than the number that must be handed over."

WHAT WILL HAPPEN TO THE CHILDREN?

There we are. All three speeches have been heard. No calm has settled on the crowd's tormented spirits as a result. Just the opposite: the more hours that pass by, the more their throats clench to a close and the more like stone their hearts become. While a whole day has already passed since they first heard about the children and elderly, now, after the speeches, they've also learned the fate of those sick with tuberculosis. With this "license to kill" in effect, with a third category now included, those sick with tuberculosis, how can one be sure that matters will stop there?[12] Who would be examining these patients with the pressure turned up to the extreme to determine whether their

12. "License to kill" echoes the language in Exodus 12:23, where the Israelites were instructed to place blood on the lintels so the Destroyer would not have license to kill their first-born.

lungs contained the bacilli or not? Who will insist that a patient who looks to be in terrible shape, but who is not ill with tuberculosis, must not be deported? What about all those who move about the ghetto with their faces looking like obituary notices? Who will prevent them from being deported? And isn't every single inhabitant of the ghetto, one way or another, seriously ill?

The mothers who held their children tight, nestled to their chests, no longer knew what to do, having listened to all three speeches to the end. They understood the utter logic of the chairman's explanation, but everyone in such a situation thinks that such logic must apply to someone else, not to themselves. For what living mother can imagine the act of giving away—of killing off—her own living and breathing child? Fearful scenes began to play themselves out on the ghetto streets, full of spasms of hysterical sobbing. Two women who are complete strangers, unknown to each other before this, meet on the street with their little ones in their arms. Each looks into the eyes of the other, seeing in them her own terror and sorrow, which would be invisible without such a mirror.

"What will you do, my little golden one?"

"What can I tell you, my little star?"

"Heaven forbid! What can we do? People—tell us what to do, save us!"

"Heaven forbid! What are we going to do? There's no place for us to go!"

And both mothers, overcome with fear by their own dreadful cries, run off on their different paths, both wetting the stones with their tears.

Two fathers are standing nearby, their faces twisted by sorrow, and begin a conversation.

"What are you going to do?"

"I won't give them my child!"

"What do you mean?"

"I'll kill him with my own hand instead! That way I'll know he won't have to suffer their tortures long, and I'll know where his bones have been laid to rest!"

The first father replies, speaking more to himself than anyone else. "I know. You can give your child away to a grandfather, a grandmother, to a father or mother—and things will be better or worse. You know, that sort of thing is understandable and happens all the time. But to give a child away like this! To whom? For what? For how long? And to what end?"

Such are the fates that Jewish fathers and mothers imagine. The mothers can't bring themselves to utter statements like "I'll kill my own child." Instead, a mother says, "They'll have to kill me first to be able to take my child away." A father is harder: he would kill his child with his own hand to prevent it from being tortured, and what will happen to him afterward? What will they do to him? He doesn't think of that.

There are those who try to console themselves and their neighbors. "It is simply impossible that they could take thousands of children and simply slaughter them just like that! Then what will they do with them? Maybe they've built shelters for them somewhere so that, like Warszawski said, they will be safe from air attacks! I know—maybe they want to make a camp of 'hostages.' And what do you think we are? Aren't we hostages already? Aren't we always at their beck and call? Why are we fenced in on all sides with barbed wire and guarded day and night—to save us from the evil eye?"

Such is the talk that circulates about the fate of the children. No one on either side—whether among the authorities or the Jewish community—has let slip a single word as to the fate of the children and the elderly who must be deported from the midst of the Jewish collective of Łódź. Nobody expects anything other than certain death for them, and such a thought is so difficult to convey—a shuddering terror with which no one can come to terms.

TWENTY THOUSAND JEWS FROM BĘDZYN AND SOSNOWIEC

The sun sinks farther into the west. Twilight arrives. With the loss of the sun, everyone senses the approach of what awaits the ghetto. No one believes in miracles. What everyone heard from all three speakers today was clear and unambiguous: that the decree was absolutely irrevocable, and thus twenty thousand Jews were to be deported from the ghetto. Permanently deported. Never to be set eyes on again. Twenty thousand Jews—one-fifth of the entire ghetto population, meaning that every fifth Jew must report himself or be seized as a sacrificial victim. Who can have any certainty whatsoever that he or she will not be that fifth?

Today's sunset is like no other. On other days, sunset might have brought a kind of respite—rest, so to speak, for the exhausted, over-worked, and hungry body. Some other time, sunset might have been greeted with praise on our lips—"In your blessed name, praise be unto God that we have come through another day." At another time, sunset might have been awaited with longing: after an entire day of separation at their different labors, a time to rest for husband and wife. After a long day apart, a time to come together over a sparse evening meal, parents and children together. The time when neighbors would meet in the courtyard of their building, pouring their hearts out to one another and filling their lungs with air that was stale but still better than their cramped apartments. Sunset was a time that was longed for each day. Today, however—how many years of their lives would people gladly have given up if they could just keep the sun from setting once more, to draw out this day longer and longer and make it last without end, so that a terrifying and tragic tomorrow would never come? Today, where is the Joshua who will cry out, "Sun, stand still in the ghetto!"[13]

But as long as the sun continues to shine, as long as it remains light, as long as daylight remains, people retain their hope. They feel a bit more certain: people meet one another, hear a lively word, and can—amid the sobs and groans—imagine a word of consolation, empathy, and confidence. It's genuine and heartfelt: a hollow and empty word, but because the will to believe is so powerful, as is the desire for hope, even an empty word has enough force to enter their brains and run in their blood, and following its own cold and sober logic runs through their mind and quickens their pulse, flooding their hearts with waves of "Maybe it's not going to happen" and streams of "Still, what if . . ." But as soon as nightfall arrives everyone quivers at the sight of their own long, drawn-out shadows. It is still, or so it seems, your own shadow, that shadow of your own, familiar "self"—so still

13. Based on Joshua 10:12: "Stand still, oh sun, at Gibeon."

that it seems to have become the tongue of your own hideous, mocking demon, a tongue stuck out to mock your hideous and mournful life, which is so hard for you to leave behind.

The sun wanders more deeply into the west. Twilight descends. No one gathers in the courtyards of the buildings today. What's the point? Their withered lungs have taken in so much gall and pus earlier today that no amount of air would be able to cleanse them. They tremble at the slightest sound or rustling—their nerves react to the sound of the breath of those nearest to them; their hearts stop at the sound of their groans. So what's the point of gathering with others? Who has a word to share with someone else? So people sit in their apartments. Many of them do not even bother to turn on a light. What for? Why be able to look into someone else's face and see your own sorrow and pain? In other apartments, mostly in those where there are children subject to the evil decree, the lights remain lit. Tonight the children will be allowed to sleep in the best beds. Mothers and fathers stand around them not to watch over their children's sleep or to chase off the vicious ghetto flies and bedbugs, but to use the few, numbered hours that perhaps remain to be together and to etch their little faces permanently in their memories.

Like the shadows of wandering dogs on a moon-drenched night in a faraway village, the elderly shuffle miserably along the walls of their rooms. Children have parents to cry and watch over them; children have parents who can at least try to do something on their behalf. Children have a hope of escaping the slaughter—there is so much talk about them and the different outcomes their fate may take; maybe there's a grain of truth to be found somewhere in all that empty talk! But for them, the miserable elderly who can barely drag themselves from place to place: Who is looking out for them? Their children? They are scattered all over the world; they have no idea what is happening. So who will look after the elderly? Who will stand up for them? Their neighbors, you say? What do total strangers have to do with them? The elderly do not have the slightest chance of obtaining the chairman's "passport to peace"—a work permit! There's no way they can work! Old, sick, and weak and incapable of any kind of work except coping with life in the ghetto, which is the hardest form of labor they can perform. No one says a word about the fate that awaits the elderly; they're not given the slightest chance. From the very first moment it's as if everyone read the same seal, stamped upon their bowed and aged shoulders: To Be Tossed Aside Like Scrap.

They shuffle along the walls of their rooms, the elderly, walls that have now become dear and precious to their hearts. Every shred of spiderweb and the marks of bugs left on the walls become treasured possessions. After all, they're in their own room, something that belongs to them . . . and who knows what tomorrow will bring or how the day after will look? Whether it will even make sense to talk about a room or instead about a common pit filled with two hundred, even a thousand people—men, women, and children all thrown together— filled with all the discarded "scrap"? Oh—to have lived, toiled, slaved, and worked themselves to the bone only to finally come to such an end—to end without burial in a Jewish cemetery and to leave no memory, no sign of their existence, behind!

All at once their bug-infested beds have become dear to them. The beds they had feared, which had always pinched at their elderly bones! The same beds which, on dark but warm summer nights, had unleashed armies of stinking, biting bedbugs to feed on their old and withered bodies! The same beds that, on fearfully cold winter nights, had let an iron, icy cold penetrate to the very marrow of their bones and freeze it! That very same bed has all at once become precious and near to them, as if their own bed has become the doctor in the house, providing them with hours of recovery and rest! In the dream visions it provides they can see the shapes of their dearest children and grandchildren, as clear as the light of day! In those beds, how many magical, wondrous stories can be told! In their final allotted hours, how dear such a bed becomes to the elderly! Will they be able to think of anything like it when tomorrow comes? His bed draws the miserable old man to that netherworld—that dreamland of life— while the four blank walls carry his thoughts beyond life itself. There are four walls, however, and only one bed; the walls win in the end. For who can sleep away his final hours? Who could spend his last hours lying there calmly? You'd have to be a person without a heart. A person who has reviewed the course of his life and reflected on its meaning, perhaps. But the decree arrived so unexpected and suddenly—with so little warning—that the few hours that possibly remain are filled with thought: mainly that he still has so much to do! He can't simply pick up a life in which so many years have been invested and throw it away like a dead skull!

Slowly, like the long, crooked legs of green spiders, the hands creep around the clock. With each passing minute, the pulse of the ghetto becomes fainter and less steady. The life of the ghetto is ebbing. From an open window whose location cannot be identified, a heartbreaking cry can be heard, like the sound of a string on a musical instrument that has suddenly snapped. The sobbing of a choking throat can be heard, sounding like the bleating of a calf whose throat has been slit. Somewhere a child lets out a cry in restless sleep, like the last leap of light from a guttering candle. The ghetto sinks into mourning and darkness; it is dressed in a sackcloth made of tears. From the life that goes on outside—life beyond the barbed wire—the ghetto can now and then make out the sound of a passing streetcar or hear the scratchy, hoarse pitch of a gramophone. As it plays, the record sounds like the mocking laugh of a staggering, reckless vagabond, cackling at the life that remains for a camp of a hundred thousand rabid ghetto dogs. Tomorrow, or the next day, they will be counted off by fives. "Cling, clang—every fifth one on the scrap heap. Zip zap—every fifth one—a Jew."

Suddenly, in the middle of the night—without any clear sense of who says so or how they know—the following news is heard: "Twenty thousand Jews from Będzyn and Sosnowiec will be settled in the ghetto." Maybe it's true that walls have ears. Perhaps the prophet had it right: "For a bird from the sky shall carry the sound."[14] Twenty thousand Jews out, twenty thousand Jews in: just shuffle the deck. Like a game. So maybe it's possible that not everybody is going to the scrap heap. From Będzyn and Sosnowiec to Łódź, and from Łódź to Będzyn and Sosnowiec; in fact, when cards are shuffled, some get torn, some eventually wear out and become too faint to read, but most of them remain in play, and the game goes on. A real game played with human lives, but still just a game and not always taken seriously. Isn't it

14. Hebrew in the Yiddish text: Ecclesiastes 10:20.

still possible that the children and the elderly will come out winners? Twenty thousand here, twenty thousand there—lives will be broken but not dug out from the roots; lives will be effaced but not erased . . . perhaps. The need to hope is so strong, and so is the will to believe.

THE CASE OF ROSA STEINER

This is the story of an elderly Jewish woman. Her name was Rosa Steiner, and she entered the ghetto in October 1941. Along with several thousand other Jews, she was deported, an old woman, from Vienna. She came with a small sum of money and a few possessions—an uprooted, but not broken, woman. Officially and according to her passport she was born in 1876. But judging from her attitude and the way she carried herself she looked thirty years younger than that. Tall, slender, and attractive, with a striking face, no one would have guessed her to be sixty-six years old. What did she do in Vienna? Not important. But isn't it worth recalling that in Vienna she had led a life full of energy and zest? And to report that she was active, before the war, in Irene Harand's movement and published articles and opinion pieces in different Viennese newspapers and magazines?[15] Perhaps it is also deserving of mention that her deceased husband had been an active member in the administration of the official Jewish community of Vienna and that her son was one of the city's most prominent doctors, a much-admired figure active in JEAS (Central Jewish Emigration Society) and a close colleague of Professor Chajes?[16] These are perhaps important details in the life of an older woman—though they have

15. Irene Harand (1900–1975) was a Catholic leader in Vienna and an outspoken opponent of Nazism and anti-Semitism. Her organization was the Harandbewegung: Weltverband gegen Rassenhass [The Harand Movement: World Organization Against Racial Hatred]; her Vienna journal, *Die Gerechtigkeit*, was published under the running head, "I fight anti-Semitism because it is harmful to our Christianity." In 1968 Harand was awarded the Righteous Gentile award by Yad Vashem in Jerusalem. See Gershom Greenberg, "Irene Harand's Campaign Against Nazi Anti-Semitism in Vienna, 1933–1938," in *Christian Responses to the Holocaust: Moral and Ethical Issues*, edited by Donald J. Dietrich (Syracuse, N.Y.: Syracuse University Press, 2003), pp. 132–150.

16. Hirsch (Zvi) Perez Chajes (1876–1927) was the chief rabbi of Vienna and a Zionist leader.

little pertinence to the story at hand. Besides, in the collective in which she lived, at No. 45 Limanowski Street, she was treated no better and no worse than her other sisters and brothers in fate.

Not better, but also not worse. She slept with everyone else on the bare earth, freezing with the others and worn down with hunger like all the members of the collective, suffering the same pain as them all. Or maybe a little bit more. She was more intelligent, alert, and impulsive. Amid the general apathy she was far less frozen into inaction than everyone else. Unlike 90 percent of the collective's residents, she was unable to organize her day according to the following schedule: hours for sleep, hours for gossip, and "louse hours" for delousing. Unlike her neighbors in the collective, she could never devote whole days to discussing the thinness of the soup, the hunger that continually plagued them, or the far-from-clean toilets and the shortage of toilet paper. Strong in nature and restless in soul, she neither wanted nor was capable of allowing herself to go under. Rosa Steiner was constantly on the lookout, rummaging around to find some way to help. She wanted to do something—to make a contribution, just as she always had back home. But the world back home was no more; for here, there was no "always" and certainly no new "home." She lacked the proper surroundings and sufficient space to spread her wings. That's why she appeared to be always on her feet and why you could always run into her on the street. Always those fiery black eyes, still young and generous in their quest—a quest that took her into the unknown, looking for a bit of home, for something intimate and warm. And as she searched, so did she find: in a small, cramped but spick-and-span little room in the ghetto, she discovered the family of a Yiddish poet.[17] The languages they spoke were entirely different, and their temperaments were just as divergent, as were their convictions on important matters as well, but they discovered their spiritual affinity immediately: he, the young Yiddish poet with a Jewish disposition toward suffering, and she, the old Jewish woman with a young, secular outlook prone to unrest.

On hard winter evenings in the most despondent hours of ghetto life, and at their hungriest and most despairing moments, they would

17. It is not clear who this poet was.

often console each other in the following manner: "You'll see, you'll be traveling back home soon, and I'll be taking you to the train and helping you get your luggage on board"; "You'll have to come to Vienna to do a reading of your work there; you can stay with me." In this way, an old Jewish woman from abroad created an environment that reminded her of home. And so a suffering Yiddish poet happened to find a friend, someone he could pour out his heart to in simple Yiddish and feel that he had been understood in the deepest way.

When the collective on Limanowski Street was liquidated along with all the rest, Rosa Steiner, together with her brothers and sisters in fate, finally arrived at the old-age home. Not at an old-age home that had previously existed in the ghetto but in the new one opened with the specific purpose of housing them—the "foreign" Jews. On her arrival Rosa Steiner was in fact treated quite a bit better than the others, and neither her passport, her appearance, her temperament, nor her attitude won her this coveted spot. According to her passport, at least, she would have needed to be born two years earlier to earn a place in an old-age home. People younger than sixty-eight were not being accepted, and then you'd have to be helpless and broken down too. Having someone to pull some strings on your behalf, however, is the most important factor in getting something done everywhere, and the ghetto is hardly an exception. And what did the young Yiddish poet actually achieve with his intervention? He created a kind of asylum for her. He gave her a place where she could lay down her old-young head until a time of peace and quiet would return. The time would come when he'd be able to keep the promise he'd made her: "When you make your return trip to Vienna, I'll take you to the train station myself."

She was much better off in the old-age home than she had been in the collective. Here she at least felt free of the atmosphere created by what she called the "lousy hours" she spent there, freed from endless discussions about the cleanliness of the bathroom. And if she didn't quite fit into the stale atmosphere of senescence, she was still Rosa Steiner, someone who could create an atmosphere all her own! She sat at a distance from the others, outside the circle, alone with a book in her hands—she, Rosa Steiner and a book, created a separate world.

And whenever she became lonely, she always knew where and when her friend could be found and so where she could feel "at home" once again. As it turned out, however, she wasn't to live in peace for long at all. The clouds of deportation once again began to gather over the heads of the foreign Jews. More than five hundred souls had already been deported from the old-age home in April. And on the list of those newly scheduled for deportation stood Rosa Steiner's name. She did not cry or tremble with agony, nor did she jump from a second- or third-story window as so many others did. She simply went to visit her friend and gave him to understand the following: "As long as I am not forlorn, and as long as I feel protected, I will not give in. I don't have the strength to endure the wear and tear of travel, and you will keep your promise, I imagine, just as I will keep mine."

There was not the slightest hint of trying to coerce her friend, the young poet, into some great action or to trick him into pulling strings on her behalf. She spoke in her customary manner; you had to know her to be able to understand what she meant. Rosa Steiner was never out front in her meaning. She always spoke indirectly, and when she wished, she could switch to a more explicit voice. Anyway she thought that what lay ahead of her was "the wear and tear of travel," not a trip to the "scrap heap." Therefore she felt no need to resort to overly direct or inflammatory figures of speech. At almost the very last moment, as she stood there with her suitcase in her hands, a note arrived in Polish: "Rosa Steiner *zostaje*" ("Rosa Steiner stays"). How proud she was of the tiny note that arrived, as she put it, "at almost the very last minute." And how coquettishly she asked for help as she pronounced the original Polish *"zostaje"* with her German accent, *"tsaztaye,"* adding *"Nicht wahr, mein Freundchen?"* or "Isn't that right, my little friend?"

No. Rosa Steiner was no longer lonely. Rosa Steiner felt more confident of her fate. With a friend with enough power to save her from the "wear and tear of travel" at the very last minute she could simply wait calmly until he kept his promise. But Rosa Steiner was not that kind of person, and sitting and waiting was simply beyond her powers. The tiny note—"Rosa Steiner stays"—could sit quietly and wait, and Rosa pasted it to the head of her hard and narrow bed. Left to her own devices she could never sit still. As it happened, the officials who ran the old-age home had children of different ages. Little children are beautiful, with their lovely eyes; their tongues, however, are usually silent, and starting up a conversation with them is quite a task. They don't speak a word of German, and Rosa Steiner absolutely loves to talk with children—you can learn so much from them! Isn't that true, my little *Freundchen*?

So Rosa gathers the children, whips together a German class, and begins to teach. No—she can't sit there quietly and wait. She keeps up her visits to her friend, who declares, "She can still be useful. There's all kinds of different work she can do, and she's not looking for any handouts." In this respect, however, her friend is powerless. There are so many young workers for whom work is a matter of life and death, since work is the only possible place for them to get their soup. So many of them are unemployed, with no jobs for them to fill. How could he possibly justify his effort to find work for Rosa Steiner, who needs a job only for what the Germans call a *Zeitvertreib*—a way to while away the time—and not to support herself? But Rosa Steiner still can't sit on her hands. Perhaps it's hunger that makes her restless; people in the old-age home are just as hungry as they are in the ghetto as a whole! It's true—people are no hungrier there than anywhere else, but not a bit less hungry all the same. Rosa Steiner has her own amulet, of course, which she has pasted at the head of her narrow little bed—"Rosa Steiner *zostaje*"—but its magic won't do a thing to quiet her hunger pangs.

Therefore, when she's finished running the children's class, and her eyes are too tired to read her book, she takes a piece of paper and writes a bedtime prayer—her *Dämmerungsandacht,* or evening's devotion, in her German. Clearly reflecting the state of her restless soul, the prayer describes it as "fettered with a coarse rope—the soul's wings are so precious, and the ropes so rough, that they are all but severed. Because they are so coarse, in fact, those ropes are gradually fraying the connection, until one bright day her soul will be wholly deprived of its wings." The very idea leaves her in the throes of an ominous and terrifying pain. Rosa Steiner, however, is not one to show her pain. At least she doesn't show it to her friend the poet. She continues to visit him with a smile on her face and with the same fire in her youthful black eyes. Only once did she visit him with a faced etched with pain and sorrow. Only once did she come without the little fire burning in her eyes, when instead they reflected her state of panic and dread. And then he never saw her again.

It was the third of September in the year 1942. Subdued, ominous voices began to make themselves heard throughout the ghetto, like the sound of an approaching storm—there was already loud talk about the deportation of the children and the elderly. "What do you advise, my friend?" she asked him. "What do you think? Isn't the old-age home the most dangerous place to be? In the city they have to search, while here they can scoop people up by the ladle. What do you think, my friend? Maybe just discharge myself and leave?"

How could a young, impractical poet possibly give her advice? So he called two older friends for help, two people with more life experience and practical know-how, and asked them for advice. "So what do you think: How should Rosa Steiner act in this situation? Where would she be safer—in the asylum she's found in the old-age home, which would be protected and spared anywhere in the civilized world, or in the abandonment of the ghetto, where you can be snatched off the street like a stray and useless dog? What's the advantage in leaving the old-age home then? First there's the legal question of whether they'll let her sign herself out at all and take her ration card along. Let's assume for the sake of argument that, through connections and inside pull, she's able to sign herself out legally and gets to take her ration card with her. Where will she go to get her food rations? Now that the records department has been sealed, going to the office and getting transferred to another distribution point is impossible. And where will she find a spot on the first night to lay down her tired, old-young head? Even assuming such arrangements can be made—that she finds a place to stay the first night and gets something to eat—what will she do tomorrow and the day after? What will she live on? She'd be left to survive on what she can buy on the private market. Does she have enough money or valuables for that?"

No, she doesn't. She and her close acquaintances in the old-age home went hungry for far too long for that to be the case! It wasn't that her hunger had diminished, just that her treatment was better; other people weren't allowed to take their belongings out of the home and sell them on the outside, though she was permitted to do just that. And she had her amulet: "Rosa Steiner *zostaje*." So people looked the other way as she left. No—she has nothing left whatsoever. All her belongings have already been sold. The best advice that anyone could come up with was the following: "For the present, go back. Meanwhile we'll find some kind of work for you to do. When you get a work permit—the 'passport to peace' in the ghetto—it will get easier to sign yourself out from the home, to find a roof over your head somewhere else, and to get rations; you'll become what passes for a 'free' person in the ghetto." This was no doubt the right advice, the most logical way out that anyone could come up with for her. It was also advice that she liked, so that, and nothing else, is what she set out to do. Early the next morning she planned to go out and pick up her work permit. She'd then say her good-byes at the old-age home and, at her ripe old age, begin to lead a fresh and different life. Wouldn't that have been interesting? A whole new start?

Unfortunately, she never came back when "the next morning" arrived. On that day—September 4, 1942—she was able to scribble down these few words with a trembling hand to her friend: "From early morning on, the institution has been surrounded by the Jewish police. No one can go in or out. Save me, friend! Do whatever you can. I am not ready to die. Rosa Steiner." Because it was a small piece of paper, and because her hand was trembling, she wrote in large, crooked letters that filled the entire sheet with those few words, and only the margin was left for her to add the following two words: "My watch." The messenger who brought the letter placed a metal wristwatch next to it. It was an old-fashioned kind of timepiece—ready to be thrown on the junk heap. Whenever her friend who survived her, the poet, would take a look at the watch, he would furrow his brow, trying to puzzle out what she meant by leaving it behind for him. Did she mean it as a symbol of the fate of the elderly that she shared with them, limping along like an old watch themselves, waiting, like the watch, to finally be thrown out like so many pieces of fat? Or did she simply mean to leave the last of her possessions to him, her friend, who had made her a promise he could not keep in the end?

—*The Sabbath, September 5, 1942*

THE GHETTO HAS NO FOOD

The factory *ressorts* are closed. Yesterday at closing time the announcement was made to the workers that they were not to come to work today. All offices are also closed. Yesterday all officials were told at quitting time that they should not bother coming to work today. It is the Sabbath. A day of rest—no work, which also means no food. When the workers don't work, and the officials are idle, they don't receive the *ressort* soup, their fundamental reason for and condition of their employment.[18] No one in the ghetto will work today, so no one will eat either, setting the tone for the rest of the day. Morning has just arrived. People, however, have little desire to see it break through the darkness. Come what may, in the face of everything that might happen—if they only knew what "that" might be—people would normally wish to end this life of endless night and all its darkness and uncertainty! Their nerves can't take any more! More than on edge, they're taut and stretched to the limit. Just a little bit more and they'll snap: the next bit of tension will bring the ghetto to its knees.

Today is a Sabbath unlike any other. No work is going on anywhere. It is as if all the *ressorts* and offices have been turned to stone. Only in the population registry does work continue at a feverish pace. Additional staff has been added at the population registry, several other offices having lent their personnel to do the worthless and hopeless work of copying the registry onto individual sheets of paper. Every residence in the ghetto gets its own sheet bearing the names and ages of all its residents. These sheets are to be given to the deportation commission lest, God forbid, they get lost during their strenuous labors and are not able to move from house to house and, aided by the list, find all those subject to be deported to hell. The list making is done feverishly, hastily, and is completely unnecessary—why bother? Why

18. Saturday, the Jewish Sabbath, was a regular workday in the ghetto.

assemble an entire staff of officials who, instead of receiving their normal soup ration (the kitchens are closed), receive bread and sausage instead? Why waste so much paper rewriting one hundred thousand names when each building has its own official record book that contains exactly the same information that is now being transcribed? The fact of the matter is simple: no one knows what to do or what his job is. They've all lost their heads. A deportation commission has been created, and so that it looks like it has something to do, it does useless make-work and performs tasks that no one needs.

THE RACE FOR POTATOES

Like throats that have not been completely choked and hearts that have not yet turned completely to stone, stomachs are demanding what is theirs. Hunger, especially in the ghetto, is a merciless beast. That beast compels you to be constantly awake and on the alert. Can there, for example, be a greater source of agony and woe in a family than the death of one of its members? Of course not, and especially not among the Jews. Nevertheless, when someone dies in one of the ghetto's apartments, however depressed and despondent the mourners may be, the first thing the vast majority of the ghetto's inhabitants do is to hurry out to get the foodstuffs still valid for pickup on the deceased's ration card. If those rations can be picked up tomorrow—at the earliest— then the deceased will have to wait until tomorrow, or the day after, or even three or more days later, to be carried away. People almost never report the death while the ration card of the deceased still has valid food coupons that can be detached and redeemed for food. The main explanation is not that mourning and its emotions have lost any of their power and effect—though this may be true to a certain extent. Pitiless hunger remains the driving force behind such behavior, compelling people to be constantly alert and to be cunning and devilishly calculating in looking to profit from even the greatest calamity.

All the *ressorts* are closed. All offices are locked. Food distribution centers, however—where people can pay for potatoes and receive the last of eight kilos per capita ration—have remained open by special decree. Although business plods and limps along there, for who among the staff can keep his head in this situation or has nerves strong enough to go about his business as if this were just another day, with the centers besieged by hundreds and thousands of people, ignoring the sword of Damocles that is descending, every minute a bit closer, toward the heads of their children, their elderly, and their sick? Living in dread of the beast called hunger, their first priority is the race for the potatoes. Those who managed to pay for their potatoes yesterday or the day before lay siege to the vegetable distributors to get them however they can. They want to eat as much as they can before they are seized for deportation, and this may be their final chance to eat their fill.

IT HAS BEGUN

The clock reads a few minutes to seven in the early morning. All the people—almost the entire ghetto—are in the streets. Whose nerves are not on edge? Who can sit inside? No one. While everyone knows that a curfew, or a *Gehsperre,* will be declared, no one knows when it will begin or how long it will last. Given the meager food rations that have been distributed, no one can sit at home and wait for a miracle to occur, for staying home would mean the following: not receiving the *ressort* soup and thus having nothing to eat. To do so would mean starving to death, even if one managed to survive the decree and avoid deportation. Under no circumstances can anyone remain inside. Everyone runs into the streets. People literally "run"—they push themselves along and hurry as if someone were cracking a whip at their heels. Whoever hasn't yet paid for their last potato ration at their distribution center rushes there in order to pay. Whoever has no money left (and there are, unfortunately, plenty of those in the ghetto) rushes elsewhere to sell or pawn something or to find a loan of some kind or other. People who have already paid run to the distribution center, clutching their food coupons in their hands. Whoever has already received their potatoes and brought them home is off running somewhere else, looking for a gardener who might be able to sell him a few vegetables or a little cabbage to have something "extra" to add to the potatoes. Wherever anyone needs to go today, they don't walk but run. Everyone's on the hunt—everyone is in a rush, and each tries to push in front of the other. The sooner you get where you're going, the greater the chances that your effort will have some effect. And while no one knows when the curfew will take effect today—in an hour, perhaps—the uncertainty only makes everyone push to arrive at their destination that much faster and to get back home just as fast.

As a result, from early morning the ghetto streets have been active as never before. It is a strange kind of activity—quiet and deathly, if such adjectives can be used. People don't speak to one another, as if everyone had left their tongues at home or wanted to forget they had tongues at all. People who know one another exchange no greetings, as if they were ashamed to be seen, and practically turn to stone as they walk. Lined up, they stand there like a series of petrified figures in front of the distribution centers and in the huge lines in front of the vegetable distribution points. In the ghetto a deadly stillness now reigns. No one ventures a sigh or a groan—for huge black stones have today been laid on the hearts of all the ghetto's residents. People run through ghetto streets like the wandering souls of the dead, metamorphosed into other shapes to atone for their sins as they pass through the underworld. That's what they look like, with bitter silence on their sneering lips and the terrifying dread in their eyes turning them into different creatures altogether. People stand in line—like those sentenced to death, perhaps—looking as if they are on display and waiting their turn, when they too will be taken to the hangman. Petrified, suffering from a nervous breakdown, from dread, from fear—none of these accurately describe all the feelings that are stirring and bursting from so many different hearts that can't even cry or scream. There's no ear sensitive enough to detect their deafening, silent, and stony cry that turns you to stone with its deafening quiet.

They swarm over the three ghetto bridges like hundreds of hydra-headed snakes. Back and forth—the snake swarm moves back and forth. People push, rush, and hurry, and the air is heavy with pressure. Amid the crush, macabre tidings hang in the air. The dark sky is swollen and ready to burst, about to explode. And from the void will pour forth an absolute horror that will engulf all that is real:

IT HAS BEGUN!

No one knows what was actually said. No one knows who said it. No one knows how, since after all everyone was silent and after all no one was even looking at anyone else, avoiding one another the way a thief evades his pursuer. So who was the first to let those three terrifying words fall from their lips:

IT HAS BEGUN?

No one—no one actually uttered those words. No one would let those macabre tidings pass through his mouth. It was the heavens themselves that exploded—it was then that the visceral news belched forth that

IT HAS BEGUN.

It happened in one corner of the ghetto, and in that same moment the entire ghetto from top to bottom felt a collective shudder. That's the way it's always been in the ghetto: no one knows what has actually happened, but everyone senses it in advance. Where did it begin? Some people report as follows: that it began at the old-age home on Dworska Street, where they're already taking the elderly out of the building. Others say that the elderly are already being removed from the old-age home on Gnieźnieńska Street, and still others that a wagon is being loaded with children and the elderly on Rybna Street. Unfortunately, all these accounts are correct: people are being taken from here, there, and everywhere and already being "loaded" on Rybna Street.

IT HAS BEGUN.

For now the Jewish police have started in. They've started their work by attacking the point of least resistance—the old-age home. There, as the saying goes, their bread has already been buttered and the table is set. Everyone can be seized as is—no exclusions to determine or cases to decide: everyone there is old, and therefore everyone can be tossed in the waste bin like so much excess "scrap." This truly is the point of least resistance, for who will take their part or waste a single word in defense of elderly people who have already lived for weeks and months at the charitable expense of the Jewish community? Who would waste a word on behalf of the "foreign" elderly on Gnieźnieńska Street, with no relatives or saviors to spare a single tear for their fate? The elderly will have to mourn for themselves. All they can manage is to emit a weak sigh—so weak, in fact, that hearts of stone cannot even hear it, much less be touched or moved by the sound. Meanwhile they are being placed on the wagons by the police like sheep going to the slaughter and being taken to what is called the "collection point." There they might receive a full hangman's supper, to include, according to rumor, a soup heavy with potatoes and horse bones. Later they will be led away from the collection point and—

THROWN AWAY LIKE A PIECE OF "SCRAP"

In the old-age homes, the police can perform their work in a quiet, calm, and businesslike manner. There no one disturbs them or gets on their nerves, and no one "drops the ball." An old man and an old woman are tossed onto the wagon like so many pieces of old clothes. Only their moans and groans are heard, and here and there a sigh. Here and there someone sheds a tear, but who is moved by tears in the ghetto? The most important thing is of course this: that the work goes forward quietly and in a businesslike fashion.

But things are proceeding in anything but a quiet and businesslike fashion on Rybna Street. The police have been forced to pull people from their rooms, and they have encountered resistance. There the police must cut living, quivering members from the bodies to which they belong—babies are torn from their mothers' breasts and healthy molars are ripped from people's mouths. On Rybna Street, older children are taken from beneath their parents' sheltering wings. Husband is torn from wife and wives are ripped away from husbands. Together for forty to fifty years, having lived through both sorrows and joys together, having raised a family with children born and children lost. They've lived for forty or fifty years as almost a single body, only for the following to occur:

After entering the ghetto, one member of the couple adjusts better than the other. The husband still more or less resembles a human being, while the fact that she was made in the image of God becomes less apparent. Or sometimes the opposite situation obtains: she remains a proper Jewish woman who can perform many different kinds of useful ghetto labor, while he can barely get onto his own two feet. In either case, one or the other must be tossed away with the "scrap" into the trash. A husband is torn from a wife he's lived with for forty or fifty years.

On Rybna Street the sick are also being seized—the sick who risked their lives escaping from the hospitals, whose terror of death gave them the strength and courage to leap over fences—the same sick to whom people gave their last piece of bread, last bit of sugar, their last bit of potatoes to keep them going a day or a week or a month longer, until perhaps the war would come to an end and they'd be able to get back on their feet. Now they're taking the sick.

So they slice living members from the body. Healthy molars are ripped out too. Live, quivering bodies are cut in two. And the pain is correspondingly immense. Any attempt to translate the pain into words will inevitably fail. Anybody who tries to bear the pain will simply fall apart. Is it any wonder that people turn to screams? It is terrifying and fearsome enough when death is encountered directly. But death in the ghetto has become such a natural, everyday, taken-for-granted occurrence that a different kind of logic has emerged: "Just ignore it, dead and gone—everyone is going to die eventually, and whoever is still alive has no say in it anyway; they have to go on living." Suffering that can be explained away, that becomes an everyday, logical routine, is suffering cut in half and not nearly so immense. The kind of sense-less suffering produced in tearing a living, breathing child from the arms of parents, or the kind of illogical sorrow produced by tearing a husband away from his wife or a wife from her husband, is much dif-ferent. Add to that all the meaningless, senseless pain caused by toss-ing patients from their sickbeds, the elderly from their old, familiar four walls all together; treat the man, the wife, the husband, the child, the patient, and the elderly like useless sacks of garbage to be thrown on Moloch's altar and set alight—the kind of pain and suffering that causes is unbearable and cannot be described!

People are screaming. Their cries are terrifying, dreadful, and pointless, just as terrifying and dreadful and pointless as the action that is the direct cause of those laments. The ghetto is no longer sim-ply frozen in fear—now it twists in convulsions: the whole ghetto has become one huge, monstrous spasm, leaping out of its own skin and then falling back upon the barbed wire. Oh, if only a fire would come and burn it all to the ground! If only lightning would crash down from the heavens and destroy it all in a single blow! There's scarcely a person in the ghetto who has not muttered something like this wish through parched lips—regardless of whether they're directly, indirectly, or not at all involved with the scenes now playing out before our eyes. Every single person is ready to die on the spot as it begins, for at this moment the horror and dread are impossible to bear. At this moment it is simply impossible to listen to the screams and cries of one hundred thousand fettered oxen, those being slaughtered but not yet dead. It is impossible to look at the twisting and writhing of their throats, those that have been cut but not yet slit through, allowing them neither to die nor to truly live.

THE JEWISH POLICE

What happened to the Jewish police that allowed them to do this dirty work? Did their brains atrophy? Were their hearts removed from their chests and replaced with stones? It's difficult—very difficult—to answer such questions. One thing, however, is certain: there is no reason to envy them! There are many different kinds of executioners. There's one kind of hangman who, for a penny from Judas Iscariot, will turn his hand against his brother, and another for whom the traitor's payoff is not enough and who must be fired up with liquor as well so his worthless hand will not tremble in the act. There are also hangmen who carry out their bloody work in the name of an idea after others have convinced them in something like the following manner: "Mr. so and so, son of so and so, is not only without redeeming social value but also a source of active harm and must be rooted out." So they get rid of the bad apples.

The Jewish police were bought. Then they were gotten drunk and given a kind of hashish: their children were exempted from the deportation decree, and they were provided with a kilo and a half of bread per day in exchange for this bloody piece of work, enough bread to eat their fill and an extra ration of sausage and sugar. At the same time, the police were given a rationale to justify their acts: "If our molars are ripped out, our living limbs chopped off, and our bodies cut in two by our own, familiar Jewish hands, perhaps it will not be as painful as the same acts carried out by strangers, with their rough and dirty ones." The point could be heard in each of the three speeches given quite openly: "If you don't do it, we'll have to." To prevent that possibility, they preferred to do it themselves! And who better to do it than the Jewish police, who were at the same time bribed, plied with alcohol, and brainwashed?

No—there is no reason to envy the Jewish police.

The so-called "white guard"—the porters who work at the Bałuty market and the food department—should have their names inscribed in black on the bloody page of history that records these events. Afraid of losing their soup during the period of the curfew, they offered to help in the manhunt in exchange for the same benefits enjoyed by the police: bread, sausage, sugar, and the exemption of their families from the decree. Their offer was accepted—and they voluntarily participated in the *Aktion*. May the names of all those officials who tried to participate in the ancillary events surrounding this *Aktion* also be inscribed in black letters on the same bloody page that records its history, listing those who joined in just to get the bread and sausage instead of the soup they would have received if they had sat at home. Perhaps this is the case—but who really knows? Who can plumb the depths of the Jewish soul? Perhaps they thought they were achieving something entirely different, were engaged in some act of rescue, if such were even possible. Perhaps . . .

THE COMFORTER IN THE POTATO LINE

There's already a wagon standing on Rybna Street. On it are several children with bulging eyes, looking completely lost, who've already been grabbed. The poor things have no idea what anyone wants with them. Why are so many people milling about and looking at them with such mournful and devouring expressions? Why are all these people sobbing? Why are they wringing their hands in despair? The children themselves have no desire whatsoever to cry. They're completely content; people have put them on a wagon and are taking them for a ride! When does a child in the ghetto ever get the chance to go for a spin in a wagon? If there weren't so many people standing around them crying, and if their parents hadn't broken out in such terrifying sobs and cries as they were being loaded onto the wagon, the children would have jumped for joy onto the wagon themselves! They are still going for a ride on a wagon, but the screams and cries, the wails and laments—all of it unnerves them and casts a dark shadow on their joy. Inside the wagon they keep walking up and down the length of its high walls as if lost, and they look about with their bulging eyes. "What's going on? What do they want with us? Why aren't we leaving on our ride?"

A wagon stands on Rybna Street, and on it sits a hunched-up old woman, a woman who has looked gnarled and twisted for the better part of the year. Since the beginning of the year, in fact, when it was her misfortune to have her thirty-three-year-old son shot down and killed while in her arms. Half paralyzed, half blind, and half deaf, she had become a constant burden on the back of her daughter, the last of six children who was left to her. A daughter? Only a pale shadow of her daughter remains—just skin and bones! She pulls her own little cart and can barely manage to return with it and her purchases. Who, alas, does she have to lean on? She'd rather die than do anything like that. In hindsight, she's even satisfied with her current situation: "Whatever else, I've removed the burden from my daughter's shoulders, lifted from her head the heavy state of mind I've constantly meant to her." So there she sits, curled up in the wagon, her furrowed face wearing a frozen smile. She takes no notice of what's unfolding around her. Screams and cries strike her ears like the echo of a distant thunder. Perhaps that's why, from time to time, she raises her blind eyes to the heavens, as if that's where the black storm clouds could be found. Her maternal and grandmotherly instincts, however, sense the little children who are "living peacefully" next to her in the same wagon, and every time a child stumbles by her, out stretches her blind and trembling hand, trying to pat the little child on the head. The heads of little children are so silky, smooth, and soft, and it's been so, so long since she's been able to stroke one with her hand. The children skip by her much more quickly than her blind and trembling hand can reach, wanting only to pat a child's little head, so she ends up stroking the air and its emptiness . . .

A wagon stands on Rybna Street. In the corner an old man stands and sobs. An old man left miserable and alone in the world, with nothing left to lose. All that was his is now gone: his wife died in the city, before they entered the ghetto. His unmarried daughter was killed while trying to escape to Warsaw. His son, the married one, died last winter of tuberculosis, and his younger son was taken from the hospital several days ago. So he has nothing left to lose. He is, however, a believer, this Jew. He believes that his soul will live on in eternity and that this soul has not been lost to him yet. He still possesses a soul which, perhaps today and perhaps in just another hour, will have to account for its actions in the world beyond. That soul is the only thing left to him, and this old Jew refuses to lose it. So there he stands, a Jew in the corner of the wagon, summing up all the deeds he has performed in this world—and so he chants the viddui.[19] Can one really, on the spot like that and in a moment of such turmoil and confusion, sum up all the details of a long life, a life of insignificance, a "vanity of vanities"? He beats his chest at the thought, and his sobs and tears, old tears, ripe and serious as they are, fall onto the floor of the wagon that is covered with filthy and tattered straw, the way overripe fruit would fall from old, giant trees and be thrown in the trash . . .

A wagon stands on Rybna Street. The wagon is long and wide and enclosed by four high walls. Similar wagons are usually seen in the city, for it was exactly this sort of vehicle that the dogcatcher would use to round up stray and abandoned dogs. The only difference was that those were much smaller and narrower. In the first place, an abandoned dog doesn't take up as much room as an abandoned human being, and second, there were never as many abandoned and homeless dogs in the city as there are now homeless and abandoned Jews in the ghetto. The wagons in which the dogcatcher would throw the dogs he'd managed to capture were covered from top to bottom, for if the pound wagon had not been covered the dogs would have been able to jump out and flee. Who could stop them? The whole world stood open for their escape. All four sides of the city were still open to them— wide open! And so the dogcatcher's wagon had to be enclosed. But the wagon for catching Jews needs no such enclosure at all. Who could escape from it? Who would try to jump? The hospital patient, the old

19. The *viddui* is the traditional confessional prayer recited on Yom Kippur and before death.

man, or the child? Where could they possibly run—into the fenced-off ghetto? The wagons in which the dogcatcher would throw the dogs he'd managed to chase down were always painted black, sometimes with shiny black lacquer, so that, at least from the outside, they'd look sharp and fancy in some people's eyes. After all, these wagons were meant to carry living creatures—and dog meat is today strongly preferred by certain palates. Canine fat is weighed out to the last gram in the pharmacies, and dog skins are worked and processed into the finest articles of feminine apparel. At least those wagons carried creatures of some worth and not Jews, Jews destined to be thrown on the pile of garbage as so many excess pieces of "scrap."

A wagon stands on Rybna Street. This wagon is there to snatch up human beings—as rumor has it—and take them to their deaths. A little farther on, just a few steps away in the market around the former butcher shops that surround the yard where potatoes are distributed, hundreds of people are standing in line waiting to pick up their ration of potatoes: eight kilos per person. At the last moment, people are trying to grab up their potatoes to stay alive during the period while the curfew is in effect. On one side of the street stands a waiting wagon that will carry death, and a few steps farther on stand the already dead—people who have all but expired out of fright—who are waiting for life. The dead and the living brush up against one another, and since the dead are always stronger, the line of living human beings seems dead as well. As if in a frozen, deathly trance, the living just stand there and stare, with choking throats and sunken heads and dark, extinguished eyes. Their bodies display only a final, weak flicker of life. The instinct of self-preservation forces them to use their last ounces of strength to remain on their feet and resort to whatever means they can: we don't need stories; even a word is enough. Just a give us a word—just one single word of consolation or hope!

An old Jew stands in line. An empty sack dangles from his back like a single leaf on an empty tree, fluttering in the autumn breeze. He sits, however, like a leaf firmly attached to its branch, refusing to give in and fall, clinging with his last ounce of strength to his spot. With his last wheezing words, the old Jewish man tries to console himself and others as well.

"Jews—I'm already an old man, worn to the marrow of the bone, without a single tooth left in my mouth. Come closer, take a look—and you know what? That's right, I still want to eat my potatoes! I don't know why—I just feel it in my heart, and I'm absolutely sure about this much: no one will be able to wipe out the Jews! Jews have always existed, and will survive! Of course those who are struck down, poor things, will suffer a bitter, bitter fate—but the *klal*—the Jewish community as a whole?[20] The *klal* will remain! Listen to what I'm telling you!" Thrilled with his own words and amazed by their effect, he excitedly continues and gets carried away.

"And when they charge the enemy on the battlefield with bayonets fixed, don't hundreds and thousands have to fall? Doesn't every soldier have to look death right in the eye? So what kind of soldier stands there and says, 'I don't want to go'? He still has to go! That's what it means to be a soldier! Jews, dear friends, are soldiers, and what kind? Beaten and battered soldiers! No one asked us whether we wanted to be soldiers or not. Now the enemy is charging us with bayonets fixed. Hundreds and perhaps thousands will fall, but the army as a whole? Have you ever heard of an army falling and being wiped out to the last man? I certainly haven't . . . Thank God, I'm now an hour older than I was . . ."

Gradually a crowd gathers around him. The Jew is not really telling them anything they don't already know. But there's so much intensity in his gestures and in his simple, heartfelt, down-to-earth way of using the popular voice that the small crowd gathered about him grows larger and larger; he begins to draw encouragement and strength from the sound of his own words. Soon he forgets that he is standing in the middle of the market with death lurking just a few steps away. His words begin to be voiced in a *nigun*, in the melody and cadence of a maggid, a traditional preacher—not one who castigates his people but who offers them consolation instead.

"It happened after Sukkoth, dear friends.[21] I was sitting at the table and catching a little nap when suddenly I felt a sharp, prickly feel-

---

20. *Klal Yisrael* (Hebrew) is a traditional term for the Jewish community as a whole and its collective responsibility.

21. Sukkoth is the Jewish Feast of Tabernacles that takes place in the fall.

ing in my cheek. So I gave it a slap, and what do you think it was, dear friends? Just a little fly! Then I swept the fly off my face with my hand right onto that table and asked him straight away, 'Tell me, fly, why me? What did I ever do to you to deserve such a painful bite?' The fly heard me out, dear friends, and then gave his answer: 'I never had anything against you personally, and I didn't want to bite you at all. But look what's happening outside—rain and wind, leaves falling from the trees and the sun beginning to disappear; it feels like my end is near, so why shouldn't I take a bite today when tomorrow I won't be able to at all?'"

He possessed a strange kind of power, that old Jewish man. His tone and the way he spoke seemed to lift stones from the hearts of the crowd, loosening the nooses around their necks. Here and there you could hear a sigh emerging from the group that had gathered round, or a groan—those in line were no longer frozen in place but began to move; their ability to groan had already been restored as well as their ability to cry. But that was not the reward the old Jewish man deserved. Instead of sighs and groans, they should have hoisted him onto their shoulders and smothered him in kisses! The story ends differently, however: Who could possibly raise him on their shoulders, the old Jewish giant, and who could possibly cover him with kisses, when almost no one had enough strength left to sigh or to groan?

NOT JUST THE JEWISH POLICE

Is it really true? The Jewish police weren't able to handle the job themselves? Perhaps. Who could possibly be strong enough to pick and probe for hours at a time at their own open wound, making it wider and deeper, before their hands would begin to grow faint? Here is how they tell it: a policeman fainted and suffered a nervous breakdown. There's even a rumor making the rounds about a suicide attempt! Who knows whether these stories and rumors have any truth behind them? Even when people can eat a kilo and a half of bread a day—an art easy to perfect, given the general hunger in the ghetto—going insane is just as easy to do. It's a lesser art to faint. And if life can become abhorrent to everyone else, why can't it be the case that a policeman could find life abhorrent to him and seek to bring it to an end? So people have begun to say the Jewish police will be unable to cope with the task. People say they will not be able to deliver the number of human beings that have been demanded, and more: the Jewish police are weak and unable to gain control over the situation. People say that the police are in despair and ready for the worst. People say . . .

But this common wisdom is nothing but a pack of lies! It's a lie when they say the Jewish police will not be able to cope! Who was it, after all, who carried out the previous deportations if not the Jewish police themselves! Who rounded up and deported the last group of twenty-seven thousand Jews if not the Jewish police? It is a lie when they say the Jewish police are too weak! Six or seven hundred police, assisted by the fire department and the entire camp of the "white guards," deployed against an exhausted, starving, overworked, suffering, foot-swollen Jewish community that can barely get itself to move—that's the strongest police force in the world! It's a lie to say they can't control the situation! The deportation committee has mobilized an entire staff of officials who sit there performing the senseless, useless work of copying the population registry volumes over onto individual pieces of paper, according to residence. With such a piece of paper in his hands, indicating the street address of every building and how many are to be deported from each apartment therein, a Jewish policeman could extract dead bodies in a pinch!

People who spread these rumors about the Jewish police are actually doing them a great injustice, engaging in an act of slander against them. The police were bought and paid for, gotten drunk, and given an ideological justification for their "work." One or two, of course, may grow faint at the task; a few may suffer nervous breakdowns; and a few others may try to commit suicide. The result would only mean two, four, or six fewer policemen! The remainder would carry out their "work" as fully and as thoroughly as has been the case up until now.

Given this situation, are people actually lying, secretly whispering into one another's ears—since no one would dare say it out loud—that the Gestapo has joined in and is helping to carry out the *Aktion?* Not in the least. Especially when bad news is concerned; that's when you can rely on the "voice of the masses." In fact, the echoes of gunfire can already be heard—and who do you think is doing the shooting, the Jewish police perhaps? There have already been reports of one person shot here, another murdered there, and these accounts include names and addresses—so who do you think did the shooting? Who committed these murders? You think it's the Jewish police? No. A kind of paradox has been at work—a beastly, terrible, murderous paradox. The German police have been pitching in to help the Jewish police do their "work." Out of mercy? Help driven by purely humanitarian concern? No; the paradox at work here is of a different sort: it is simply a matter of the beast getting the scent of blood.

The smell of blood has been in the air, but he hasn't yet tracked it down. He follows the trail but hasn't been able to spill any blood himself. Now he's left the forest, if only to enter that "soiled" and "diseased" Jewish territory to see that blood with his own eyes and to spill it with his own hands. That's why one killed here, someone else shot down dead in his tracks over there, is nothing in comparison with what people imagine with fear and trembling, their thoughts drenched with blood. The beast will not satisfy himself with a shooting victim over here and a murder over there; it will be a mass slaughter, a pogrom, in order to give full and literal expression to the Nazi anthem "When Jewish blood spurts from the knife."[22] First a slaughter via pogrom and then an expulsion, following the method used in Zduńska Wola and other towns, or so goes the rumor now being whispered from ear to ear. In matters of this sort, everyday people are a much more reliable source of information than the chairman, who only yesterday assured the public from his podium, "I will not permit firearms to be introduced to our streets, and blood shall not be spilled . . ."

PEOPLE ARE NABBED FROM THE STREETS

Oy—God, Jewish God—how cheap Jewish blood has become. Oy—God of all humanity—how cheap human blood has become.

The streets are running with blood—shed in the courtyards of buildings and inside their very apartments. It is not red, healthy blood that is being spilled—that type doesn't exist in the ghetto. Three years

22. A Nazi SA (storm trooper) fight song and youth anthem from the 1930s, whose full verse went "When Jewish blood spurts from the knife / Then all goes doubly well."

of war and two and a half years of ghetto life have devoured all the red corpuscles. Pus, however, can be found in the ghetto, and a constant stream of bile—dripping, streaming, and pouring from the eyes and running through the streets, courtyards, buildings, and the apartments themselves. How could the constant shedding of blood possibly slake the thirst of the beast? All it can do is whet his appetite—nothing more!

It is no longer just rumor or idle gossip but a certainty: the head of the ghetto administration, Hans Biebow, who is usually the one most concerned with the existence of the ghetto and keeping it alive, has taken point position in the *Aktion:* he is now the one leading the "resettlement" himself. The kidnappings have begun. The Jewish police are snatching people from the streets—and are doing it mercifully, according to instruction: children up to ten years of age, the elderly sixty-five and older, and the sick certified by doctors as having no prospect of recovery. The Jewish police snatching people off the streets can be bargained with by afflicting their conscience in every possible way; at least people can cry in their presence, try screaming at them, while other people are snatched by what are called "mixed committees." A few of the Jewish police, a few firemen, a doctor (a mute figure who cannot bring himself to utter a single word, because no one asks him for his opinion), a nurse (there strictly as window dressing), several porters from the "white guards" (whose job is to load the "express merchandise" onto the wagon), and—a single figure in uniform, with a revolver in his hand.

The kidnappings have begun. Here is how people are being nabbed:

First the Jewish police arrive—along with a whole gang. Wearing police hats, firemen's hats, and porters' caps. The building is surrounded, the central entrance blocked—the building where you've lived so long and felt so safe and at home is suddenly transformed into a prison. Everyone must remain inside as soon as the announcement booms out from the courtyard. In this way people are driven like mice toward the mousetraps. Your world narrows down to your own four walls. Your apartment becomes too small. Your eyes feel too small for their sockets, your chest too small for your pounding heart—eyes grow wide with terror, bulging out from your face. Your throat clenches with agony, swelling until it feels as if it will burst, as if encircled not by a slender noose that might slice it in two but a coarse piece of rope that grabs you and chokes until you can barely breathe, leaving neither here nor there, letting you neither live nor die.

The Jewish police have the addresses. The Jewish police employ the Jewish superintendent of each building, and each super has a registry book that lists each and every tenant. The addresses supply the following information: in such and such an apartment lives a child who was born on such and such a date. The addresses tell the story: in apartment so and so lives an elderly man who is such and such years old. A doctor enters each apartment. He examines everyone present and determines who is actually healthy and who is just putting on an act of being in good health. He's had far too much practice at it in the ghetto—a quick glance is all it takes for him to separate those who are healthy from the deathly ill. It's no use for a child to grasp at his mother's neck with both of his little hands. It's no use for a father to throw himself in front of the door and bellow like an ox being slaughtered, "You'll take my child over my dead body!" It's no use for an elderly man to clutch at the cold walls with both of his bony hands, pleading, "Let me die in peace." It's no use for an old woman to fall at their feet, kiss their boots, and beg them: "I've got grown grandchildren older than you." And it's no use for a patient to bury his feverish head in his damp, sweat-soaked pillow and shed what is probably his final tear.

It's no use. The police must deliver their quota. So they must kidnap the required number of people. No mercy is allowed. They—the Jewish police—nab their victims in an organized way. And as they nab people, they help them as they moan, sob, and cry. The police who take people away try, with their hoarse voices, to offer them words of solace and comfort and to make excuses for their pain. They speak with the bedside manner of serious, conscientious doctors who are talking to someone with a life-threatening condition, trying to convince the patient to undergo a delicate operation. Thus when a father and mother hand over their child, they at the same time have the feeling that they've entrusted their offspring to Jewish hands. Only later, when they glance at the now empty corner of their apartment and notice the empty bedding that belonged to their child—only then does the reaction begin to set in. Only later does the brutal pain begin to make itself felt—just as the brutal pain of a tooth ripped from the mouth begins to hurt only when the narcotic begins to wear off.

Even when the Jewish police have to use force (and even when they use it mistakenly), they apply it mercifully. The Jewish police understand, as well as sense, that they must beat those who are already beaten and afflict the already afflicted. They carry the child away in their arms. The old man is propped up carefully. They look for a comfortable spot in the wagon to put the sick. The pain is immense, but it is the pain of pouring iodine on an open wound—a burning, tearing feeling that can drive you mad, but the iodine must be applied lest the wound fester and spread gangrene throughout the body. The Jewish police do their work with this awareness: if they do not pour iodine on the wound of the Jewish body, others will come and rub salt and pepper into that same wound. If they don't continue to nab people, others will do the job in their place and . . .

IT'S ALTOGETHER DIFFERENT WHEN OTHERS DO THE JOB

They enter a courtyard, and right away there's a stray shot from a handgun. That clips everyone's wings at once. All blood immediately runs cold, and everyone feels as if molten lead has been poured down their throats. As the lead begins to harden, the *oy* or *ahhh* that had been on the tip of the tongue is unable to leave their mouths. They tremble—no, trembling is an act that needs blood flow in order to be carried out, and blood has ceased to circulate in their bodies; it has stopped flowing, like water on a frosty night! People stand there in an awkward, dumbstruck form of paralysis, clumsily waiting for what is to come . . . until a harsh, laconic, and draconian order is suddenly screamed high and loud, then repeated by the Jewish police: "Everyone must report to the building courtyard in the next two minutes. No one can remain inside. All doors must be left open."

Who could describe, who could paint a picture, of the insane, wild rush that follows: half dead human beings, barely able to move, throwing themselves down several stories of stairs, hurrying to carry out the order in time? No one can. Old sclerotic legs, twisted by rheumatism, stumble on the crooked stairs and over the sharp paving stones. Young, limber legs that can spring like a deer zoom by them with birdlike quickness. The clumsy, tripping feet of the sick who've been chased from their beds bend like bagels as they run. The swollen feet of the starving scrape and shuffle along like the blind finding their way. Everyone runs, everyone hurries and throws themselves into the courtyard, because woe be unto whosoever is late. He won't be able to finish the last leg of the journey—unless he swims it through his own blood. Woe be unto those who stumble and trip as they make their way—they'll never get their footing again and will slip and fall on their own blood. Woe be unto the terrified child who wants to scream out one single word—"Mama!" He'll only manage to get the "Ma—" out of his mouth and will never be able to reach the "ma." A revolver shot will slice the word in two right in his throat. "Ma—" will emerge, while "ma" will curl up and fall back into his heart, like a bird shot down on the wing. The experience of the last two hours has made this a bloody, realistic fact.

When the Jewish police come they grab whoever they can get— whoever is nearby. If someone is hiding out and can't be found, he isn't grabbed. When *they* come to take specific persons, however, they take whoever is at home in place of whoever is missing, then go on to find whoever is hiding out and take him too. When they find him he doesn't have to be led away but carried off. When the Jewish police come to take people, they make sure they get their "take" on the side as well. It goes without saying that ghetto currency is not accepted— valuables only. The transaction is conducted quietly and stealthily, and when no one can see or hear, those who still have something left to trade can buy themselves out. When others come to take people, there's only one precious currency you can pay them with—your life. You can, of course, choose not to go with them. But you'll never go anywhere again.

When the Jewish police come to take people, they move them from their rooms and try to send them on as if they are human beings. They allow them to bring along the little amenities that people require: a piece of bread wrapped in a bundle, a bit of sugar in a piece of paper, the shirt on their back, and if they want, a book of Psalms in their pocket. When *they* come to take people, however, they snatch them away like dogs from the street, take them on the spot and just as they are. People are tossed onto the wagons, packed in, and shipped away. When the Jewish police seize them, there's a certain method to their madness, and the method makes a kind of sense: anyone is taken who is unable to work, who is a parasite and a useless mouth to feed, from the ghetto's youth up to age ten, those older than sixty-five, and the sick with no prospect of recovery. When *they* come to take people, there's no sense or logic to it at all. "Swollen feet? Onto the wagon with you. A hunch in your back? Into the trash with you too. A head full of red hair, without any gray in it? You're going too." No order to it, no logic—anything goes. They just grab whoever is within reach, just because.

The line wends its way throughout the courtyard. The color of every face is pale and drawn, the light in every eye has long been extinguished, and he—he's still got a revolver in his hand, firing off a shot whenever he likes. Who would go up to him and explain, "That child over there turned thirteen last winter"? Who's going to tell him, "The lady over there with the gray hair is only forty-five years old and isn't too old to work—she's had a steady job for the last year and a half"? Who will tell him, "That man over there with the swollen feet, he's just hungry—if you let him eat his fill for two weeks, he'd be a competent, useful human being again"? Who would do such a thing? No one, of course! In the end, the revolver sits in a steady hand, a hand that remains steady after cutting down a hundred, and even a thousand, of the "accursed Jewish rabble." The experience of the past few hours has made that perfectly clear.

THE BOILS FINALLY BURST

When a boil finally bursts on its own, pressure is released, and there's a feeling of relief. But in this situation, when the stone is finally moved that's been sitting on your heart and you spit the lead from your throat and can finally scream, does it really make you feel any better? Has the stone that's been sitting on your heart simply worn itself down to dust? They've blown it to bits with dynamite, and everything around it is also damaged. When you cry, do you cry tears that can cleanse and wipe away the bitterness that clings to your life like dust? It's only pus, little bits of bile that stay with you, just showing up in a different place.

The whole time you stood there lined up in the courtyard, trembling in your petrified trance, you lost all sense that you have a child, a wife, a heart, and a brain. Your head is held in a sturdy vise, your neck surrounded by a coarse noose, and heavy stones weigh upon your heart. The dearest person to you in the world could be shot down in your arms, your own child could be ripped away from you, together with a chunk of your own breast, and you—standing there in your deaf and dumb, narcotic torpor—you wouldn't move a single nerve or show even the slightest twitch of a reaction. You'd stand there quietly like a rough piece of wood, and with all your tortured senses dulled you react only to the cold steel of the revolver barrel when you feel it press against your temple. But when you're back in your apartment—once your senses can partially free themselves from their deathly cramp— your eyes begin to open and all at once notice that you've come back without your child who you've just been holding in your arm. Then it suddenly sinks in that you've returned without your wife, without your dearest companion—that they've taken the best and most precious people in your life. And when you suddenly notice the empty bed, where you cared for a patient who was so dear to you, the person closest to you in the world—what else can you do but cry?

But did you? Did you cry like a human being and shed human tears? No, you howled! You roared, you bellowed, you wailed and wailed, making sounds like every beast in the forest: howled like a dog, like a wolf, like a jackal! You roared like a lion, like a tiger—a menagerie of sound with only one voice missing: the human one. After all, your woe was not a human one that could evoke human tears; human beings simply aren't strong enough to bear this kind of pain. Animals might be. So the answer is no—you did not cry. Your neighbor? The one who left his own daughter lying down in the courtyard in a pool of her own blood just because she didn't understand a word of German and showed them her work permit before they asked to see it? He didn't cry either. He let out wild shrieks instead: a wild shrieking like the sound made by an old cat, when someone has snuck up on her and snatched her young, half blind kittens from under her warm belly and then—in front of the cat's very eyes—tossed them into an old, muddy swamp.

And your neighbor's neighbor, whose two sons were like crutches under his lame arms, propping him up on his swollen feet, sons they tossed like another piece of shit onto the pile in the wagon, right on top of everyone else; he didn't cry either. He huffs and puffs, the way an old, senile lion must sound. And your next-door neighbor who went down to the courtyard to take her place in line together with her husband, in whom she always took such pride. She straightened his folded-over collar with her own hands so that she could tuck away and hide his stately beard. Then with her own eyes she watched as a calm, gloved hand pulled the collar back down, peered inside, and put a bullet in his throat. Even she—your next-door neighbor, when she'd managed to carry herself back upstairs into her room on the fourth floor—even *she* didn't cry. All she could do was emit a stream of gruesome hiccups, the sound that a female hyena gone mad must make, and every gurgle you hear is like a sharp arrow with a poison tip headed straight for your heart.

And then there's your neighbor's neighbor—who was widowed when her husband, as they were trying to save him from the hospital, was shot down like a runaway rabid dog, leaving her with three wonderful children, like three young giants—she too did not cry. Instead she ripped out a handful of hair from her dusty head with each of her hands and emitted a wild and abandoned wanton laughter, something like the sound that jackals must make in the dark of night as they lap up the blood of their prey. In every dwelling a different boil bursts, completely unlike the quiet opening that occurs with painfully infected skin. A fiery volcano of emotion lets loose in every room, and those eruptions can be heard: bellowing, wailing laments; screaming, terrifying sobs; and wild, abandoned laughter. The lava pours out of the open windows, through the wide-open doors, through the courtyards, and down to the streets below. Each apartment infects the next, each building the one next to it, every street the neighboring street, until the whole ghetto lets loose with a wild, deafening roar.

The boils are bursting.

Now the boils that have burst are being sprinkled with salt. A new order has appeared, printed on "Jewish-colored" paper, the yellow color of the despised. The text of the ordinance is as follows:

Announcement No. 391
Subject: General Curfew in the Ghetto

As of Saturday, the Fifth of September, at 5:00 p.m., and until this order is revoked, the ghetto will be under a

GENERAL CURFEW.

Exceptions Include:
Firemen, transport department workers, sewage and sanitary department, incoming-goods department workers at Bałuty Market and the Radegast railway station, and pharmacy personnel.

Street passes must be obtained from the Head of the Order Police—Hamburgerstrasse 1.

All Building Superintendents
will be required to keep any and all non-resident individuals from entering the buildings for which they are responsible, and to permit residents only to reside in them.

Those found on the streets without passes will be evacuated.

Building Superintendents
must remain in their housing blocks with their building registration files available.

Each building superintendent must have his work permit with him.

Ch. Rumkowski
Eldest of the Jews in Litzmannstadt

The coarse hangman's noose has just been pulled a little tighter around everyone's throat. In the not-too-distant future, everyone will be loitering about with their eyes bulging even farther from their sockets, with their tongues hanging motionless from their mouths like tongues covered with hardened pieces of manure teeming with loathsome, nasty worms. And then they forbid us to walk the streets, forbid us to exchange a human word with anyone else. You're not even allowed, in times like these, to find out what's happened to your brother who lives the next street over. No one is allowed, in times like these, to find out what's happened to your parents in the building right across the street. You must live not only trembling in fear for your own life but also in a quivering, trembling fear for the lives of those nearest and dearest to you. If it is your fate to remain alive, so you must go on living not just in your own despair but in frantic despair about the fate of your next of kin.

No one is allowed to enter the street beginning five p.m. today. From five o'clock on people must sit in their own rooms like animals in their cages. How long will people remain confined? The ordinance gives no hint of an answer. There one can find only the following: "until this order is revoked." Who, however, will revoke it, if it is to be revoked at all?

The new ordinance turns everyone's thoughts to the darkest possibilities. "Who really needs them, the one hundred thousand Jews sitting there soiling the air, needing food, whether good or bad—who needs them? Maybe a few people take an interest in work the ghetto can perform, but who really needs this ghetto business anyway?"

People wonder whether they've used the following as an excuse to pull the wool over their own eyes, for while they tell themselves, "The Jews have become necessary. Jews are useful. Jews work and earn every meager piece of food they get," they see with those same eyes that the other side can get by without Jewish usefulness and Jewish labor—that the curfew will continue and all workplaces will remain closed for an undetermined period of time, "until revoked." For when someone is pulled from line indiscriminately who is neither young nor old, with a work permit in hand, isn't that proof and confirmation that Jewish workers and their labor are nothing but a joke to them— that they can go to hell, for who needs them? Today, since that same Jewish labor is no longer needed, what further right to exist, alas, can the ghetto as a whole claim to possess? Why should Łódź in particular be an exception in all of Warthegau and sustain a community of one hundred thousand useless Jews who are no longer needed? The *shpere* in this way provokes many different thoughts and reflections. Not one of them brings any cheer. No happy outcome whatsoever comes to mind. No one has the strength to articulate such a thought.

What intent lies behind the new ordinance? The idea is that no one will be able to run and hide. Residents of one building will not be able to hide out in another one that has already been "worked over." A kind of cat-and-mouse game thus ensues. Even a cat lets a captured mouse loose from its claws for a bit, lets it run around free to enjoy a little fresh air, knowing full well that the poison it has sunk through the back of its neck, penetrating through to the brain, will not fail to have its effect. The mouse will never escape. Everyone will be perfectly free to pace back and forth in their rooms, and even run around a bit in the meantime, but saving yourself—that is no longer a possibility; the poison has gone too deep and has already begun to take effect. Later the cat will come and get the mouse—no one has any place left to hide.

People pace back and forth in their rooms, numb on their shuffling feet. With eyes glazed over, bulging eyes staring off into the distance, they gaze out the windows: Is that them? Are the kidnappers coming? Ach! They might as well come and take us! Whatever is to come—let's just get it over with, and it will all be done! Done once and for all! Only the wildest and most dissolute young street hoodlums would be able to toy with human life in the wanton, frivolous way they play with rats: soaking them with kerosene and setting them on fire, letting them run around in circles until they go mad. This is just how every resident of the ghetto feels: set alight and now surrounded by fire on all sides, able to run around in circles only between his own four walls, able to find neither refuge nor advice.

THE STREETS ARE CLEARED

At five o'clock the curfew begins. From five o'clock on people will no longer be allowed on the streets. Now it's only three p.m., with two hours left until the locking of the gates. Another two hours and your fate will be sealed. Those fates will be varied. "Who will live, and who will die?"—it will be decided who will be snatched and thrown on the wagons and who will simply walk right by, and even who will be tossed on the wagon and then, by some miracle, are able to survive and escape it . . . even cases like these have been known to occur.[23] "Who will starve, and who will eat his fill?"—the difference between those who've already gotten their eight kilos of potatoes home and thus been able to salt them away "at the first call," and those who haven't yet been able to get their potatoes and so will probably never obtain their ration at all.

It is therefore truly the case that "they that are slain with the sword are happier than those slain with hunger."[24] For hunger takes longer and brings a miserable and exhausting death in its wake, and since everyone trying to obtain his potato ration does so not just for himself but also for those nearest and dearest to him, the line has gradually become more pushy and rough. In this effort people spend the last ounces of their dying strength. Everyone wants to get a little closer, get there a little bit earlier than the next—to get there a little bit earlier and so get a little closer to the front. The line which, until this point, had not moved at all, as if a spell had been cast over it, now begins to take on a little bit of life. It begins to move. Bodies that seemed to be in the first stages of rigor mortis receive the spark of life. The line begins to "bubble," as it were, and soon it will simmer and boil—begins to bubble like water that is about to boil over and spill from the pot as the din of impatient voices make themselves heard, like the dull and far-off sounds emitted by a volcanic crater just before the fiery lava begins to explode.

The curfew starts at five o'clock. The clock has already struck three. Only two hours are left to move about freely, to breathe free. Two hours total left to work the potato yard, and the line is not only not getting any shorter but longer by the minute. The hands of the clerks at the scales begin to tremble. So do the hands of those in charge—each one of them feels the responsibility that weighs all the heavier on their shoulders with each minute they waste. Every minute that passes allows them to help another person, and no one outside the line is

23. The closing of the gates refers to the Ne'ilah, or closing prayer on the Day of Atonement. The rest of the passage mimics the High Holy Day liturgy.
24. Quoted in Hebrew from Lamentations 4:9.

standing there just for the fun of it. Every minute thus means saving other human beings from death by starvation. The guards at the front of the line become unimportant and are no longer tense; they let forty, fifty people in at a time to give the line a little push, shorten it up, make it less conspicuous. It's dangerous to let so many people hang around in such a small space! The clerks working the scales have stopped weighing the potato rations so precisely—no more tickling the weights on the scale to get the amount just right—and if the ration comes out a little heavy, just take your potatoes and be well! And nobody knows whether the lucky winner of the extra half to a whole kilo of potatoes that the scale has awarded them has already been consigned to an entirely different fate—will it be "Onto the wagon with you!" tomorrow? So the guards look the other way; they understand what the time of day means. Now, when so many people are waiting—now, when the work being done places the lives of so many people into their hands—now is no time to play around and go by the book.

Forty and fifty people at a time crowd themselves into the potato yard, and a few, bent over buckling from the load, run off with their potatoes through the other side of the yard. The load is too heavy for no one. They are not hauling potatoes in their sacks. Their bent and buckling backs are hauling sacks full of life for several members of their families—life for themselves and those nearest to them! There will be a *shpere*. But what will be its duration and how long will it last? Who knows? "Until revoked," as the new ordinance reads. What about bread? Who knows when it will be distributed again? Normally the distribution would have taken place on Tuesday, and now any bread that anyone had left over is already long gone. Oh Master of the Universe, couldn't their trembling hands have weighed out another two hundred and fifty grams for a boy, an old man, or someone seriously ill—and done it today, yesterday, or even the day before? The next "ration," if the "normal" schedule is followed, would be distributed on the tenth. That's why no one simply walks as they carry away their potatoes, even if the weight of the potatoes presses their heads even closer to the ground and makes their feet even more clumsy and unsteady; everyone runs. Each person carries life in his sack, and each wants to get that life home as quickly as he can to share it with those nearest and dearest to him, who have become even closer and more dear to him in the last few days. And by the way—

The curfew begins at five o'clock, and it is already three p.m. The hands of the clock move as slowly and deliberately as an old miser's, scrutinizing his accounts with a sharp pencil. Those who've already managed to make it back from the street don't want to stare at their own four walls, which usually make them feel so at home. Those friendly confines will transform themselves into prison walls soon enough! At the same time, these are the same rooms that have soaked up so many tears, so much sorrow, and so much mute woe and pain. The walls of home become oppressive reminders of a brooding heaviness instead. The courtyard is larger and more expansive; it's freer, or at least that's the feeling it provides. So people wander about the courtyard of the building. But they don't gather in twos and threes to shoot the breeze as usual. No one has the patience to stand still. Conversations don't take, and break off quickly. Everyone has heard things that are so terrifying and ominous that it's better not to let them cross your lips. No one who is condemned to death wants to hear his sentence read out loud, though he knows that it has been signed and sealed and cannot be appealed. No groups gather in the courtyard for conversation. People circulate individually, like animals pacing in their cages. Everyone walks alone, carrying individual burdens, sorrows, and personal woes.

Those who haven't managed to make it home from the streets— though their backs carry no life-saving sacks since the potato yard has closed, since its employees and guards have to get home as well—they push themselves along as well. They hurry. They run. No one walks in the ghetto today. Everyone runs, propelled by sheer nerves. Tired, stumbling feet expend a last burst of energy, kicking like people who are drowning and struggling to reach the shore. Swollen feet pinch against their clumsy cloth shoes, but look at their quickness and speed today: people will do anything to keep from being on the street, where the air is aflame and dust sizzles with hatred that falls like the dew, with destruction, as the pavement burns under their feet. And so in dribs and drabs the streets begin to clear. Here and there a straggler can still be seen, running with terror in his eyes. As he runs he often becomes confused, unable to recognize the entrance to his own building. This is the way Jews run into the synagogue the eve of Yom Kippur when they are late or the way pious Jews tremble on the day when their fates will be determined, when they throw themselves at the mercy of their severe judge and wait for him to deliver judgment: "life" or "death."

It is now five o'clock. The *shpere* has begun.

The everyday ghetto street—ugly and miserable as it is—takes on a new appearance. The street is somehow tinged with a festive air, if "festive" can be used to describe the stillness of a city whose residents have been struck down with the plague or cholera. A deathly and desolate emptiness now haunts the ghetto streets. The dread, the horror, and the fear so firmly lodged in each individual heart during the last two days now assumes a clear and external form in the visage of the empty street—that form is death, its visage the void and emptiness its shape. Hats alone pass through the street: the hats of policemen and firemen's hats, along with the hats of transport workers. These hats are the guardians of death—they stand watch over the void and prevent the emptiness from being filled. If someone wearing a different hat walks the street, he is immediately stopped by one of the official hats and is allowed to proceed further only if he produces a small slip of paper that reads (in German) as follows:

Special Pass

The Bearer by the name of _____ residing at _____
will be permitted passage through the streets of Litzmannstadt during the period of the curfew, day and night included.

Reason granted: the above-named individual is employed by

_____.

Litzmannstadt Ghetto, the _____

The pass must be validated with two different stamps: the round stamp of the deportation committee, to be signed by two members of the committee itself, and the round stamp of the Jewish police, to be signed by an officer on the force. Woe unto the person without official headgear who is caught on the streets and is unable to produce a piece of paper bedecked with two different stamps and three signatures!

The curfew ordinance has a special provision regarding the *shpere:* all persons discovered on the streets without a pass will be deported. It is five o'clock. The *shpere* has begun.

THE BUILDINGS EXPLODE

The streets are empty. Black and melancholy. The courtyards are empty—scrubbed perfectly clean. People are sitting in their apartments, fettered like oxen waiting for the butcher, hands bound like *kapores,* the sacrificial hens.[25] After being twirled overhead, they then sit and wait, all tied up, waiting for the slaughterer to come. The slaughterers move from apartment to apartment, and every hallway is marked by blood—Jewish blood. Every step of the way wrenches tears from more sets of eyes. Sobs. Terrible cries and terrific shrieking and screaming, forming vast puddles of tears. Jewish tears, as their last remaining wellsprings break loose, pouring out with voices raised to a shout. Mothers let loose, tearing the last little bits of lungs they have left from their chests. They are taking their children. The elderly emit their last cries as they are taken from their four familiar walls. The sick force their last moans and groans from their hearts as they are taken from their far-from-comfortable ghetto beds. Buildings that had until now been awaiting death in something like a frozen trance . . . now those buildings begin to explode—people scream, shriek, and wail their lament as a cacophony of voices breaks loose, building on itself. Loud, wild, pulsating, impulsive screams are heard, each one topping the next, almost like an earthquake. The heavens let loose all their fire and fury—lightning and thunder rage as the storm cuts loose that will swallow everything in its path, destroy everything. The world will once again become formless and void.

The slaughterers go about the slaughter. Their hearts don't tremble at all, and their hands are steady. The slaughterers proceed with the slaughter. Cold-blooded? Indifferent? Who can know? Who has ever peered into the heart of a slaughterer as he wields the knife, stands over the ox whose feet are bound as it looks back at him with its own

25. Ironic invocation of *kapores,* the sacrificial hens that are part of the Day of Atonement purification ritual, which is performed as described here.

murderous, bloodshot eyes? Perhaps at that moment the slaughterer's eyes are no less murderous and bloodshot than those of the ox! Who has tried to plumb the depths of the slaughterer's thoughts as he stands over a calf that looks back at him with its two blue, innocent eyes, calling out to him for so much sympathy and mercy? Maybe at just that moment a warm feeling floods his heart, reminding him of the human traits known as sympathy and mercy! Who has attempted to dissect the feelings of a ritual slaughterer as he stands holding the knife between his teeth, bends the weak little head of a dove bound for slaughter, and meets its glassy eyes as they faint with fright? Isn't it possible that at that moment his heart becomes just as faint and his eyes just as glassy and numb with fear as those of the dove? His hands, however, must remain steady. Feelings are feelings, the heart is the heart—but his hands cannot be allowed to tremble. For if the slaughterer's hands tremble, the product is considered forbidden meat.

Who then could possibly peer into the hearts of the Jewish police when they tore a child away from the hands of its father, and the father, in his wild and wanton despair, threw a hatchet or a knife at them? The possibility exists that at that very moment they grabbed the child in a fit of murderous rage! Who has tried to plumb the depths of the Jewish police as they carried off a child whose eyes are glazed over in mute, unconscious terror, like those of a dove being chased by a sparrow hawk? Perhaps at just that moment their hearts are flooded by a warm wave of mercy! Who has tried to dissect the feelings of the Jewish police as they carried a tuberculosis patient from his bed and encountered his naive and sickly eyes? Perhaps at that moment they become just as sick as he! However, their hands must not tremble. Human emotions must not be allowed to enter their hearts. The quota must be met: three thousand people a day. If their hands become unsteady or their hearts begin to feel pity or fill with other human emotions, the slaughtered victims would become impure. Blood would be spilled in a gratuitous and senseless way, and it has in one building after the next. But what difference does it make to the victim whether his slaughter is kosher or impure? The slaughterer is simply doing the best he can and tries to keep his emotions under control—but not his victim. So long as his slaughter has not yet been accomplished, as long as he lives and breathes, he shows his reactions, and so—

THE BUILDINGS EXPLODE

The way the building at 45 Limanowski Street exploded. Just now the police had been "working" that address. Not a minute went by after they left the area before the building erupted with screams and roars, letting loose with an immense chorus of shrieking voices as if from the depths of hell. The earth began to tremble, as if devoured by a massive flood.

That was the building from which they took old Mr. Krell. Because—

What did old Krell know how to do his whole life long other than to carefully guard his beard and his side locks and the Jewishness of his Jewish god? Absolutely nothing at all. His material needs had always been attended to by somebody else. When he was small, it was his parents. When he grew up and was orphaned, this role was taken on by the families of the town where his yeshiva was located. When he was ripe for the wedding canopy and took a bride, it was his wife. She became the one who prepared his breakfast and lunch and placed them under his nose and who washed the shirt that he would change each Friday at the ritual bath; she paid the attendant his fee. On his own he knew from nothing. When alone, Krell saw the world with the innocent eyes of a child that belong to a naive yeshiva boy. While the townspeople were exiled from their homes under a hail of pistol and rifle fire, mocked and ridiculed as if a steady stream of boiling water were being poured over their heads, and shipped to the ghetto, Krell knew one thing and one thing only: he must take his Talmud volumes with him. These books were the only burden he brought. His refined and delicate hands, unaccustomed to any sort of manual labor, could not manage to haul the entire Talmud, so he took as many volumes as he could and wheezed and panted his asthmatic breath. The trouble he took was worth the effort. It was worth the pulmonary disease he began to suffer as he breathed hard while dragging them along. If he hadn't brought his Talmud along, what would he have filled his empty and poverty-stricken days with? If he hadn't taken the difficult passages of the Talmudic commentary along with him, how would he have filled those difficult, hollow, and sleepless nights?

That's how he'd always lived his life, old Krell, and so he remained. No one had ever seen him in the courtyard with a group of neighbors. What could he possibly talk about with them? Hunger? As far as he was concerned, he had enough. Whatever his wife gave him would suffice. It was either one or the other: if she had something, she would give him something—and if she didn't? That would have to do just as well! If she didn't give him any more, it followed that she had nothing left. So there was no point talking to the neighbors. Especially today, on the Sabbath day. What was the day of rest created for if not for sitting, and if you cannot sit, then to lie down and to study and praise God for the mercy he has bestowed on his good people by granting them this precious Sabbath day? As for the goings-on in the street with the frightful decree, the terror and turmoil now hovering over Jewish hearts—old Krell knew nothing about it. That was his wife's department. But she wouldn't tell him the stories she'd heard. What for? Just to worry him? So old Krell just lay there studying his Talmud the way he did yesterday and the day before when suddenly the Jewish police came in and took him away.

What had old Krell done his whole life other than carefully guard his beard and his side locks and the Jewishness of the Jewish god? Absolutely nothing. His material needs had been taken care of by his wife. How could old Krell possibly know what it meant that he was being "taken" today? Nothing. He had no idea whatsoever and knew only how to express his surprise: What did the police want with him? And why were there so many of them? If a single or even half a police had come, would he have shown any resistance at all? Wouldn't he have gone along? What did old Krell know about it? When the police come calling, isn't one obligated to follow the Talmudic doctrine known as *dina demalkuta dina*—the law of the land is binding by definition? Why would they need so many police? It's probably just a mistake that would be cleared up shortly. What would old Krell know? Nothing at all. But of course his wife knows quite well. Oy, does she ever! She hasn't been able to get a single wink of sleep for nights on end.

Over the course of the last several nights her pillow has been soaked through with her tears. She trembled the entire time, tormented with worry about him, and now she stands there, rips out her hair in great swatches, bites her cheeks—and remains silent. With all her strength and the last shred of nerves she has left, she holds it all in and keeps herself from screaming, from screaming out the burden that's been laid on her heart for the last several days. Why should she make him fret, the old man? But after he's been carried away, when he's already on the other side of the courtyard, when he's already standing on the wagon and is too far away to hear—then she could begin to cry and let her shrieks carry the pain that has been afflicting her heart. Who could possibly hear her screams and not break out in screams of their own? Who could possibly listen to her cries and keep from crying themselves? No one! In this way—

THE BUILDING AT LIMANOWSKI 45 IS EXPLODING

There are many children in the ghetto who belong not just to their parents but to the building as a whole. Such children as a general rule are lovely and far more intelligent than their age would indicate. Rysiek Fein was just such a child, everybody's darling. No neighbor, whether male or female, no stranger could pass him by without giving him a pat on his clever little head. No neighbor, whether male or female, could pass little Rysiek by without offering some version of the following: "My little Rysiek, what will you do when the war ends and we all get out of the ghetto?"

"When we get out of the ghetto I want to buy myself a—a roll." Because he was constantly hungry, was Rysiek Fein. No less hungry than hundreds and thousands of other children in the ghetto, but he was smarter than most other six-year-olds. When he was hungry (and when was he not) he would not, as was the habit with other children, constantly nag people and complain. He would suffer his hunger in silence, like an adult. Because Rysiek knew and understood that even if he cried all day long he wouldn't get any more than his twenty-five decagrams of bread. And even if he nagged until the next morning he wouldn't get anything more than his sparse and meager bit of soup. So when his mother would steal a little bit from her own ration—

break off a little piece of bread and give it to him, and when she'd pour a little bit of her soup into his bowl—he didn't need to nag or pester her at all. If his mother had something, he knew, she'd give it to him on her own.

A clever child he was, Rysiek Fein. But he was no longer just a child. He was jealous of Józek, his eleven-year-old brother. Józek had already gone to work. Every day when he went to work Józek took a bowl along with him, and before he got home he had already gotten some soup— a bowl of soup that was his alone. All to himself. Rysiek was not jealous of the soup that Józek received and that he did not—he was still too childish for that; only adults begrudge the good fortune of others. He was simply jealous of the fact that Józek had to get up so early and go to work while he had to stay home the whole day all by himself. This was perhaps the reason that one of Rysiek's favorite pastimes was to play "*ressort* worker." With a piece of string he would tie a pot to his waist and march around the courtyard, walking back and forth across it just like Józek, with his strong and steady gait. And when neighbors would ask him, "Where are you hurrying off to, my dear little Rysiek?" he'd reply, "I'm hurrying off to work." "And why do you have that pot tied on you, Rysiek?" "To get my soup." And then he would laugh. He was a child, but a clever child, and knew his game was just that: "I'm just playing this game because I'm hungry," he'd say, "and Mama hasn't come back yet from the *ressort*." During the last two days, when his mother gave him—like all Jewish mothers in the ghetto gave their little children—her last little piece of bread, spreading it with the last tiny bit of margarine and sprinkling it with the last tiny bit of sugar that was left, Rysiek asked her, "Mama, why are you giving me so much food, and such good food to eat? I'm not sick!"

A clever child, Rysiek Fein. He knew that they "nab" children—he knew more about it than his neighbor, old Krell. The only thing he didn't quite understand was that this nabbing was also meant for him. When he was younger people used to threaten him by telling him that if he didn't behave, the gypsies would come and carry him away . . . but that was so long ago! Maybe he misbehaved back then, but today— these days everybody says he's so sweet. Anyway, there are no more gypsies in the ghetto. So who would snatch him? And why? Rysiek

Fein, however, is still just a child—a six-year-old child. So they took him. And since Rysiek Fein was one of those children who belonged not just to their parents but to the entire building, none of the neighbors were able to look on when his father smashed his head against the wall in wild despair, and no one was there to hear when his mother shriekèd out her dreadful pain.

THE BUILDING AT NO. 47 HAS EXPLODED

The house next to the two aforementioned buildings—the adjoining one at 5 Urzędnicza Street—was smaller but built on a solid oak foundation. Old Berkowicz built it. Fifty years ago when he did, he was still a young man just learning the ropes. There was a young wife back then too, a round, plump, and warm woman—one of our own—a full-fledged housewife and mother hen who wanted to rule her own roost and build it through her own efforts, not those of strangers. She didn't want outsiders peeking into their home. "Let the house be one stride wide," she'd say. "At least it will be our own." So her husband, who was still a young man back then, built her a house. He did anything she'd ask; if she'd wanted him to pluck a star from the sky, he'd have done that for her too. As the years went by he built a tannery in the courtyard of the house as well. As old Berkowicz used to put it, "All you need to live is a wooden roof to cover you—but to work, for that you need four solid walls." So he built himself a tannery—not a fancy, overwhelming, world-class establishment that catches your eye but a tannery where they could set to work with their own hands. In that tannery the wife also worked, as did the child once he was old enough to become part of the family livelihood.

The years flew by. Children were born and came of age and eventually brought new sons- and daughters-in-law into the little house. And while the house—may the evil eye not be tempted—was eventually filled to the brim, it stood fast and strong, never coming close to tottering and falling as it bore the heavy steps of new sons- and daughters-in-law and their children with ease. Nor did it totter when the roof of the little house had to be taken down so that a second floor made of wood could be added to alleviate the crowding that came with the years. A solid foundation had been laid, and the grandchildren born into this house likewise came from the strongest oaken stock—the old Berkowicz blood. No doctor had ever set foot in this house save the midwife, who came to help a daughter or daughter-in-law to give birth. No shouts or screams were ever heard in the little house save the cries a woman makes in the midst of her birth pangs. No crying was ever heard in the little house save that of a child who was awakening from a bad dream. What a warm and homey place that house became— for parents, their children, and their children's children; it was just the kind of home that Berkowicz's wife had longed to have. A place where all the children could find work—the tannery fed all of them in the little house at number seven, and the anchor for them all was the father, old Berkowicz himself. His word was final and his opinion the only one that mattered: "That's what Dad said" or "That's what father-in-law thinks" or "That's what grandfather wants" is all you'd hear.

The same holds true even in the ghetto now that the tannery has passed into the hands of the community and has become the property of "the eldest of the Jews," the head of the Judenrat, and is being run by a "manager," a "kierownik," as they call them in the ghetto, whom no one knows or respects. Old Berkowicz is still calling the tune and remains in charge of all the tannery workers in everything but name—that is, of his children and grandchildren. All this despite the fact that by now old Berkowicz was in fact very old, and despite the fact that, poor thing, he'd already had to bury a number of his grandchildren in the ghetto, and that many of his children, as well as sons- and daughters-in-law, are now wandering about with feet swollen from hunger. His wife spends more time in bed than on her feet and is something less than a human being at the present time. In the face of it all he alone remained the same old Berkowicz—the solid old oak. He was the first one to show up at work in the morning and the last to leave at the end of the day. Even on the Sabbath, old Berkowicz goes to work. What's done is done, and "if we have to, we have to," was how he looked at it, while conceding to end the workday early only on the Sabbath itself. Then he washes his hands and recites some Psalms or a few verses from *The Wisdom of the Sages*. It makes no difference what anyone says to him; the main thing, according to him, is remembering that you're a Jew: "That's what Papa said" or "That's what grandpa thinks" or "That's the way Grandpa wants it" was always the response.

So he sits there, old Berkowicz, reciting his verses from *The Wisdom of the Sages* or reading a few Psalms: it's Sabbath afternoon, after all, and he's got a little time on his hands. Suddenly the house is surrounded by the Jewish police, who take him, old Berkowicz, along with his wife, who's been lying there, alas, for several weeks and is no longer a fully human being. She doesn't understand what anyone could want from a woman of her years, why they were "driving" a woman in her old age to the police. And he—he just stands there and laughs. "Ha-ha, look how many militiamen they've sent for His Honor! They must think I'm still the old Berkowicz, the one who could take on a whole county fair full of Polish peasants and knock them silly! Ah children, my little children, things aren't what they used to be! Three years in the ghetto could bring even a Cossack to his knees." Still, the whole thing amazes him as it unfolds. "Why, my little children, why? Did I ever sin at the feet of the golden calf?"

After all, what does old Berkowicz know about being "taken"? All he knows is he's the first to come to work and the last to leave and how to read verses from *The Wisdom of the Sages* on Sabbath afternoon, or a few Psalms. What could being "taken" have to do with him? He's still a worker! Aren't they only supposed to come and take those no longer able to work? But his children know all about it. They gather around the old man, wringing and pounding their hands.

"They're taking Dad?"

"Mama?"

"Father-in-law?"

"Mother-in-law?"

"Grandpa?"

"Grandma?"

For the first time in the fifty years that the house has been standing, screams and cries are heard pouring from within; building No. 7 has exploded.

AND THERE WILL BE HANGINGS TOO

It's a lie when they say that people are losing the strength to go on. Human beings are incredibly strong! And it's a lie to say that people's nerves are gone. For if people had nerves of iron or even of steel, even then they would have surely been broken by what has transpired today! And yet oddly enough there's no report whatsoever of anyone going mad. In spite of it all the day goes forward in a kind of monotony, as if nothing of significance requires mention. It's as if people are being roasted slowly over an open fire—they shrivel and begin to evaporate, become stunned and paralyzed, lose their sense of awareness, but do not perish: for human beings are incredibly strong!

Today was a strange day—almost every possible physical and spiritual impulse could be felt. One blow came after another, each one worse than the one before, as the reports coming in became worse and worse; the day unfolded with events and tidings that could match those of Job, with more still to come. The day is not yet over, and within its hidden recesses more blows surely await us.

In the ghetto we hear not only about the events themselves; the collective sense of smell captures the scent before they arrive. Before they become facts, people already know all about them; they have already been sensed, since the ghetto air has already transmitted the scent of their existence. Anyone whose sense of smell has not yet decayed, along with the rest of his five senses, already knows that something new is in the wind; everyone senses that today's events have not yet uttered their final word and that a surprise lies hidden beneath its wings. The dazed minds of the ghetto population are about to receive another stunning blow. All sense that the blow is unavoidable and have a feel for where it may be delivered. But no one knows when it will fall and who it will strike, although people can make good guesses. In the meantime, people live in—could it be called *terror*? That cannot be the proper designation for the feeling that people are experiencing at the present time. With the amount of terror and dread that people have already been through, and with fear and shock that people have already survived today, could terror really have any effect? The human organism has, so to speak, already habituated itself to this poison and can ingest it with indifference. The remainder of the day will therefore be experienced in a state of "expectation," as they try to determine with greater certainty what will transpire without relying on their sense of smell alone. Everyone wants to determine with precision what that "what" may be. But no matter what this "what" finally turns out to be, nobody will be surprised. For what could possibly be worse than ripping a piece out of a living heart? What could be worse than the amputation of a quivering limb? And when all is said and done, what could be worse than finally dying, once and for all? Perhaps there's one thing that is worse: to live through the kind of days the ghetto has gone through recently, hearing building after building explode—and to know that "something" else is coming without knowing what that might be.

"The sun sets bloodily in the west—the western horizon swims in blood from end to end"—it would be both ridiculous and foolish eloquence to say that the colors of the heavens reflect the blood that has been wrung from, and poured out, in the ghetto today. Heaven is too far from the earth for this to be the case! And it's not just that the ghetto's screams and cries have failed to reach on high—even the echoes of their echoes fall short. You see, it was all for naught. The screams and the cries. No one saw them. No one heard them at all. "The sun sets bloodily in the west" is therefore simply a fact that symbolizes what has happened during the ghetto's bloody day. "The western horizon swims in blood from end to end"—a fact that simply describes the situation as it stands at nightfall. But the day will continue to wrestle with the evening before giving way to the night. That day is not over yet, and "today" is hardly eager to come to an end; for the measure, it is almost certain, has not been filled. The final tidings of Job are yet to be announced. What iron resolve and strength the present day must possess—it is as long as the Jewish exile, as heavy as Jewish woe. What dark powers human beings in the ghetto must possess! After three years of hunger, after three years of bitter slavery, they can still survive a day like today! Their hearts must be made of copper! Their minds must be made of iron, and their nerves of steel! Have these three years, perhaps, eaten away at their hearts, bit by bit, the way rust does iron, so that there—where their hearts should be—stones have grown instead? Have these past three years dried out their brains so that ghetto men now wander about aimlessly, with hollowed-out and empty skulls? Have they caused human nerves themselves to shrivel, making the figures wandering about the ghetto now little more than dummies, able to bear all that comes quietly, as if they were made of stone—and so are scattered about the way stones can be found in mud and sand?

Not at all! If these people no longer had hearts, they would never have sensed the pain that surrounded them! If their brains were no longer intact, they would not have understood and felt the pain of their sorrows. If they no longer had functioning nerves, would they have been able to express their pain with such shrieks and cries? What dark power they must possess—just like beaten dogs or trained soldiers for whom one blow, then another and another, means nothing at all. This day has played its loathsome tricks on the Jews of the Łódź ghetto—and may it be cursed for that! May it also be cursed for the innocent Jewish blood that has been spilled today! May it be blotted from memory for the millions of tears ripped from Jewish hearts today! May it be erased from the count of days for the marrow of Jewish bones that has been turned to ice on the spot! Let today be accursed, erased, and banished from conscious awareness for the final, most terrifying and draconian tidings the day delivered before coming to an end. For in the *ressort* that produces fancy goods out of wood, work was mandatory today. A brand-new gallows was erected there. Twenty-two Jews are scheduled to be hanged upon it.

A gallows for twenty-two Jews has been erected in the *ressort* that produces fancy goods made from wood, in the section where children's toys are produced. And it all makes sense; the gallows is nothing but a plaything for the uncles of the same children for whom other sorts of toys are being made. The gallows couldn't have been erected anywhere else. For a gallows is not an everyday piece of merchandise—it's a luxury item, a plaything, and so it must be produced in the *ressort* where toys are made.

A gallows for twenty-two Jews. And you, Son of Man, wander about choking on the news! Feel the noose being tightened around your own throat, and feel your powerlessness as well. You can't even take your sharp fingernails, you insignificant Son of Man, and dig them into your throat to rip it apart piece by piece and throw it to the dogs! You have no nails, the ones you do have are not sharp, and you are not allowed to have dogs in the ghetto! You must remain, you insignificant Son of Man, both still and powerless! You can't even scream and howl anymore—all your screams were expended as the day progressed. Nothing is left for you to do, you insignificant Son of Man, except to simmer at a low heat, without being able to burn away, and for this too you must survive, thanks to the dark powers that human beings in the ghetto possess—their hearts are made of copper, their brains of iron, and their nerves are made of steel.

SUNDAY, SEPTEMBER 6, 1942

THE LONG AND DREADFUL NIGHT

How long is a night in the month of Elul? In "normal" ghetto times, exhausted and overworked people would plop down on lousy mattresses, on hard, bug-infested beds, turn over once or twice, and just like that it would be time to get up. But last night—how long it lasted! And with the terrifying way it drew itself out, and how immense—how dark and sorrowful—it became. For who could have slept last night? Mothers, whose children had been taken from them? Husbands, whose wives had been snatched from their sides? People whose sick were snatched from their beds? Or perhaps their neighbors, who have absorbed all of their sorrow and tears? The entire ghetto tossed and turned from one side of its mattress to the other and found no sleep at all. Their legs were painful and wasted and made them unable to lie still. The mind of the ghetto was feverish, with nothing cool to provide relief. Every kind of scream and cry has fallen on their hearts, the moans and groans coming from every open window and door and passed on into the silence of the night. And on you, Son of Man, the tears from your neighbors' rooms have fallen like red-hot pins and needles, with their points piercing your heart. It is as if your bed had been made with sheets of fire, making you unable to lay yourself down or even sit upon it. But you cannot get dressed and leave your bed either, because your feet feel as if they've been sawed off and have no desire to carry even your worn-out, emaciated body.

How dreadful was the pain when you laid yourself down on your bed, made with those sheets of fire. Your body was being roasted, and

it felt as if stones were falling on it from all sides—from the neighbors next door and from your neighbors above and below. All of their
agonies entered your room through the open window, crawled all over
your feverish body like disgusting green maggots. Go ahead and try,
Son of Man, to close your window—it won't do any good! The slightest
crack will be enough, the smallest keyhole sufficient, to let them come
crawling through and besiege you and to chew away at the last bit of
marrow that remains in your bones. And the window, if you close it
that last crack, will leave you choking on your own sickly sweat. Hours
have already gone by since the victims were dispatched. Hours have
gone by since the pain was inflicted, and the effect has not diminished
one bit. None of the mothers have ceased their shrieking. None of the
fathers have exhausted their tear ducts, and the silence of the night
makes the screaming and crying sound twice as loud and twice as
piercing. No other sound, Son of Man, reaches your ears—just that
wailing. No thought other than death crosses your mind, and your
heart dwells on nothing except destruction.

And you, Son of Man, whose fate it was to witness the execution
of twenty-two Jews of the ghetto—you who saw their hanging bodies
swaying wantonly like twenty-two leaves fluttering from a withered
branch—you, Son of Man, whose nights are still sleepless thanks to
their shadows, there you lie on your hard and uncomfortable ghetto
mattress, your skin creeping as if besieged by repulsive, crawling
green maggots gnawing away at the last bit of marrow in your withered limbs while your eyes, bulging wide open, dance with the ghostly
shadows of the twenty-two Jews that were hanged. Their tongues lick
at your dried-out throat, slobbering their spittle on your brain with
those long, twisting tongues until you can't wait for morning to arrive.
Your night is terrifying and long, Son of Man, and so you dread going
to bed the next day. You know what the new day will bring—and that
there's no limit to how much worse things can get.

GERMAN COMMITTEES ONLY

It has indeed turned out to be the case that there is no limit to our sorrows. It turns out that there's no limit to how much worse things can

get and that all last night's tears and pleas to God were for naught. Today is much worse than yesterday, much darker and more terrifying. Yesterday it was just the Jewish police doing the snatching. Yesterday we were dealing with Jewish bandits, and in some of their faces we could still discern a trace of the fact that they'd been made in the divine image—some of them refused to harden their hearts and still recognized friends and acquaintances. They were still Jews, and among them were some who still sheltered feelings of mercy somewhere in the farthest reaches of their hearts, and there were still some people who managed to find a path to those impulses. There were those whose fingers knew how to pluck the strings of those feelings and so to survive. Yesterday it was the Jewish police doing the snatching, and if in a few cases they only "assisted" the Germans, and Jewish blood was spilled on just a few streets, how will it look today, when the Jewish police have lost their "autonomy," having handed over their right to act "independently," and become the means by which the official executioners carry out their acts?

Today, the Jewish police no longer have anything to say about the life of the Jews; the ability to say which Jews will live has been taken over by others. From today at five o'clock in the morning, German police are directing operations all by themselves. These German committees are composed of a single German overseer accompanied by an indeterminate number of Jewish policemen, Jewish firemen, a few of the "white guard," a doctor, and a nurse. Together they decide which Jews will live. Police precinct number two has, since five o'clock this morning, been "worked over." A few revolver shots can be heard in each building. Are the shots hitting anyone? Is anyone crumpling over, swimming in his own blood? Or have the shots missed their targets entirely? Whatever the case may be, those same shots are definitely making people shudder and tremble to the very marrow of their bones and turning their faces pale, while the executioner himself doesn't examine things all that carefully. It's not just the young, the sick, the "freeloaders" living off the dole who are pulled out of the lineup and loaded onto the wagons but those whose faces have gone pale as well—anyone who was terrified till his bones froze to the marrow, anyone whose fear made their feet stumble as they walked—

they're all garbage to be tossed onto the wagon. There's only one other choice left to them—to refuse to go and be felled on the spot.

That's how the committees are "operating" today.

JEWISH WOMEN DOLL THEMSELVES UP

With a dry and crisp report, like stones striking against plaster walls, revolver shots echo off the Jewish buildings. Those particular shots must have been the warning that orders were to be carried out completely and to the letter. Two minutes after the shots have been fired, absolutely everyone who lives in the building must appear in the courtyard and line up for inspection. All those in line must remain quiet and calm, for "order" must prevail. It all has to work with the precision of a watch—"Do you understand? German punctuality!" Not a peep, not a sound of any kind, is allowed. No one is allowed to make the slightest face, for that could be taken the wrong way and interpreted as something still worse.

The people must line up like horses for inspection. A horse can let out a neigh, can stomp the ground with his feet, and can even flash his big, ugly teeth—but in the end it's only a horse, and more is not to be asked. Human beings, however, are expected to stand there in dignified fashion and remain quiet, even when looking death straight in the eye. A human being is not permitted to utter anything approaching a neigh until the scream he lets loose in his death throes—he can paw the ground only in his final death throes. And so human beings must line up like horses for inspection. A horse, however, will sometimes receive a pat on the mane from his inspector, get a friendly slap on the back, or even stretch out his snout to reach a sugar cube. After all, horses will be horses! Creatures who are useful whether alive or dead! A horse can be ridden or can carry a load, and when he's no longer able to do either there's always his hide, from which boots can be made, and a carcass that can be thrown to the ghetto Jews as scraps of food. But the Jews themselves, they're nothing but Jews—you certainly can't ride them, as they need every last ounce of their strength just to carry themselves around. Their hides and carcasses, which must have some use, are in fact worth absolutely nothing, not even as trash. Who indeed would want to besmirch his hand, even his gloved hand, by giving a Jew a little pat on the head? To deliver his own kind of caress, every executioner carries a riding whip in his hand instead. Why should he make the slightest effort to give a Jew a friendly slap on the back when he can give him a much better blow with a boot to the stomach? And what Jew is so spoiled that he expects to find a sugar cube with his snout? A slug of lead from a revolver is too precious for him!

The people must line up like horses for inspection. Horses, however, are thoroughly examined from top to bottom, and according to strict and immutable regulations, while people are taken as they are. With horses the matter of pedigree is considered along with the nobility of their ancestry and their stock. In cases such as these, even the old ones are not sent to the tannery, even when they're weak and good for nothing in any practical sense. But Jews! What good would any certificate of pedigree do, and what kind of noble ancestry and stock could they possibly have, alas? Send them all to "the skinner"—to hell with them all! In point of fact, no one in the ghetto actually knows the best way to present themselves during inspection—whether to pinch their cheeks so they look rosy and healthy and thus fit to work, or to look ill in order to wring the last spark of pity from the executioner. No one knows what to do while going to the courtyard for the inspection. If they go down to the courtyard as usual, without hat or coat, it might seem as if they are not taking the committee and its inspection seriously instead of giving it the respect it deserves. Or should they go down to the courtyard ready for anything that might befall them, wearing both hat and coat? At the same time, so much had already been heard from early that morning that nothing anyone tried had any effect. If someone had red cheeks they were considered a "lazy good for nothing," since if someone really worked in the ghetto their cheeks would certainly not look rosy and red. If their cheeks were pale, on the other hand, that could only mean they were incapable of work altogether. If you came down to the courtyard wearing dirty clothes, that meant you were not taking the whole procedure seriously, whereas wearing a hat and coat was met with the following response: "Well, since you look like you're ready to travel, we might as well send you on your way!"

And while everyone's fate hangs on a mere nothing or an evil whim, people are in a dilemma and don't know what to do: Should I act this way, or choose the other alternative? Neighbors gather in whispers, trading conflicting advice on what to do. Jewish women, in any case, report to the "inspection" as if they're heading off to a wedding—Jewish wives who have become gloomy and depressed in the ghetto and lost their Jewish grace and charm, Jewish wives who, on account of the difficult conditions and meager nourishment they have endured, have lost their feminine beauty prematurely. Jewish wives who are ashamed to reveal their naked bodies to themselves after having lost any sense of grace and attractiveness in their own eyes, let alone in the eyes of their husbands—these same Jewish wives have, in the face of all that, decided to make themselves look "pretty." Their premature gray hair has been smeared with artificial color, and when no hair coloring is available, they hide their prematurely gray hair coquettishly under a silk scarf—God forbid someone might spy a strand of gray dangling down and take them for one of the elderly. Starving bluish and faint lips have been smeared with red. When no actual lipstick is available, red pencil or a piece of red paper works in a pinch. Their pale cheeks have been rouged in the same way. One neighbor looks carefully at the other, and they give each other advice on how to make themselves look prettier, make themselves look younger, and how to hide their premature signs of aging. Their husbands stand nearby watching, nodding their heads in sorrow. "Our modest and loyal Jewish wives—who are they getting so pretty and dressed up for anyway?" There's one thing these Jewish wives don't have to do as far as makeup goes—there's no need to add to the streaks underneath each of their eyes with any kind of color or blush. After their decimation by hunger, the struggle to survive, and the continuous sorrows of ghetto life, the eyes of these Jewish women have been underlined by the most delicate and precious shade of blue, a color created as their eyes looked the most difficult terrors imaginable straight in the face—sights that no color and no makeup in the world would be able to mask.

The people must line up like horses for inspection. Horses don't know what people want from them or what their fate will be, and people here don't know what is wanted of them or what their fate will be either. Horses, however, before they're lined up for inspection, have been treated to a generous meal, have had their coats brushed so that they will shine and their manes specially braided and decorated with red ribbons meant to ward off the evil eye. Everyone knows how to do it; this is the best way to get the highest price. When people line up for inspection, however, they have been fed only with threats, fear, terror. No one has groomed them, and they can't even be sure that dolling themselves up is the right thing to do. Jewish wives have cleaned themselves up and made themselves look pretty not to please others or to be selected, but just the opposite: to be turned aside, to get the lowest, cheapest price for themselves—to be overlooked so they can remain part of the lamentable, terrifying, and miserable ghetto and its way of life.

The people are forced to line up like horses for inspection. Horses, however, do not have the sense to know what is actually at stake in the examination and so stand there unafraid. People, however, sense it all. They know that some of those standing with them will soon be tossed in the trash like an extra piece of garbage and so are fearful and afraid: oy, how they stand there in fear . . .

AN ASYLUM FOR THE EXEMPT

Policemen, firemen, and the "white guard" wagon drivers, like others at work in this deportation, obtained an official exemption beforehand for their children and close relatives. Others had different kinds of pull with the authorities who had some say, were able to get exemptions for themselves or their dependents. The kinds of middlemen for obtaining these favors are various: the bureau in charge of work *ressorts* run by Jakubowicz at the Bałuty Market square obtains exemptions for the family members and dependents of the *ressort* managers. Gertler also has gotten quite a few people off.[26] Exemptions are also issued by police headquarters. Richter, the German commander in charge of trans-

26. Aaron Jakubowicz administered the ghetto's system of factories under Rumkowski; David Gertler was "head of the *Sonderabteilung* (special unit) and special agent of the Gestapo." See Isaiah Trunk, *Łódź Ghetto: A History*, translated and edited by Robert Moses Shapiro, introduction by Israel Gutman (Bloomington: Indiana University Press, 2006 [1962]), p. xl.

port, issues them too, along with others. These exemption certificates take different forms but contain the following information: "By the power vested in the bureau, Jakubowicz presiding" or "Through the power vested in Mr. Gertler" or "The headquarters of the Ghetto Police declares," followed by the names of those "exempt from deportation. Names: _____. Address: _____." The exemption certificate is then rendered official by a round rubber stamp and by the signature of the head of the ghetto administration, Hans Biebow.

When panic breaks out, however, when the guns do the talking, then even someone with the ironclad guarantee of an official certificate of exemption in his hand cannot be certain of his fate. In all the confusion that ensues when someone starts to explain his situation, there may not be time to reach into your pocket, take out the certificate, and prove that you are indeed exempt. A rule has therefore been issued to the effect that all those possessing exemption certificates must remain, until the storm blows over, in special centers established just for them: children at the collection point located at 33 Łagiewnicka Street and the elderly at Marysin. These special refuges were set up early this morning. Everyone agrees that these centers are a good and necessary innovation, a beneficial arrangement, so long as people can be sure that the guarantee of safety for those with exemption certificates will be honored. Everyone's hearts are so aggrieved and their spirits so desperate that nothing, absolutely nothing, can be believed any longer. But they have no choice. Fathers who still retain a bit of their masculine strength of character take their children by the hand—facing whatever sorrows that may ensue—put their exemption certificates in their pocket, and throwing all caution to the wind set out into the streets, despite the curfew, and head for the refuges to place their children in a secure location. By doing so they can have the feeling, at least to all appearances, of having done something for their children. Later these same fathers return home without any feeling of calm. In fact, they have brought their children to a more secure location, but they know they cannot fully believe in that security. These fathers are the ones pacing back and forth in the courtyards like shadows. Neighbor seeks out neighbor, and each whispers so that their wives will not be able to hear.

"So what do you think, are our children really safe?" one tries to console the other, with both trying to find strength in the consolation.

"Well, you know, they promised us."

Of course, promised—on paper. Such things have been heard of before. Afterward they must return to their rooms, be strong, and put on an upbeat face that will reassure their wives, who shed tears with every step they take.

"Praise be to God, our child has been brought to safety."

PEOPLE GO INTO HIDING—WHERE IS THERE TO HIDE?

Mothers with weak maternal hearts—mothers who are unable in any way, shape, or form to part from their children, even to send them to a more secure refuge, and who are unable to give their children away without hesitation—these mothers are the ones who scream, "As long as I live, I will not hand over my child with my own hands." Others without an "ironclad certificate" and unable to send their children to a more secure location, the elderly for whom there were no wagons to take them to the "refuge" for the old, and the sick, their hearts still shivering in feverish agony for another few days or hours of miserable life—all of these people are desperately trying to go into hiding. Mothers want to find a hiding place somewhere for their children. The elderly want to find someplace to stash themselves for their final years, and the sick wish to hide their illness somewhere as well. But where? A mother runs with her little one up to the attic, looking to stash herself away with him somewhere in the most distant corner and to enclose her child in the deepest recesses of her heart so that no one will hear a peep that he makes or hear a single breath that he takes. She'll stand there quivering and trembling until the committee has left her building. Everyone worries about his own hide, because a child is considered contraband in this kind of business. Or so the neighbors shriek, with this warning on their lips: "They're just as smart as you are, you know . . . they know where the attics are too. And if—God save us from the very thought—they should find you, it's not just those hiding who are playing with their lives. You're putting all of us, the whole building and all the people in it, at risk . . ."

With this warning, the mother's wings have been clipped—clipped but not yet reduced to ashes. She wants to save the fresh, innocent life of a child she is tied and bound to by every tender fiber of her heart. So she places her stumbling feet on the staircase, wanting to go down to the cellar to hide with her child in the deepest and dankest corner she can find and to lie there until the building has been "worked through." Once again the neighbors warn her. "God forbid! The cellar is the first place they look!" With that, the despairing mother's wings have been burnt, but a single feather within them always remains untouched and a single ray of hope remains. As long as her arm still has the strength to carry her child, the Jewish mother will not put him down or let him fall; instead, she'll head for the larder. She tells them to lock it and keep it locked from the outside. It's a huge lock that strikes your eye immediately, and anyone who enters will see that it's been locked from without. But the people are worried about their own hides and continue to warn her. "And what happens, God forbid, if the child starts wailing when he hears a gunshot, hears someone get shot, gets frightened, and starts to cry? In that case all of us—everyone in the building—is put at risk!" The mother's wings have been singed but not yet consumed by the flame. They can't fly very far this way, but they still have the strength to keep her airborne. So a mother decides to hide herself with her child inside the toilet. They wouldn't look there, would they? And if they did, it's not going to involve anyone else: Doesn't everybody have to go there? But . . .

That's where her wings finally bring her back down to earth. Her child's little head slumps to his chest like a slaughtered hen; he's turned blue from top to bottom. His weak little lungs can't find enough air there to breathe. When he begins to gasp for breath, no mother will make her child fight for breath while holding him in her own arms— let them take him from her alive, not as a corpse choked to death . . .

And then there are children who, all by themselves, could teach you a thing or two about ghetto life, who came to maturity here— six- and seven-year-old children who can stand in line for hours in the worst heat and the strongest rain just to bring home their piece of bread—to bring home their ration of sausage or meat once every ten days—six- and seven-year-old children who are impossible to cheat at the scale and who'll never let you slip too many pieces of bone into their ration of meat. These are children who, by their sixth or seventh year, have already became practiced traders, who can deal in contraband, whether "well-made," that is, cigarettes made in the apartments, "heart medicine," the homemade sweets sold by peddler children, or saccharine—such children are counted among the lost.[27] They are regarded as ghetto criminals who are then marked for "resettlement." Such children have learned their lessons so well that by age six or seven they've already learned how—at risk of their lives—to snatch a potato or another vegetable from the carts. These are children who know how to fend for themselves. They hide on the highest roofs, lying there with their eyes closed while getting baked by the sun, and cover themselves with rags and the kind of refuse you find lying around when they crouch in the lofts and attics or squeeze their tiny, limp bodies into any damp, filthy space in the cellars. And when the roofs are too low and visible for hiding or the attic too accessible with a good and solid set of stairs, or when there's no cellar at all in the building, the children hide themselves between the potato plants.

These children are lying hidden everywhere you turn: in the attics, on the roofs, in the cellars, and in the fields where the potato plants are grown. They lie there for hours, expiring from heat and hunger, keeping still for so long that spiders attach their webs to them. There they lie, trying to protect their young lives, but quite often they fail. Many times, and often at the very last minute, they succumb to fear or, weakened by hunger, ultimately fall into the hands of those sent out to nab them.

The elderly and the sick don't even have this much of a chance! With great difficulty they inch along with a weak and stumbling step, moving from their apartment to the attic and from there down to the cellar, then from the cellar to the pantry. Wherever they turn, they confront people with dread in their eyes, warning them with trembling lips to go away. The potato field is too far away. Their feet can't run like the children's, and they can't risk such a lengthy trip. During the *shpere* their eyes bulge from their sockets and their minds shudder with a single thought until it leaves them petrified: *Go hide. Got to hide. Where to hide?*

27. *Treyf*, meaning nonkosher food, was code for contraband in the ghetto; *gute gemakhte*, meaning "well-made," was code for homemade cigarettes.

What time must it be? Only ten o'clock in the morning. How large can the ghetto be? All told, the size of a single stride. But how many days feel as if they've passed during those few early morning hours! Just days? Years! Centuries! How much time will it take for the ghetto to finish its return to the Middle Ages? Just a few days more, and maybe just a few hours! And how unbelievably wide the ghetto has suddenly become! Just listen: stories about developments two buildings over, when they reach you, seem to have crossed wide open expanses to arrive, as if they've come from over the sea. The curfew has divided building from building, street from street, making them feel as if they're located on different continents. So you listen to these various stories as if they were chronicles from some ancient, bygone era. You listen to them as if they were legends read out from old, musty scrolls and end up shrugging your shoulders. "Are these stories true or false? Where does the truth end and fantasy begin?"

Because it's only human nature: whatever the force of logic cannot fathom, and wherever the power of reason no longer helps, we confront a steel wall of doubt and disbelief. That's why so many people no longer believe in God and do not wish to hear about those evils done by the Crusaders. That's why people just shake their heads in doubt when they read the stories of Chmielnicki and his marauders.[28] That's why in our own time people shrugged their shoulders and expressed disbelief when we read various newspaper accounts of what was being done to Jews in Berlin and other cities. Every one of us had his own skeptical grin. "Well," we'd chuckle, "our writers really aren't lacking in the imagination department." We ourselves—as actual eye- and ear-witnesses—we who have seen with our own eyes and heard with our own ears the senseless actions and measures we've been subjected to—we will not be any different in the future if enough strength and years are granted us to survive it all. A few years will be all it takes before we too begin to shake our heads doubtfully once again, and in

---

28. The massacres led by Bohdan Chmielnicki were carried out against Jews by Cossacks in the Ukraine in 1648–1658.

just the same way. "Well," we'll say, "our writers really aren't lacking in the imagination department."

But won't the truth nonetheless remain "true"? That truth will grate and shriek: "Not only is everything that has been written absolutely honest and correct, but no pen in existence and no human power exists that would be able to fully describe these events as they actually occurred. It's not just that the pen would be unable to offer a description of the entire ghetto; it wouldn't even be able to give an hour-by-hour account of the events that have unfolded over the last few days. There exists no pen and no language with the vocabulary to convey every range of emotions that overtake a human being forced to see and hear all that has occurred in the last few days . . . And—"

Son of Man: Even if, with all the years of Methuselah, you were able to invent the kind of language that is required, were able to discover the fitting words, to use pen and ink to express and describe everything your eyes had seen, everything your ears had heard, and all that your human heart had felt—what would you really have achieved? In the end, you'd finally get a grip on yourself and break out in a cry: "It can't be true!" Even after seeing it all, hearing it all, and feeling it all yourself, in the end even you won't believe it, for the limited capacity of your intellect won't be able to grasp what has occurred. The truth is universal, vast in its immensity, in its beauty and ugliness alike, while intelligence and logic are exercised individually and limited as a result.

Blimele was her name, a girl age six, seven, or maybe eight. Her father was a Yiddish poet.[29] The devoted and quiet wife of the Yiddish poet was her mother. Blimele had hair that flowed in golden locks, blue eyes, and teeth that sparkled white. Her father read his most beautiful poems out loud as she came into the world. All that was most luscious in his lyrics—the morning dew of his deepest gift—seemed to have been poured directly into her limbs. A child—a song—and Blimele was her name.

---

29. Simcha Bunem Shayevitsh (1907–1944), a poet of the Łódź ghetto and author of the epic poem "Lekh-lekho," set in the ghetto. (Roskies, ed., *The Literature of Destruction*, sec. 91.) Blimele is the addressee of this, as of his other surviving poem written in the ghetto.

Her sister had no name. Today, at ten o'clock in the morning, she was exactly thirty-three hours old. Friday's terrors had brought this little sister into the world a few weeks early. She was born at the beginning of the ninth month: such a tiny little girl, whose two tiny, curled-up fists had already found their way to her mouth. Her two quiet, frozen eyes had not yet said a thing. As yet she had no name. She was weak, the new mother: the tormented wife of the Yiddish poet in the ghetto. Only a few hours after giving birth, trembling but joyful tears could still be found about her eyes and at the corners of her care-worn mouth. The new mother was utterly exhausted, and her trembling husband, sitting nearby, chased the irksome ghetto flies from her face. The flies he could flick away, but the wolf still landed at his door. Yesterday, the Sabbath, in the late afternoon, the police arrived and took his Blimele from him. The most beautiful poem of all his poems: cynically and brutally, they profaned his song of songs. The mother was weak. She lay in fever, childbirth fever, while next to her, the infant with no name tried to grasp the nipple on her withered breast with its toothless little mouth but was unable to do so. The mother was spent, and the father remained helpless. Blimele had been taken, and the only one to cry out was the tiny, newborn child with no name, cried out when it was unable to hold the withered breast nipple in its little mouth. And screamed itself half to death.

The mother became weaker and more feverish, so the father, the Yiddish poet, had to become the hero. He must not allow his drawn, worn-out face to make any kind of gesture or show any expression. The new mother must not be allowed to see a single mark of sorrow on his brow lest the sight of it make her even weaker or make her fever worse. His must not shed even a single tear. Certainly not now: for he, the poet who had so often made fantasy pass for reality, was now faced with the task of denying a blatant and bitter truth. He had to use every ounce of that talent to comfort her with his words. And each of those words pricked him like a pin or a needle, given their utter untruth: "They won't take Blimele . . . if they do, it will just be overnight, and maybe the day after . . . it could be all over in a couple days . . . then they'll bring her back . . . The Jewish police would never take a child away from a Jewish poet, now, would they?" He stated it all with a completely straight face: as he is a Jew, that's what he did. Just let her see how calm and full of confidence he is about Blimele's fate. After all, the poet's wife knew full well how beloved Blimele was to him. So in fact what he says must be true. Knowing him, and how beloved his Blimele was to him, it all just had to be true. If he had felt even the slightest suspicion or the smallest doubt, she must have thought to herself, how could he sit there so calmly?

The postpartum mother is weak with fever and lies there half asleep. Twilight has fallen. The lamp cannot be turned on—its light would be too bright and might hurt the small, still expressionless eyes of the little nameless one. As a result she, the newborn's mother, was unable to see that the poetic forehead of her husband was glistening with moisture and was unable to notice how every hair on his disheveled head was drenched. She was unable to sense that his entire body was swimming in anxiety and that his soul was even more feverish than her weakened body. He shielded his eyes from her using stones from his heart. Thus his tears could find no direct outlet—so instead they dripped out of every orifice, and his hair wicked them up, and then they trickled in rivulets down his body. Perhaps, many years from now, there will be a researcher—a super sage—who will declare that tears that do not find their proper exit are not, properly speaking, tears at all. The poet, however, did not engage in research; every drop of his now-damaged blood was crying out within. Every single word he spoke to calm and console his weak and feverish wife after childbirth had been a lie. These were not simply lies but beautiful falsehoods that the po-etic imagination had transformed into truth and repeated many times over. The poet had given such passionate support to these lies, and sworn to their veracity with such strong and solemn oaths, and had argued for them so logically and convincingly, that he himself began to believe they were true. His own powers of reason began to believe in them, because—because it's simply human nature: whatever his limited, individual capacity for reason can grasp is transformed into a universal truth, and that which his individual intellect cannot grasp is considered doubtful or simply unbelievable.

The Jewish poet believed in the truth of his lies for an entire night. And he believed in the truth of his lies for another three hours into the current day—until nine-thirty in the morning. At nine-thirty the

German committee arrived and pulled the Yiddish poet away from the bed of his sick and feverish wife—and then took his wife along with his tiny, newborn tot, who was then exactly thirty-three hours old and who still did not have a name. These are the facts, and 100 percent true ones at that. But the writer of these lines would not hold it against anyone who harbors doubts about them, just as this additional fact will seem unbelievable: that the father, the Yiddish poet, ran about in circles, taking this enormity to heart, while retaining his clarity of mind, which made him believe that he would somehow see this weakened, feverish mother of his newborn child again. He believed that his most beautiful poem of all would be returned to him—his Blimele—and along with her a beautiful, fresh and kicking little girl, a newborn who would now have a name.

The tidings delivered by the neighbors are more than sad. They're dreadful—senseless. In fact, they're unthinkable. The mind simply cannot grasp them, and still they represent the absolute truth!

At 7 Żytnia Street . . . isn't Żytnia Street far from here? Is the whole ghetto really that large? Just listen, in any case, to what people there are saying and believe it, though it sounds so far-fetched, so old and so strange. There at 7 Żytnia Street lived the wife of Dr. Zember, the "doctoress," as the neighbors used to call her, as she was no doctor herself. Her husband was the doctor. The crucial word here is "was": he had tried to escape from Dachau and was shot, or so they informed her. She had been deported to the ghetto from a little Jewish village, together with her four-year-old daughter, a tiny little angel with eyes as blue as the sky. She lived at No. 7 Żytnia Street; she was taken from her apartment, along with her daughter, down to the courtyard, where the "inspection" was under way. There she held her daughter's little hand tightly as both smiled at each other. The child is happy that her mother has brought her down to the courtyard—after all, today the world is bright and beautiful outside, and the sun is simply delicious. And the mother—the mother was forced to smile. It was necessary to put up a good front so that one would look healthy and able to work, in order to not be tossed on the trash heap.

The young girl's freshness, her rosy cheeks and skin as smooth as milk, made an immediate impression. Good party man that he was, however, he could never allow himself to revel in the beauty of a Jewish child. As a good party man, he had been born to exterminate all that was Jewish, so only one decision was left him: "Get rid of the bitch." But she, after all, was a mother, and so—the answer was no! She would not hand over the girl or let them tear her child away from her as long as she remained alive, and so she went on smiling. What else could she do? Let him enjoy her tears? Let him take pleasure in the spectacle for free by laying bare the emotions on her face? Instead she stood there and smiled and let her face show her emotions. She stood there and smiled, resolute in her refusal to hand over the child.

He replied by twisting his face into a derisive grimace. "You don't say! Really? She actually intends to resist?"

Yes. She actually had managed a smile, but that did not prevent her from remaining a devoted and serious mother—she would not simply hand over her child! Let him do what he would. His training, however, had been too good. His courtly Junker education had drilled into him the importance of chivalrous behavior toward women. He simply wasn't clear whether these general rules of decorum applied to Jewish women as well. After smiling, then smiling again in a kind of embarrassment, he pulled the Jewish woman and her daughter out of line. His excellent schooling took the upper hand and was not without some effect; he gave her three minutes to think it over. Three minutes on the dot.

The neighbors were thrown into convulsions at this prospect. Neighbors who were themselves standing in the longer, general line snuck a tearful glance at the two who had been taken aside, standing there smiling at each other—the child content that she could still remain at her mother's side, and who continued to hold her little hand, and the mother who was content that she still had her child at her side.

Three minutes—and not a second or a moment more.

So what will it be? What has she decided?

For her, it was no decision at all. From her point of view nothing at all had changed in the three minutes that had gone by; as far as she was concerned, nobody was going to take her child from her hands while she was still alive. For her, nothing at all had changed during those three minutes, including her smile. His smile had, in the meantime, become darker and more sinister. This was perhaps the reason that he had forgotten the rules of politeness in dealing with women and thus was all but shouting as he gave the command, "Up against the wall!" With the same smile as before she turned and faced the wall. The only difference was that now she gripped her little girl's hand with a convulsive strength, and this was perhaps the reason that the child turned her little head up toward her mother. The child probably wanted to complain about the slight discomfort that the firm grip of her mother's hand had caused her. And this internal change remained a secret that both mother and daughter shared: outwardly the mother looked no different, while for him it was apparent to all that his smile began to tremble into the lines of a twisted grimace as he tried to summon the strength to maintain it. Later, after he had shot down both the mother and her child with his small revolver, the extra effort was no longer necessary. The twisted smile on his face had petrified into a permanent one, and if anyone had asked him why he was smiling and what his smile actually signified—cowardice, bestiality, or simply nonsense?—he probably would have not known that he was smiling at all and that the truth was that a moment ago he had calmly, politely, and "graciously," as the Germans say, murdered two human beings, a young and vibrant mother and her four-year-old child, whom she was holding by her little hand. In answering he might have cried out the same thing that people will probably cry out decades from now, when they read about these events: perhaps he himself would have screamed, "It's all lies! A bunch of nonsense!" However, it actually happened, as unbelievable and senseless as it may seem.

How far is the building at 40 Lutomierska Street from the one at 7 Żytnia? A few dozen steps at the most. Make the tiny effort required, Son of Man—go and listen to a story that you will not believe. Listen to a tale that might have taken place in the far and distant past in far-off Africa among a tribe of wild negro cannibals. Shake your head, shrug your shoulders, but know that it is the truth—a truth that is impossible to believe. The superintendent of that particular building is a young man with a wife and a five- or six-year-old child, the sum total of all he possesses. Even the single bed that stands in his apartment has been borrowed and does not belong to him. In the eyes of their parents almost every Jewish child is marvelous; every Jewish father's child is the absolute best, and every Jewish mother's the most beautiful of all. And Abbaleh had turned out well in his father's eyes, beautiful in his mother's eyes, and was considered clever by both his parents and the neighbors.[30] "An exceptionally clever little lad" was the description that received unanimous consent from all who knew him.

The father had it tough in that particular building—he was constantly at work. Abbaleh worked as hard as he could at his side, helping him with everything he could, as far as his childish strength would permit. Abbaleh thus did not want to be deported under any circumstances. And so for two nights he had not slept at all, in dread lest someone would come and snatch him. During those final days he did not act like a child who could divert himself from his sorrow and terror with childish games; he behaved like an adult whose sorrow was written across his face and who was hunted by terror from behind. That is, he behaved just like his father and mother, passing the days with suppressed sobs and moans and his nights with muffled cries. A five- or six-year-old child who turns out well is a child who can often pass for a mature, intelligent young man. Abbaleh had even begun to eat like a grown-up during those final two days—to keep from starving to death rather than to enjoy the taste of what he ate. During those last two days he became restless. He ignored his father completely and no longer helped him with his work in the courtyard as he had done before; he trembled and dreaded going down to the building's courtyard at all. Whenever he heard an unfamiliar step on the stairs his tiny little heart would begin to pound in his chest, and he would bury his tiny little fists all the deeper in his mother's dress. Completely unlike himself, he began to act like a normal little five- or six-year-old child.

During those fearful days and sleepless nights, his parents resolved that Abbaleh would go into hiding, in a place where no one would find him, in a distant corner of the courtyard: a dark place, a spot that was almost impossible to see. It was a place you could pass by ten times and not notice even once. There was room for ten people to hide there without being seen, making it all the safer for a little tyke like Abbaleh, who was already familiar with the spot. As soon as word got out that

---

30. Abbaleh is a diminutive of Abraham.

the hunt was on, and that people were being snatched from nearby buildings, Abbaleh would slip away like a little mouse into that dark and far-flung corner, and there he would remain as long as necessary, until he was sure it was safe to come back out. Abbaleh—he was someone you could really depend on.

The problem was that no one could depend on her—the fine lady from Düsseldorf with her dyed hair and rouged and puffy cheeks. If she—as she maintained—had to savor the taste of resettlement and be shipped off to this pigsty of a ghetto, why shouldn't the Polish Jews get to try it as well? In vain they tried to make her understand that this deportation had nothing to do with any kind of "resettlement," emphasizing the German word. In vain they struggled to make her see that what was going on here—to use the current expression—was that children and old people were being taken to the trash heap. Does the lady from Düsseldorf with the dyed hair and the rouged, puffy cheeks understand what it means to tear a child out of the heart of its mother and father? Doesn't she herself have three children? Three little children of her own also subject to the same decree? And by the way, what kind of plan does she have going for them? Oh well, no one is going to tear out his hair worrying about *her* children! *They* haven't been coddled and pampered like the children of those accursed Polish Jews! And when they come to take her children away, what happens to them will be no worse than what happens to thousands of other innocent German children being killed during those barbaric air attacks. Don't tear your hair out worrying about *her* children! There's no way she will try to hide them!

And so the question arises: If the lady from Düsseldorf thinks it so far beneath her to tear out her hair worrying about the fate of other people's children, then why is she so concerned about Abbaleh, who is nothing more than "someone else's child"? The excuse she offers is the following: Abbaleh should not be allowed to have it better than what her own children will be getting. The only reason she is even troubling herself about the matter is this: Polish Jews are cowards and hide their children. She's ripping out her hair with concern because Polish Jews lack discipline and do not amount to anything more than a "pile of shit"—because Polish Jews are "disloyal good-for-nothings" and do not know how to "knuckle under" to the law. They're lucky to have her living in the building at all, she tells them, so don't worry—she will see to it that nobody will evade the law, even if it means that all the tenants will face a firing squad. She will tell them where the young punk has been hidden away. And so the lady from Düsseldorf goes from stairwell to stairwell and neighbor to neighbor with the explicit intent of warning them against any attempts to get around the law. The whole courtyard resounds with the claims of the lady from Düsseldorf with the dyed hair and the flushed red face: she will not be hiding her children, and she simply will not allow other children to be hidden either.

The neighbors shudder—they stagger. Everyone kisses her hand. People offer her lavish gifts; if they have a morsel of bread, they ask her to come by and take it. If someone has not yet touched their entire potato ration they received only yesterday, they ask her to stop by and help herself to as much as she likes; no one will say a thing to her in the hope that she will keep quiet herself. Maybe she has plans to hide her own children? She's still a mother after all—she's given her blood, sweat, and tears for her children, just as other mothers have.

The lady from Düsseldorf with the dyed hair and the rouged, puffy cheeks just laughs. She makes fun of them all. Imagine these Polish Jews thinking that a German woman would allow herself to be "bribed." As far as her own children go, no one should tear their hair out worrying about them, as she's already told them all. When they come to snatch them, she'll simply hand them over. And take them they did, along with Abbaleh and many other children from the building at 40 Lutomierska Street, while the wailing and screams from their devastated mothers ripped open the hearts of even those people with no children to sacrifice to Moloch, the god who devours them. It was then that the lady from Düsseldorf took a kind of triumphant victory lap, going from apartment to apartment and neighbor to neighbor, telling them, "A terrible, undisciplined pack, these Polish Jews. Their children are taken and they scream and cry—what a yammer they make!" And what happened to her? Of course they took her three children! Three children, but that's the way it is—discipline is everything! Because she knows what is most important: the law is the law.

It's only ten in the morning and already the street brings tidings such as these.

When someone who has died is removed from his apartment, people follow. He is accompanied on his final journey and people watch as they carry him to his resting place. Until the last shovel of earth is tossed on his grave and still longer, people remain by his side. Today when someone is snatched alive from an apartment you can neither accompany him nor hear the last things he has to tell you as he sets forth on his final journey. Like a dog on a chain, the curfew, or *shpere*, as the Germans call it, ties you down. Like a dog on a chain, all you can do is growl, and that only when no one is paying attention. In this kind of situation, it is completely natural and goes without saying that no one knows anything about what happens to those who have been snatched, or "carried off," by the "nabbers." For the very same reason that today, people are chained up like dogs, without any freedom of movement, so that every nerve is set on edge and fixated, interested only in what may have happened to their next of kin who have just been snatched—people acquire an immediate and sudden sixth sense for the slightest occurrence that plays itself out on the streets of the ghetto. Perhaps the experience of being tied up has allowed people to acquire a doggish sense of smell and a doggish acuteness of ear? Perhaps. In the ghetto, every sort of impossibility becomes possible. In the case of child snatchings, for example, do people really react any differently than dogs? What does a dog do when her master sneaks up from behind, snatches her newborn puppies from under her warm belly, and takes them off somewhere to be drowned? Does the dog do anything more than whimper and howl? It's almost unheard of for a bitch to catch her master in the act and rip out his eyes. Just the opposite; tomorrow, and sometimes as soon as the same day, she will lick his hand if he lets her eat her fill.

What is known about those who have been snatched? The only thing known for certain is that they will not be shipped off today and that the transport will begin tomorrow. The wagons will deliver the snatched from their residences to the collection points, where they will remain until tomorrow, when they will be shipped off for good. In the Łódź that existed before the war, there were similar vehicles known as equipment wagons, running routes from building to building and from courtyard to courtyard. These wagons were manned by what were called shippers, who would pick up the merchandise, count it, and give a receipt for it. The raw material would then be delivered to the finishing floor. But the material was not delivered from the shipping wagon to the vat. The merchandise would first be transferred to a warehouse for sorting by type, and only then be sent on to the finishing plant. That's how the system functioned in the textile industry of prewar Łódź. Once the war began the raw material was no longer available, the Jews who worked with it were no longer in the city, and so no textile merchandise whatsoever was being produced. There seemed to be no way—at least any foreseeable one—for Łódź to remain a center of textile production, so the wagons proceeded to transport raw material. Instead of the textiles they had carried before, they now carried away the people who had turned it into merchandise—the same wagons run from building to building and courtyard to courtyard as before and the same shippers load them up. Only now their loads of "material" are not counted, and no receipts are given. As before the war, it is not unloaded from the wagons and turned directly into the finished item; it is first taken to the warehouse, in this case the collection point. Will the material that is unloaded there be "sorted" as well? No one has the slightest bit of information about that.

What is known about those who have been snatched? The only thing known for certain is that only the former hospitals located on Łagiewnicka and Drewnowska Streets and the former old-age home are being used as the collection points this time. Additional collection points are located in Marysin and at the central jail on Czarniecki Street. If these "shelters" are not typical (for deciding what is "typical" should result from a logic which, though right or wrong, is usually associated with a thought process that, whether correct or incorrect itself, is governed by an accurate or seemingly accurate idea and cannot be chaotically or randomly determined), they are still symbolic—every person who has been taken is sick and broken and 100 percent qualified to enter a hospital. There the comparison ends, since these hospitals have nothing close to a bed to lie on and certainly no doctors who are willing and able to heal the sick; each of the snatched is fully qualified for a place in the old-age home, whatever their age—even the children who still have their baby teeth. Everyone who has been snatched up and taken away in the wagons does suddenly become old, broken, and gray. The actual residents of an old-age home, however, expect their stay to last years, or at least weeks, while those who have been snatched expect a stay of only a few days, a few hours, or a few minutes.

Every one of the snatched, even those with a conscience as clean as polished gold and crystal, is 100 percent qualified for the central prison; the mere fact that he has been snatched up and taken proves that he deserves a spot. The yellow patch that he bears on his back and chest shouts out in the shrillest voice, "A Jew! A criminal!" And what better place for a criminal than a prison? For every one of the snatched, the simple act of being taken is qualification enough for Marysin, where the ghetto cemetery is located. Of course, those who reach the cemetery in the normal fashion have reached the end of their road and are no longer terrified by death and do not try to return, while the snatched who are carried on the wagons to Marysin are absolutely terrified, with their hearts pounding with fear and every bone in their body screaming, "Go back! Try to live!" Those normally carried off to Marysin received a little spot, but still a place, that their nearest and dearest knew about, while the snatched receive no place at Marysin at all and will tomorrow be sent off to parts that will remain unknown, and no one will know what happened to them.

What is known about those who have been snatched? The only thing known for certain is that at the collection points, each receives a daily bread ration of twenty-five decagrams and a bowl of good, thick soup served with bones. Are any of the snatched able to eat this bread and soup? Wouldn't the food stick in their throats? At the moment, no one knows the answer to these questions.

"THE RETURNED": WHAT STORY DO THEY TELL?

The clock already reads twelve noon—one of the full-blooded days of summer. It is impossible to sit inside; no one can tolerate that. The reason is perhaps that you are forced to sit inside with your fellow apartment dwellers around you, to whom you have nothing to say. You yourself are very young, and you yourself have your work permit that proves you to be a useful citizen of the ghetto. Your wife is also young, and her work permit is also in good order. Your fourteen-year-old son is younger than both of you and is already at work as well. He's tall and thin, with a handsome face and a good build. You yourself have no reason to fear, and neither does your wife or son. But then you sit inside listening to the wailing and moaning of your neighbors, to their screams and their cries, just a day after pieces were ripped from their limbs—you sit inside and every minute hear the screams of another neighbor, both men and women, sickened to death by the immense sorrow weighing on their hearts. You sit in your room and every minute hear another scream from the door of a neighbor who, in the depths of despair about his children who have been snatched from him, is trying to end his life by hacking himself to death with a knife. Or you hear another neighbor as he throws himself out the window of one of the highest floors. As you sit in your room wallowing in your own sorrows—anguishing over your own wife and child and about the sorrows of all of your neighbors and the Jews as a whole—as you continue to sit there, the mirror shows you each time you look the picture of an emaciated and fallen figure; "You too are a candidate for the trash heap!" is the story it tells. When you sit in your room and steal a furtive glance at your wife, who has aged decades in the last two days, then turn from your wife to look at your beautiful son and see a dark, broken figure with the terror of death lurking in his deep black eyes, the general turmoil suddenly pierces you as an individual dread and fear for yourself and your wife and fear of the threat that hangs over your trembling child! You are all candidates for the trash! All of you with that sallow, dark, and withered look! Those are the ones they're looking for—those are the ones who get snatched.

All things considered, it's better to leave your room. Things are already a bit better when you reach the corridor and run into the neighbors, who have already stumbled upon this technique—going out instead of staying inside. And when the screams and cries chase after you from the doors that are open a crack, you leave the corridor—go down to the courtyard instead! The announcement of the *Gehsperre*, or curfew, never said you could not stay within the confines of your own courtyard! It's only the strange ones in which you're not allowed to tread!

In the courtyard you nonetheless run into neighbors from the surrounding area. These neighbors have presumably already worked the system and received special permission; the whole courtyard is full—may the evil eye cast its glance elsewhere—with neighbors as a result. You know them intimately, these neighbors. Living conditions in the ghetto have made sure that you know every detail of their lives. Today, however, you barely recognize them, so much have they changed overnight. It's not just their outward appearance that's different but their spirits and innermost selves. The neighbor, for instance, who always loved to crack jokes with his lips wide open and a sardonic look, always on the verge of laughter, now keeps those same lips clenched tightly shut. The one known as "Mr. Consolation" among the neighbors is, sadly enough, today seeking a word of consolation from others, and even if he were able to find it he wouldn't be able to take it to heart. "Mr. Pessimist" wanders about with the same gray and ashen face as always. Even the sworn optimist has wrapped himself in a strange, gray overcoat of despair and is unrecognizable; all your neighbors and acquaintances have transformed their inner and outer countenances overnight.

Especially in the light of day and in the middle of the courtyard, people feel utterly alone, and because no one actually wants to be alone, and since everyone is in constant dread of being left alone with their thoughts, neighbors gather in the same small circles as they did in "normal" times in the ghetto. Little by little, one by one, they begin to unburden themselves of their thoughts. But people speak differently today; the rhythm of their speech has changed. And the voice of each individual has undergone a change, as they're overcome by shock—their senses are dulled and uncertain, and their voices sound as if they're coming out of throats that have been slit or from the bottom of some deep pit, like the voices of those who have been called back and returned from the abyss. People in fact are discussing these "returnees" in small circles, and those who have returned fall into two predominant groups: those who never got as far as the collection points and managed to escape from the wagons en route and those who succeeded in escaping from the collection points themselves. As far as the first group is concerned, there is really not that much to tell. Resourcefulness, a friend who works for the police, sheer luck—any one of these could have been the reason they were able to slip off the wagon. But to have had one foot already in the grave—to have arrived at the collection point and then come back home to walk down the street without being stopped—that's a matter that arouses curiosity right off the bat. That is something in which everyone has a flesh-and-blood interest—in knowing when, what, how, and why.

People who have returned relate the following: those who didn't lose their minds and could still think straight still had hope of passing through the seven gates of hell and coming out in one piece. There were different ways and means to open the doors of the collection points. The most reliable and effective one was money. It should go without saying that this didn't mean paying with "Rumkis."[31] But even Rumkis, if you had enough of them, could be the coin of the realm. Dollars were excellent currency, not to mention gold! German marks were also accepted if you had enough. But since not everyone who had a sufficient amount of hard cash at home had had the presence of mind or chance to bring it along to the collection point, the deciding factor was often those valuables that the snatched happened to have on their person. Gold watches of well-known brands, for instance, or a few diamonds or diamond earrings. Loaves of bread and other staples were less in demand. First because the "liberator"—the Jewish policeman of today—is not suffering as powerfully from hunger as usual. He's getting paid for his "work" on top of his normal ghetto ration, another kilo and a half of bread per day as well as sausage, sugar, and other items. Second, in this kind of situation one hand has to wash the other, as the saying goes—you hand over the goods, and I'll open the door. In the case of foodstuffs, the liberator would have to take it on faith that he'd get paid, as no one had their food reserves along with them. There were even cases where a policeman traveling with the wagon or working at the collection point would discover a friend

31. The ghetto currency, named after Rumkowski.

or a close relative among the snatched and would free the person in question without any payment, then drive them back. Most of this variety of the "liberated," however, like those who were "liberated" illegally, never made it back home. They usually found a hiding place in another part of the ghetto where no one knew them and thus where there was no danger of getting turned in by a jealous neighbor. The only thing known about them is that they're somewhere at large, and nobody knows where. At present, no one can speak with them face to face and hear the story they have to tell.

Others of the deported, however, were liberated in a legal and completely kosher manner. These too fall into two groups. The first are those whose relatives succeeded—through money, inside connections, or other bribes—in obtaining release certificates for their snatched relations and getting them out from the collection points. The second category consists of the lucky—it sometimes happens that an officer appears at the collection point and tells the police to let this or that person or that one go. Such cases, it is true, are rare, but they happen nonetheless. The first group of those who were set free legally have not returned home. They were sent from the collection points to secure shelters, thanks to their release certificates. The only ones who've returned home are those set free by sheer luck. When someone in this situation returns to his building, people stare at him as if he had returned from the next world or as if he were a sheep snatched from the maw of the wolf. Even if the curfew is still in full force, it's suddenly forgotten, and people run through the courtyards and jump over fences just to receive greetings conveyed from their nearest and dearest who remain at the collection points and had no such luck. But the greetings they receive are full of despair and tell them almost nothing at all. What, after all, can be said about a flock of sheep whose feet are already bound and lined up in a row for the slaughter? Every time the door opens, your blood runs cold. Every new face of the snatchers that appears heaps a little more ice on your soul. Everyone knows what it means and has done the math for himself: someone is getting thrown on the trash heap.

True, they are still distributing the daily bread ration, all twenty-five decagrams of it, and it makes no difference when you get there—in the early morning, at noon, or even at night. Who? What? When? How does it happen? No one cares; is there bread or not? To eat it or not to eat it? Who could squeeze bread down their throat at a time like this? If there is someone standing there with blank eyes chewing it down, he's eating it only because he's got nowhere to put it and doesn't want his hands to have to carry the extra load. Almost no one goes to get soup. Everyone is flat and exhausted from continually standing on their feet. There's nothing to sit on and no place to sit when there is— nothing to lean on when your last moments approach and nowhere to lay your hot and feverish head unless it's on someone else's. No one is able, however, to carry even their own weight. Everyone maintains a grim silence. No one says a word to anyone else. They stare at each other mutely in lament. Even the children are quiet. Even the children who don't know what awaits them have no appetite for their bread. Every time a door opens they shoot innocent and expectant glances in its direction—maybe Papa has come back, or maybe Mommy's returned home. They don't want to be "there" . . . they want to be home. In fact, you don't get such large pieces of bread at home as you do there, but home is still better. It's not good there! For the love of heaven! How do you get out of there?

Such is the story that the returnees, the snatched, have to tell.

FEAR AND BOREDOM

How dreadfully a summer day like today drags itself out, even a day off. Every day in the ghetto drags itself out in a slow and lazy way. A laborer glances at his watch a few times every hour—that is, if he has one. A few times every hour and at every opportunity, another one asks what time it is. In the ghetto, a gray and tired life drags itself forward with the slowness and difficulty of a stalled caravan in the desert that has lost track of its path and its destination. Life drags itself out with its last reserves of strength, because just laying down is not an option, so people drag themselves forward, as long as they can still move.

How often the following questions are heard: "What for?" "Why bother?" "Sooner or later, no one will be allowed to make it any farther than Marysin anyway!" Though this view is shared by 70 to 80 percent of the ghetto's inhabitants, no one sits down and says that he won't drag himself forward one more step. Suicides are rare in the ghetto. As long as someone can still move his feet he'll drag himself a little farther on. Dragging yourself forward this way is actually quite boring, because there is no goal or purpose involved. The work is tedious and brings no satisfaction, like a tasteless soup, since it provides the human organism with no nourishment other than apathy and depression.

When boredom befalls you on an ordinary day, you turn to just this kind of work to drive it away, even when the work itself has no purpose or meaning for you. Today, however, you've been forced to take a holiday. Today, thanks to the curfew, or *Gehsperre,* as the Germans call it, you can't go to work, and your wife and child have nothing to do. You're not working today, and you and your family are being worked on. They're tanning your hide. They haven't skinned you yet, but they're working on your hide from the outside—a whole new tanning system is being tried. So you wander aimlessly around the courtyard of the building, because thanks to fear and boredom it's impossible to sit in the apartment. It feels as if your knees have been poured full of lead. Every hint that something might be afoot makes its way into the courtyard from the street, pours into your knees, fuses with the lead already there, and begins coursing through your veins, making itself felt throughout your whole body until it collects on top of your soul, where it hardens and cools. When you pace back and forth with the weight of that lead on top of your soul, it pushes your head down toward the ground, forcing high-pitched yawns from your twisted throat laden with all the sorrows of your heart, while you yourself don't know exactly what's wrong. Are you hungry? No, that's not it; it's not the continuous pangs of hunger that make themselves felt with such a sharp and pronounced sting each day. Today the feeling is dull and numbed, and you feel it as if through a fog. When they give you something to eat, you eat, but you have no idea what or how much you've eaten and no sense after you've finished of being more full than before. You could have gotten by without any food—you're not even hungry. Perhaps you're sleepy after the long, sleepless night? Just the opposite: just try to see if you can lie still for even a single minute and you'll feel as if you'd laid yourself down on top of an anthill. Your terrified and restless blood assaults you from every side, giving you a feeling of poking and pounding and burning that makes it impossible to lie down. No, you're not sleepy! When you're really drowsy, you can sleep no matter what.

So you just wander through the courtyard with your eyes ripped wide open, but today the two poor eyes you have in your head just aren't enough—and even if you had ten pairs of eyes today, they wouldn't be enough for all there is to see. So you prick up your ears. Today is an exceptional situation—a day turned upside down, more perverted than any other. In normal circumstances, your eyes can see much farther than your ears can hear. Today your ear reaches farther than your eyes, your vision becomes dependent on your ability to listen. Your ear, as it were, sees first, and only after that does your eye begin to hear. And when you finally are able to focus, what is it that you finally see? Nothing that is distinct and explicit, and not the filled-out shapes you usually descry; all you see appears as if through a fog, just the outlines and not the things themselves, as if cataracts have obstructed your sight. Perhaps it's better this way—better for your eye to be masked so as not to see the naked debauchery that is taking place. Maybe it's healthier for your eyes today to be dependent on your ears, because you don't actually know how your eyes would react to seeing your own living skin being tanned like a hide still fully attached to your trembling body. If your eyes were to gaze at that, wouldn't your ability to see shut down at once—wouldn't that be enough to make you go blind?

HOW A MOTHER GOES INSANE

They called her "Putzi" or "Poppy," nothing else. She never had any other name. She was born in Danzig and came to Łódź by way of Zbąszyń at the end of 1938, along with hundreds of other children, without a father.[32] He had been deported earlier, to Dachau. She arrived with only her mother, who had a sister here. She was a remarkable child, this Putzi or Poppy. Neither pretty nor clever, with a pointed head, a face round like a ball, two ruddy legs of equal length, and two

32. Zbąszyń, a Polish town on the German-Polish border, was where Jews expelled from Germany were housed in a transit camp in the "Polenaktion" of October 27–29, 1938.

large black, almost motionless eyes, she sometimes looked more like a clown in caricature than an actual child. She never showed herself to be particularly gifted, and at five or six she could have been much smarter for her age. Younger ghetto children could have "sold her in a sack," as the saying went. Although neither pretty nor clever, Putzi or Poppy was well known in the building where she and her mother lived. Young and old alike knew who she was. Her nature was such that anything could make her cry at the drop of a hat. Not the kind of child who would burst into tears and then let herself be comforted, Putzi or Poppy would indulge her tears all day long, and no one and nothing except her mother was able to console her. She would begin just before daybreak. As soon as her mother wanted to get dressed to go to work, Putzi or Poppy would let loose with a terrific outburst, which meant either "you should take me along" or "stay home." When her mother left anyway, Putzi or Poppy would traipse about and wail, starting down in the courtyard. Then she would move to the stairways, performing on each one of them individually, and then in front of every door. She had no desire to enter any apartment and didn't want to play with any other children at all; she just continued to cry. No one ever saw Putzi or Poppy eat anything, but at dusk, when she would peer through her tears and see her mother coming, she'd rise like the wind and run to her so fast that no other child could catch her, bursting into her mother's arms with the full force of her running start. There she would remain—as the neighbors tell it—refusing to let go of her mother's arms until the next morning, when her mother would leave for work and leave Putzi or Poppy screaming and crying again.

So the cycle continued, day in and day out. The neighbors were astonished. How was it possible for a child to cry her eyes out, and her heart out, every single day for a full eight hours and look as well as she does—to look as well as other Jewish children without any of her woes? The astonishment of the neighbors meant nothing to Putzi or Poppy; she cried and looked fine for reasons all her own. She was a strange child. The neighbors called her "Lyalka," the crying doll. To her mother, however, she was only "Putzchen," or "Pupchen," and she carried her about like a precious stone sixteen hours a day, never putting her down. Putzi or Poppy even had to sleep in the arms of her mother. Or so the neighbors say.

She was very much like her mother, right down to her figure, with the same round face and the same large, immovable eyes. The resemblance ended there, however; Putzi or Poppy would scream and cry all day long, and no one ever heard a peep from her mother. Neighbors who didn't live nearby even thought that she was unable to speak. Yesterday Putzi or Poppy started her day in the usual manner, wandering throughout the building and crying as she went. As always, her mother left for work before dawn. Other women would go to work and "just throw something on," as long as they were somehow presentable. Who in the ghetto, after all, sets much store on appearances? Putzi or Poppy's mother, however, always went to work "fully decked out" in a coat, with her hair carefully combed and clutching her purse in one hand and a bag with a soup pot in the other. "The Lady from Danzig" was what they called her in the building. She had that "citified" look that was stylish and always well put together, with every hair in place and carrying her purse as if it were an accent to her look. She spoke so quietly you could barely hear her, and then it was in German. It was bad German, but that is what it had to be for "the Lady from Danzig."

The ghetto already knew about the decree yesterday morning. The snatchers had been about their business on several streets. At six o'clock, as the Lady from Danzig set out for work, nobody knew precisely when the enforcement of the decree would actually begin. Some people had the feeling it would begin the next day—that is, on Monday. In the meantime, all hope was for a miracle. Perhaps, despite all the evidence to the contrary, the decree would be canceled at the very last moment. So everyone went to work. Putzi or Poppy, of course, woke up yesterday as she did every other day—that is to say, in tears. But before the "crying doll" could begin her tearful journey through the courtyard, she noticed her mother already hurrying back quickly and with urgency in her step. Her hat was askew, and the hair it exposed flew in every direction. Her hand purse had been stuffed into the bag with her soup bowl, and with the red handle of her soup spoon tucked under her arm she looked nothing at all like the Lady who, even in the ghetto, placed such importance on her appearance. In her great surprise, Putzi or Poppy—caught between one stairway and the next and between one sob and another—went stone-cold silent and did not sprint to her mother as usual. Perhaps that was why her mother, after entering the courtyard and not seeing her Putzchen or Pupchen, let out the terrible and ear-piercing shriek of "Puuuu-tzzziiiiii!" That sounded nothing at all like the Lady from Danzig, who always comported herself in "citified" fashion, talking so quietly you could barely make her out, and then only German at that.

At work, or perhaps while still on the way there, she discovered that the execution of the decree was to begin that same day. So she ran home and took Putzi or Poppy in her arms and locked herself in the apartment. And yesterday, the whole day through, no one heard a peep from them for the first time any of the neighbors could recall. The Jewish police arrived shortly before six a.m., taking away Putzi or Poppy—a child with no father—from a mother without "protection," who almost never raised her voice and when she did speak, spoke only German. This time the roles were reversed: this time the child walked off like the "Lady from Danzig," all dressed up in a jacket and wearing a little hat, with a child's little hand purse under her arm. She looked like a bouncing ball, walking alongside the tall, stiff policeman, with her large, round, inexpressive black eyes staring straight ahead. This time it was her mother who let loose a shrill, inhuman, terrifying scream that echoed off the courtyard and into the stairwells so that every apartment could hear the grating, shrieking, animal sound of her cry: "Puuuutzzziiiiiii . . ." She then made her rounds of the building for hours until late in the evening. Afraid of the consequences that would ensue if her screaming were heard on the other side of the barbed wire, located quite close to the building, the neighbors, with great struggle, finally managed to bring her inside.

She then paced fitfully the whole night through, moving from one corner of her room to the other, screaming and roaring the monstrous and grating sound of her "Putziiiii!" and crying bitter tears. But she was hardly the only one in the building! And her cry was not even the loudest one to be heard, lost as it was in the dreadful voices and embittered cries of hundreds of other Jewish fathers and mothers that could be heard in this building and from others nearby. When they tried to single out her screams from the others and make out her grating, shrieking cry, consisting solely of the word "Putzi," they were able to suffer and bear it long after the bellowing of others had left their nerves in shreds. Others were wholly justified in their complaints, and their screams and cries were like knives in your heart. But who could not listen to hers? An embittered mother flung far from her home, alas, repeatedly screaming the name of her only child, a living piece of herself ripped from her chest. At the crack of dawn she went down to the courtyard with a shriek, just as Putzi had always done. And from the courtyard she walked from stairwell to stairwell, then from neighbor to neighbor, for hours on end, just as Putzi had done.

Just like Putzi, but not like her at all; Putzi cried and shrieked for eight hours straight, all day long uttering only one single word, and that was "Mommy." For Mommy herself, throughout the long night and eight hours of the following burning hot and feverish day, could not just cry out "Putzi." The name had probably lost its effect on her ears, which heard it simply as a wild, un-Jewish, animalistic kind of sound. At dusk, she began to scream, or rather bark, a series of different Jewish names: "Perele, Peyle, where did I leave you, Pay-le? Who tore you from my heart?" This was the sound of a Jewish mother screaming her Jewish pain from the depths of her Jewish heart, and this was probably why her neighbors, instigated by the unusual, inhuman cries she emitted, discovered a doctor to come and take a look at her.

The doctor's diagnosis was that she was suffering from a fit of insanity. Was the evidence behind this diagnosis that a Jewish mother was crying out in Yiddish, from her Jewish heart?

A MOTHER WHO WEIGHS AND MEASURES

Young, fair-haired, and outgoing, Rivka K. was able to withstand every blow the war had dealt her. Often, in her most difficult moments, she'd offer an apology something like the following: "It's inhuman; you'd have to be raised on lion's milk to be able to get through it." She had in fact already gotten through a great deal: she'd already lost her husband in the city, when they snatched him up early on. One morning he went out to get some bread, and that evening she found him in the morgue at Poznanski Hospital. All the fingers on his left hand were broken. Two ribs on his right side were broken, and he had two holes in his head. That was all that remained of a man they pulled out of a bread line and marched off to forced labor. Three days after his death, Rivka gave birth to twins: a girl and a boy, both alive. The boy looked like his father—dark with narrow, black eyes—while the little girl was the spitting image of her mother, fair-haired and lively with two gray-blue eyes, as if the two hadn't been born from the same womb within minutes of each other.

Two days after she brought her two children into the world at the beginning of March 1940, she was awakened in the middle of the night by the crack of a gunshot. The bullet whizzed by her ear, meant not for her but for her fifty-four-year-old mother sleeping at her side in her husband's bed. Two drunken voices came at her from two murderers, standing next to her bed with revolvers in their hands, commanding her with dark fire in their eyes, "Get out of this apartment right now—now!"